PHILOSOPHERS LOOK AT CANADIAN CONFEDERATION

LA CONFÉDÉRATION CANADIENNE: QU'EN PENSENT LES PHILOSOPHES?

PHILOSOPHERS LOOK AT CANADIAN CONFEDERATION

LA CONFEDERATION CANADIENNE: QU'EN PENSENT LES PHILOSOPHES?

editor
Stanley G. FRENCH
éditeur

THE CANADIAN PHILOSOPHICAL ASSOCIATION

L'ASSOCIATION CANADIENNE DE PHILOSOPHIE

MONTREAL 1979

Canadian Cataloguing in Publication Data
Main entry under title:
Philosophers look at Canadian Confederation = La Confédération canadienne: qu'en pensent les philosophes?
Text in English or French.
Bibliography: p.
0-9690153-0-5
1. Federal Government—Canada—Addresses, essays, lectures.
2. Quebec(Province)—History—Autonomy and independence movements—Addresses, essays, lectures.
3. Federal-provincial relations (Canada)—Addresses, essays, lectures.* I. French, Stanley G., 1933- II. Canadian Philosophical Association. III. Title: La Confédération canadienne: qu'en pensent les philosophes?
JL27.P48 321'.02'0971 C79-090099-8E

Données de catalogage avant publication (Canada)
Vedette principale au titre:
Philosophers look at Canadian Confederation = La Confédération canadienne: qu'en pensent les philosophes?
Textes en anglais ou en français.
Bibliographie: p.
0-9690153-0-5
1. Gouvernement fédéral—Canada—Discours, essais, conférences.
2. Québec (Province)—Histoire—Autonomie et mouvements indépendantistes—Discours, essais, conférences.
3. Relations fédérales—provinciales (Canada)—Discours, essais, conférences. I. French, Stanley G., 1933- II. Association canadienne de philosophie. III Titre: La Confédération canadienne: qu'en pensent les philosophes?
JL27.P48 321'.02'0971 C79-090099-8F

Printed in Canada
by Concordia University
Montréal H3G 1M8

Imprimé au Québec
par l'Université Concordia
Montréal H3G 1M8

Legal Deposit — 4th Quarter 1979
National Library of Canada

Dépôt légal — 4e trimestre 1979
Bibliothèque nationale du Québec

MONTREAL

THE CANADIAN PHILOSOPHICAL ASSOCIATION

L'ASSOCIATION CANADIENNE DE PHILOSOPHIE

1979

TABLE OF CONTENTS / *TABLE DES MATIERES*

AVANT-PROPOS

La publication de cet ouvrage marque une étape importante dans l'arrivée à l'âge adulte de la philosophie au Canada et au Québec. Je ne veux pas dire que tous les articles qui y sont réunis sont rigoureusement scientifiques. Quelques-uns le sont, d'autres sont plutôt polémiques, mais chaque article tente d'appréhender, d'une façon rationnelle, les concepts incertains et vexants qui sous-tendent les discussions sur l'avenir du Canada.

Par "arrivée à l'âge adulte", j'entends, en partie, rappeler qu'il y a vingt ans, il y avait peu de philosophes autochtones au Canada et que ces derniers étaient pour la plupart des Québécois. A cette époque, celui qui se préoccupait des problèmes pratiques était taxé de non-professionnel et celui qui mentionnait le Canada, de provincial. Même en 1971, à un colloque de l'Association canadienne de philosophie à Terre-Neuve, c'était avec trépidation que j'ai prononcé une conférence sur l'engagement social de la philosophie.

Ces généralisations concernant la philosophie canadienne s'appliquent moins au côté francophone. Par exemple, Louis-Adolphe Pâquet (1895-1942), dans un discours intitulé: *Vocation de la race française en Amérique* (1902) déclare entre autre:

> Oui, sachons-le bien, nous ne sommes pas seulement une race civilisée, nous sommes des pionniers de la civilisation; nous ne sommes pas seulement un peuple religieux, nous sommes des messagers de l'idée religieuse; nous ne sommes pas seulement des fils soumis de l'Eglise, nous sommes, nous devons être du nombre de ses zélateurs, de ses défenseurs et des ses apôtres. Notre mission est moins de manier des capitaux que de remuer des idées; elle consiste moins à allumer le feu des usines qu'à entretenir et à faire rayonner au loin le foyer lumineux de la religion et de la pensée.

Le discours de Pâquet fut, par la suite, connu comme "le bréviaire du patriote canadien-français" .

A l'instar du colloque dont il tire son origine, ce livre s'inscrit dans la pratique d'un bilinguisme passif, tel que Storrs McCall le décrit dans son introduction. C'est-à-dire que chaque auteur a écrit dans la langue de son choix. De ce point de vue, l'ouvrage n'est pas compromettant; il rappelle la pièce *Balconville* de David Fennario qui a été joué, avec succès, au théâtre Centaur en janvier 79. Selon les besoins de la situation, les acteurs ont parlé anglais ou français; quant au public, il a dû rire et pleurer comme le font les Montréalais. Le lecteur bilingue profitera davantage de cet ouvrage, mais les articles, qu'ils soient en français ou en anglais, peuvent se lire séparément.

Cet ouvrage a adopté l'organisation des trois ateliers qui furent à l'origine de ces articles soit: nation, état, souveraineté et autodétermination; formes d'association, contrat social et constitution; droits des individus, de la collectivité et des minorités. Deux articles font exception: le discours d'ouverture de Charles Taylor intitulé "Why Do Nations Have To Become States?" et le dialogue que j'ai échangé avec Storrs McCall, publié en grande partie dans *The Montreal Star* (79-04-21).

La première partie traite des concepts de nation, d'état, de souveraineté et d'autodétermination. Dans le premier article, French et McCall tentent de clarifier ces notions (p. 63); suit une réponse d'André Paradis qui soutient que "le débat constitutionnel n'est pas, à mon sens, un débat qui gagne à être posé *in abstracto*" (p. 67). Le lecteur trouvera ensuite les articles substantiels de David Copp (p. 71) et de Frank Cunningham (p. 97). Copp maintient que, si la majorité des Québécois(es) choisit de former un état national et si cet état pouvait être créé en déplaçant les frontières, le Canada aurait le devoir de ne pas intervenir. Cunningham prétend que c'est dans l'intérêt des Canadiens (ceux qui habitent le Canada, sauf les résidents du Québec) de promouvoir le droit des Québécois à choisir leur propre avenir, même si cela signifie la séparation de la confédération. Pour eux, la seule façon de convaincre les Québécois de leur bonne foi est de réellement encourager l'autodétermination de ces derniers. Selon Paul Gagné (p. 103), la nation canadienne-française arrivera à la formation de fait d'un état souverain indépendant, s'il n'y a pas reconnaissance au niveau d'une nouvelle constitution canadienne de son droit à l'autodétermination.

Il est stimulant de lire à la suite les articles de Francis Sparshott, de Christopher Morris, de Leslie Mulholland et de Dan Goldstick. Sparshott (p. 107) démontre que l'idée de souveraineté s'avère incohérente, mais que, dans la pratique, elle demeure une notion vitale, car elle permet au commerce mondial de déterminer d'une façon plus précise qui dirige et contrôle n'importe où dans le monde — l'on doit savoir qui soudoyer. Morris (p. 117) soutient que la notion de souveraineté-association est un concept incohérent et nous suggère de considérer la demande de souveraineté-association comme une tentative pour obtenir une plus grande indépendance et de nouvelles négociations des ententes coopératives. Mulholland (p. 125) conclut que, du point de vue de la fraternité, on pourrait justifier la création de clauses légales et politiques spéciales pour le Québec si son peuple le désire. Selon Goldstick (p. 133), le principe d'autodétermination sera subordonné au principe démocratique lorsqu'il y a conflit entre les deux.

Il est intéressant de noter que trois des francophones participants à l'Atelier I ont choisi indépendamment l'un de l'autre le concept de l'idéologie. Guy Lafrance (p. 141) décrit et contraste l'idéologie fédéraliste et l'idéologie de la souveraineté politique. Jean-Guy Meunier (p. 145) couvre aussi l'étendue du sujet, mais d'un point de vue différent, montrant que l'incompatibilité des paradigmes idéologiques se retrouve aux divers niveaux de l'analyse tels ceux de la description, de l'explication et de la justification théorique. Il vaut mieux, selon Vincent Lemieux (p. 157), commencer par une science critique qui fasse éclater ces notions idéologiques, plus utiles aux combats politiques qu'aux débats scientifiques.

La deuxième partie du livre comprend plusieurs analyses de différentes formes d'association, de constitutions et de contrat social. Dans le premier article, David Gauthier (p. 193) soutient que nous devons considérer la confédération canadienne comme une entente entre des parties se définissant chacune selon leurs intérêts et pour qui la confédération a dû sembler accorder des avantages mutuels et équitables. Gauthier conclut que nous ne devons pas nous mettre en quête d'une nouvelle constitution. Robert Ware (p. 201) et Michael McDonald (p. 211) contestent l'opinion de Gauthier. Ware démontre que le peuple du Québec n'a jamais renoncé au droit de chercher à établir une nouvelle entente et qu'il n'y a aucune justification pour leur refuser une nouvelle négociation du contrat original. McDonald réfute l'argument de Gauthier pour deux raisons: dans la pratique, les antécédents du Canada ne corroborent pas la théorie du marché équitable; et d'un point de vue philosophique, l'applicabilité et la justesse morale de la théorie contractuelle peuvent être mises en doute.

Les articles de di Norcia, d'Armour et de Mathie abordent la question d'une façon différente et s'attachent à la notion de communauté. Vincent di Norcia (p. 217) montre que l'ordre politique du Canada s'appuie davantage sur la force et l'autorité que sur le consentement et le contrat. Le Canada n'est ni une nation, ni une fédération, ni une démocracie dans le vrai sens de chacun de ces mots. Leslie Armour (p. 225) préconise un fédéralisme personnel que soustendrait une attitude qu'il qualifie d'anarchiste communautaire. William Mathie (p. 233) examine les perspectives de l'unité politique au Canada par le biais de descriptions philosophiques des communautés politiques telles que générées par la conception libérale du contrat social et par le nationalisme.

Dans l'ensemble des textes par Robert, Stevenson, et Pestieau, on met l'emphase sur un autre point encore, qu'on peut caractériser de "realpolitik and utopianism". Selon Serge Robert (p. 239), au lieu de considérer l'organisation politique de la société comme un contrat social librement consenti entre individus rationnels, il sera plus fertile de penser que les décisions politiques sont déterminées par des contraintes économiques. En ce qui concerne la constitution canadienne, le statu quo est impensable. Jack Stevenson (p. 245) essaie davantage de montrer ce qui, en pratique, est désirable dans notre situation concrète et historique, plutôt que ce qui serait désirable d'une manière ultime dans une situation idéale. Son analyse l'amène à la conclusion que nous devons modifier d'une façon importante la règle de la majorité absolue et que nous aurons besoin de développer un processus pour satisfaire l'élite afin d'atteindre et de maintenir une nouvelle entente réalisable. L'hypothèse de Joseph Pestieau (p. 255) est qu'il est inhérent au nationalisme québécois de soulever des attentes excessives, de soulever ce que des opposants perçoivent comme du fanatisme — "En politique, un bluff qui réussit n'est-il pas une hypothèse qui s'avère juste?"

La dernière partie du livre traite des droits des individus, de la collectivité et des minorités. Nous commençons par l'article de Nicolas Kaufmann (p. 297) dont la thèse est que c'est l'histoire récente qui a renoncé à la protection des minorités en mettant l'accent sur les garanties générales des libertés fondamentales des individus. Il propos l'adoption d'une constitution confédérale où la majorité et la minorité ne s'opposeraient plus sous des rapports numériques, mais se sépareraient en tant que deux entités distinctes pour lesquelles il existerait des droits.

Les articles de Marsha Hanen et de David Braybrooke font état d'une convergence d'opinions intéressantes. Hanen (p. 301) soutient que l'intérêt national serait peut-être mieux servi en discourant moins sur les droits, car les droits sont trop facilement considérés comme absolus, et en focalisant sur les compromis politiques. Dans le même esprit, Braybrooke (p. 311) démontre qu'invoquer un droit — par exemple, le droit de se séparer — invite une réponse de même nature tout aussi agressive. Au lieu des droits, pensons aux opportunités. Pour favoriser l'épanouissement de leur minorité francophone, les provinces autres que le Québec peuvent mettre en place des mécanismes qui se fonderaient sur le centre vital de culture francophone qu'est le Québec.

Virginia McDonald et Michael McDonald se préoccupent des droits individuels et des droits collectifs. Virginia McDonald (p. 325) croit que, légitimement, des droits peuvent être invoqués par les collectivités qui, selon des critères subjectifs et objectifs, peuvent être qualifiées de "soi" . Michael McDonald (p. 333) explique la justification des droits en montrant qu'ils sont basés sur l'intérêt. A l'encontre de ses membres, une collectivité peut exercer certains droits. Pourtant même si les collectivités (par exemple, les nations) peuvent être les bénéficiaires de certains droits, cela ne devrait pas être, car à vrai dire, seuls les individus ont des intérêts dans le sens moral pertinent.

Cette partie du livre se termine par trois articles qui s'éloignent du sujet, mais qui, néanmoins, sont intéressants et valent la peine d'être lus. Des discussions sur les droits des minorités au Canada, Maryann Ayim (p. 343) tire des leçons sur les droits de la femme qui, comme les autres groupes dominés, cherche son autonomie, mais d'une façon différente à cause de sa situation différente. Brenda Baker (p. 349) examine une variété de raisons qui pourraient supporter les revendications provinciales pour le droit de posséder et de contrôler leurs ressources naturelles. Finalement, nous avons l'appel de Serge Morin: délivrez-moi de vos droits!

La bibliographie de Myrna Friend est sans aucun doute un des aspects importants de cet ouvrage. Elle fait partie d'un projet plus vaste, commencé en 1976, qui est de compiler une bibliographie de la philosophie au Canada. Les principaux chercheurs de ce projet originaire de l'Université de Toronto sont Myrna Friend et Jack Stevenson.

Un nombre impressionnant de personnes et d'institutions ont apporté une contribution importante à la production de cet ouvrage. Durant ma vie de chercheur, j'ai parcouru rapidement d'innombrables listes de remerciements dont les lecteurs les plus avides sont ceux qui y sont nommés. Pourtant, il m'importe d'écrire que cet ouvrage n'aurait pas été achevé sans la collaboration des personnes nommées ci-après. J'ai reçu de l'aide professionnelle de Stephanie Manuel qui a travaillé avec moi dès le début, et a maintenu l'ordre dans le chaos; de

Jeanne Jobin, la responsable du service des thèses de l'Université Concordia; de Pamela Mitchell du service d'imprimerie de Concordia; de Denis Rose, pour la maquette de la couverture et la mise en page; de Susan Hudson, pour la mise en page; de David Braybrooke, de Jacques Plamondon, de Jack Stevenson et d'Arthur Monahan qui formaient le comité consultatif d'édition; de Sylvia Potvin pour la mise en marché; de Anna Black-Hopkins, de Frances Bauer, de Aida Melkonian, de Shona French et de Sean French qui ont corrigé les épreuves; d'Anne Peacock et de Lucie Lequin qui m'ont assisté dans la préparation finale de cette édition. J'ai aussi été moralement supporté par Storrs McCall, Susan Hudson, Stephanie Manuel, Keith French et Ewan French. Un remerciement historique est dû aussi à Gwyneth Frayne. L'Association canadienne de philosophie et l'Université Concordia m'ont aussi apporté leur soutien. Il me fait plaisir d'exprimer ma gratitude.

Stanley G. FRENCH

INTRODUCTION

In May 1978, at its annual meetings held that year in London, Ontario the Canadian Philosophical Association sponsored a panel discussion on the subject of Canada's future. Following that discussion it was decided to form a special CPA Committee on the Confederation Debate, whose aims would be twofold: (a) to see in what areas of the Confederation debate the special skills and talents of philosophers would be useful; (b) to attempt to involve philosophers from all parts of Canada in discussions concerning Canada's future.

The committee was formed during the summer, and comprised the following ten members: David Braybrooke (Dalhousie), Frank Cunningham (Toronto), Marsha Hanen (Calgary), Nicolas Kaufmann (Université du Québec à Trois Rivières), Guy Lafrance (Ottawa), Storrs McCall (McGill, chairperson), André Paradis (Université du Québec à Trois Rivières), Jacques Plamondon (Sherbrooke), Serge Robert (Université du Québec à Montréal), Jack Stevenson (Toronto).

Work on the planning of a conference began in the fall of 1978, and the conference took place in Montréal over the weekend of April 20-22, 1979. Its program included a public meeting on Friday evening, at which Charles Taylor of Oxford University spoke on the subject "Why Must Nations Become States?", and a dinner-symposium on Saturday evening at the Windsor Hotel. The latter meeting included a panel discussion with symposiasts Gerald Beaudoin (Université d'Ottawa), Donald Smiley (York University), Robert Boily (Université de Montréal), and Richard Simeon (Queen's University). At this symposium food, wine and talk flowed freely, and the discussions lasted until 11:30 p.m.

The meetings during the day of Saturday, April 21 were devoted to workshop discussions. Three themes were proposed, with a separate workshop for each theme:

I. Nation, State, Sovereignty, and Self-determination.

II. Forms of Association, Social Contract and Constitution.

III. Individual, Collective and Minority Rights.

The structure of these workshops was a little unusual, it being stipulated that each participant had to submit a 3-5 page summary of his ideas in advance, these summaries then being circulated to all other members of the same workshop. By this means lengthy opening statements of their positions by participants were avoided, and each workshop could proceed directly to discussion. The summaries of the participants form the basis of the present volume.

The Committee on the Confederation Debate intends to continue its work, believing as it does that the free and open exchange of ideas that resulted from its conference cannot but be of value in the context of the current discussions over Canada's future. A rule which we adhered to, and which we found beneficial, was the principle of "passive bilingualism" — each participant spoke in the language he knew best, and if anyone failed to understand he asked. Simultaneous translation, which serves as a screen to real communication at many conferences, was not used.

In conclusion I would like to thank all the members of our committee for working hard in the interests of a cause they believed in: Nicolas Kaufmann for much correspondence and worry over the telephone, Frank Cunningham for looking on the brighter side of things when the news sounded glum, Guy Lafrance for handling all money except what was handled by Serge Robert, David Braybrooke for marrying his daughter in haste so that he could arrive on time, André Paradis for taking charge of accommodation and maps, Jack Stevenson and Myrna Friend for weeks of careful work on the bibliography, Jacques Plamondon for gallantly tending his newborn child all night so he could come to the workshops, Stan French for undertaking the thankless task of being editor, Marsha Hanen for flying more miles in a good cause than any of us, and Serge Robert for persuading the Windsor Hotel to give us two wines for the price of one. If all Canadian committees could work as well as this one, we wouldn't have to worry about the future of our country.

Storrs McCALL

WHY DO NATIONS HAVE TO BECOME STATES?

Charles TAYLOR

There are three major modes of political justification in the modern world: welfare, rights, self-government. Nationalist modes of thought have become involved in all three, and point towards the need for nations to become sovereign states.

The initial locus of nationalism as a political justification was in the context of the aim of self-government. The notion that self-government is a good in itself, that men live a higher life who are part of a free, that is, self-managing people, returns early in the modern world. I say 'returns', because it was seen as an ideal that the ancients had lived by and that needed to be recovered. It returns first in Renaissance Italy; Machiavelli stands at the end of the first return of the tradition of civic humanism. But then we find it again in the English 17th century, and it becomes part of the mainstream of European thought in the 18th century, with the American and French revolutions. Both look back to republican Rome as their models for a free people. Freedom cannot simply be defined as independence for the individual relative to state interference; it is no longer enough to demand 'laissez-faire, laissez-passer'. Free men are self-governing men.

This had a natural link with the nascent nationalism. The ancient tradition of civic humanism stressed that self-government was only possible for a community, where the members identified strongly with their public institutions, to use modern language, or where men love the laws, to use the old terminology. Self-government was possible, because men were willing to die for the *patria*, for the laws, because they devoted themselves to *res publica*. They had what Montesquieu called 'vertu'. Men who were devoted above all to private goals, or spiritual goals which by-passed the fatherland, were fit politically to live in despotisms, but not in a free state. Machiavelli and Rousseau both made this point.

Thus in both the American and French revolutions, the term for those who were partisans of self-rule was 'patriot'. This expressed one link between self-government and love of the *patria*. The idea of a democratic régime where the people lacked such dedication was still foreign to 18th century believers in self-government. But the term expresses the link with modern nationalism. For today it has above all a nationalist ring. And we think ironically of patriotism as the motive which may have pushed many Germans to follow Hitler, many Russians to condone Stalin, etc., where the beneficiary of this sentiment is now as much despotism and tyranny as free states. So has the term evolved. Many people even think now of free governments and nationalist feeling as being enemies, in the last analysis incompatible.

The connection is clear historically. Nationalism didn't arise out of the value of self-government. The causes of modern nationalism are very deep, and have to do with the erosion of earlier communities and identifications: the withering away of local community, the decline of religious identifications which often by-passed nationality. Indeed, the very notion of a group identification founded on a relation to the supernatural is strange to many moderns in Atlantic civilization; and the local neighbourhood society cannot have the place it once had. But people need a group identification, and the obvious one to take the place of the earlier forms is the one that springs to the attention of the speaking animal, viz., nationality as based on language.

But once nationalism arises, it cannot but take the place of patriotism in the aspiration to self-government. Civic humanism needs a strong identification with a community. But this is the form that community-identification takes among modern, emancipated men (emancipated from church, from locality, from hierarchical allegiances). So patriotism comes to mean nationalism.

And the context in which nationalism comes first to count politically is that of the revendication of self-rule. What is demanded here is self-determination. Men can only rule themselves if they are grouped in their *patriae*. Only men who form together a *patria* can achieve self-rule, not just any agglomeration of humans who happen to be contiguous with each other. So the ideal demands that *patriae* be given some sort of political personality.

I use the vague term 'political personality', rather than saying bluntly that *patriae* ought to be sovereign states, because the 18th century already saw our modern dilemma. They saw that the close identification with fatherland, and the demands of universal participation, require a small face-to-face society; whereas modern nations are very large and spread over vast areas. The solution, as propounded by Montesquieu and Rousseau, as adopted by the nascent United States, was federation; smaller societies joined in a larger union. Both the political ideas which dispute for the soul of contemporary Québec were born in the 18th century, and from exactly the same source, the aspiration to self-government. This demands that the *patria* be given a political expression. This could be taken to mean independent statehood, sovereignty. But given the size and nature of modern nations, it could also require federation. Of course, these two solutions were not necessarily seen as alternatives. The nation could demand independence, and then adopt a federal structure.

The paradigm case is, of course, the USA. The fathers of US independence convinced themselves that they formed a nation, that they could justifiably secede from the English nation to which they had seen themselves until quite recently as belonging (notably when they had fought together against us, e.g., at Louisbourg). They felt justified in this, because they saw themselves as betrayed by their ex-compatriots, denied the rights of Englishmen, relegated to a dependent status.

So the modern idea was born. Self-determination is the right of a nation, because it is the condition of self-rule of the people who form the nation. This, either because since they form a nation, the only *patria* they can identify with is that nation, and hence this must have political expression; or, as in the case of the USA, because since they form a dependent group which can only achieve self-rule by breaking away, freedom demands that they found a *patria*, and hence become a nation.

So the first and most important reason why nations had to become states is that it was seen as a condition of self-rule. The demand for the self-determination of nations was thus part of the aspiration to self-government, to popular rule. It was a demand of the Left in the nineteenth century. It spread out with the ideas that flowed from the French revolution. The term 'self-determination' was coined later; in the aftermath of the first world war it came into its own. And in this age, the revendication made sense because it was seen as the inevitable condition and concomitant of self-rule. The new nations were achieving self-determination by carving up what had been autocratic or at least authoritarian-ruled empires: Russia, Germany, Austria.

The second great wave of self-determination comes after the second world war, and involved conferring statehood on the ex-colonies of European imperial states. Here too, self-rule and self-determination were but two sides of the same coin. Or so it was thought. The régimes that now exist in many of the ex-colonies are indeed very far from the tradition of civic humanism, and would shock our 18th century forbears (as would many aspects of our own régimes, to say the truth). But even so, the link is not entirely broken. All modern régimes pay obeissance to the ideal of popular rule. All are supposed to be expressions of the popular will, however bogus. All require some formal expression of this through plebiscites, or mass elections, or other modes of ratification. For the ideal of self-determination is still conceptually inseparable from that of self-rule.

So nations have become states in order to rule themselves. But do they have to? Certainly they do, if they are otherwise hopelessly dependent. If you're a colony, then you have as a nation no choice. This paradigm predicament is clarified once and for all by the 18th century Americans. And then repeated endlessly in the period after 1945. This is why the rhetoric of independence slips naturally into the claim that one lives in a colonial predicament. We see this in the language of Québec nationalists: clearly, in the terrorism of the FLQ (echoing the Algerian FLN); but also among more sophisticated.[1]

Of course, there is some historical truth here. Québec was a colony. But are we "colonized" now? This would be the shortest way to demonstrate that we must become a sovereign state. Well, we obviously aren't in some straightforward sense, not as the 13 colonies were in 1776; nor like, say, India in 1947.

But it is claimed, there are other forms of dependence, other relations which make it such that the only road to genuine self-rule lies through independence.

In order to understand these, we have to look at the other ways in which modern nationalism has become intricated in our political arguments and justifications.

Nationalism, I said earlier, is a modern form of group identification, one prevalent among emancipated peoples. But to probe deeper, we would have to say that this very idea of identification, of having an identity, is modern. We can speak anachronistically of the identity of mediaeval man. But this is anachronistic, because a mediaeval man didn't have the question to which identity is the answer.

The question is 'who am I?' The answer points to certain values, certain allegiances, a certain community, perhaps, outside of which I couldn't function as a fully human subject. Of course, I might be able to go on living as an organism outside of any values, allegiance, or even community. But what is peculiar to a human subject is the ability to ask and answer questions about what really matters, what is of the highest value, what is truly significant, what is most moving, most beautiful, etc. The conception of identity is the view that outside of the horizon provided by some master value, or some allegiance, or some community membership, I would be crucially crippled, would become unable to ask and answer effectively these questions, would thus be unable to function as a full human subject.

The judgement about identity is a judgement about me in particular, or about some particular person or group. There is no claim that others will be unable to function outside my horizon. The horizon necessary for me is not essential for human beings as such. There are some things which we might judge universally necessary: for instance, a minimum of freedom from crying need, or a minimum of love as children; we might argue that without these, no-one could become a fully human subject.

But the claim about identity is particularized. I may come to realize that belonging to a given culture is part of my identity, because outside of the reference points of this culture, I couldn't begin to put to myself much less answer those questions of ultimate significance which are peculiarly in the repertory of the human subject. Outside of this culture, I wouldn't know who I was as a human subject. So this culture helps to identify me.

We can see how the question about identity is a modern one; it belongs to modern, emancipated subjects. For our mediaeval forbears, there couldn't be a question about the conditions of human subjecthood for me, or for us. There were conditions for man as such, in a sense, especially a relation to God, which he could turn his back on with eventually catastrophic results. These conditions were unrecognized, or seen only distortedly, by pagan and infidel. That was their great misfortune. There was no question of their having *different* such conditions.

The idea that this can be so is inseparable from modern emancipated humanism. Being human is not just a matter of occupying the rank assigned to humans in the cosmic order. Our humanity is something each one of us discovers in him/herself. What it is to be human is not to be discovered in the order of things in which men are set, but rather in the nature that men discover in themselves.

Of course, emancipated humanism doesn't lead of itself to the notion of identity. It is a necessary but not sufficient condition. The first versions of emancipated humanism of the 17th century give us a picture of man as an atomic subject, fulfilling his purposes as a producer, and setting up a political order as his instrument. There is no place here yet for the notion of identity, for the question of what horizon of meaning will be essential for this or that person's being-human. The need for a horizon of meaning is ignored altogether. And hence individual and national differences are of no moral relevance.

The sense of the importance of these differences comes in the Romantic period; and it comes with what I have called the question of identity. For each man to discover in himself what his humanity consists in, he needs a horizon of meaning, which can only be provided by some allegiance, group-membership, cultural tradition. He needs, in the broadest sense, a language in which to ask and answer the questions of ultimate significance.

The Romantic subject can never be the atomic subject of 17th century thought, of Hobbes and Locke for instance. Even the most individualistic of Romantic aspirations, in seeing the need for a horizon of meaning, sees that men are essentially social; for this horizon, this language comes to us within a society. Romantic individualism consists in the demand that we break away from group conformity, that we elaborate an original statement. But it has no place for the 17th century myth of the state of nature, the view that we could see our *original* condition as one of solitary agents of choice.

Since the Romantic insight is that men need a language in the broadest sense in order to discover their humanity, and that this language is something we have access to through our community, it is natural that the community defined by natural language should become one of the most important poles of identification for the civilization which is heir of the Romantics. Romanticism is a deepening of the modern aspiration to what I have called emancipation, to finding one's human purposes in oneself, autonomously, and not in some cosmic and hierarchic order in which we fit. Hence nationalism, the singling out of linguistic nationality as the paradigm pole of self-identity, is part of this modern drive to emancipation. It connects naturally with the demand for self-rule.

But at the same time, the Romantic conception of identity, and also therefore nationalism, comes to modify the other modes of political justification which belong to the modern aspiration to emancipation: in terms of welfare and rights. Just a word about these.

The modern notion of rights is of what has been called 'subjective rights'. We can speak of subjective rights when we couch our claims about how it is licit and illicit to act in terms of privileges which are seen to belong to subjects. This big change comes also (naturally) in the 17th century. Instead of saying: 'it is the law of nature that no-one ought to take innocent life', we now start to say: 'men have a right to life'. This way of putting it makes the norms governing people's behaviour towards us appear as a privilege, as it were, that we own. The point of this semantic transposition of natural law is first, that it accords us a certain autonomy in deciding how the norms should be applied to us (if I have a right to life, then presumably I can waive it, a possibility not allowed by traditional natural law, and which the modern theorists felt they had to block, by inventing the notion of an 'inalienable right'.); and second, that it underscores the dignity of the person. The point of natural law is now seen to be respect for the integrity of human subjects, who are seen as having a certain dignity. Rights talk is plainly part of modern emancipated humanism.

Similarly with modern justifications by welfare. These arise with the principle that the political and other structures in which men are set have no inherent value. They are no longer to be seen as commanding allegiance because, say, they represent the hierarchical order of things, or the chain of being. They are only instruments set up by men to accomplish their purposes. Men and their purposes becomes the only source of political value. Political structures and policies are to be judged instrumentally. The criterion of welfare is a natural extension of this way of thinking. It only requires that one define welfare as what fulfils human purposes. In the influential utilitarian mode of thought, which has been so important in our civilization since the 18th century, it is thought that these purposes can be defined more narrowly in terms of desire-fulfilment. But defined narrowly or broadly, the welfare criterion of justification looks to the effects on human welfare of any structures or policies. It is consequentialist, if not always utilitarian.

Now Romantic conceptions of identity involve transformations in both of these modes of justification. The core of the modern conception of rights is that respect is owed the integrity of the human subject. This obviously entails his having a right to life, to liberty; on Lockeian assumptions also to property. But if we also add the Romantic understanding of identity, as essential to human subject-hood, then plainly there is something else here to which we have a right, viz., that the conditions of our identity be respected. If we take the nationalist thesis that these are primarily our belonging to a linguistically-defined nation, then we have the beginnings of another justification of the rights of nations to political expression, which does not pass through the aspiration to self-rule, or not necessarily so.

A parallel point can be made about justifications in terms of welfare. But what I should like to explore here is the argument which springs from rights along with the Romantic premisses of identity; because this is the richest and most important source of contemporary thought, feeling and revendications.

This involves three key notions of post-Romantic thought: expression, realization and recognition. 1. The conditions of my identity are a horizon of meaning; a language in the broad sense in which I can ask and answer questions of ultimate significance. These I have access to through a culture, that of my community. Thus it is essential for me that this culture be a rich and healthy one, that it be a going concern. If one takes the nationalist line that this culture's health is synonymous with that of the natural language of my community, then this language must be a going concern.

But languages and cultures are only going concerns to the extent that they are continually recreated through expression, be it through works of art, public institutions, or just everyday exchange. Keeping a language healthy involves giving it scope for expression. And so if we have a right that the conditions of our identity be respected; and if these are primarily concerned with the health of our natural language; and if these depend on its expressive power, and hence also opportunity; then we have a right that our language be accorded scope for expression. This is what lies behind one of the most insistent demands of our contemporary debate, for what are called collective language rights.

These are demands for linguistic rights, but not for those of an individual, e.g., to speak to the public authorities in his own language, or to be tried in a language he can command. They are for the rights of a community's language to receive the scope it needs to maintain/increase its expressive power, which is in turn seen as a common condition of the identity of all speakers of the language.

2. The need for expression shades over into the need for what I have called realization. A language gains expressive power in being used for the whole gamut of human purposes. This includes also being used in public life, the world of economic management, of technology, of learning, and so on. This in turn requires that the community speaking the language be achieving something of their own in these fields. If all the important realizations are brought about by other peoples, then the language of public life, of economic-management, of technology, etc., will almost inevitably be a foreign one.

This conclusion is reinforced if we take account of another important dimension. The language/culture which defines our identity must be one which can command our allegiance. We have to see it as valuable. If it comes to be depreciated in our eyes, and if it remains the indispensable pole of our identity, then we are in a catastrophic position; one in which we cannot avoid depreciating ourselves, tied as we are to an impoverished culture.

That many people in modern times have felt the pain of this kind of self-depreciation is undeniable; as is also that it has sometimes been the basis of catastrophic reactions, especially the attempt to compensate by hyper-chauvinism. The argument between nationalists and anti-nationalists concerns only the remedy. For the latter, self-identification via the nation is contingent and avoidable; and so the pains of belonging to an impoverished culture can be overcome by cultivating individuals, if necessary in some other language, and breaking their identification with the nation. For nationalists, this identification is necessary, indispensable for men; the remedy can only therefore be the promotion of the national culture.

If we take this nationalist line we can see that the national community has an even more vital need for self-realization. It is not just that the language risks losing its expressive power if it is not involved in the achievements of technology, the economy, etc. It is also that the community cannot be without achievements in these sectors, because these are the sectors that modern men value; and a community without realizations of this kind will inescapably come to depreciate itself; and thus find its identity undermined.

For contemporaries, the crucially prestigious sectors are: artistic creation, technological innovation, economic productivity, and of course, political self-rule itself.

But now we can see the basis of another justification of nations becoming states, which can disconnect itself altogether from the aspiration to republican self-rule, from the tradition of civic humanism. The argument could be that the condition of a people's having its own realizations in the field or art, or technology, or the economy is that it become a sovereign state, perhaps because this is the only condition of its insulating itself from some powerful and pervasive foreign pressure. Or the argument could go more directly, that political self-rule is a crucial realization which is necessary in itself for self-respect.

But note that this is crucially different from the argument for self-rule in the tradition of civic humanism, the argument which presided over the original demand for self-determination. For it is not necessarily crucial for this demand for realization that the self-rule be republican, i.e., that it involve real free popular participation, argument, persuasion, competition for rule among equals. It suffices that it be rule from within the community rather than outside. The rule of a charismatic dictator can also serve to prove to a people that it is capable of political success; and a despotic government may preside over great economic, technological, artistic realizations.

This is why many Western liberals have come to accept as a valid fulfilment of the demand for self-determination the establishing of despotic régimes in Third World ex-colonies. For these governments, however non-republican, are indigenous, and thus can meet this need for indigenous realization. One can learn that black is beautiful under an indigenous dictatorship as one never could under semi-liberal colonial institutions; so runs the argument. Whether it doesn't involve an inescapably patronizing element is another issue.

But this separation of self-determination from its republican roots has relevance to our country in a different way. The purely republican case for Québec independence is surely very weak. All rhetoric about colonialism aside, it is clearly not the case that separate statehood is the essential pre-condition of self-rule, as it was for the 13 colonies. In a federally-structured representative democracy, clearly we *have* self-rule. That is why we are capable of going about the political business of deciding among ourselves whether we will go independent or not; this through the normal political process. This is not how things happen in a real colonial predicament.

But we can construct another argument for political sovereignty out of the need for realization. The argument could go that Québec needs an independent political instrument in order to ensure participation in economic direction, a role in technology design, and the like; either because of the overwhelming force of the neighbouring Anglo-Saxon culture of 250 millions, the richest and strongest economically in the world; or because of the greater political clout that the English-Canadian majority inevitably exercises in Canada; or both. In short, that an independent political entity is necessary to insulate Québec to some degree from forces that threaten to occupy the whole space of economic management and technological innovation, not to speak of a good part of those of political organization and the formation of public bureaucracies.

Something like this has been an important argument of nationalists in Québec. One of the most popular arguments among independentists is to the effect that the majority in federal Canada has favoured the economic development of Ontario over Québec, that therefore the requirements of economic realization include an independent Québec government with the major responsibility for the economic management of the province's economy. The argument ramifies far. Its relevance is not only to what we have called realization. It is also an argument about welfare: provincial underdevelopment has meant impoverishment of Québécois, it is claimed. But realization is also an important element in it. I am not concerned here to weigh the argument, but just to record it as the form which this mode of justification of sovereignty takes in the present Québec debate.

And of course, political independence has a more direct relation to realization. Political sovereignty is itself a realization, and one which puts a people on the map.

3. This brings us to the third important notion mentioned above. I spoke above about a political status "insulating" Québec from the invasive influence of North America. Independentists usually object to this kind of language; they protest that their intention is not to turn inward but to have access to the outside world, which being buried as a minority in federal Canada has denied them.

They touch here on a very important point, which a study of the Romantic conception of identity can also clarify. Because the language/culture we need for our identity is one which we always receive from others, from our surroundings, it becomes very important that we be recognized for what we are. It is extremely difficult for anyone to maintain a horizon of meaning by which he identifies himself, if this is denied, or set at nought by those who surround him.

This obviously applies to the individual, growing up in a community, and living his life in it. But it also applies between communities. This is especially evident when we appreciate how important is the self-respect of a culture. This self-respect is gained through realization; but the value of realization depends also to a great degree on the recognition of others, on how a people is seen internationally, by the world at large.

There is therefore among a small people, whose self-confidence has been shaken by living in the shadow of the contemporary world's most powerful language/culture/technology, a tremendous hunger for international recognition. This goes a long way to explain the impact of the famous 'Québec libre' speech of de Gaulle in 1967; which was appreciated far beyond the ranks of independentists.

And it can provide us another reason for demanding independence. For sovereignty, and precisely in its formal trappings; exchange of ambassadors, seat in the UN, etc., is the paramount form of international recognition today. That's what it means to be internationally recognized. This incidentally, is why it is very hard to conceive of the independentist movement in Québec willingly making a deal for a renewed federation short of sovereignty. For precisely the legal status of sovereign country is essential to the goal they seek. This can be caricatured by their enemies as the desire on the part of an élite to ride around in limousines in foreign capitals, and cut a figure at international conferences. But it also has a more serious side in the need for recognition, for an acceptance by the world community that one counts for something, has something to say to the world, and is among those addressed by others; the need to exist in world public space as a people.

We are now in a position to sum up this rather rambling set of answers to the question: why should nations become states?

A. The first answer might be: because sovereignty is the condition of republican self-rule. This is the answer we can retrospectively put in the mouth of the American independence leaders; except that they had to become a nation at the same time. They made a patria-state, but all in order to rule themselves. It is the answer of the peoples of central Europe between the wars, of the colonies struggling for liberation after the second World War.

But it is hard to apply this to our situation. So we turn to:

B. There is another set of arguments which turn on rights. We can argue:

1. The conditions of our identity are indispensable to our being full human subjects.

2. For moderns a (in some versions, the) crucial pole of identification is their language/culture, and hence their linguistic community.

   thus

3. The availability of our language/community as a viable pole of identification is indispensable to our being full human subjects.

   Now

4. We have a right to demand that others respect whatever is indispensable to our being full human subjects, e.g., life, liberty.

   Therefore

5. We have a right to demand that others respect the conditions of our language/community being a viable pole of identification.

The conditions mentioned in 5 can be spelled out to include: the health/expressive power of our language, a certain realization in crucial sectors on the part of our language community, and some degree of international recognition. And these, with other premisses, can be made the basis of language legislation such as we now have in Québec (collective rights), and also of political independence as a *matter of right*; because supposedly indispensable to realization and recognition.

What we think of this argument will depend partly on our detailed conception of the conditions mentioned in 5; which may be different from those adumbrated above. But it may also depend on what we think of premisses 1, 2, and 4. Of these, 2 is the only controversial one today. It simply states what follows from our definition of identity. One would only challenge this if one wanted to challenge all talk about identity. No doubt many philosophers would, but in fact it is hard to see how much of our modern self-understanding could get on without some concept of this kind.

4 is similarly basic to political thought and argument in the 20th century.

The big disagreements concern 2; whether to affirm or deny it, and if the former, what variant to affirm. For some espouse 2 in a strong, exclusive form, which makes the language/community the all-important, over-riding pole of identity; while for others it is an extremely important, but not the sole basis of a modern identity.

Over against both of these, there are those who reject 2 in any form, for whom it offers an aberrant pole of identification, one which tends to cloud over, or even crush individual difference, autonomy, and originality. On this view, each human being must elaborate his own identity; this can never be submerged in that of a group. Hence the moment of greatest imposture, for this conception, is when society imposes rules (like language legislation) in the name of some supposed group identity.

For others, (e.g., classical Marxists), the ultimate identity is indeed that of a group, but of no national society, rather of the world community of liberated mankind. Proletarians have no country, as the Communist Manifesto assures us.

Now for anti-nationalists of either individual or collectivist stripe, the above argument doesn't go through. There is no justification for restrictive language legislation; and no justification for sovereignty outside of A: its being indispensable for republican self-rule. Since this clearly doesn't apply to the Québec-Canada case, the demand is rejected out of hand.

We can see the shape of the battle which is joined between those who affirm 2 in its most uncompromising form, and those who deny it in any form; a battle whose general lines are perhaps distressingly familiar to us.

But what if you think (as I do) that neither of these is right? That it isn't true that the most important pole of identification is the national one, that making it the only one is liable to stultify human development, and justify repressive policies; while at the same time, you cannot accept that group identification is of no importance at all for our identity? On the contrary, you think that it is very important for everyone, and in certain circumstances (when the culture is menaced), can be truly vital. If you also think, as I do, that something like these circumstances have existed in Québec during the last two centuries, then you will have trouble aligning either with the ultra-nationalists, or with the anti-nationalists.

One thing will certainly be true, if you feel like this: the Canadian scene will be perennially frustrating for you. Because the extreme positions always seem to win out here. That ultra-nationalism should win in Québec is perhaps not too surprising. Perhaps what's more surprising is the resistance to it; and what's hopeful is the fact that the final round is not yet played out here, in spite of the election of an independentist party.

But what perhaps needs more comment is the anti-nationalist stand of the rest of Canada. I don't mean by this that there isn't a lot of Canadian nationalism around, both healthy and unhealthy. I certainly don't mean that there isn't a lot of linguistic and cultural narrowness and bigotry in English-Canada. From the standpoint of Québec we are painfully aware of this. Intolerance of the minority there has certainly been. And it is really this, more than anything else, which makes the cause of Canadian unity seem desperate in the long run.

But English Canada has not been nationalist in the sense characterized here. The intolerance and bigotry, the suppression of French schools and the French language, were never carried out from a sense of a threatened identity. Indeed, sharing a language with our giant neighbour, English Canadians rarely had any sense of how language can play a crucial role in identity.

Hence, when faced with the demands of a French Canada for some recognition of its rights as a nation, where this took the form of the right of French speakers, or the powers and jurisdictions of Québec, the rest of Canada has been generally hostile and uncomprehending. When pushed to a justification of its refusal, it has generally taken up the language of anti-nationalism, indeed, often gone even farther, and rejected even 1, the whole language of identity. English Canadian spokesmen have taken refuge in the crassly philistine contention that language is just a medium of communication, that we should choose our media for greatest efficiency, hence English should predominate; or else they have argued that a society needs a minimum degree of unity, and this precludes allowing wide rights to all minority languages. French is assimilated, on this argument, to all the languages spoken by new-Canadians, and this assimilation by itself shows a complete misunderstanding of the nationalist revendications of French Canada and more latterly Québec.

Politically, our situation seems to be this: while the argument of A is generally understood to be irrelevant for Québec, by all except the minority with an insatiable taste for self-dramatization, some form of the argument I tried to formulate in B is accepted by the vast majority of Quebecers. That is, even opponents of independence and the Parti Québécois accept some moderate variant of 2, that language and the language community form a crucial part of the horizon which defines their identity. They are not willing to sacrifice everything to it, as are the ultra-nationalists, but its place cannot be denied. A stand like this is almost inevitable on the part of a small people whose language and culture has been so beleaguered for so long. The alternative would have been a most stultifying fatalism.

It is because of this identification that one can speak of a French Canadian nation, and latterly of a Québec nation. Nations exist not just where there is the objective fact of speaking the same language and sharing a common history, but where this is subjectively reflected in a people's identifications. To parody Marxist jargon, nations can't only be *an sich*, they must also be *für sich*.

And hence some variant of the conclusion of B, 5, is almost universally felt to hold by Québécois. The argument is over what the conditions are for the language/community being a viable pole of identification. Do they require sovereignty? Certainly it requires some kind of political personality for Québec. This, argue federalists, it already possesses as a province in the Canadian federation.

Two things prevent this being a satisfactory answer for (as it appears) most Québécois: a) it is not clear that the province has all the powers it would need to ensure the level of realization it aspires to, and b) the French fact in Canada still lacks international recognition.

Sovereignty-association claims to fill these two lacunae. Whether it could really deliver as promised is a big question, but at least it looks on the face of it as if it could. A new form of Canadian federation could as well, one which was founded on a recognition of the duality which is basic to the country. A public acceptance that the country was the locus of two nations could allow the international recognition which has hitherto always been muted.

I can't hide that I consider the federal solution much the preferable one. Sovereignty-association seems to me near-disastrous for two reasons: (i) there will in fact be too much divergence of interest, coupled with bad blood, to work it. If it got off the ground at all, our association would start breaking up almost immediately. This the more so, in that the will to make it work is absent among ultra-nationalists in Québec, for whom the association is only a stop-gap measure to make separation less abrupt and traumatic, and thus also to make it saleable to the majority in the province. Even if it were to get off the drawing board, sovereignty-association would almost surely end badly. (ii) sovereignty-association is the project of the ultra-nationalists; if it wins, their vision of Québec will be correspondingly strengthened. But few things are more spiritually destructive for a community than to have ultra-nationalism win out, and a full-blooded affirmation of 2 in its most extreme variant made the basis of its social life. First, it breeds a willingness to sacrifice everything else on the altar of the nation; and then nationalism itself becomes an obsession with power.

But as things stand, only a renewed federation based on duality can be a long term alternative to separation. That is, no long term solution will be viable which fails to come to terms with the place that variants of argument B have in Québec. But such a solution would require that English-Canada come to have some understanding for B and hence for Québec. And of this there is very little sign.

I have been discussing why nations have to become states. We have seen that beyond the traditional justification A, there are a possible complex of arguments adumbrated in B, which can justify statehood. But whereas A seems to give sufficient grounds for demanding sovereignty, since this is the necessary condition of republican self-rule, the predicament defined by B is more complicated.

The requirements of expression, realization and recognition may push us towards sovereignty as a solution. But there may also be good reasons pushing us the other way. The advantages of supra-national collaboration are more and more evident to us. These are partly economic and technological, as has been stressed in the European community, and in some of the arguments for maintaining Canadian unity. But they are also spiritual, in opening not only a wider identification, but also a plurality of poles of identification. This can help protect us from the stultifying, repressive obsession with the nation, which is one of the standing dangers in modern civilization.

That is why federation remains an important option, just as Montesquieu and Rousseau saw two centuries ago, when our modern ideal of self-rule began to establish itself. In the best world nations wouldn't *have* to become states. It should be one of their options (self-determination), but not the highest, not *the* option, to quote the title of a recent book. A higher aspiration is to supra-national unity, following the best of the modern political tradition.

NOTE

1. e.g., Charbonneau et Paquette, "L'acte de 1867, une constitution colonialiste" *L'option,* 125.

CANADA-QUÉBEC: A DIALOGUE*

Stanley G. FRENCH and Storrs McCALL

McCALL Let me see if I can state what I take to be the main points of agreement and disagreement between us. We both support the maintenance, spread and flourishing of French language and culture in Quebec. Stanley believes that this can be accomplished only through Quebec assuming effective control over such major culture-related institutions as education, immigration, social policy and economic policy. Furthermore, he believes that Canada in its present form is not a viable political framework for the preservation and promotion of Quebecois language and culture, and that Quebec sovereignty is necessary for the realization of this end.

At this point we part company. In my opinion, Canada precisely does provide a viable framework for the preservation and promotion of Quebecois language and culture, and the rapid evolution of Quebec society for the past ten or fifteen years shows this to be so. Furthermore, the million or so Francophones who live outside Quebec stand in need of protection, as all minorities do, against the domination of the majority, and here too the federal framework performs a useful, even indispensable role. If we were to ask in general what democracy was, we would be as inclined to answer that democracy meant protection against tyranny as that democracy meant majority rule. As long as Canada stands foursquare for minority rights — the rights of women, Francophones, native peoples, children, old people, ethnic minorities of a hundred different languages and traditions — then Canada is the best option for all of us. If Canada were to condone discrimination against Quebecois, or deny us our democratic rights, then I agree that Quebec's independence would have to be seriously considered as an alternative.

FRENCH From the point of view that I represent, your preliminary remarks contain a number of claims, not to mention attitudes, that reflect the articulate anglophone side of our historical two solitudes.

---

* Pour la version française voir l'appendice.

For example, you imply that francophones are just another Canadian ethnic minority, to be treated, of course, in a "foursquare" manner. Contrast your view with the position that there are two (or three) founding peoples in Canada, anglophones and francophones (and native peoples).

The francophone founding nation has not enjoyed the same rights and privileges as the anglophone in this state called Canada. Anglophones in Québec have had their own publicly supported school system. Francophones in Canada have not. Anglophones in Québec have received medical and other services in their own language. Francophones in Canada have not.

You refer to the rapid evolution of Québec society in the past decade or so, and conclude from this that Canada does provide a viable framework for the preservation and promotion of Québécois language and culture. There are two difficulties in this line of argumentation. The first is that, as one of the founding peoples, the Québécois(es) should not have been placed in the position of requiring rattrapage. Secondly, when one has been discriminated against, a gradualist solution is unsatisfactory. One wants justice now.

Canada does not stand foursquare for minority rights. The rights of women (although not a minority), of francophones, of native peoples, have since the 1960's received only grudging recognition, and very little in the way of positive action. The Canadian Bill of Rights has not been incorporated in the constitution, it does not take precedence over previously existing legislation, and it has proved to have little if any practical significance. We establish Royal Commissions and then ignore their findings and recommendations. Conscious members of victim groups must weigh the advantages of continued association against the disadvantages of sometimes intolerable situations.

McCALL I'm glad to be called "articulate", but not so glad to think that I'm still locked into one of the two solitudes. Still, let me do my best. I didn't want to give the impression that I regard Francophones as just one of Canada's many minorities. I do believe in the notion of two (or three) founding peoples, just as you do, Stanley.

I also agree that the francophone founding nation has not enjoyed the same rights and privileges as the Anglophone. Examples are the 1890 Manitoba schools legislation and Regulation 17 in Ontario. But to dwell solely on the injustices of the past does not bring us any closer to their resolution in the present. Certainly progress has been slow. But there has been progress nonetheless, and it is continuing. In the last few months, for example, British Columbia has passed legislation giving the right to public education in French to any group of 10 or more Francophone children in a community. From one point of view this is gradualism, but from another one cannot help but admire the direct and prompt way in which the B.C. government has acted.

Would B.C. have so acted had they not been part of Canada? I doubt it.

I agree that Canada has moved very slowly on minority rights. We have not, as you point out, seen fit to entrench a bill of rights in our constitution. But now the mood seems to be changing. Half the provincial premiers were in favour of entrenchment at the last premiers' conference. Is it not time to act now, and push for explicit recognition of individual and minority rights, rather than give up and say that Canada might as well die?

FRENCH I think, Storrs, that now we are approaching the heart of the matter. It is clear that you place a high value on the continued existence of a Canada that includes Québec. I understand, because this has been — indeed, is — one of my own values. In one of my personae I would seriously regret the creation of yet another state in the world. As an anglophone Canadian living in (say) London-Ontario, Québec is that feature of Canada that I most admire. Take away Québec and you take away the uniqueness of Canada, the soul of Canada. Then Ontario may as well annex itself to the United States.

But as a Québécois I have no interest, really, in the maintenance of Canada. I neither know, nor care, where London-Ontario is. Your history is not my history. Your geography is not mine. My home is Québec, not Canada. Visiting Toronto or Edmonton is like visiting a foreign country. In fact, I am treated with more courtesy and respect when I visit New York, or Miami.

Think of Canada-Québec as a marriage that is disintegrating. One partner says that, on the whole, he has enjoyed the marriage. Although occasionally unfaithful to her, he loves his wife. Without her, he would be seriously diminished. They are already separated, but not legally so. Some children live with the father, some with the mother. The children must be protected through the continuation of the institution. Divorce will result in economic hardship for both parties. Let's be practical, make a list of our differences, seek compromises, perhaps see a marriage counsellor.

I reply that somehow you are missing the point. To begin with I was forced into the marriage. I was used. I gave more than I received. Because of my language (my gender), you assigned rôles to me that suited your convenience. By and large I did the dirty work, the tedious work, the household chores. You said that this was the natural order of things.

You deprived me of my dignity, my self-respect. Time is running out for me. Now, before it is to late, I want to be autonomous.

I want to live alone, to make my own decisions. I am willing to make the necessary economic sacrifices. The anglophones in my custody will be treated with at least as much consideration as the francophones living with you. I hope that we shall remain friends.

There is no point in our seeing a counsellor because I am not motivated to try to save the marriage. It is typical of you to think in terms of a finite list of negotiable grievances. Of course I have serious grievances; but in the end my desire for autonomy is a non-quantifiable, non-negotiable feeling. Let me live alone for awhile. Allow my self-respect to become firmly rooted. Then perhaps we can form a partnership of equals based upon mutual respect.

McCALL You paint an emotional picture, using the powerful simile of an unhappily married couple moving towards divorce. But I am not sure how appropriate this emotional picture is. First, I am not sure how many Quebecois share the feelings you portray. My own experience is that many or most do not. Second, what are important in a discussion of this kind are not emotions but arguments. What would justify separation? Not merely a sense of past injustices, or a desire for independence. What is required is an argument to show that these injustices are irremediable: that Canada does not, and in all likelihood never will, provide a framework in which Quebec can live, grow and have her being. So far I have not seen such an argument produced.

In fact, as far as arguments go, it seems to me that most of the weight lies on the other side. French language and culture have never been livelier in Quebec than they are now, and new life is being breathed into the francophone communities outside Quebec by her example. These changes have taken place within confederation. Depending on what happens over the next few years, we have the opportunity to create in Canada something very rare in the world: a society in which more than one language and culture live together for the mutual benefit of all. The alternative is to risk locking ourselves into narrow, inward-looking and exclusive national states.

Before it is too late, and before attitudes on both sides harden past the point of no return (attitudes of "let them go" outside Quebec are even more destructive than separatist attitudes here) let us act to bring people together. Canada needs to be re-created, not destroyed.

FRENCH I want now to delineate some of the options available to Canada and Québec. One can distinguish a range of possibilities, from (1), maintenance of the status quo, through (5), Québec sovereignty as a nation-state.

I shall say nothing about (1) other than that, in your comments thus far, you seem sometimes to favor the status quo ("Canada precisely does provide a viable framework..."), and at other times to support another model ("Is it not time to act now, and push for explicit recognition of individual and minority rights...").

(2) *Constitutional Reform* This model involves (i) transfer (patriation) of the British North America Act from Britain to Canada; (ii) amendments to the Act, including substantial changes in the division of powers (federal-provincial); (iii) a bill of rights enshrined in the constitution, including language rights, and the right to an education in French or English. In (2), Canada remains one state with two (or three) founding nations. There is one constitution. The reformed constitution may delegate certain powers to Québec subject to the constraints of a charter of rights. There is some evidence that you would support (2), but it is logically possible that you would accept (3).

(3) *Special Status for Québec* Like (2), this model requires patriation of the constitution and constitutional reform. The amended constitution would explicitly recognize that Québec is pas comme les autres. Québec would be guaranteed powers that the other provinces do not enjoy, powers relating to the preservation and promotion of the Québécois language and culture. The bill of rights envisaged in (2) may be anathematical in (3). Still, we have one state with one asymmetric constitution.

(4) *Sovereignty-Association* Now we have crossed the watershed. We have not one, but two constitutions. The constitution of Québec grants it unlimited sovereignty over A, B, and C (e.g., immigration, communications), while X, Y, and Z are shared with Canada (e.g., defence, the Canadian monetary system). In my next interjection I shall attempt to unpack and defend (4).

(5) *Sovereignty* Here we have two states, Canada and Québec, each with unlimited sovereignty. Québec is the 146th member of the United Nations. We have our own army, our own monetary system, our own state-supported, deficit-earning, prestige-motivated national airline, and so on. Neither of us favors (5), although our reasons may be somewhat different. I would opt for (5) over (1), whereas you, Storrs, almost certainly would not.

I invite you to spell out the position you are defending.

McCALL I'm glad we're now getting down to discussing, in a more concrete way, possible models for Canada and Quebec. Yes, you are right, I favour something in the range of models (1) - (3), and I don't support (4) or (5). I'm not a constitutional expert, and I can't say very much about just what would be the best type of "federalisme renouvelé", except that I do feel strongly about enshrining both human and linguistic rights in the constitution. However, I have serious misgivings about your model (4), sovereignty-association, which I shall attempt to state.

You say that in (4) we have not one but two constitutions, one for Quebec and one for Canada. Presumably you mean that under (4) Quebec is "sovereign" in a sense in which she is not sovereign under (3). What sense is this? This question is important to answer but also difficult, the word 'sovereignty' being ambiguous and having not one but at least two distinct senses.

In the first of its senses, sovereignty is one and indivisible: either a population or nation is sovereign or it is not. If it is, it constitutes a nation-state. If it is not, it constitutes something less than a nation state, for example a province, territory, district or, in the case of the Soviet Union, an autonomous republic. These units lack sovereignty because they are subject to the laws of a higher authority, and the choice of whether to so subject themselves either is no longer, or never was, theirs to make.

In the second sense of the word, sovereignty is something that can be shared; something that is a matter of more or less. In Canada, it is said, sovereignty is shared between the federal government and the provinces, the former being "sovereign" in matters of national defence, the latter in matters of education. In the same vein, members of the European Common Market are said to have ceded or delegated some of their sovereignty to the European parliament. It is important however to note that Britain and France, in spite of having ceded some of their sovereignty-in-sense-2, are still sovereign-in-sense-1. This is shown by the fact that if they so decided, they could withdraw from the Treaty of Rome. Sovereignty-in-sense-1 is genuinely indivisible in that it cannot be shared, though it can of course be given up in toto, meaning that the state which gives it up places itself under the jurisdiction of another state.

In your model (4) you say that we have not one but two constitutions, one for Quebec and one for Canada. Does this mean that Quebec becomes sovereign-in-sense-1? I assume it does. In that case, presumably Quebec would no longer elect representatives to Parliament in Ottawa, and the sovereignty-in-sense-2 that she would share with the remainder of Canada in matters of defence, monetary system, etc. would be exercised through joint ministerial committees. Is this feasible? Can a sovereign state entrust matters like defence and monetary policy to a committee which is not controlled by its own elected assembly? I doubt it.

If Quebec is going to be sovereign she really will have to be sovereign, and control her own money and her own army from her own elected assembly. A sovereign state can of course enter into a customs or monetary union with another state or states, as is seen from the example of the European Common Market, but to do this requires first a period of sovereignty-in-sense-1 and no shared sovereignty-in-sense-2, followed by negotiations and a collective decision to enter a period of sovereignty-in-sense-1 and some shared sovereignty-in-sense-2. Note however that in Europe there is a European parliament, and that so far there is little or no shared sovereignty in matters of defence.

More important is the suggestion that French language and culture can receive adequate protection only within the confines of a sovereign state. This does not seem to me to be true. Furthermore, as I said before, the transformation of Quebec into a sovereign state means the abandonment of the French-speaking minorities outside Quebec, whose language and culture would be unlikely to receive the support they do in our present federal system.

FRENCH In this last exchange you have done something that I find puzzling. Two things, in fact. First, you have refused an invitation to make clear the position(s) you are advocating, on the ground that you are not a constitutional expert. I shall return to this.

The second puzzle is that you do not hesitate to criticize (4), the sovereignty-association model, although this has not yet been fleshed out. Tant mieux. Your criticisms should be helpful in this process.

A constitution is the system of fundamental principles according to which a nation, state, or group is governed. In (4), the Québec nation has a constitution in which Québec has absolute sovereignty (sovereignty-in-sense-1) over such institutions as A, B, and C — generally speaking, those institutions which allow the preservation and promotion of language and culture. Québec remains, in some sense, a part of Canada. Institutions not directly relevant to the preservation and promotion of language and culture are the sovereign-in-sense-1 business of Canada-Québec and its constitution.

In the special status model, (3), Québec does not have sovereignty-in-sense-1. In (4), Québec has sovereignty-in-sense-1 over A, B, and C.

In (3), Québec is not a nation-state. In (5), Québec is. In (4), Québec is a borderline case: a nation with absolute sovereignty over A, B, and C, within a state having absolute sovereignty over X, Y, and Z.

To answer one of your questions, there would be a Canada-Québec parliament (possibly analogous to the European parliament) in which elected representatives from Québec and from Canada would exercise legislative power over X, Y, and Z. Canada and Québec each would have a national assembly to deal with A, B, and C.

What reasons may be given for preferring sovereignty-association over special status? First, one assumes that the preservation and promotion of language and culture will be better served when Québec has sovereignty-in-sense-1 over A, B, and C. With the ceded special status of (3), the preservation and promotion of language and culture is not constitutionally guaranteed, it is subject always to the good faith of the anglophone majority.

Another reason for preferring (4) to (3) is that sovereignty-association is more likely to nurture the sought-after dignity, or self-respect. With (3), one is still, by one's very special status, a second-class citizen.

The most telling argument against sovereignty-association — apart from the fact than no precedent exists — is that the rights of minorities in Québec, and in Canada, may suffer. Here I assume that, in negotiating the new constitutions of Québec, Canada, and Canada-Québec, each nation will attempt to protect constitutionally the relevant minorities living outside.

Returning now to the points made in your penultimate paragraph concerning the European Market model, these it seems to me apply more to (5) than to (4). What you say may apply also to the version of sovereignty-association envisaged by certain members of the Parti Québécois. About this we cannot be certain, since the Parti Québécois has steadfastly refused to say what it means.

I quote from the *Bulletin de liaison* of the Parti Québécois (janvier 1979, p.4): "La souveraineté-association n'est pas encore définie, mais le terrain est déjà 'balisé', comme les ponts de glace sur les rivières durant l'hiver." Such reticence — one is tempted to say political canniness — is not however the exclusive domain of the Parti Québécois. The federal Liberal member for Westmount has this to say in *The Westmount Examiner* (11 January 79, p.5): "What should the position of the federal government be if, say, 60 percent of Quebecers vote 'yes' to a referendum question asking whether Québec should negotiate sovereignty-association with the rest of Canada?. . . My view is that no disclosure of federal strategy should be discussed in advance of knowing what the question will be and what the actual results are riding by riding and region by region."

As philosophers we may rush in where politicians fear to tread. You say that you feel strongly about enshrining both human and linguistic rights in the constitution. Will you give some specific examples? Should the right to an education in French or English be entrenched in the constitution? If you answer in the affirmative, as apparently you do, how do you respond to the claim that such a step actually would undermine Québécois language and culture?

McCALL I like your statement to the effect that philosophers rush in where politicians fear to tread. In this discussion we are certainly freer than most, and can explore the realm of ideas with equanimity. But there are, nevertheless, some constraints. Your concept of sovereignty-association strikes me as being internally inconsistent. This is something that must be straightened out.

Under sovereignty-association, would Quebec be sovereign-in-sense-1? Your answer is a sort of yes-and-no. She would have sovereignty-in-sense-1 over institutions which allow the preservation and promotion of language and culture. Over other institutions it would be not Quebec (and not Canada) that would be sovereign-in-sense-1, but a new entity called Canada-Quebec. "Canada", i.e. the other nine provinces, would presumably be sovereign over its language and culture in its territory.

This model won't work, because it is incoherent. Either one is sovereign-in-sense-1 or one is not. One cannot share sovereignty-in-sense-1. What can be shared, and what is shared in federal Canada and in the ECM, is sovereignty-in-sense-2. So it does not make sense to say that Quebec might have absolute sovereignty-in-sense-1 over language and culture-related institutions, but not over other matters.

You have to choose between two alternatives. Either Quebec will be sovereign-in-sense-1, in which case she will ipso facto be sovereign over all language and culture matters, or she will not be sovereign-in-sense-1. If the latter alternative is chosen Quebec will be, as she is now, part of some larger state that is sovereign-in-sense-1. However, within that larger state, it would still be possible, with respect to language and culture matters, for Quebec to be sovereign-in-sense-2. But you can't have it both ways. That is why I keep asking whether, under sovereignty-associaton, Quebec will be sovereign-in-sense-1.

You may think that these questions about sovereignty are legalistic and pedantic. They are not. They go, in fact, to the heart of the notion of sovereignty-association. Let us suppose, for example, that Quebec were sovereign-in-sense-1, that she entered into a customs and monetary union with the rest of Canada, and that in 10 years' time she became dissatisfied with these economic arrangements and decided that she wanted to issue her own currency. Being sovereign-in-sense-1, she could do so. She could withdraw from the monetary union. The decision would be hers, and hers alone. If, however, she were not sovereign-in-sense-1, the decision would not be hers alone. If she wanted to issue her own currency, or raise an army, she would have to seek permission from the sovereign state of which she was a part, and it is unlikely that such permission would be given. The only way to avoid the necessity of obtaining the agreement of others is to be sovereign-in-sense-1.

Let me turn now to the question of enshrining human and linguistic rights in the constitution. This, as you say, is a project dear to my heart. I believe that the following linguistic rights, among others, should be enshrined:

(1) The right of every Canadian to communicate with and obtain services from the federal and provincial governments in either French or English.

(2) The right of every Canadian whose mother tongue is French or English to have his children educated in their mother tongue, where numbers so warrant.

(3) The right of every Canadian to receive health care services, and to appear before the courts, in French or English, where numbers so warrant.

Why are these rights important? They're important because, without them, we don't have any clear idea of what citizenship consists in. What, after all, distinguishes me from an American, or for that matter from a citizen of France? Surely one very obvious thing is that I belong to a country which is in some important sense officially bilingual. No matter where I choose to live in Canada, no matter whether I am French or English-speaking, I can be assured at least that I will be able to receive some government services and that my children will be able to be educated in their mother tongue. These minimal elements of Canadian citizenship must be spelled out in the constitution, and it will be a measure of the goodwill of all Canadians how generous provinces are prepared to be in specifying the "where numbers so warrant" clauses.

You, I gather, have two misgivings about letting Canada rather than Quebec be the vehicle for promoting language and culture. First, you say, such promotion would always be subject to the good faith of the anglophone majority. Of course you are right in that no constitution which represents an agreement among contracting parties is workable without good faith on all sides. But if linguistic and cultural guarantees are built into the constitution, then the preservation and promotion of French language and culture will rest upon something more than just good faith. Secondly, you wonder whether a guaranteed right to education in French or English might not actually undermine Quebecois language and culture. Could you spell this out? Would the restriction to mother tongue French or English allay your fears?

FRENCH For the benefit of those of our readers who have been patient enough to come this far, I should explain, Storrs, that we have engaged in this dialogue for a number of reasons: because we both are deeply concerned about the future of Québec and of Canada; so that we may provide some input to the CPA conference on the future of Canadian federation; and also for the sheer enjoyment that one derives from such philosophical activity.

I hope that our concern, and our enjoyment, will lead us to continue this dialogue in the critical weeks and months ahead. This will be, however, my last contribution prior to the CPA conference. I wish therefore to say a few general things before turning specifically to what you have written above.

We seem to share the following goals. We actively support the desire to preserve and promote the Québécois language and culture. Neither of us supports Québec sovereignty in the sense of the creation of yet another world state, model (5), although I would prefer outright sovereignty to the status quo. We are concerned about minority rights. We favor patriation and reform of the constitution. We feel a certain sense of pride and identity as citizens of a two- (or three-) nation bilingual state. I particularly like the passage in which you talk about what distinguishes you from an American, or from a citizen of France.

At this stage in the dialogue we have been unable to find agreement concerning the means to these ends. Using the oversimplified models that I set out so that our discussion might become more substantive, I have attempted to defend a form of sovereignty-association for Québec. (I shall come to your criticisms in due course.) Another model that I am prepared to explore, as a second choice, is special status for Québec. You are certainly opposed to sovereignty-association. You are probably opposed to special status. And although you are reluctant to commit yourself, it does seem from your previous interjection that constitutional reform is the limit of your willingness to negotiate.

Turning now, briefly, to what I take to be the beginning of your exposition and defence of a constitutional reform model, I would make the following comments. (a) In your (2) you should of course have written "...his/her children". (b) What is the rationale for these rights? Do you regard them as self-evident?

(c) Why these particular rights, as opposed to certain apparently similar alternatives? Take your (2), for example. We have the following possibilities:

2.1 The right of every Canadian to an education in French or English;

2.2 The right of every Canadian whose mother tongue is French or English to have his/her children educated in their mother tongue...

Why have you opted for 2.2 rather than 2.1? You do not say.

(d) The rights proposed by you are each designed to protect certain minorities, francophones in Canada, anglophones in Québec. The protection of such francophone rights in Canada may cost money, and may cause certain inconveniences and resentments, but the dominant anglophone culture in North America will not be threatened. On the other side, it can be argued that the protection of these rights in Québec, for the anglophone minority, does pose a threat to the survival of the Québécois language and culture. For example, if your (1), (2), and (3) were enshrined in the Canadian constitution, anglophone Canadians would once again find Québec an attractive place to live and work in their mother tongue, they would migrate to Québec for economic and other reasons, the embattled Québec majority, which is a North American minority, would continue and accelerate its slide into powerlessness and merely token existence. I think that I am not indulging in empty rhetoric. There is an important sense in which protection of minority rights, while no doubt desirable for francophones in Canada, tends to undermine the attempt to make Québec a secure francophone national territory. Do you not acknowledge this as a special problem?

Turning finally to your critique of my sovereignty-association model, it seems to me that we have gotten into a typical philosophical conundrum. Earlier in this paper you defined 'sovereignty', 'sovereignty-in-sense-1', and 'sovereignty-in-sense-2'. This was done a priori, so to speak. Now you say that my "concept" of sovereignty-association is "internally inconsistent", and that my "model" is "incoherent". Your argument is based upon your definitions of 'sovereignty'.

Let me try to defend my position. Concerning sovereignty-association, four questions interest me: (1) Would it be possible *in fact* to establish the type of two-nation state outlined above? I think that it would be possible; and you have not argued the contrary. (2) Even though possible to establish in fact, would such a two-nation state work? Again, I think so, but more modeling needs to be done. (3) Do the advantages-disadvantages of sovereignty-association outweigh the advantages-disadvantages of the status quo, of constitutional reform with the protection of minority rights, of special status, and of outright sovereignty? I think so, but would like to explore special status further before finally making up my mind.

(4) Is sovereignty-association logically possible, conceptually coherent? Your critique is limited to this question. Now it seems to me that if a model could be implemented in fact, and if it would work, then if there is a logical or conceptual problem, we must return to our definition of 'sovereignty' to resolve the confusion. This is what I propose to do.

The word 'sovereign' means greatest in rank or power, independent of the control of other governments, the final arbiter, so to speak. Now, one is sovereign *over* something, just as a property is a property of something. One can be sovereign over *some* of the institutions (in Rawls' sense) in a society, or one can be sovereign over *all* of the institutions. Thus, when we write that "either a population or nation is sovereign or it is not", we should write, to be exact, that either a population or nation is final arbiter over all of its institutions, or it is not; if not all of its institutions, then the population is final arbiter over some, or none of its institutions.

There are then several distinctions with respect to sovereignty that must be made. One may be final arbiter over all, some, or no institutions. One may have ceded authority over all, some, or no institutions. In the above I am talking about legal authority; but there is also *de facto* sovereignty. A population may be the constitutional final arbiter with respect to institution A, or it may have legally ceded authority over A, or it may have *de facto* authority over A, or it may have no authority over A.

The basis of your critique seems to be the definitional assumption that either one is the constitutional final arbiter over all institutions (the traditional sovereign state), or one has only ceded powers. This is why you write that I "have to choose between two alternatives". Well, there are more than two options, as I think I have shown.

Sovereignty-association cannot be defined out of existence.

McCALL You are right. Sovereignty-association cannot be defined out of existence. The trouble is, you have not yet succeeded in defining it into existence. This is not surprising, in view of the fact that there must be a dozen different conceptions of sovereignty-association floating around Quebec today. Nevertheless, until we can get straight about at least the general form of sovereignty-association, we shall not make any progress in discussing its merits.

As you point out, a people can be legally or constitutionally sovereign over some of its institutions, or it can be sovereign over all of them. Only in the latter case is it sovereign-in-sense-1. Note that among the institutions which fall within the purview of sovereignty-in-sense-1 is the constitution itself. A people sovereign in this sense can amend its own constitution, it can change the terms of its association with other peoples. A people which has only sovereignty-in-sense-2 cannot. To be the constitutional final arbiter with respect to some but not all of one's institutions means that one possesses sovereignty-in-sense-2 within the framework of a larger state which possesses sovereignty-in-sense-1. As I said before, sovereignty-in-sense-1 is an all-or-nothing matter. Either you have it or you don't. You can't be sovereign-in-sense-1 over some institutions but not others.

From what you have said, it seems clear that under sovereignty-association Quebec would not be sovereign-in-sense-1. I may be misunderstanding you on this point, but I believe what I say is correct. Under your option (4) of sovereignty-association above, "the constitution of Québec grants it unlimited sovereignty over A, B and C (e.g. immigration, communications), while X, Y and Z are shared with Canada (e.g. defence, the Canadian monetary system)". What you do not make clear is whether under (4) Quebec could unilaterally alter the terms of her relationship with Canada. In all probability she could not, since you say later on that Quebec would "remain, in some sense, part of Canada." So be it. If Quebec must seek approval in a Canada-Quebec parliament for constitutional and other changes she may desire, she is not sovereign-in-sense-1.

Two things follow from this. The first is that your model of sovereignty-association, Stanley, differs radically from that of the Parti Québécois. Under their model Quebec would not elect representatives to a Canada-Quebec parliament. She would not be subject to legislation enacted by such a body. She could unilaterally alter her relationship with Canada, and she could amend her own constitution. The Parti Québécois position, therefore, is one which is souverainiste in the full sense of the word. Yours in not. Secondly, if under sovereignty-association as you conceive it Quebec is not sovereign-in-sense-1, your model (4) does not differ fundamentally from what we have now. Under (4), as far as I can see, Canada would still be a federation. It would be a renewed federation perhaps; a federation with a new constitution; a federation in which Quebec had more powers than she has now; maybe even a two-member federation instead of a ten-member one; but it would be a federation nonetheless. Your option (4), therefore, falls within the range of federalist options, albeit at one extreme end of the range.

To sum up, you have attempted to carve out some middle ground, under the name of sovereignty-association, between sovereign statehood and the various types of federalist option. But there is no middle ground. If Quebec is not to be a sovereign state, the next greatest degree of autonomy she can possess is to be one of the partners in a federation. To believe otherwise is an illusion.

Let me now say something about the entrenchment of language rights in the constitution, in reply to your questions. You ask why I selected just the rights (1), (2), (3) that I listed, and what the rationale for them was. Well, I didn't try to be exhaustive in my list, but merely to present certain rights that seemed to me essential if Canada was to continue as a bilingual country. By this I don't mean a country in which everyone speaks both languages, but one in which all citizens have at the very least the right to receive certain government services in English or French, and to obtain education in their mother tongue for their children. If these rights are not available, what meaning can we attach to being a citizen of a bilingual country? You ask whether according such rights to the anglophone minority in Quebec might not pose a threat to Quebecois language and culture, and you raise the possibility that anglophones from other provinces, encouraged by entrenchment of the right to mother-tongue education for their children, might not rush to Quebec in sufficient numbers to swamp the "embattled Quebec majority". Are you joking, or are you serious? For those of us here in Quebec, the question is not whether the anglophone community is going to swallow up the francophones, but whether in ten years' time there is going to be an appreciable anglophone community left.

To conclude on a rather more positive note, I am delighted to see the list you drew up of points on which we agree. The list is a substantial one: promoting Quebecois language and culture, avoiding the creation of a new nation-state, concern about minority rights, patriation and reform of the constitution, a sense of pride and identity as citizens of a two- (or three-) nation bilingual state. To me, the list points to one thing and one thing alone: the urgent need for a renewed constitutional framework, within the overall context of Canada, which can encompass and sustain each one of these points of agreement. As I said before, now is not the time to destroy Canada, now is the time to create her as she should be created. It ought not to be beyond man's powers to find a constitutional formula which does this, a formula which gives Canada's own particular answer to the question whether people of different languages and different traditions can learn to get along. We must work to build together a society and way of life which, based upon two cultures, draws its strength from both.

NATION, STATE, SOVEREIGNTY and SELF-DETERMINATION

NATION, ETAT, SOUVERAINETE et AUTO-DETERMINATION

PARTICIPANTS

ROBERT BINKLEY
Philosophy, University of Western Ontario

VENANT CAUCHY
Philosophie, Université de Montréal

DAVID COPP
Philosophy, Simon Fraser University

FRANK CUNNINGHAM
Philosophy, University of Toronto

STANLEY G. FRENCH
Philosophy, Concordia University

PAUL GAGNE
Philosophie, Université du Québec à Trois Rivières

THEODORE GERAETS
Philosophie, Université d'Ottawa

DAN GOLDSTICK
Philosophy, University of Toronto

BRUCE HUNTER
Philosophy, University of Alberta

GUY LAFRANCE
Philosophie, Université d'Ottawa

VINCENT LEMIEUX
Science politique, Université Laval

STORRS McCALL
Philosophy, McGill University

JEAN-GUY MEUNIER
Philosophie, Université du Québec à Montréal

CHRISTOPHER MORRIS
Philosophie, Université d'Ottawa

LESLIE MULHOLLAND
Philosophy, Memorial University

ANDRE PARADIS
Philosophie, Université du Québec à Trois Rivières

JACQUES PLAMONDON
Philosophie, Université de Sherbrooke

SHELDON RICHMOND
Philosophy, Acadia University

STANLEY BREHAUT RYERSON
Histoire, Université du Québec à Montréal

FRANCIS SPARSHOTT
Philosophy, University of Toronto

LEON THIRY
Philosophy, Wilfrid Laurier University

FREDERICK VAUGHN
Political Studies, University of Guelph

JUDITH WUBNIG
Philosophy, University of Waterloo

WORKSHOP I REPORT

ATELIER I RAPPORT

Introduction

This workshop was composed of some 27 participants. Because of its size and the fact that few opinions were advanced not already contained in abstracts of papers, the rapporteurs have not attempted to take account of the details of the various discussions and debates. Instead we summarize the main points raised around three questions — What is a nation? Is there a right of national self-determination? What is sovereignty? — and take note of some themes that recurred through the discussion of each of these questions.

Nation

A la question "qu'est-ce qu'une nation?", les opinions exprimées pourraient s'énoncer comme suit:

a) Un nombre très minoritaire de participants ont soutenu que le concept de nation est un concept qui n'a aucun référent sur le plan de la réalité socio-culturelle puisque empiriquement il n'existe et ne peut exister en fait que des individus. En conséquence, on ne peut parler qu'improprement d'une nation, c'est-à-dire dans la seule mesure où elle réfère à un contrat toujours susceptible d'être abrogé entre des individus.

b) Une opinion a été émise à l'effet que le concept de nation fait sens mais qu'il s'agit là d'un concept archaïque qui renvoit à une représentation aujourd'hui périmée. S'il était conséquent de parler de la nation au XVIIIe ou au XIXe siècle, il faudrait plutôt de nos jours, compte tenu du développement économique et politique mondial, parler non plus de la nation mais de l'Etat comme facteur de cohésion et d'unité des peuples et des collectivités géographiquement situées.

c) De façon très majoritaire, les participants de l'atelier ont convenu qu'il existe bien une entité telle que la nation et que cette entité est irréductible à celle d'Etat. Mais les critères qu'on peut évoquer pour définir la nation ne font pas consensus. Ces critères peuvent être la territorialité, le sentiment d'appartenance, une langue et une culture commune, des habitudes d'interaction, la viabilité économique, la capacité concrète d'une collectivité de générer un Etat propre, l'histoire, l'altérité et le sens de l'identité qui résulte de conflits avec d'autres collectivités. Il n'y a pas unanimité ici sur la priorité de l'un ou de l'autre de ces critères ni sur la définition exacte qu'il convient de leur attribuer.

Self-determination

Those who thought that there is no viable sense of "nation" obviously thought there are not natural rights of national self-determination. All the other participants agreed that there is a *prima facie* right of national self-determination. The main discussion turned around such questions as whether or how this right could be overridden and whether a right to self-determination entails a right to secession. There was some discussion about whether or in what respects the rights of non-seceding parts of a state should be taken account of in such a situation.

Souveraineté

La discussion s'est engagée sur le concept de souveraineté. Il en est ressorti que la souveraineté peut:

a) soit être entendue comme absolue, indivisible et non susceptible d'être partagée;

b) soit être entendue comme divisible et susceptible de faire l'objet de négociations entre deux ou plusieurs partenaires.

A la première acception, on a objecté que des états peuvent partager ou céder une partie de leur pouvoir à d'autres états tout en demeurant souverains au sens fort du terme. En outre, la souveraineté d'un état peut, dans certains cas, ne pas être reconnue par la communauté internationale ou encore, dans le cas où elle est effectivement reconnue, ne pas impliquer pour autant la reconnaissance du droit pour une nation d'être représentée ipso facto dans des organismes internationaux comme l'ONU.

Recurring questions

Three questions, given a variety of answers, recurred through the day's discussions:

1. Can (and/or should) one think of Quebec or of other such entities collectively, or should such things as collectives and collective rights be thought of individualistically?

2. Are there different ideological commitments that shape both philosophical and political debate concerning the confederation question? If so, what are they, and what are their effects on the debate?

3. To what extent do (or should) considerations of political economy enter into the understanding of the workshop's themes, and can specifically philosophical issues be treated in isolation from them?

Frank CUNNINGHAM and André PARADIS

NATION, STATE, SOVEREIGNTY, SELF-DETERMINATION, THE POPULAR WILL AND THE RIGHT TO SECESSION. NOTES TOWARD THE ELUCIDATION OF THESE NOTIONS IN THE CONTEXT OF THE DEBATE CONCERNING CANADA'S FUTURE.

Stanley G. FRENCH and Storrs McCALL

1. **State** A state is an independent political entity, sovereign (see below), both possessing and able to amend its own constitution. (Of the 145 members of the UN, Canada is the only one which requires legislative action on the part of another state to amend its constitution.)

2. **Nation** The word 'nation' is frequently taken to be synonymous with 'state'. Thus we speak of "international relations", "the national debt", etc. But 'nation' is also used to refer to populations of individuals ("peoples") who do not constitute a state. Candidates would include the Scots, the Basques, the Bretons, the Latvians, the Nagas, the Croatians, the Ibos, the Wallons, the Armenians, the Kurds and the *Québécois.* Whether or not all these are nations has been and will continue to be the subject of debate. Current usage favours the word 'nationality' in some contexts: thus it is natural to speak of the Swiss republic as comprising four "nationalities" rather than four "nations".

In order to constitute a nation, what common characteristics must a group of people share? It has at various times been claimed that nations are populations bound together by a common language, history, soul, spirit, destiny, homeland, race, culture, or some combination thereof. Nations are not arbitrary collections of people. Nor could they be bound together by a fortuitous characteristic such as left-handedness. There must be something that unites them, yet no one characteristic has emerged to serve as the defining criterion of nationhood.

Although a single objective property of nationhood eludes us, a subjective or attitudinal one can be found. This is, that the members of a nation must be conscious of or identify themselves as such. To belong to a nation, therefore, would seem to require if nothing else that the people in question call themselves a nation, and are so called by others.

3. **Sovereignty** This word is ambiguous, and should be used with great care. In the first of its senses, sovereignty is one and indivisible: either a population or nation is sovereign or it is not. If it is, it constitutes a nation-state. If it is not, it constitutes something less than a nation-state, for example a province, territory, district or, in the case of the Soviet Union, an autonomous republic. These units lack sovereignty because they are subject to the laws of a higher authority, and the choice of whether to so subject themselves either is no longer, or never was, theirs to make.

In the second sense of the word, sovereignty is something that can be shared; something that is a matter of more or less. In Canada, it is said, sovereignty is shared between the federal government and the provinces, the former being "sovereign" in matters of national defence, the latter in matters of education. In the same vein, members of the European Common Market are said to have ceded or delegated some of their sovereignty to the European parliament. It is important however to note that Britain and France, in spite of having ceded some of their sovereignty-in-sense-2, are still sovereign-in-sense-1. This is shown by that fact that if they so decided, they could withdraw from the Treaty of Rome. Sovereignty-in-sense-1 is genuinely indivisible in that it cannot be shared, though it can of course be given up *in toto,* meaning that the state which gives it up places itself under the jurisdiction of another state.

This ambiguity in the meaning of the word 'sovereignty' is harmless, provided it is clear which sense is being used. If it is not, those who debate over whether and to what extent Québec is already "sovereign" risk talking at cross-purposes.

4. **Self-determination** Self-determination is an act or process whereby a group of people take a collective decision as to how they wish to be governed. The alternatives are either to be self-governing, i.e., to constitute themselves into a sovereign state, or to be governed by or in association with others, i.e., to put themselves under the jurisdiction of another state. Two major problems concerning self-determination are: (i) Who has the right to self-determination? (ii) What procedural norms should be satisfied by the exercise of this right?

Under (i), it seems clear that not every group of people has the right to self-determination. Few if any jurists would accord it to, say, the residents of Longueuil, or Martha's Vineyard. Historically, the right to self-determination has been recognized almost exclusively in only two types of case: nationalities emerging from the break-up of the

Austro-Hungarian, German, Russian and Turkish empires following the first world war, and ex-colonies which achieved independence following the second. It is questionable whether candidates for a third wave of self-determination — ethnic minorities within already existing states — would achieve similar recognition for their right, given that in their case opting for independence would involve the added step of separation or secession. Conditional recognition of the right, i.e., recognition of the right to select options up to but not including secession, is conceivable, but is not tantamount to self-determination in the full sense of the word.

Under (ii), problems arise concerning how the right to self-determination is to be exercised. Is it to be by free choice of the electorate? Following full and fair presentation of the options? What majority of the vote would be required? For these questions see below.

5. **The Will of the People** Although it has been argued that the will of the people, or the national will, may in certain conditions be incarnated in the figure of one man (Louis XIV, Churchill), modern democratic traditions regard it as expressed through an act of collective choice, defined as the aggregation of individual preferences. For the moulding of these preferences in the case of an act of self-determination, public access to information and the right of individuals to campaign freely are essential. Various difficult problems concern the vote which determines the collective choice. First, the question posed on the ballot must not be capable of misinterpretation. Second, in a question which may determine the future of a people for a hundred years or more, a plurality of 50% plus one vote is not sufficient. By the same token, unanimity is out of the question. What figure between these two extremes would be a reasonable one is open to debate: perhaps two-thirds. If the population engaging in the act of self-determination itself contains a substantial minority, as in Québec, the position becomes yet more complicated.

6. **The Right to Secession** Self-determination on the part of a sub-population of a state implies, among other options, the option of secession. Because of the effects of secession on the non-seceding parts of the state, the right to self-determination cannot be regarded as an absolute right, nor can it be regarded as identical with the right to secession. What justifies the latter right? Something else, surely, than simply the desire for independence. If, for example, there were discrimination, or if the secessionists had been denied their

democratic rights, then separation might be justified. Even so, it would have to be shown that the wrongs suffered by the disaffected party were too deeply ingrained to be corrected within the framework of the existing state.

ETAT, NATION, SOUVERAINETE ET AUTODETERMINATION: EN REPONSE A MES COLLEGUES STANLEY FRENCH ET STORRS McCALL

André PARADIS

Le débat constitutionnel n'est pas, à mon sens, un débat qui gagne à être posé *in abstracto,* comme s'il suffisait de poser au départ quelques définitions et quelques principes de base pour pontifier, à partir de telles prémisses strictement normatives, sur ce que doivent être ou peuvent être les alternatives acceptables et tolérables d'une collectivité nationale. Faut-il se rappeler en effet que l'histoire politique s'est presque toujours chargée de démentir ce que les tenants du statu quo avaient érigé en vérités et en dogmes immuables. Pour les monarchistes, les revendications parlementaristes de la bourgeoisie ont toujours été *en principe* hors de propos et pourtant l'impuissance de la monarchie à prévenir et à enrayer le développement du capitalisme commercial a scellé son propre sort. De même, doit-on penser que l'Acte d'Union et la conclusion du pacte confédératif canadien n'eussent été possibles si n'eut d'abord été créée brutalement une situation non de droit mais de fait (a matter of fact) à savoir la conquête militaire britannique de la Nouvelle-France et la subordination politique des canadiens, français et anglais, au leadership et aux intérêts de la bourgeoisie coloniale empressée de promouvoir l'unification commerciale du continent. C'est dire que pour juger d'une question politique, il faut être attentif à l'histoire politique et que la résolution effective d'un débat se joue, non pas au niveau des principes, fussent-ils philosophiques, mais au niveau des rapports de force atteints entre les diverses composantes d'une société. Les considérations, les principes philosophiques, si louables soient-ils, s'inscrivent eux-mêmes dans ces rapports de force et ne font que ponctuer, sur le plan de la légitimation et de la lutte idéologique, l'état de tension qui marque le passage toujours difficile d'un ordre ancien à un ordre nouveau. Il m'apparaît donc superflu d'ajouter que si le présent colloque se veut philosophique, il ne saurait prétendre à l'aseptie politique.

Venons-en néanmoins aux mots et aux questions de principes.

A l'encontre de mes collègues French et McCall, il me semble élémentaire d'admettre qu'il existe bel et bien un état québécois. Pour peu que l'on entende par état un ensemble cohérent d'institutions politiques, juridiques et administratives régies par des règles de droit entérinées par une assemblée législative élue au scrutin universel et promulguées par un parti gouvernemental (en régime capitaliste libéral), institutions qui exercent leur autorité sur un ou plusieurs groupes ethniques, l'existence d'un état québécois tombe sous le sens. Que l'état québécois ne soit pas par ailleurs souverain, qu'il ne dispose pas d'une constitution propre, qu'il se définisse en outre, dans le cadre confédératif, comme un état provincial, cela est d'autant plus évident que la revendication péquiste de la souveraineté politique n'est signifiante que par là. Le tort de mes collègues French et McCall est, me semble-t-il, de n'opérer que dans une perspective statique et étroitement sémantique où l'on présuppose, aux fins d'une classification "rationnelle" et comme si cela allait de soi, qu'un état est et ne peut être par définition que souverain, faute de quoi il ne saurait passer à l'existence. Nous parlerons donc volontiers d'un Etat québécois dans le sens même où l'on parle volontiers d'un Michigan State, d'un State of California, d'un State Attorney, d'une State prison ou même des United States.

Faut-il dire en l'occurrence que là où se situe précisément l'une des contradictions épineuses qui alimente le présent débat constitutionnel est que l'Etat québécois peut légitimement prétendre représenter la volonté politique d'une collectivité nationale sans ne constituer pour autant un *état-nation,* c'est-à-dire, un état déjà habileté dans les faits à exercer sa propre souveraineté politique. Compte tenu de l'histoire politique récente du Québec où, pour la première fois, un parti politique accède au pouvoir après avoir manifestement rendu publique son option souverainiste, et compte tenu du fait que d'aucuns pourraient soutenir que la légitimité de la souveraineté politique de l'Etat binational canadien (à moins que celle-ci ne soit tout simplement imposée) tient à la délégation de pouvoir *consentie* par les états provinciaux, la crise constitutionnelle actuelle apparaît d'autant plus intraitable que l'Etat fédéral prétend lui aussi, à juste titre, représenter la volonté politique des québécois. Un tel dilemme n'a rien de théorique ou de philosophique. Il exprime un état de tension — limite atteint historiquement par la double structure de pouvoir fédérale-provinciale et ne peut être résolu démocratiquement que par la tenue d'un scrutin référendaire.

Admettre que l'impasse constitutionnelle actuelle ne peut être résolue que de la sorte, sans recours à la violence militaro-politique, implique en outre que l'on admette non seulement le caractère *national* de la collectivité québécoise mais aussi l'habileté que l'on reconnaît à toute nation de s'autodéterminer, jusqu'à et y compris la séparation politique. Faute de quoi on ne saurait que parler fictivement du droit à l'autodétermination et nier en principe ce que, de toute façon, on n'est prêt à reconnaître que conditionnellement dans la pratique. J'aurais souhaité entendre mes collègues French et McCall se prononcer clairement sur cette question plutôt que de tergiverser en distinctions sémantiques qui les conduisent à un constat d'incertitude (Whether or not all these (including Quebec) are nations has been and will continue to be the subject of a debate.) Un tel "constat" ne peut, à la rigueur, que cautionner l'arbitraire politique. Est-il en effet nécessaire de préciser encore que si les québécois francophones sont jusqu'à nouvel ordre de citoyenneté et de "nationalité" canadienne (par référence au concept d'Etat bi-national canadien) ils n'en forment pas moins une nation tant par leur histoire et par le territoire qu'ils occupent que par leur langue, leurs coutumes, la représentation qu'ils se font d'eux-mêmes, leurs institutions et l'intégration géo-politico-culturelle des régions qu'ils habitent. Que faut-il de plus à mes collègues? L'hésitation de mes collègues à reconnaître clairement le peuple québécois comme peuple-nation constitue un point crucial dans leur argumentation car elle leur permet, en soulevant un doute et en s'abstenant sur une question de reconnaissance de principe, de nier au surplus, à partir de considérations utilitaires cette fois, le droit des Québécois à la séparation politique. Toutes les nations qui ont accédé à l'indépendance politique, soit par voie de négociation, soit par voie révolutionnaire, ont forcément limité le pouvoir des états auxquels elles étaient annexées et reconnaître aujourd'hui leur légitimité c'est reconnaître aussi les effets de limitation de pouvoir que leur sécession a occasionnés.

Que la question du référendum doive enfin être claire et dépourvue d'ambiguïtés me semble tout à fait essentiel. Quant aux procédures, je me limiterai à constater que mes deux collègues sont d'habiles comptables. Un vote majoritaire au scrutin référendaire devrait-il obligatoirement équivaloir au moins à 67% des voix exprimées pour traduire adéquatement la volonté politique des québécois? Mes collègues French et McCall répondent enfin clairement: oui. Je leur soumettrai donc le cas suivant pour éprouver leur cohérence. Si la question du référendum devait se lire "Voulez-vous que le Québec demeure dans la Confédération?" et que le décompte des votes positifs n'atteigne que 60% des voix exprimées, conclueraient-ils, en toute logique, que les Québécois ne veulent plus vraiment du pacte confédératif?

Le véritable débat, une fois reconnus la nation québécoise et son droit à l'autodétermination, y compris la séparation politique, devient celui-ci: "Est-il préférable et plus avantageux pour les Québécois de revendiquer leur souveraineté politique?" La réponse à une telle question ne peut que venir d'eux. Etre démocrate, c'est accepter la nécessité irréversible d'un tel débat.

DO NATIONS HAVE THE RIGHT OF SELF-DETERMINATION?

David COPP

There are three main questions which are addressed in this essay. First, what is a nation? Second, do nations have a right to self-determination? Third, is Québec, or are the Québécois, a nation, and does it, or do they, have a right to self-determination? With respect to the first, I contend that nationhood is a matter of degree, and that there are three factors which must be weighed in deciding the degree to which a given group is a nation. I argue, concerning the second question, that democratic principles can ground the claim that nations have the right of self-determination, but only subject to certain qualifications which may mean that some nations do not have this right. Democratic principles do not provide a privileged place for nations as opposed to other groups. The characteristics a group must have to be entitled to be self-determining are possessed to a sufficient degree by most, but perhaps not by all nations, and are also possessed by some non-nations. Finally, I contend that questions of nationhood are largely irrelevant to the constitutional issue facing Canada and Québec. On democratic principles, majority rule should decide the issue, but there are difficulties in applying the democratic procedure in a principled way to complex situations, such as this. I mention some scenarios in which the nationhood of the Québécois would be important.

1. WHAT IS A NATION?

In the relevant sense of "nation", a nation is not a state, although the people of a state may comprise a nation. I say this while aware of the fact that the word is sometimes used as a synonym for "state". We speak of a national flag, a national capital, international relations, and so on, and we have the United Nations. However, when we ask whether nations have the right of self-determination, we are asking whether groups of some other kind have the right to form or to maintain a national state. We are interested in whether a nation has the right to create for its members an independent state. This is not a question about the rights of states, at least not directly, but about the rights of collectives of some other kind, about the rights of "nations". It is in this sense of the word that it has often been said that there is no Canadian "nation"; and it is in this sense of the word that it has been claimed there are "two nations" in Canada which had a role in founding the state. Clearly then, in the relevant sense of the word, whatever a nation is, it is not a state, although the people of some states may constitute a nation.

Nations are sometimes supposed to be identified by a shared language and culture. Thus it is supposed that the two nations of Canada are identified by the two widely shared languages and cultures. But this will not do, as was pointed out by Ernest Renan.[1] In the first place, a consideration of examples shows that linguistic and cultural similarities and differences are not decisive. Despite a sharing of language and culture, the English and the Americans do not form one nation. Even if many English-speaking Canadians share language and culture with the Americans, I presume they are not all members of one American nation. Similarly, I presume the Québécois are not merely a part of a single French nation. It may be thought that in these cases there are relevant linguistic and cultural differences. The French spoken in Québec is in some ways different from that spoken in France, and the cultural traditions are also different. But the French spoken in Paris, and the cultural traditions of the Parisians, are also somewhat different from those of the people of Carcasonne. This is not enough to show there is not one nation embracing the people of these two French cities. Linguistic and cultural difference is not sufficient to establish difference of national affiliation, nor is linguistic and cultural similarity sufficient to establish one national affiliation. In the second place, I would think that a nation could be joined by people with divergent linguistic and cultural backgrounds, or rejected by people who share its language and culture. Thus, one might not only leave one's state, but renounce membership in one's nation, and one might seek not only new citizenship, but membership in a different nation. An ideological emigrant from Germany in the 1930's might illustrate the former, an ideological immigrant to the United States the latter. Of course, one who sought a change in national affiliation might also seek to change his language and to adopt a new culture. However, the change in language and culture need not take place hand in hand with the change in national affiliation. A person could be accepted or rejected as a member of a given nation without his having yet accomplished a change of language or culture, or vice versa. In short, the conditions under which one may change his national affiliation, together with the examples mentioned above, suggest that linguistic and cultural similarities and differences are not decisive of nationhood.

Joining a nation would seem to involve identifying with the nation's tradition and history and being accepted as a member. This suggests an account on which a nation is a group whose members identify with a common history and tradition, and are accepted as members by others who so identify.[2] Identifying oneself with a given tradition and history can be thought of as consisting in so regarding oneself that one feels pride in certain events in that history or tradition which one regards as accomplishments of some person or group, shame or regret for certain events which one regards as failures, and resentment concerning certain events which one regards as offences committed against certain persons, or against a group. One who does not identify might admire the accomplishments and despise or condemn the failures and offences, but he would not feel pride, shame or resentment. Let us say that a number of people identify in the same way with a given tradition and history if, and only if, they identify with it, and feel pride, shame and resentment with respect to the same events in it, or would do so if they were equally well informed about it. Someone might identify with the tradition of a group in the same way as all of its members, but not be accepted as a member. Here, accepting someone as a member of a group with whose tradition and history one identifies can be thought of as being disposed to regard significant accomplishments or failures of his as part of the tradition, and objects of pride or shame. Thus, we can perhaps say that if a group of people is a nation, then the members of the group identify with a certain history and tradition in the same way and accept one another as members.

This obviously would be a poor place to stop. For one thing, even a family could fulfill the given requirement, as could an ethnic or religious group, a group aspiring to create a nation, and a part of a nation. What distinguishes a nation from groups such as these? Also, many groups we would consider to be nations do not fulfill this condition. Must *every* member of a nation identify with the tradition in the same way? Could there not be disagreement among the members about the merit of certain of the events in the tradition and history so that some take pride in events which others regard as shameful? Could there not be disagreement about the boundaries of the relevant tradition and history so that some regard as shameful certain events which others regard as not committed by a member and therefore not part of the group's history? Could not a nation be split by class conflict so that one class does not identify with the contribution to the nation's history made by another class? Could not one be a member even if the other members would regard only one's accomplishments, and not one's failures, as part of the tradition? Let us try to solve some of these difficulties.

It would be impossible, I think, to give necessary and sufficient conditions of nationhood. A group may gain or lose its nationhood gradually over time, and there may be periods during which a group is neither clearly a nation nor clearly not one. Think of nationhood as a matter of degree, akin to baldness. One understands what baldness is when he knows the factor, variation in which makes a person more or less bald, and when he knows, so to speak, the direction in which baldness lies. Similarly, I suggest, we will understand what a nation is when we can identify the factors variation in which makes a group more or less a nation, and we know the direction in which nationhood lies.

The first factor, or cluster of factors, has to do with the members' identification with a history and tradition. A group is more a nation, *ceteris paribus*, first, as more of its members identify with a more extensive history and tradition; second, as it includes a greater proportion of those who so identify; and third, as more members accept other members *as* members. In the first place, we expect members of a nation to have similar attitudes to key events in the nation's history and tradition. And, as the history with respect to which members of a group identify becomes more comprehensive, the group seems more like a nation, *ceteris paribus.* In the second place, other things being equal, a nation includes all or most of the people who identify in the right way with the relevant history. Of course, some outsiders may identify. But if a group is a nation, and not part of a nation, we expect there to be few such outsiders in comparison with the number of members who identify with the tradition. Finally, the members of a nation may not identify with all of the accomplishments and failures of all other members. But, as more members are disposed to identify with more of the accomplishments and failures of more of the other members, a group is more a nation.

The second factor is political. The first cluster of factors may be satisfied to a high degree by an ethnic group which is not a nation, or even by a family. One central difference between groups such as these and nations is that members of nations have some desire to live in a national state. They have some political aspirations or sentiments. Of course, the members of an ethnic group might desire to live in an independent self-determining state. But if what they desire, in particular, is that there be a state which includes basically all and only the members of the group, the group is like a nation, at least in this respect. Members of a nation desire to associate politically with people who identify with the same tradition they identify with. The second factor, then, is that a group is more a nation, *ceteris paribus*, as more of its members desire that a political entity be formed, or be continued, comprising, to a greater degree, all and only members of the group, and that that entity be to a greater degree independent and self-determining and otherwise have the attributes of a state.[3] This implies that a group is more a nation as more of its members have some description which effectively picks out that group and its members and desire that the people who fit that description form a state. This factor can explain why families, ethnic groups, religious groups, and groups aspiring to create nations typically are not themselves nations. Variations in this factor explain variations in our tendency to regard Scotland as a nation. This factor also explains why we think it important for a state's stability that its citizens comprise a nation, and why we think a country comprising two or more *nations* is unstable in a way that a country comprising two or more ethnic or religious groups need not be.

The third factor has to do with the feasibility of creating a national state. A group is more a nation, *ceteris paribus*, as geographical and economic factors are such that it would be more feasible to create, or to continue, a state comprising to a greater degree all and only members of the group as citizens. This factor explains why a small group of deluded crackpots who fulfill the first two conditions to a high degree is not normally a nation. It also explains why we would not speak of the existence of a Jewish nation during the Diaspora, or, even assuming they desired to form a state, of the existence of a nation of all English speakers. The territorial distribution of a given population may be such that great population dislocations would be required to create a national state. Because a state is a territorially based political entity, the lack of a territory occupied by members of a group detracts from the feasibility of creating a national state. Moreover, the division of the group's territory among different states, or its being physically separated by territory occupied by other groups, or its being jointly occupied by several intermingled ethnic groups, can detract from the feasibility of creating or maintaining a state exclusively for the group in question. Prevailing economic circumstances also can detract from this. Admittedly, a group may be regarded as a nation even if the creation of a separate state for it would be difficult for one of these reasons. But there are degrees of feasibility and degrees of nationhood. Also, difficulty of creating a national state may be counterbalanced by the other two factors mentioned. In addition, a strong national sentiment can sometimes make feasible what would otherwise have been unfeasible. It should be noted that some circumstances which undermine the feasibility of creating a state for a group do not count against the group's being considered a nation. For instance, the Tibetan people's nationhood is not diminished by the Chinese occupation merely because this makes Tibetan independence difficult to attain. External political factors which make statehood unfeasible should not be taken to detract from a group's nationhood.[4]

Of these three factors, the second is perhaps most important and most controversial. A territorially based ethnic group, sometimes called a "nationality", could satisfy the first and third conditions to a high degree. But not all such groups are nations. It is sometimes said, unhelpfully, that the members of a nation must think of their group as a nation.[5] This idea is captured, I think, by the second factor. According to this factor, the members of a nation desire that there be a national state. They think of the group as an appropriate candidate for independent statehood. A territorially based ethnic group need not have this characteristic, and to the degree that it does not, it is less a nation. That this is so may be blurred by polemical uses of the term. One might speak of such a group as a nation in expressing one's own desire that the group form an independent state, or in order to raise in the group a desire for independence. I regard this as indirectly confirming the importance of the second factor. We see further confirmation of this in the efforts of states to reduce minority nations within their boundaries to the status of mere ethnic groups by eliminating the desire for independence. Consider for instance the case of Tibet. However, it is important to understand that this second factor is quite compatible with the existence of harmonious multi-national states. It implies that a group is more a nation as more of its members desire independent statehood for the group. It does not imply that the members of a nation would rank this desire above all others, would choose, vote for, or fight for, independence. Moreover, the second factor is compatible with the harmonious existence of ethnic minorities within national states. It implies that a group is more a nation as its members desire that there be a state comprising to a greater degree all and only members of the group. It does not imply that the members of any nation would desire the expulsion of minorities. It does not imply that the members' desire to live in a state composed of fellow nationals would be strong enough to lead to chauvinistic actions. However, it does imply that a desire to live in a national state will be present to a greater degree as a group is more a nation. The members of almost every group will desire to live in some independent state or other, if they are politically aware at all. The members of a group which is clearly a nation will desire, by and large, to live in an independent *national* state.[6]

There are three main factors which must be weighed in deciding the degree to which a group is a nation. First, the identification of members of the group with a unified tradition and history and their acceptance of other members as members, in the sense explained above. Second, the desire of members to form or maintain a state. And third, the feasibility of forming or maintaining a state for the members of the group. Thus, some would be inclined to follow Max Weber in saying that a nation is a group of people who have a sentiment of belonging together and sharing a common destiny, the desire to form or maintain a state, and who normally live in a particular territory.[7] The account suggested here is similar to this, differing mainly in that it does not give necessary and sufficient conditions of a group's being a nation. Groups are nations to different degrees, and there are at least three parameters which must be weighed in assessing the degree to which a group is a nation.

The account given here can accommodate many of our ways of using the word "nation". For example: Cobban distinguishes between political and cultural conceptions of the nation.[8] The political ideal is to weld a nation out of the population of an existing state with the purpose of contributing to the unity and stability of the state. The cultural ideal is to create a state for the population of an existing culturally-unified nation. It is a virtue of the present account that it accommodates both conceptions. It is immaterial whether people identify with a common tradition and history as a result of political propaganda, or as a part of sharing a language and culture. The doctrine that nations have the right of self-determination may have been used primarily to advance claims on behalf of culturally, linguistically or ethnically unified nations. But it is a virtue of the present account that a nation need not be a group of one of these kinds, although it may be, and although it must be a group with some non-frivolous political aspirations. Finally, one notable characteristic of the word "nation" is its vagueness. The present account preserves this characteristic and explains why we have difficulty deciding whether given groups are nations.

2. THE RIGHT OF SELF-DETERMINATION

Let us now turn to the second main question. Does a nation have a right of self-determination? This question can be rendered more precise. We will assume that a nation's having a right of self-determination would be its having a right to form or maintain a "national state", *viz.*, a state which is legally independent and politically self-determining and which comprises more or less all and only the members of the nation. The right of self-determination must include at least this. To be self-determining a group must have a political organization, and if it is fully self-determining, the organization must not be legally or politically subordinate to other organizations. Moreover, the right could not include more than this. It is the right of a nation to determine its *own* course which is in question, and this right cannot expand into the right to determine the course of some larger group which includes the nation as well as some non-members. Let us say that the right in question is the right to form or maintain an independent national state.

The claim that nations have this right does not imply that existing states have a duty to ensure that the international order is reorganized in such a way that every nation has its own state. Neither does my right to swim at the beach imply that anyone has a duty to ensure that I swim there. The mistaken view that there is this implication pays insufficient attention to the choice of the members of the nations concerned. In my account of nationhood, some fairly large proportion of the members of a nation will desire that the nation form a state. But it does not follow that they would *choose* to have a national state created. *A fortiori*, it does not follow that the nation as a whole would choose this. It is important to see that the view that there is this implication is mistaken. The doctrine of a national right of self-determination is not as destructive of the international order as it might seem to be. It does not imply a duty to see that nation and state coincide, as some have thought.[9]

The claim that nations have this right also does not imply that a nation would never be wrong to exercise the right. The right of self-determination is not an absolute right. Although a nation's right to self-determination implies that others have a duty not to interfere, this duty is not absolute and may be outweighed by other considerations. Difficult and important moral and political issues are involved here. A nation's right of self-determination may conflict with the need for international security or for political stability. In contemporary circumstances, we more often see the contrary case, perhaps, where denying self-determination undermines security and stability, but circumstances may change, and have been different.[10] The right of self-determination may also conflict with the rights and needs of persons. It might well be wrong for a nation to exercise its right of self-determination by seceding from an existing state, if this would involve leaving in poverty those living in what would be the remnant of that state. It is important to realize that the right of self-determination is not absolute. If nations have this right, they have a moral claim to constitute a separate independent state. It does not follow that this claim should always prevail.

The right of self-determination would be the right of a nation not to be *interfered* with in forming or maintaining an independent national state if it should choose to do so. In Feinberg's terminology, it would be an active negative claim right.[11] If any nation has this right and chooses to form or maintain a state, then other existing states and individuals have a duty not to interfere. Let us regard the right in question as the right not to be interfered with in forming or maintaining an independent national state if the nation so chooses. Does any nation have this right?

I will pursue two lines of argument. First, I will consider whether there is any theoretical barrier to a nation's possessing rights. If there is, our problem can be disposed of quickly. But I will claim there is no such barrier. Second, I will consider whether any cogent arguments can be mounted to show in particular that nations have the right of self-determination.

3. RIGHTS OF COLLECTIVES

The question whether nations have the right of self-determination could be answered quickly if we could agree with Cobban that "rights are rights for individual ... men and women, or they are not rights at all."[12] Cobban makes this claim partly on the political ground that, in practice, the assertion that a collective political entity has rights has led to authoritarianism and the denial of individual rights. If he is correct, then it would be prudent to deny that nations could have rights. Nevertheless, there may be many claims which, though true, it would be prudent to deny. I am interested in whether it is true that collectives lack rights. Cobban does have a more pertinent argument. He claims that if there is a national right of self-determination then a nation must be a "single self" "capable of determining itself", and moved by a "single will", a "General Will". This he thinks a nation is not. The argument amounts to this. If an entity has a right not to be interfered with if it chooses to do a given thing, then it must be capable of doing the thing in question, and capable of choosing to do so. A nation is not capable of making choices, or of performing actions, so it cannot have any rights of this sort, and *a fortiori*, cannot have the right of self-determination.

Against this line of argument, I claim that nations are capable of making choices. Many collective bodies of many sorts make choices and perform actions. States choose governments and declare wars. Corporations choose product lines and fix prices. A family may choose a site for a picnic and move a picnic table. Moreover, as this last example shows, a collective need not be an organized body with an institutionalized decision procedure in order to make a choice or perform an action. Many groups not of this kind, including families, audiences, classes, and mobs, can make choices and perform actions. Therefore, the fact that a nation is a collective, and that many nations are politically unorganized, does not show that all, or even some nations cannot choose or act.[13]

Nevertheless, there may be special reasons why a politically unorganized nation typically cannot make a choice, or why its choices cannot be identified with any certainty. The choice of a nation must be understood to be a function of the choices of its members. That is, it must be understood to be determined by the choices of the members according to some collective decision-making procedure.[14] But, contrary to what Hobbes sometimes seems to have thought,[15] there is no "natural" procedure. There are different, equally satisfactory, procedures for translating individual choices into a national choice. These different procedures may derive different "collective choices" from the same set of choices made by individual members of the group. Hence, one cannot speak of the choice of the group *simpliciter*, but only of its choice *relative to* some decision-making procedure. This is so, not only for politically unorganized nations, but also for any collective which lacks an institutionalized decision procedure. It is true that if the members of the group are unanimous, or nearly unanimous, in choosing some alternative, then we can speak of the group's having chosen that alternative, even in the absence of an established decision procedure. No credible rule for deriving the choice of an unorganized collective from the choices of its members would fail to assign to the group the unanimous or near unanimous choice of its members. This explains our assignment of choices to groups like the mob which stormed the Bastille. But it is unlikely that any group as large as a nation would ever choose anything unanimously. This seems to undercut the right of self-determination. We cannot speak of a politically unorganized state choosing *simpliciter* to form a national state, but only of its choosing relative to a decision procedure. Hence, alleged breaches of the duty existing states have not to interfere with a nation's exercising its choice will also have to be assessed relative to a decision procedure. If there is no natural decision procedure, and no unanimity, then there will be no non-arbitrary way of determining whether the right of self-determination has been violated. This means the right is effectively undercut.

This argument can be regarded from another point of view.[16] Suppose the problem has arisen of determining whether a given politically unorganized nation chooses to form a state. This can only be solved if a collective decision procedure can be chosen for the nation. The nation cannot make the choice itself, for its "choice presupposes the very rule that it would establish".[17] Further, if some authority made the choice, then, unless it chose the unanimity rule, its choice would be arbitrary. "There is no rule which is obviously suitable."[18] Even the majority decision rule which suggests itself so naturally to many of us would be unsatisfactory. This is because, if a particular alternative were preferred by a narrow majority, "it would be misleading to report that the nation as a whole preferred (it)," and "almost one-half the nation may be forced into a political arrangement which it does not desire."[19] Consequently, there is no non-arbitrary way of solving the problem we began with, and the right of self-determination is undercut.

It is true that under the majority decision rule almost one-half of the numbers of a group may be forced into a political arrangement it does not desire. But whether it would therefore be misleading to report that the group has chosen this arrangement would depend on circumstances, and, in particular, on how the majority rule is regarded by members of the group. If nearly all the members regard the majority rule as the legitimate decision-making procedure for the group, they may all accept the result as indicating the group's choice. In this case, it would not be misleading to say the group has chosen this arrangement. It need not be unfair to enforce a choice made in this way. To refuse to enforce a choice made in this way would be to allow a minority to force a majority to accept a political arrangement it does not desire. This would be unfair, especially if nearly all the members regard the majority decision rule as the only legitimate one.

The flaw in the above argument is that it ignores tradition and political culture and the fact that the members of a nation identify with a given history and tradition. This may mean, and in many actual cases it will mean, that there is a decision rule which is the appropriate rule to use in determining the choices of the nation in that it would be regarded as legitimate by nearly all members. For example, the tradition of the nation in question may be that putative group choices are legitimate if and only if they are agreed to by the majority of adult members, or by the majority of adult female members, or by the majority of the adult members who express a preference, or, in important matters, by two-thirds of the adult members, or what have you. In this way, the tradition may identify some decision procedure as the appropriate one for the nation in question. If so, it may be that the members of the nation would generally accept results of the traditional procedure as indicating the choice of the group. They would be nearly unanimous in answering the question what the group had chosen with respect to some issue, even though they were perhaps not even nearly unanimous in their own choices with respect to that issue. In this circumstance, it would not be arbitrary, and it would be appropriate, for anyone to regard the result of the traditional procedure as indicating the choice of the nation.

It is true that a group may be so deeply divided on a given issue that a large segment of the membership would not accept the result of the traditional procedure, or of any other, as indicating the choice of the group. In such a case, perhaps, it would be a mistake to regard the result of the traditional procedure as the choice of the group. However, on the above account of nationhood, the members of a nation identify with a tradition and history and desire the formation or maintenance of a national state. Of course, they may still decide not to choose, or vote for, a national state. But if a serious split of this sort occurred in a group over the question whether the group should form a separate state, we would have some evidence that a large segment of the membership did not desire a separate state. We would have evidence that the group is less a nation than it could be. To the extent that there are deep divisions over the statehood question, and divisions of sufficient depth to undermine the legitimacy of any putative group choice, there is evidence that the group is less a nation, other things being equal.

Can it be assumed that there will be a suitable non-arbitrary rule for *every* politically unorganized nation? The tradition of the group may not extend to this. Even so, a non-traditional procedure may be regarded as legitimate by nearly all the members. International law might prescribe use of a plebiscite of a given sort, and the members of the nation might accept such a procedure nearly unanimously. Still, there may be cases where no procedure other than the unanimity rule itself would be accepted. In such cases, we could fairly speak of the group's choice only if that choice were the result of applying the unanimity rule.

The present line of argument suggests a "convert to near-unanimity" rule for all politically unorganized nations. It suggests, that is, that a choice is appropriately treated as the choice of a politically unorganized nation if, and only if, nearly all the members of the nation would accept it as such, if they knew the distribution of members' choices. If nearly all the members would choose alternative *A*, they would likely also accept alternative *A* as being the choice of the group as a whole. Alternatively, even if a large segment of the members would not themselves choose alternative *A*, they might accept alternative *A*, as being the choice of the group, provided that they regard as appropriate some decision procedure which would yield alternative *A* given the individual choices of all the members.

It is important to notice that I am not claiming that a near-unanimity rule is the appropriate rule to use in settling all political issues. I am only claiming that the above "convert to near-unanimity test" is an appropriate test to use for the particular task of deciding whether a given choice can be imputed to a politically unorganized nation itself. I would apply the same test to any group which lacks an institutionalized decision rule. Did the family choose to picnic here, or was it simply a choice of the parents? If the "parental guidance rule" is accepted in this instance by all members of the family, then they will accept that the family's choice has been made when the parents' choices have been made. If the parents' choice is accepted as the family's choice by all members, then their choice is fairly treated as the choice of the family. There will have been a "conversion to unanimity", even though there may not have been unanimity with respect to which site should be chosen. Did the nation choose to form an independent national state? If nearly all the members accept that this choice has been made by the nation, then it is fair to say the nation has chosen this. There has been a "conversion to near-unanimity", even though there may not have been unanimity with respect to whether the nation should choose to form a state.

The conclusion I reach at this point is that even politically unorganized nations may make choices, and hence, may choose to form independent national states. Similarly, a nation may choose a particular constitution, and choose a particular government. I see no theoretical barrier to attributing to a nation a right the possession of which presupposes the ability to make choices.

4. DEMOCRACY AND THE RIGHT OF SELF-DETERMINATION

Let us now turn again to the specific issue whether any nation has the right of self-determination. Recall that to the extent that a group is a nation, more of its members will identify to a greater degree with a common tradition, and will desire to form or to maintain an independent national state, and it will be more feasible to create or maintain such a state. Do any of these characteristics of a nation secure a foothold for the right of self-determination?

It seems plain that the fact that a group identifies with a common tradition cannot gain for it the right of self-determination. The librarians at some university may identify with an ancient tradition reaching back to the earliest libraries, but they have no right to form a separate state on this ground. It would be completely unfeasible for them to do so, even if no person or collective interfered, and I assume that this disposes of the matter. However, lack of feasibility cannot be argued with respect to any group which is very much a nation. Do the feasibility and the desire conditions sufficiently ground the claim that a nation has this right?

The right of nations to self-determination seems to be a corollary of democratic principles. Democratic principles imply, of course, that political decisions of states ought to be made on the basis of the choices of the governed. But if the choices of those who are governed should rule in states, the choices of those who are to be governed should rule in deciding what state is to govern a given people. The allocation of a particular group of people to the jurisdiction of one state rather than another can have very significant consequences for the life of each member of the group. The decision that a given group shall be governed by one state rather than another may mean that it is governed by a state where important political issues are resolved differently than they would be in that other state. This may be so even if the decisions of each state are and would be taken on a democratic basis. The preferences of the people of the states in question may ensure this. This means that important political decisions may effectively be taken by the decision as to which state is to govern a given people and territory. If this decision is not taken on a democratic basis, important political decisions may effectively be taken on a non-democratic basis. Hence, to ensure effective democracy, the choice of the people to be governed should be the basis for deciding what state is to govern them. Now, given that the members of a nation desire that they be governed by a separate national state, there is a *prima facie* case for their being governed by such a state. They may not choose this, all things considered. But if they do choose this, then democratic principles would seem to imply that a separate national state ought to be formed. As John Stuart Mill says,[20]

> Where the sentiment of nationality exists in any force, there is a prima facie case for uniting all the members of the nationality under the same government, and a government to themselves apart. This is merely saying that the question of government ought to be decided by the governed. One hardly knows what any division of the human race should be free to do, if not to determine, with which of the various collective bodies of human beings they choose to associate themselves.

An example may help. The state of Israel has different policies than would a state governing all of the Levant. It seems likely that this would be so even if the hypothetical state and Israel were equally democratic and followed the same kind of democratic decision-making procedures. Thus, it would seem that democracy would effectively prevail only if the choices of the Israelis were the basis for deciding what state would rule the Israelis. Equally, it would seem that democracy requires that the choice of the people of the West Bank be the basis for deciding what state will rule them.

The argument purports to establish that it is a corollary of democratic principles that a group has the right to decide, by democratic procedures, what state it is to be governed by. It would seem to follow that a group has the right to form or to maintain a separate self-determining state if a majority of its members chooses that it do so. It clearly does not follow from this principle that nations have an unconditional right not to be interfered with in forming a national state. Although many of the members of any nation desire that an independent national state be formed or maintained, it does not follow that a majority of the members of any nation would *choose* this. Many things which a person desires he does not choose. He may have desires which conflict and which he takes to be more important. One might desire that an independent national state be formed but have a stronger desire for a socialist state and believe that the best chance for socialism lies in the existing state. Even a group which is clearly a nation may not have a majority which would choose a national state over any other political arrangement. Therefore, even granting the above principle, it does not follow that any nation has an unconditional right to form or maintain an independent national state. A conditional right would follow. It would follow that any nation has a right to form or maintain a national state *if* a majority of its members chooses that it do this. But this self-determination right follows directly from the above principle, and it follows from this principle that *any* group has the right to form a state, even if it is not a nation. This result surely throws the principle into doubt.

This unrestricted principle implies that any group has the right to form a state consisting of all and only its members if a majority of the group chooses this. The librarians, the people of Westmount, the residents of a given region rich in resources, the Québécois — all of these groups, and the group consisting of you and I, have this right. In the case of many groups, it would be completely unfeasible to form a separate state, even if no person or collective interfered in any way, and I assume this to show these groups do not have this right. Moreover, the unrestricted principle undermines democracy. Suppose the majority in collective C chooses state S. Then C has the right to bring about that it is governed by S. But the group of dissenters in C has the right to ensure it is not governed by S. That is, the unrestricted principle, followed strictly, undermines the rule of democratic majorities.

It is evident that the principle needs to be restricted in its range. It could be restricted to apply only to existing states. The citizenry of a state has the right to decide, by democratic procedures, what state it is to be governed by. It has the right to maintain the existing state, or to dissolve it in favour of government under some other state. But this is both too strong and too weak. It would sanction a state's continuing annexation of a smaller state, China's annexation of Tibet, for example. For, once the annexation is accomplished, if the majority of the resulting state chooses to continue the annexation, this state has the right to do so even if the residents of the formerly independent state continue to be almost unanimously opposed. Moreover, democratic principles would imply that the annexed state has the right of self-determination, given the almost universal sentiment of its residents. But the narrow principle yields no such right. It is both too strong and too weak.

The range of our principle must neither include all collectives nor be restricted to existing states. Of course, the principle must extend at least to states. Democratic principles imply that the people of an existing state have the right to decide, by democratic procedures, whether to maintain or dissolve the state. But the case of the annexed smaller state suggests that the principle must also extend to groups which could feasibly be states. Now, nations are groups of this kind. The result is that the range of the democratic self-determination principle should include states, nations, and other collectives which could feasibly be states. The principle is that any state, nation, or nation-like group has the right to form or maintain a separate self-determining state if a majority of its members chooses that it do so. Call this the "democratic self-determination principle" (DSP).

If we take the range of the principle to include all and only states, nations and nation-like groups, we avoid some of the problems mentioned above. The principle does not undermine the rule of democratic majorities except where the dissenters on the issue whether to form or maintain a given state are the majority of a state, a nation or nation-like group. The case of the annexed smaller state suggests that this is appropriate. The principle undermines the rights of China over Tibet. The Tibetan nation would have the right to secede from China if a majority of its members chose that it do so, and even if a majority of the citizens of greater China chose that it not do so. In short, the plausibility of our principle seems to be enhanced if its range is specified to include states, nations, and nation-like groups.

Does this mean that DSP, with an appropriately defined range, yields the right of national self-determination? It does yield the conclusion that a nation has the right to form or maintain an independent national state if a majority of its members chooses to do so. But there are at least four problems.

First, DSP does not ensure the priority of the right of national self-determination. Many would think it ought to take priority over any right a state which includes a nation might have to prevent that nation from seceding. Suppose the majority of Québécois chose Québec independence, but the majority of Canadians chose to preserve Canadian unity. On this showing the rights of Canada and Québec would conflict, and we would have no ground for saying the right of Québec should take priority. It is true that democratic principles need to be restricted in scope. It may be that no right can be derived therefrom to violate others' rights. But this restriction does not help because we have no ground for applying this scope restriction to deny that Canada has the right to maintain unity rather than to deny that Québec has the right to secede. Canada's maintaining unity would violate Québec's putative right to secede, but Québec's seceding would violate Canada's putative right to maintain unity. The situation seems to be symmetrical, so the scope restriction does not give the nation's right of self-determination priority over the larger state's right of self-preservation.

However, the argument we began with suggests a sense in which a state is a voluntary organization. States, and groups which could feasibly be states and whose members desire a separate state, cannot rightfully be forced to accept government by a state where this arrangement would not be chosen by a majority of their members. This idea suggests a priority principle to the following effect. Where there is a conflict between rights secured by the democratic self-determination principle, a given group's right takes priority, other things being equal, on two conditions.[21] First, overriding that right would mean that that group, or a "significant" part of it,[22] would be forced to accept government by a state other than a majority of its members has chosen. And second, securing that right by forming or maintaining a given state would not mean that any group within the range of DSP, or any "significant" part of such a group, would be forced to accept government by that state against the will of a majority of its members.

Let me illustrate this priority principle. Suppose a majority of North Americans prefer that there be one North American state, but that a majority of Mexicans prefer to maintain Mexican autonomy. Then DSP would imply a conflict between the rights of Mexico and the rights of the group of North Americans as a whole. The priority principle implies the conditional priority of the right of Mexico. The right of the larger group cannot take priority because creating a North American state would force Mexico to accept an arrangement rejected by a majority of its citizens. However, the right of Mexico may take priority. First of all, overriding it would mean forcing Mexico into the North American state. Thus, Mexico's right takes priority if, within Mexico, there is no nation or nation-like group, and no significant part of such a group, a majority of whose members would choose to be governed by some state other than Mexico. It is true that this asks that the democratic choice of the North Americans be frustrated. But securing that choice would violate another group's democratic choice. The priority principle says that even a democratic majority has no right to force a group which is potentially a state into a state it would democratically reject.

Notice that this priority principle does not give priority to the rights of nations as such. Where DSP yields a conflict of rights, the right of a nation, or of a state, or of a nation-like group may take priority, depending on the circumstances. The relevant properties of groups, as far as DSP is concerned, are those of choosing statehood and of being feasible candidates for statehood. I cannot see why a group's rights should be enhanced if the group has the additional characteristic that its members identify with a common history and tradition. I cannot see that this characteristic is at all relevant to the present issue except insofar as it contributes either to the group's choosing of, or to the feasibility of, statehood for the group.

The first problem, then, is to defend a plausible priority rule. The second problem arises because the feasibility of forming a state for the members of a group is a matter of degree. Is it then a matter of degree whether a group falls within the range of the democratic self-determination principle and so a matter of degree whether a group has the right of self-determination? This seems to be simply wrong. We wish to say that entities either have or do not have a given right, and not to allow that an entity may have a right "to some intermediate degree". This raises the problem how to justify regarding a given group as falling within the range of DSP, and having the right in question, but regarding a different group, for which it would be slightly less feasible to make a state, as falling outside the range of the principle and the right. This basic problem is to specify a non-arbitrary threshold which indicates the degree to which statehood must be feasible for a group to have the right of self-determination. Moreover, with respect to the issue whether all nations have the right of self-determination, the problem would be to show that the degree to which statehood must be feasible if a group is a nation is not less than the degree required for having the right of self-determination. If it less, some nations may lack this right. I call this the "slippery slope problem".

The third problem is related to the second. Only one of the parameters relevant to assessing a group's nationhood is relevant to assessing whether it is in the range of the right in question. Hence, a group may lack the right of self-determination because if falls outside the range of DSP, even though it is *more* a nation than some group which has the right. It may be more a nation because many more of its members identify with a much more unified history, but fall outside the range of this principle because it would be slightly less feasible that it form a national state. In this way, depending on the locations of the relevant thresholds, it could be that some nations are outside the range of the principle. I call this the "conflicting factor problem".

The final problem is whether the right derived from the democratic self-determination principle is properly attributed to a nation rather than to the majority of people in a nation. I call it the "right-holder problem". I claimed above that a nation's right of self-determination is a right not to be interfered with, and that it implies that other agents have a duty not to interfere if the nation should choose to form an independent national state. However, the argument from DSP suggests that it is not necessary that a nation *itself* choose to form a state in order that other agents have a duty not to interfere with its forming a state. The right of self-determination should not be understood in such a way that the correlative duty not to interfere is conditional on the nation's making a choice *itself.* The democratic choice of its members suffices. This does not directly controvert the view discussed in part three, that a nation's having any right is conditional on its having the capacity to make choices. However, it might suggest that the national right of self-determination derived from DSP is best thought of as a right of the majority in a nation, rather than as a right of the nation itself. The duty others have not to interfere is to protect the choice of the majority, not the choice of the nation itself. On a beneficiary theory of rights, since it is the interests of the majority which are to be served by the duty others have not to interfere with the formation of a state, the right which correlates with this duty is a right of the majority, not of the nation itself.[23] However, we might question whether the interests of the nation are not directly served. Since the interests of a nation are presumably some function of the interests of its members, and since a large proportion of the members of a nation desire the formation of a national state, the duty not to interfere with the formation of such a state presumably will directly serve the interests of the nation. If so, we could attribute the correlative right of self-determination to the nation. In any case, I cannot pursue this issue any further.

The conclusion I reach is that democratic principles can, with certain reservations, ground the claim that any nation has the right to form or maintain an independent national state, if it is feasible that it do so, and if a majority of its members chooses that it do so. Thus, I will say that nations have the right of self-determination. Strictly speaking, however, this claim may be too strong. Even if we ignore the priority problem and the right-holder problem, the remaining two problems suggest that some nations may lack this right.

5. QUÉBEC AND CANADA: A CASE STUDY

Complications can be expected to appear when theoretical principles are applied to a real case. In this section, I apply the principles developed in the preceding section to the case of Québec and Canada. Is there a nation in Québec which has the right of self-determination? The complications we encounter in answering this question should reveal some of the strengths and weaknesses of the arguments we have been considering.

First, we must distinguish between the people of Québec and the Québec people of French ancestry, the Québécois. The population of

Québec includes, of course, many people of British ancestry, and of other European and non-European ancestries, as well as the Québécois. Now, the people of Québec probably do not constitute a nation. The division in loyalty between those of French and those of other ancestries means that the group of Québec residents does not rate strongly with respect to its identification with a single tradition and history. Moreover, although it would be feasible for Québec to form a state, it seems unlikely that a majority would desire that Québec form an independent state, and less likely that a majority would *choose* to form an independent state. Thus, the people of Québec are not a nation. Nevertheless, the democratic self-determination principle would give Québec the right to form an independent state if a majority of its residents chose that it do so.

The Québécois presumably do constitute a nation. Presumably, at least, they would identify largely with a single history and tradition. Unfortunately, the other two parameters are more difficult. It would not be simple to form a state consisting of all and only Québécois. The population of the province is about twenty percent non-Québécois, and the non-Québécois form an even larger percentage of the population in the Montréal region. To form a national state there would have to be substantial population movements, or a redrawing of boundaries, and this counts against the nationhood status of the Québécois to the extent that these measures would not be feasible. Also, it is not clear what proportion of the Québécois desires the formation of a Québécois national state. A reasonably large proportion may desire Québec to be a state, but to the extent that Québec would include people not in the group, the Québécois are less a nation. On balance, the Québécois likely do constitute a nation, but even if so, the group is weak on two of the relevant parameters of nationhood. Now, given the position developed above, does the Québécois nation have the right to form an independent national state if a majority of its members chooses that it do so? Recall that this right is the right to form a state consisting essentially of all and only members of the nation, a "national state". As we saw, it would not be a simple matter to form such a state. Hence, given the conflicting factor and slippery slope problem, it is not entirely clear whether DSP extends to the Québécois, even if this group is a nation. On balance, however, it seems likely that it does. We may conclude, then, that the nation has the right to form a separate self-determining national state for the Québécois if a majority of Québécois chooses this.

However, this does not end the matter. As there are two peoples in Québec that must be kept separate, the Québécois and the people of the province as a whole, so there are two potential objects of constitutional debate. The preceding discussion shows that debate may focus on the constitutional future of the present Québec and Canada, or on possible new territorial and constitutional arrangements for the Québécois. The former is the present focus of debate. Also it seems likely that the Québécois would prefer to keep Québec intact, and would reject the option of a national state if that would involve redrawing boundaries. Thus, the fact that the Québécois have the right to form a national state if they choose to do so may be irrelevant to the present constitutional and political issue in Canada.

It is important, therefore, to notice that the DSP does not imply that Québec has the right to form a state if a majority of the Québécois choose this option. This conclusion would be anti-democratic, for it holds that Québec would have the right to form an independent state if a majority of a sub-population of Québec chose this.[24] However, the above conclusion just does not follow from the democratic self-determination principle. Let us assume that the Québécois are a nation, and that the right of self-determination extends to this group. It would follow that if a majority of the Québécois chose to form a national state, the nation would have the right to do this. However, an independent Québec would not be such a national state. Hence, the duty others would have not to interfere with the Québécois nation's forming a *national state* would not imply a duty to allow *Québec* to achieve independence if a majority of the Québécois chose this.

There are, then, two possible scenarios with respect to which DSP would yield interesting implications. In the first, a majority of Québec residents choose statehood for Québec. In the second a majority of Québécois choose that a *national* state be formed, rather than that the present Québec form a state. Let us assume this could feasibly be done by redrawing boundaries. In both cases, Canada would have a duty not to interfere, and the group in question would have a right to achieve statehood. However, we must not ignore the priority problem. It might well be that a majority of Canadians would choose to maintain Canadian unity. In this case, DSP implies that Canada has the right to do so. In this case, the rights of Québec, or of the Québécois nation, conflict with the rights of Canada. Where does priority lie?

In neither case would Canada have priority. Securing Canada's right would mean that a group within the range of DSP would be forced to accept government by Canada against the choice of a majority of its members. In the first scenario, the frustrated entity would be Québec, in the second, it would be the Québécois nation. This is enough to show that Canada's right of self-preservation does not take priority. If, in the second scenario, the Québécois chose a national state to be created by redrawing boundaries, this right of the Québécois would take priority. Overriding this right would mean that the Québécois would be forced to accept government by Canada against the choice of a majority. But securing that right, assuming boundaries are redrawn to create a national state, would not require forcing any group in the range of DSP, or any significant part of any such group, to accept government by the new state. This shows the right of the Québécois to create a national state would take priority over Canada's right. However, the first scenario is more difficult. Even if a majority of Québec residents chose Québec independence, the right of Québec under DSP might not take priority. This is because the anglophones in western Québec are a significant part of a nation-like group. If they voted against Québec independence, then securing Québec's right would involve forcing them to accept government by Québec. In this case our principles imply that Québec's and Canada's rights would have equal weight, other things being equal. The anglophones would be a significant group, if they rejected Québec sovereignty because redrawing the boundaries could place them within Canada. There would be a feasible way to respect the democratic choice of these anglophone Québec residents. Because of this, the right of Québec would take priority, in the first scenario, only if a majority of anglophones chose Québec independence, or if Québec accepted a redrawing of boundaries.

It appears, then, that questions of nationhood are largely irrelevant to the present political and constitutional issue in Canada. On the democratic self-determination principle, Québec would have the right to secede from Canada if a majority of Québec residents choose that it secede. The fact that the people of Québec are not a nation is irrelevant to this. Moreover, a majority vote by the Québécois nation would not itself legitimate Québec independence. Still, in the unlikely event that a majority of Québécois chose that a *national* state be formed, rather than that the present Québec form a state, and if such a state could feasibly be created by redrawing boundaries, Canada would have a duty not to interfere. The right of the nation would take priority over the right Canada would have to preserve unity. Also, in the unlikely event that both a majority of Québec residents, and a majority of anglophone Québec residents, chose Québec sovereignty, then Québec would not only have the right to secede, but its right would take priority over Canada's right to preserve unity. Now, these rights are not absolute rights. But if the proposal were to create a new state in Québec in a way which respected the democratic choices of groups whose preferences could feasibly be respected, the Québécois nation would have the right to proceed unhindered.[25]

NOTES

1. Ernest Renan, "Qu'est-ce qu'une Nation?", in Henriette Psichari, ed. *Oeuvres Complètes de Ernest Renan,* Vol. 1 (Paris, 1947), p.887-906, cited in A.I. Benn, "Nationalism", in Paul Edwards, ed., *The Encyclopedia of Philosophy*, Vol. 5 (New York, 1967), pp.442-5, and p.443.
2. The basic idea is suggested by A.I. Benn, *op. cit.*, pp.443-4. See also J.S. Mill, "Considerations on Representative Government", Chapter XVI, in *On Liberty, The Subjection of Women, etc.* (London, 1924), intro. by M.G. Fawcett, p.380.
3. This raises a number of questions. One important question is whether it matters *why* these people desire to form or continue the state. Would desiring this merely for commercial or economic advantage count toward making a group more a nation? Or, must the members desire this because they wish to associate politically with people who identify with the same tradition they identify with? Perhaps the group is more a nation the more members have this desire for the latter reason.
4. Of course this raises a number of questions. Can one distinguish clearly between purely political inhibitions to statehood, and others, such as economic ones? Can one distinguish clearly between political factors external to the group and others?
5. S.I. Benn and R.S. Peters, *The Principles of Political Thought* (New York, 1965), p.294.
6. This discussion raises further questions. A group is more a nation as more members desire the creation or maintenance of a national state. But desires can be of varying degrees of importance in a person's overall hierarchy of desires. Does it matter to the question whether a group is a nation whether many in the group have conflicting more important desires? Does the nature of these conflicting desires matter? For example, suppose everyone in a group desires the formation of a national stae, but has a stronger desire for the maintenance of the existing multi-cultural state. Does the fact that the members have the latter stronger desire count against the group's status as a nation? Or, suppose everyone is dissuaded from choosing the formation of a national state by the claim that they would face slight financial losses.
7. H.M. Johnson, *Sociology: A Systematic Introduction* (New York, 1960), p.315. See M. Weber, *From Max Weber: Essays in Sociology,* trans. and ed. H.H. Gerth and C.W. Mills (Oxford, 1946), pp.171-179.
8. Alfred Cobban, *National Self-Determination* (London, 1944), pp.56-63.
9. *Ibid.*, p.49.
10. For a discussion of the conflict between these considerations see Cobban, *op. cit.,* especially chapters III and VIII.
11. Joel Feinberg, *Social Philosophy* (Englewood Cliffs, N.J., 1973), pp.56-61.

12. Cobban, *op. cit.,* p.47.

13. For a discussion of these claims see my "Collective Actions and Secondary Actions", *American Philosophical Quarterly,* 16 (1979), pp. 177-186

14. Kenneth Arrow, "Values and Collective Decision-Making", in *Philosophy, Politics and Society,* 3rd series, P. Laslett and W. Runciman, eds. (Oxford, 1967), p.223.

15. Thomas Hobbes, *Leviathan,* ed. C.B. Macpherson (Harmodsworth, England, 1968), p.221.

16. The following is based closely on an argument stated by Stanley French and Andres Gutman in "The Principle of National Self-determination", in *Philosophy, Morality and International Affairs,* Virginia Held,*et. al.,*eds. (New York, 1974), pp. 150-152.

17. *Ibid.*, p.151.

18. *Ibid.*, p.152.

19. *Ibid.*

20. "Considerations on Representative Government", chapter XVI, *loc. cit.*, p.381.

21. Even if a given group has the right of self-determination and even if this right takes priority over conflicting rights sanctioned by DSP, this is still not an absolute right.

22. This raises the question what counts as a "significant" part of a nation or nation-like group? I have in mind, as significant parts of such groups in given territories, the portion of the Basques which is in France and the portion which is in Spain, and the portion of anglophone Canadians which is in Québec, assuming anglophone Canadians are a nation-like group. However, the portion of Spaniards who are in Paris, or the portion of anglophones who are in the Gaspé region, would not count as significant. "Significance" here is a matter of degree, and is partly a matter of numbers. I will say a portion of such a group which is in a given state is more significant as it is more localized in a given territory which is adjacent to the territory occupied by the rest of the group, and as it would be more feasible to unify that territory under a state which would be chosen by a majority of the group as a whole.

23. See David Lyons, "Rights, Claimants and Beneficiaries", *American Philosophical Quarterly,* 6 (1969), pp.173-185.

24. There are theories of representative democracy on which decisions for a group by a majority of a sub-group would be accepted. But the Québécois are not an elected or representative sub-population of the Québec people.

25. My views on these matters were formed over a long time by discussions with many people. For recent help, I would like to thank Steven Davis, Stanley French, and Susan Lagacé and Jan Narveson.

QUEBEC SELF-DETERMINATION AND CANADIAN INTERESTS

Frank CUNNINGHAM

This paper sketches out an argument to show that it is in the interests of those in Canada who live outside of Quebec ("Canadians" for want of a better short-hand term) to promote the right of "Quebeckers" to determine their own future, even if this determination takes the form of separation from Confederation. The full argument I have in mind (and I do not suppose it to be the only possible one) depends for the most part on the correctness of certain empirical sociological, political, and economic views which I do not intend to defend. Rather I attempt to map out one line along which an argument supporting this conclusion can be made, indicating where I think certain philosophical issues are relevant or not relevant on the way.

In lieu of definitions. When I refer to the interests of "Canadians" I am referring to the overwhelmingly large majority of Canadians who do not have some interest in denying Quebeckers the right in question so large as to outweigh an interest in promoting this right. The group excluded by this is, I maintain, very small. Perhaps Canadian owners of factories in Quebec are examples, though defending Quebec self-determination may even be in the objective interests of some of these Canadians on balance. When I refer to "Quebeckers" I mean those whose home is in Quebec. This seems to me enough for the argument sketched here, though I think the argument is supplemented if it can be shown that Quebec is a nation (and that there exists a moral right of national self-determination).

I use the word "right" to mean *legal* right for the similar reason that while I think Quebeckers do have a moral right of national self-determination, I do not think that the philosophical problems surrounding this concept need to be solved to make the case I want to argue, namely that Canadians should do what they can to facilitate Quebeckers determining the future status of Quebec. No doubt a clever, if mean, argument could be made (though I do not suspect for one minute that any member of the Canadian Philosophical Association would make it) that since now Quebec does not have a legal right of self-determination up to and including separation from Confederation there is no such right to defend, and hence a precondition of acting on the prescriptions embodied in this paper must be to oppose anything but a constitution giving Quebec this right, which in turn requires that Quebec stay in Confederation at least until after ratification of such a constitution.

To forestall such an argument, I take "promoting Quebec self-detemination" to mean "promoting the ability of Quebeckers to determine their own future *as if* they had a legal right to secede". One way to do this (and one that I, myself, favour) would be to promote a federation within which this right is actually held. Whether this is favoured or not, Quebec self-determination should be promoted by doing whatever is possible in Canada today to prevent possible military intervention or economic penalization of Quebec in the event that Quebeckers opt for separation. This means combatting anti-Quebec sentiment among Canadians in the press and the schools, exerting political pressure on elected government officials, and so on.

By "interests" I mean "objective interests". I realize this concept is problematic, but believe it can be made intelligible and defended. Roughly, I characterize the objective interests of a group of people as those subjectively motivating interests its members would have if they were in possession of relevant *knowledge* about their society and the consequences of various possible courses of action on their own and others' futures. It is an empirical question, relative to any putative interest, just what kind of knowledge this is, as it is an empirical claim that people's subjectively motivating interests change in accord with increasing knowledge. I believe it also to be an empirical truth that as objective and subjective interests increasingly come into phase, so to speak, through history, conflict of (subjective) interest diminishes. But I do not think that any of these claims needs to be defended to support the conclusion of this paper. What is supposed is that understanding the truth of the specific social-scientific theses listed below will lead Canadians to promote Quebec self-determination. This is a supposition that those who agree with the theses can put to the test by sharing their knowledge with their compatriots.

What the claim involves. The claim of the argument sketched here is in some respects a strong one. I hold that Canadians should promote Quebec self-determination even if this means separation, because (as is argued later) given the history of Quebec and existing power relations, the ability uni-laterally to separate must be defended by Canadians to make possible the kind of equality between them and Quebeckers that is in the interests of each. The claim is also strong in urging more than passive favouring of the right in question. On the other hand, the claim is not as strong as opponents of Quebec self-determination sometimes try to suggest such claims always are.

The claim of the argument is *not* that any form of self-determination whatsoever Quebeckers could imaginably choose would be in Canadian interests. For instance, should Quebeckers choose to create a militaristic, fascist state, this would not be in Canadian (or Quebec) interests, and it would be necessary to weigh the pros and cons of acting on one of two conflicting intersts. (It should be mentioned, however, that despite some of the more violent anti-Quebec propaganda and despite serious reservations many Canadians and Quebeckers have about the major present political expression for Quebec self-determination, the Parti Québécois, the onus rests on someone who perceives such a counter-acting interest to *demonstrate* that in the actual situation of Quebec today their fears are justified. It will not do just to imagine highly improbable possibilities. Also, even if there were a strong ultra-right movement in Quebec using self-determination as its rallying call, this would not justify either Quebeckers or Canadians in combatting self-determination. Why leave the field to the right?)

Promoting Quebec self-determination up to and including separation does not prohibit one from consistently favouring and urging something other than separation (e.g., Confederation on new terms). Not only is there no conceptual incompatibility here, but it can be argued that Quebec perception of a sincere preparation to defend separation on the part of Canadians is a necessary condition for establishing some workable alternative to it.

Canadian Interests. The argument that it is in Canadian interests to promote Quebec self-determination hinges on four social-scientific theses, which I shall simply state, making a few comments on some.

(1) *There are social, economic, and political problems faced by all of us so grave and inter-related in such ways that a very high degree of co-operation among Canadians and Quebeckers will be necessary to resolve them.* The kinds of problems I have in mind include: inflation, unemployment, threatened and actual stagnation of educational and cultural institutions, inability rationally to employ technology, and lack of effective control for most people over the conditions of their lives and work. In general the point is that in a modern industrialized society such as ours isolated activity in one part of the country cannot resolve such problems, but must be co-ordinated with activity in other parts.

Let me briefly illustrate the point by making reference to two problems that many see as central: foreign ownership of the economy and regional political balkanization. Those who agree that the large foreign ownership of our resources (over 50%) and manufacturing industries (over 60%) is harmful to both Canadians and Quebeckers in making both subject to the needs of a foreign economy, should also agree that co-operation will be needed in breaking this control. This is so because without it foreign-based monopolies can play Quebeckers and Canadians (and indeed Canadians and Canadians) off against one another to maintain their strength here. Also economic reprisals by multi-national corporations for nationalization will require maximum, co-ordinated use of Canadian and Quebec resources and expertise to be withstood.

The political balkanization I referred to is the present arrangement inherited from the B.N.A. Act whereby Ottawa has the money and the provinces have jurisdiction over matters of education, health, civil rights, labour matters, and other things to a very large extent. Whether any such arrangement could have worked is seen by many as a moot point, since in the historical development of Canada it has not. Funds exist for policies that do not exist and (more often) *vice versa.* Levels of government pass various economic and legal bucks back and forth rather than answering people's needs.

Especially important for the present argument is that as long as Quebec is "a province like the others" each Canadian province has to be treated as entitled to whatever it is politically necessary to accord Quebec in the way of jurisdictional independence. This creates the bind that either Quebec does not receive enough independence or the right kind or else other provinces get too much or the wrong kind, given that however different the Canadian provinces are from one another, Quebec is surely more sociologically different from all the others.

Again, co-operation will be needed between Canadians and Quebeckers to construct a more rational form of interaction. This would obviously be the case if Quebec remained in a new Confederation, since even with "special status", give and take would be necessary on all sides. It would also be necessary if Quebec were a separate state, since the continuing existence of a hostile neighbour, especially one with the close economic ties Quebec has in varying degrees with Canadian provinces, would interfere with attempts to create and maintain a rational distribution of legal and economic powers among the provinces and between them and the federal government.

(2) *The extensive co-operation required between Canadians and*

Quebeckers is such that it cannot be maintained unless the parties involved respect and trust one another. A supposition underlying much political theory is that co-operation requires either social homogeneity or else it results from at least tacit contracts among groups essentially in competition, each motivated by enlightened self-interest. It does not seem to me that these are the only alternatives, and in many instances social co-operation among sociologically heterogeneous groups requires more than just belief on the part of each party that a contract is mutually advantageous and trust that the other party also believes this. What is required instead is a desire on the part of each party that the unique aspirations and values of the other party are fulfilled (respect) and a belief that the other party has this desire regarding them as well (trust).

Examples of situations where such respect and trust are required for effective co-operation are easily found on the individual level in on-going small groups (families, neighbourhoods, maybe even philosophy departments), and I believe that the situation of Canada-Quebec is one as well. This seems to me the case for two reasons. First, confronting the sorts of problems mentioned above will involve sacrifice (e.g., a certain amount of economic sacrifice may well be needed for a time to break multi-national control), and stronger trust than that associated with merely self-interested contracts is required when such sacrifices are anticipated and experienced. Second, the needed co-operation is of long term sort and involves many uncertainties thus making the weaker form of co-operative base unreliable.

(3) *To begin acquiring the attitudes of trust and respect necessary for co-operation in facing common problems, Quebeckers must become convinced that Canadians will promote their ability to determine their future even to the point of separation from Confederation.* The main reason for this is that Quebec was brought into Confederation as a conquered land and has by and large found itself economically and politically dominated by the more powerful Canadian provinces to the economic and cultural detriment of Quebeckers. Unless Quebeckers see that Canadians respect their aspiration to determine their own future, they will (correctly in my view) conclude that Canadians still regard them as in some respects a conquered people, and if Canadian support of this self-determination stops short of preparedness to support the forming of a separate state, Quebeckers will (again correctly) conclude that respect is not sincere.

Of course, respect and trust must work both ways; so Canadians must come to trust Quebeckers as well. However, given the history of the country, I believe that the first step must be taken by Canadians. While some paternalistic employers, colonial powers, and slave holders have thought that they had the trust and respect of their employees, colonized peoples, or slaves (I do not mean to draw exact analogies here), they have found out that trust and respect never emanate from a position of inequality.

(4) *The only way Canadians can convince Quebeckers that they are prepared to promote their self-determination is actually to promote it.* You can't fool all of the people all of the time.

NATION ET ETAT, SOUVERAINETE ET AUTODETERMINATION

Paul GAGNE

Bien que ces quatre concepts me semblent s'interpréter les uns par rapport aux autres, je trouve éclairant de les regrouper en deux paires: 1) la nation et l'Etat; 2) la souveraineté et l'autodétermination. En effet, ces quatre concepts nous renvoient à deux problèmes différents: 1) A toute nation doit-il correspondre un Etat? 2) Le droit à l'autodétermination implique-t-il nécessairement la souveraineté? Le premier problème est une question de faits historiques alors que le deuxième est une question de droits.

1. *Nation et Etat: toute nation doit-elle posséder son Etat?*

Je pense qu'il est impossible de parler de nations et d'Etats de façon abstraite. Il faut se référer à l'histoire et au contexte économico-politique concret de chaque cas particulier.

Les nations et les Etats sont des réalités historiques, donc des réalités qui changent au cours du temps et même qui apparaissent à une certaine époque et qui disparaissent à une autre.

Sur le plan historique, l'Etat est une réalité politique antérieure à la nation: Les historiens ont écrit au sujet de la formation et de la disparition des Etats-cité de l'antiquité, par exemple Athènes ou Rome; ils ont écrit également au sujet des royaumes féodaux du Moyen-Age et des empires des temps modernes. Il semble cependant que l'Etat-nation est de formation historique plus récente, voire même un phénomène contemporain, bien qu'il faille faire des distinctions entre l'apparition des vieilles nations européennes et l'apparition de nouvelles nations en Amérique, en Afrique et en Asie. L'apparition de l'Etat-nation sur le plan politique semble coïncider étrangement avec l'apparition du capitalisme sur le plan économique.

Je crois également qu'il convient de rappeler que ces deux concepts visent deux choses bien distinctes. L'Etat vise l'organisation politique des sociétés alors que la nation renvoie plutôt, selon Lénine, aux notions de communauté de gens ayant une langue, un territoire, une vie économique et une culture qu'ils partagent en commun.

Sur le plan historique, on peut dire que l'organisation politique des sociétés en est venue à coincider plus ou moins avec la constitution de la

Sur le plan historique, on peut dire que l'organisation politique des sociétés en est venue à coïncider plus ou moins avec la constitution de la nation. Je dis plus ou moins, car je pense que même les cas prétendus clairs, comme la France et l'Angleterre, ne sont pas si clairs: elles ont aussi leurs problèmes de minorités. Je serais plutôt enclin à penser que l'Etat-nation correspond plus à une nécessité d'ordre économique qui a engendré une unification très souvent forçée par le groupe dominant, lequel a imposé son gouvernement, sa langue et sa culture à des groupes dominés.

En conséquence, je pense que l'Etat peut être national, bi-national et même multi-national; l'histoire le démontre amplement. Le vrai problème n'est pas là, il est plutôt de savoir si dans un Etat national donné il y a d'autres groupes ethniques dominés qui répondent à la définition de ce qu'est une nation et à qui l'on dénie le droit à l'existence en ne les reconnaissant pas politiquement et en les exploitant économiquement. Et même plus, s'il y a, à l'intérieur d'un État, exploitation de groupes ou de classes d'hommes par d'autres; car la base et la racine de l'exploitation de l'homme par l'homme est avant tout économique, comme Marx l'a si bien démontré.

2. *Souveraineté et autodétermination: le droit à l'autodétermination implique-t-il nécessairement la souveraineté*?

Dans ce qui précède, j'ai plutôt tenté de démontrer que le concept d'Etat est relativement indépendant du concept de nation et qu'un Etat peut être mono, bi ou multi-national et qu'il importait plus qu'il n'y ait pas exploitation de l'homme par l'homme ou de groupes d'hommes sur d'autres groupes d'hommes; en d'autres mots, que l'Etat soit juste économiquement et politiquement.

Pour ce faire, il faut que l'Etat reconnaisse tant les droits des individus que les droits des communautés qui le composent; car je crois qu'il n'y a pas de droits individuels sans droits collectifs et vice-versa; qu'il n'y a pas de société juste sans reconnaissance de droits égaux entre individus, groupes d'individus ou entre nations.

Le droit à l'autodétermination est le pendant collectif du droit à la liberté des individus et j'irais même jusqu'à affirmer que la reconnaissance du droit à l'autodétermination d'une collectivité est une condition nécessaire à la reconnaissance de la liberté des individus de cette collectivité; sinon il n'y a pas de libertés de langue, de culture, de religion. De plus la conséquence fondamentale de cette non-reconnaissance est la domination politique et l'exploitation économique. Le droit à l'autodétermination est donc aussi fondamental à reconnaître que le droit à la liberté des individus.

Un des problèmes fondamentaux de la confédération canadienne est la non-reconnaissance de ce droit à la nation canadienne-française dans une constitution. Le Canada se comporte comme un Etat mononational, alors qu'il est au moins bi-national.

Le droit à l'autodétermination entraîne nécessairement le droit à la séparation, si c'est là le désir de la nation qui l'exerce; donc la formation de fait d'un Etat souverain indépendant. Pour ce qui est de la nation canadienne-française, je crois qu'elle en arrivera là, s'il n'y a pas de reconnaissance au niveau d'une nouvelle constitution canadienne de son droit à l'autodétermination, i.e. de choisir et de participer au genre d'Etat dans lequel elle désire vivre; car on ne peut pas maintenir indéfiniment par la force une domination.

NATION AND SOVEREIGNTY - REFLECTIONS ON TWO CONCEPTS

Francis SPARSHOTT

I Sovereignty and Empire

Everyone says that the concept of sovereignty is ambiguous. Not everyone says that its credentials are obscure and its implications misleading. To build one's political thinking around the concept of sovereignty is to encourage the strange and vicious notion that the truth of politics lies neither in joint action nor in mutual accommodation but in *command.*

The idea of sovereignty gets its credibility from the archaic idea of *empire*. According to the latter, the human order is symbol (both part and reflection) of a cosmic order, and must therefore embody a fixed pattern of lawful power. The most clear and consistent available pattern is one with a single point of reference (the emperor as *primum mobile*) unambiguously related to an unmoved mover, or God. In theory there can be only one empire; in practice, too, there can only be one with 'barbarians' (accidental being, unformed matter) on the fringes. If two putative empires come into contact, one is a false claimant and must be eliminated (see the last sentence of Aristotle's *Metaphysics*, XII), but in real life there can be many empires so long as they are not in regular communication.

In its original sixteenth-century formulations, the concept of sovereignty reflects and seeks to reverse the breakdown of empire. Deprived of the centre that authorized them and also limited them, heterogeneous devolved powers presumed autonomy, and, lacking demarcated spheres (Rome knew no *imperium* without its correlated *provincia*), conflicted anarchically. The 'sovereign' is invoked to restore order as a *de facto* mini-emperor within a territorial domain. A single power system is once more insisted on, but without the cosmic justification. God is indeed invoked, but insanely, relying on the absolute Divine Will and not the eternal Wisdom: anointing a monarch cannot sanctify territorial bounds.[1]

That sovereignty be embodied in a single sovereign lord was never strictly necessary. What the ideal of sovereignty demanded was that the distribution of power be determinate and exhaustive, that within a given territory no class of decision should lack a decider and none should have more than one. Even so, the necessity is not a practical one. The needs of common life are met by any reliable and expeditious way of settling disputes and defusing conflicts, and that does not require that every buck should have a definite place to stop at, only that every buck should stop somewhere. In practice, divisions of political powers tend to be incomplete and inconsistent, settled by political rather than constitutional means. No limit can be set a priori to what arrangements can prevail: confederations, cordial understandings, special relationships, customs unions, privileges, fudgings, and connivings are the rule. Traditional theorists often either ignore these or construe them on the 'sovereignty' pattern as articulations of autonomy or as treaties between autonomous powers. But that is not because things are that way, it is because we are haunted by the ghost of empire.[2]

II **Sovereignty as Brigandage**

The living significance of sovereignty is in *ecumenical* politics. The idea is native to a time of conquest and exploration, colonization and exploitation. One needs to know of any territory *who is in charge here,* who can sign the concession. In contrast to empire, sovereignty becomes a necessary notion only when regular international relations are established. Paradoxically, one needs to invoke absolute autonomy *only* when it has to be compromised. Someone must keep the lighthouses and weather stations going, and everyone must know who that someone is. Technology is sometimes said to embody an ineluctable dynamic that necessarily spawns international corporations, which constitute a power structure alternative to the political, so that sovereignty is now obsolete. Not so. Worldwide commerce and industry need either sovereignty or empire, preferably the former.

Everything I have said so far points to the conclusion that the basic assumption of the principle of sovereignty, as opposed to that of empire, is territory. Sovereign power is not power over a determinate group of peoples, but power within a given geographical domain. The territorial mosaic that is the United Nations makes this startlingly visible.[3]

III **Sovereignty and Self-Determination**

Because the concept of sovereignty presupposes that the globe is divided into territories within each of which power can be uniquely located, the native peoples of Canada present an intractable political problem. Not being self-defined in a way that lends itself to assimilation to this global carve-up, they can neither have nor assign sovereignty to the lands they inhabit, cannot enter into treaties (the documents that govern their relations with the local players of the sovereignty game are called 'treaties', but are in no respect treated as such; they function merely as conceded claims to property rights and personal privileges). The Hudson's Bay Company, or whoever else is around, simply moves in and takes over, because if (for instance) Canada is not sovereign in the Arctic, someone else must be, and who would that be? The USSR, or (oddly) the USA, but certainly not the Inuit, even though the Inuit are the only people who live there. It is not that the Inuit are non-persons; they are just non-powers.[4] The Dene nation cannot be a Dene state because they do not have the entrance stakes for that game, namely, conceptual membership in the 'comity of nations', the association of sovereignty-thinkers.

The persistent illusion that sovereignty is an all-purpose concept in politics tempts us to assimilate to each other the three problems of Canadian confederation. First, the problem of provincial autonomy and potential separation is a typical sovereignty problem. Confederation was and is coalition, mostly economically motivated, of territories and potential territories. Its problems are those of dividing powers in a way that will reflect the alignments and divergences of economic concerns. From this point of view, the Ottawa government is an *imperium* with its own *provincia* no less than Ontario is, and William Davis' habit of speaking of Ottawa as a *foreign* power (which used to puzzle and enrage me) reflects a true feeling for the situation.

The issue between anglophonic and francophonic Canada is altogether different in character, a confrontation of two ways of life, two nations, even if one of them is definable only by its being other than the other. (It is because 'English Canada' exists only in contrast to French Canada that in British Columbia, where the interprovincial issue is pressing and the intercultural one only a distant rumour, and where Québec-plus-Ontario is accordingly thought of as the monolithic juggernaut of 'Eastern Canada', the whole Separatism business seems just a stupid charade; nothing in one's experience out there suggests that one might belong to any other 'nation' than Canada as a whole.) These are not territories but rather tribes, related not as two solitudes but in mutual *rejection* of otherness. (Such mutual rejection need not be hostile, because it rests on real differences — it is an organic, not merely a mechanical, non-solidarity; but if one side feels or is threatened by the other, hostility may break out, as it has here, or become endemic, as it has in Belgium.) The issue involving these two nations is one of the self-determination of self-defined groups; and it cannot be too strongly emphasized that the idea of sovereignty works strongly against that of such self-determination, because the limits of tesserae in the global mosaic can seldom coincide with the homelands of self-defined groups. The considerations determining the limits of sovereign territories make them essentially arbitrary from the cultural viewpoint. The boundaries of Lower Canada or Québec never did, do not now, and were never meant to, define the French fact in North America. Whatever the justification for a French-Canadian independent state, it would not be a justification for the independence of Québec. The justification for *Québec* separation (which might, of course, be deemed sufficient) could only be that no other *existing* sovereignty-defined territory would plausibly serve the purpose.

Entirely different from either of the above-named constitutional problems is that of the native peoples — which could also be the problem of Hutterites, Doukhobors and others (sometimes miscalled 'minorities') who have identity to preserve and a place where they live, but who lack the distribution of powers necessary to sovereign status. Within the territorially-articulated system of sovereign powers, it should be possible to make explicit and proper provision for culturally-defined enclaves that are autonomous but whose autonomy is not articulated as a system of powers. The problem of how this should be done has never been precisely defined, and the moral and practical issues have never been squarely faced.

IV **Nation**

I have made incidental use of the concept of a nation, implying that a nation consists of people who feel, and recognize that they feel or ought to feel or may be expected to feel, that they belong together, in such a way as to warrant pretensions to political autonomy. In what circumstances such presumptions of feeling may be expected to arise, and should be taken seriously if they do arise, and in what circumstances what pretensions to autonomy should be taken how seriously by whom, are questions much debatable in principle and in detail, but on which there is a broad practical consensus. What I want to say a few words about is the idea of nationality itself.

It has been said that the idea of a nation is cultural rather than political in its immediate significance. But that view seems to rest on the equation of politics with the distribution of powers, on the sovereignty model; and I observed at the start that to think in that way is to degrade the notion of politics and thus unwittingly to degrade the quality of public affairs. Of the alternative notions of what politics is, interest brokerage likewise has no special place for nationhood, though national interests could be set alongside commercial and other interests as recognizable participants in negotiations; but one could argue that this view of politics also, equating formal public interactions with trading relations, reflects and promotes a degraded view of humanity. But if we equate politics with the joint conduct of affairs in certain specifiable conditions, the nation becomes a *prima facie* political entity as consisting of those who have most joint affairs to conduct.

In a North American context, the concept of nation may have a resonance that it lacks elsewhere. As an ever-present paradigm in the back of our minds we have the maximal groupings of the Indian peoples, always called 'Nations': clearly identified, but lacking the territorial and authoritarian trappings of sovereignty, autonomous and autarchic but (in the Six Nations of the Iroquois) affording a model for federal unions, they have presented to the imagination a living reminder of an alternative political reality, all the more powerful for being essentially unknown.

In general, the idea of a nation seems to be conceived on the analogy of the extended family, and more specifically of the tribe, clearly conceived by Aristotle and his Greek predecessors as the pre-political unit of social life that becomes a 'state' when it settles down, surrounds itself with walls, and admits settlers. The analogy is justified because the familial unity of the tribe is itself imputed and notional: the tribe is that within which familial relations obtain, those relations themselves being modelled on those inevitable within the nuclear family and whatever orbits around that nucleus. The nexus that constitutes the nation is thus not solely, and perhaps not primarily, one of feeling: it is a matter of shared life and habitual interactions. My nation is defined by those with whom I feel at home, not having to think about what I do, not having to explain myself — which is why a shared language has so often been thought essential to a nation. My nation, like my family, consists of those with whom I am presumed by myself and others *not to be strangers* — whereas politics as bargaining presumes that the participants are strangers, and politics as territorial power-articulation has no participants, only status-holders.

How far an extended family extends is a matter of convention; but the relevant conventions, like most conventions, take account of miscellaneous practical requirements. Similarly, and *a fortiori,* who belongs to the same nation as myself is a matter of convention, but not of entirely arbitrary convention. In particular, we may distinguish three different ways in which nations may be experienced as bounded. First, my fellow-nationals may be separated from others by a sharp frontier, a sea or a mountain-range, in such a way that all the people I meet, and all the people *they* regularly meet, belong to an 'us' with no contrasting 'them'. Second, my nation may fade out at the edges as people become progressively more different and less connected. A native English-speaker in Canada may not have any sharp sense of *nation* at all. When moving from Britain to Canada, or from Canada to the States, or vice versa, one need have little more sense of being a *foreigner* than one would have on moving from Calgary to Toronto; and many families must, like mine, have members in the States, across Canada, in Britain, in Australia, whose commitment to the local community may be fierce or tepid, deep or provisional, depending on the style in which they have chosen to conduct their lives. And third, I may experience my nation as being confronted and sharply delimited by another nation, contrasting in language or values or way of life or in all three: different people, of whom I never know quite what they are thinking, and, especially, what they are thinking about *us.* It seems evident that at least some French-speaking Québecers experience their nationhood thus; and they often speak of what they feel confronting them as 'English Canada', a phrase that no one I have met can relate to his experience of himself at all.

V **National Rights and Individual Rights**

One is so used to the cliché that contrasts 'the individual' with 'society' that one is tempted to suppose too readily that national rights and individual rights are rights against each other and hence necessarily opposed. But if nations are pseudo-families, that supposition may be wrong. Family rights seem rather to be extensions of individual rights, in that the fundamental familial relationship is one of solidarity. My right to be myself is my right to be at ease in being what I am, and that right may be translated into my nation's right to a national life. Certainly, my family may be cloying, suffocating, hateful, that against which I rebel and from which I free myself: but its tentacles in their embrace define what my freedom must be.

The argument of the preceding paragraph is obviously specious. A nation is not a family, not even an extended family, but is the expression of a consensus sustained by and in turn sustaining a habit of easy interaction; it is not easy to see how it can be a bearer of rights, rather than (say) a fiction invoked to explain a set of presumed rights that this or that individual may wish to vindicate. Part of the problem is that although (as anthropologists used to say) "there is no nature, there is culture", and what a person is is what his society makes him, a person who migrates from one culture to another is not killed by that process, and may not even (in his own eyes or the eyes of others) be any the worse off. Nothing in the world encourages any animal (even a rational one) to claim a right to *go on in the same way.* And yet, as the framers of the Québec Act insisted and even Lord Durham conceded, a society established with its own way of life and institutions has a clear right against any conqueror or occupier to be left in undisturbed possession thereof: to act otherwise, they said, would be to offend against humanity.

VI **Nation and Sovereignty**

Should nations coincide with sovereign states? Obviously they cannot always do so, if sovereignty is based on territorial divisions and nationhood on personal relations. But, one may ask, what other basis for the demarcation of a sovereign state could have a better claim? The answer lies ready to hand: administrative convenience, and economic expediency, are just as directly relevant. But if nations are like families, they don't want to be interfered with by outsiders. When, and how far, can one be sure that one won't be interfered with? Conversely, when can one be sure that whatever one seeks to preserve by way of national identity and integrity can be better secured by a sovereign state that coincides with the national borders (if any)? If there is anything at all in our discussion, it shows that these are contingent matters, to be decided not by any principles of inherent fitness but by reasonable forecasts of the consequences of making this or that arrangement. That would be true even if one were making a new start in a new world; if the issue is one of making new arrangements in a situation in which the nation is already involved in specific relations, other issues arise which are not within the purview of this essay.

VII **Nation, Sovereignty and the Body Politic**

Three separate ideas must be held mutually distinct. First, there is the body politic, the Hobbesian commonwealth, an organization of individuals agreeing to conduct their affairs in common. Second, there is the nation, the organized society into which one is born and into which one's family merges, the people whose language and mores are identifiably one's own. Third, there is the sovereign state, a power unit (however structured) based primarily on territory and not on personal participation.

The conventional wisdom of old textbooks, distinguishing *state* from *society*, does not so much confuse these three as tell this or that lie about them in the interests of this or that ideology.

The first of them, the body politic, has hard edges, in that all and only those who have agreed have a part in the agreement. It is a pure and admitted fiction; but it represents an ideal structure of decision, in that it identifies those who can literally be said to make joint decisions and those for whom such decisions accordingly hold with unimpeachable legitimacy.

The second of the three, the nation, may have fuzzy edges or none, in that what the nuclear family merges into is an indefinite nexus of relationships. It is by no means a fiction, but its determinate identity is fictional, in that the extrapolation of familial relations rests on indeterminate analogies with the extended family of which in its turn the limits are set, if at all, by conventions that may not be clearly spelled out.

The third of the three, the sovereign state, is inherently as hard-edged as the first. But, unlike it, it is no fiction. It answers rather to a practical decision, the decision to impose a structure and observe a limit. It may or may not coincide with what anyone feels to be their home ground as nation or as body politic, but in any case belongs to a different world of thought: the Roman-imperial or Byzantine-theocratic, as opposed to the Hellenic-republican.

NOTES

1. The irrationality of this floating divine right may partly explain the apparent lunacy whereby, for instance, a Scottish King could give someone Nova Scotia as a present, without consulting the natives who lived there and regardless of the fact that the Acadians were there already, having presumably been given the same place by another king who didn't own it either. What on earth, we ask, did these people think they were doing? I suppose the answer is that anyone who has been anointed with oil in the name of an omnipresent Deity has as much, and as little, right to anything as he has to anything else.

2. The Pepin/Robarts report (*Coming to Terms*, 14) rejects the concept of sovereignty, except in a limited context, precisely on the grounds that it thus misleads about how responsibilities are shared.

3. This is especially true in Africa, where the political units have almost no relation to traditional groupings of peoples but are simply the successors to the territories carved out by colonizing powers — and are left intact largely because international relations presuppose such carved-out territories.

4. The wording of the Pepin/Robarts report is significant in this regard. "When the Europeans arrived on Canadian soil the Indians and Inuit were already occupying and using much of it", they say, and speak of "those parts of Canada

where Indian title to lands had neither been the object of treaties nor superseded by law" (*Coming to Terms*, 5). In other words, their original status is thought of as that of freeholders under an unidentifiable sovereign whom the French or British crowns superseded, not as themselves collectively the ultimate authority by which alone title could be transferred.

THE IDEA OF SOVEREIGNTY-ASSOCIATION*

Christopher W. MORRIS

What is sovereignty-association?

Sovereignty is the right of a government[1] or of a people[2] to determine the nature of public policy. According to the classical works of modern moral and political theory, the sovereign — be it an individual, an assembly or a people — is the source of legitimate authority and law. We shall call this the classical notion of sovereignty, according to which, then, sovereignty is the attribute of some political body of being the source of legitimate (moral, political and legal) authority. As should be clear, the classical notion of sovereignty finds its home in moral conventionalism,[3] especially social contract theory.[4] In this tradition the sovereign is the ultimate source of authority because in the absence of absolute government (Hobbes) or of a legitimately constituted people (Rousseau) there are no binding rules or laws. Sovereignty, as unlimited, indivisible and inalienable, as in the classical notion, is possible only within the framework of moral and legal conventionalism. Only within a perspective in which moral reasoning is a process not of discovering but of creating, can classical sovereignty be ascribed to a government or a people. Within the natural law[5] and natural rights[6] traditions, nature is the source of legitimate authority, not the will of individuals. Natural law and natural rights theorists make little reference to sovereignty; they do not need the notion for their conception of the source of legitimacy, nor is it an essential feature of their accounts of the state. Within these more traditional perspectives, government or the people are always bound by natural law and thus cannot be sovereign.

Sovereignty, in the classical sense, then, is the source of legitimate authority. As ascribed to governments or to peoples, such an account of sovereignty is possible only within moral and legal conventional-

* I am grateful to Andrew Lugg, Adam Morton and John Thorp for comments.

ism. It is this feature of the classical notion of sovereignty that renders the notion of sovereignty-association especially problematic.

An *association* we shall characterize as a cooperative activity in accordance with an accepted principle of action. Using the common understanding of the notion, we shall say that a number of persons cooperate, or act in a cooperative manner, if and only if each acts in a way determined by their mutual agreement.[7] Associations thus facilitate cooperation. We may understand trade unions, political parties, nations, clubs and agreements as associations in this sense. They are cooperative activities: individuals engage in mutually advantageous activity, acting interdependently in accordance with some principle(s) of action. Principles of action which make cooperative activity possible and which thus are part of an association impose constraints on the independent action of individuals. Action in accordance with some accepted principle of action is constrained in ways specified by the principle. This is the important point for our discussion: an association imposes constraints on the actions of its members.

Sovereignty-association would then seem to be conceptually incoherent. A government or a people is accorded the right to be the ultimate source of legitimate authority, but at the same time the same government or people is constrained in its decisions and actions by binding principles of action. The association limits and alienates the allegedly unlimited and inalienable sovereignty. The sovereign government or people is both absolute and constrained.

The incoherence of this notion of sovereignty-association emerges most clearly when one recalls the conventionalist background of the notion of sovereignty. In traditional social contract theory, prior to agreement there are no binding rules or laws; in classical terminology, individuals in a state of nature are in a position of liberty. If agreement establishes a sovereign government or a sovereign people, that is because prior to agreement or independent of agreement there are no binding rules or laws. The sovereign is absolute, as well as indivisible and inalienable, because there is no other source of moral and legal authority. The incoherence of the suggested understanding of sovereignty-association thus lies in the combination of notions of unrestricted authority and of constraints.

Let us look at the problem in its more practical forms. Canada, the Soviet Union and Japan are sovereign states according to common usage. The governments or the peoples of these states are thought to be the ultimate determinants of their laws.[8] But Canada, the Soviet Union and Japan are each bound by international law and by the rules of their cooperative agreements. Not all international law is dependent on consent; new nations can acquire obligations without consenting, either explicitly or "tacitly", as can other nations merely by undergoing some change such as acquiring new territory.[9] And not all cooperative agreements are explicit. A mutually advantageous convention may impose obligations on members without their explicit agreement; for "...an agreement sufficient to create a convention need not be a transaction involving language or any other conventional activity. All it takes is an exchange of manifestations of a propensity to conform to a regularity."[10] So Canada, the Soviet Union and Japan are sovereign states *and* are (most likely) bound by the constraints of international law and of cooperative conventions. How can this be on the classical notion of sovereignty?

The problem has been stated both in its conceptual and practical forms. How are sovereignty and association reconcilable? Of course the problem is not new. It arises, as we have seen, in the theory of international law.[11] And it arises in philosophical discussions of moral autonomy.[12] The issue is one of reconciling the autonomy or independence of an agent with constraints on its actions. The solution lies surely with the abandonment of the classical notion of sovereignty, or so I shall argue.

Individuals and nations may be bound, morally and legally, by conventions to which they do not explicitly agree. A mutually advantageous arrangement may create obligations for beneficiaries given general adherence to the terms of the convention. Hart's well-known Principle of Fairness,[13] Rawls' two Principles of Justice[14] and Gauthier's reconstruction of Hobbesian moral theory[15] can be viewed as different accounts of the conditions and terms of morally binding social arrangements. In general, traditional contractarian theory is an attempt to specify the conventional nature of morality and law.

Viewed from the perspective of social contract theory, the nation-states of the sixteenth and seventeenth centuries were independent enough that their boundaries were the natural or salient limits of moral conventions. Relations between nations, given existing independence and antagonism of interests, were state of nature relations — that is, relations unconstrained by moral or legal rules. In such a world the classical notion of sovereignty is useful and appropriate. Given the contractarian perspective, nation-states through their governments or people became the ultimate source of legitimate authority. Being in a state of nature in relation to other nations, nation-states could have no other or "higher" source of law than the will of their governments or people. Given the general facts concerning the development of nations during this period of Western history, the classical notion of sovereignty is useful.

Certain developments that have taken place since this time, however, may create binding obligations where none existed before and thus challenge the centrality and importance classical contractarian theory gives to nation-states and to the notion of sovereignty. The dangers of nuclear conflict and of other forms of modern warfare create an identity of interests that did not exist centuries ago. Such an identity of interests could give rise to new conventions and binding obligations. If only because of the shared interest to avoid nuclear conflict, most if not all nations today find themselves in the Rawlsian "circumstances of justice",[16] that is, in a situation in which moral conventions are rational. Further, problems arising from pollution, population growth and the possible exhaustion of certain natural resources may require solutions involving cooperation between nations. Different nations share interests in population control, containment of pollution and abatement of the depletion of certain natural resources. This interdependence of interests also may give rise to new conventions and obligations on the part of nations. And lastly, nations today are economically interdependent in ways not possible in earlier centuries. This important interdependence clearly creates new identities (as well as new conflicts) of interests.

The picture of the relations between nations that we find in classical social contract theory seems no longer true. Where nations were once relatively independent and where their interests were relatively conflicting, there are now important identities of interests that give rise to new obligations. Whereas the classical notion of sovereignty is at home in the old picture of the relations between nations, it does not appear as useful today. These new developments, then, when coupled with the possibility of conventions which create obligations independently of explicit consent, create a situation where the classical notion of sovereignty is no longer applicable. The "sovereignty" of most states today is rather limited.

The problem with the classical notion of sovereignty is its individualism. It is a notion perhaps well-suited for emerging nation-states three to four hundred years ago, but little suited for our own — in spite of the revival of nation-state nationalism in many parts of the globe. The classical notion is at home in a world where nations are conceived on the model of individuals in a non-moral state of nature. According to this conception the interests of nations are independent and conflicting, and no binding obligations arise between them.

Absolute, indivisible and inalienable sovereignty can easily be ascribed to the governments, or people, of such nations.

The classical notion of sovereignty is thus not very useful in our world. Indeed, it is misleading insofar as its use leads people to believe that governments or peoples are not bound by (conventionally derived) rules and norms independently of consent. The use of the classical notion today hides certain important facts and ascribes to government, or to the people, a moral and legal independence no longer possible. Yet the notion of sovereignty continues to be employed, not only in Québec but around the world. Given that the classical notion is no longer useful, it is perhaps possible to give sovereignty a new sense, related to yet different from the old. The persistent use of the notion on the part of many social critics may suggest that there are important concerns which need to be articulated by some such concept.

The important issues that are raised by contemporary references to the notion of sovereignty, I shall suggest, concern the degree and the nature of the independence of states and governments, as well as the nature of their cooperative conventions and agreements with others. A "sovereign" nation may be thought to be one which possesses a certain *degree* of independence in certain areas of jurisdiction: legal, moral, cultural, economic, etc... Granted that even the United States is not sovereign in the classical sense, what do demands for sovereignty by other nations amount to? I suggest that we interpret them, depending on the context, as demands for greater independence of a specifiable sort: e.g. greater independence in legal and cultural matters comparable to that of France in relation to other European nations. Sovereignty, in what we shall call its modern sense, is not an all-or-nothing notion, but rather allows of matters of degree. Nor will the modern notion possess a clearly defined sense. All nation-states today possess some degree of independence in some areas, and all are likely — given the factual assumptions we have made — to be bound morally and legally by some cooperative conventions and agreements. Sovereignty, then, can be nothing more than a degree of independence of a specifiable sort, something which holds only as a matter of degree. Demands for sovereignty today are thus to be interpreted as demands for greater independence in certain domains. This analysis or redefinition of the notion of sovereignty is not far from the view of the Pepin-Robarts Report:

> Observers have often noted that, in practice, sovereignty, however useful as a legal concept, was necessarily limited. . . The notion that sovereignty is divisible and limited has led to the use

of more positive concepts such as "competence" and "jurisdiction." These concepts define the state in terms of the fields of activities in which a government, be it central, provincial or municipal, exercises its authority under law.[17]

What does sovereignty-association then mean? In the context of the debate over the independence of Québec, I would suggest that Parti Québécois demands for sovereignty-association be regarded not as demands for the conceptually incoherent status analyzed earlier, but as demands for greater independence in certain domains and for a renegotiation of certain cooperative agreements (e.g. the British North America Act). It would clearly make no sense for the P.Q. to demand sovereignty in the classical sense, for even the United States does not possess it. Nor could the classical notion be compatible with association, especially with the rather intricate forms of economic association the P.Q. mentions in its public statements. Viewed as a demand for greater independence in certain domains — legal, cultural, economic (especially the latter?) — the goal of sovereignty-association loses its appearance of incoherence.

What such a demand amounts to is a call for renegotiation of certain cooperative agreements, e.g. the B.N.A. The terms of such cooperative agreements are no longer viewed as mutually advantageous by Québec (and others). We may analyze political parties and movements in terms of coalitions formed around common interests. Interests vary and change over time and place; old coalitions dissolve from time to time; new ones arise. Proposals for sovereignty-association or for the renegotiation of cooperative agreements can be understood in terms of the dissolution of some old coalitions and the formation of some new ones, a process which can often be mutually advantageous to all parties if carried on in a peaceful manner.[18]

Of course, less confusion would be created by the abandonment of the notion of sovereignty altogether, as it does not easily shed its classical meaning. Continuing to use the notion, even when reinterpreted in the way I recommend, may be due to our tendency to interpret politics in statist and nationalist terms, a tendency under challenge by the current libertarian revival.[19] In any case, although the concept may not always be used clearly, present demands for sovereignty-association can be given a coherent — as well as a reasonable — sense.

NOTES

1. Hobbes. See *Leviathan.*

2. Rousseau. See *Du Contrat social.*

3. Moral conventionalism is a "nontraditional conception" of moral reasoning. See Jesse Kalin, "Two Kinds of Moral Reasoning: Ethical Egoism as a Moral Theory", *Canadian Journal of Philosophy,* November 1975. "On the nontraditional conception, moral reasoning is not the activity of discovery, but the activity of creation. It is the activity of establishing and adopting moral principles and moral rules." p.324. A coventionalist view of ethics is developed in J.L. Mackie's recent *Ethics: Inventing Right and Wrong* (Penguin, 1977).

4. I am referring to the contractarian moral and legal theories of Hobbes and Rousseau, not to that of Locke who only has a social contract view of government.

5. Thomas Aquinas.

6. John Locke.

7. "So characterized, cooperation depends, not on common objectives, but on common principles of action. These common principles are what is necessary to achieve mutual advantage." David Gauthier, "Rational Cooperation", *Nous,* March 1974, p.53.

8. More often it is governments that are thought to possess sovereignty, perhaps because it is generally governments that issue proclamations of rights to national self-determination and governments often have a common interest in not ascribing sovereignty to their citizens. The United Nations Charter, for instance, clearly reads like a work authored by heads of states.

9. H.L.A. Hart, *The Concept of Law* (Oxford, 1961), pp.220-221.

10. David Lewis, *Convention* (Harvard, 1969), pp.83-84. See his definition of convention, pp.42,78.

11. Hart, ch. X.

12. Gerald Dworkin, "Moral Autonomy", in *Morals, Science and Sociality,* eds. T. Engelhardt and D. Callahan (The Hastings Center, 1978), pp.156-171.

13. Hart, "Are There Any Natural Rights?", *Philosophical Review,* 1955, pp.175-191.

14. John Rawls, *A Theory of Justice* (Harvard, 1971).

15. Gauthier, "Rational Cooperation" and other papers.

16. The "circumstances of justice" are the name Rawls gives to the conditions which are necessary for questions of justice even to arise. See *A Theory of Justice,* pp. 126. See also the works of Hume and Hart that Rawls refers to.

17. *Coming to Terms: the Words of the Debate,* volume two of the *Report of the Task Force on Canadian Unity,* p.14. See also Hart, *The Concept of Law,* pp.216-217. "For the word 'sovereign' means here no more than 'independent'...", p.217.

18. See *The Limits of Liberty* by James Buchanan, chapter 10 (Chicago, 1975).

19. See Robert Nozick, *Anarchy, State and Utopia* (Basic Books, 1974) and Murray Rothbard, *For a New Liberty* (Macmillan, 1973). See also Buchanan.

NATION, STATE AND CONSENT

Leslie A. MULHOLLAND

Modern democratic conceptions of the state suggest not only that particular legislatures should be responsible to their electorate, but also that the state itself morally depends for its right to rule on the consent of its people. However, there seem to be two dominant modern conceptions of the mode in which the state is morally based on the consent of the people who are subject to its rule: 1) the state is morally based on a *social contract* among the individuals composing the people; 2) the state is the form of organization for the purpose of furthering through laws the values of a multitude of persons who by virtue of their possessing a *pre-political unity* collectively consent to the state's rule. This may be regarded as the nationalist view. My aim in this discussion is to examine these two accounts and bring out their relevance to the question of the possibility of a consensus within Canada.

I assume the following formal definition of 'state': the *state* is that set of institutions which constitutionally have supreme responsibility for enacting and executing laws, as well as adjudicating conflicting claims concerning the application of laws, for a territory whose people are subject to a single constitution. To the extent that a constitution provides for distinct areas of jurisdiction within a territory, I regard the state as the totality of those institutions which have at any point supreme authority in the process of enacting and enforcing laws. A state's *sovereignty* lies in its possessing supreme authority for enacting the laws through which it governs its people. Sovereignty is *indivisible* inasmuch as there cannot be two (or more) institutions within a state which have supreme constitutional titles to enact conflicting laws for the same population. Where two legislative institutions can enact laws for a population, one must have constitutional supremacy in cases of conflict. The indivisibility of sovereignty, then, is a purely formal condition for a coherent legal system.

1. Typically, the social contractualist rejects the notion that there is any pre-political unity among the people which is morally relevant to

the authority which the state exercises. In its sophisticated forms, the contractualist doctrine does not suppose an actual historical contract. Rather, it requires that people subject to the state be regarded as having an equal moral status as persons apart from their membership in the state, and presents the state as morally obligated to act on the principle of accordance with a possible social contract among members of the population which it governs. This requires primarily that the state enact and enforce laws which protect the freedom and property of its citizens and secure their natural equality as persons. The state also makes possible collective cultural and economic policies. But these are a means to the securing of individual rights and the preservation of the state rather than an end of the political association. Provided that the state creates conditions under which individuals can resolve their conflicts in peace and pursue their private aims, it is regarded as receiving at least the tacit consent of the people.

In the contractualist account, then, individuals become a collective unity which constitutes them as a people or nation only through their organization by a state. Apart from the state, persons are considered only in their role as independent individuals, each privately responsible for the securing of the rights which he claims. The state alone can transform the multitude of persons into a collective unity by the fact that the organs of the state enable collective decisions on the laws governing freedom and property to be made.

Nationalist doctrines on the other hand tend to maintain that the state is morally based on the *collective* consent of a distinct community of persons who possess or think they possess certain common values which are relevant to political unity and which give them a sense of communal identity apart from their actual incorporation into a state. These are values which will lead persons to give their allegiance to the state, support one another in times of crisis and have the sense of participation in a common destiny. The most potent type of such values would be those based on blood — that is, the belief in a common ancestry and history which forms the basis of the experience and conventions of the community and leads the individual to feel a sense of identity with other members of the community which he does not feel with members of different communities. This in turn leads him to desire to preserve that community and forge a future in political association with its members.

In this conception, the pre-political unity of the people is regarded as natural and the community is likened to a natural person with his own special abilities and preferences. Attainment of political unity is like the coming to majority of the folk-person. Through this analogy, a nation is regarded as having a collective pre-political *right* to self-determination, i.e., to construct for itself an independent state for the sake of furthering its communal values.

2. Both these doctrines have their advantages in treating the question of consent. The contractualist position has a certain rationality which nationalism as a principle of consent lacks. Since nationalism regards membership in the state as based on *birth* in a given tradition, it places the moral ground of membership in an arbitrary characteristic of the individual — a characteristic which he cannot acquire through any action. In doing so, it tends to treat members of the national community as an elite with special privileges which others can never acquire. Accordingly, nationalism treats the state as in principle responsible only to secure the consent of the nationalist community, and neglects the feature of equal citizenship which is fundamental to the contractualist. However, should the nationalist deny that he means to promote elitism, his denial would be inconsistent with his claim to base the right of self-determination on a pre-political unity resulting from common ancestry. Non-national members of the community could not be part of the pre-political unity; hence, their consent would be irrelevant to the nationalist.

Furthermore, the contractualist position suggests a formal reason for denying that any specifiable multitude of persons has a collective pre-political right to self-determination. For if a population is not organized into a political unity, it has no structure through which it can make decisions collectively for the whole population. Such a structure is possible only if it includes an authority which can secure the adherence of the population to its decisions. But without a decision-making structure, it is impossible for a population to determine itself; hence, without such a structure, it cannot have a right to self-determination. Accordingly, it is not even possible for a nationalist group to have a collective right against some existing state or states to be allowed to form an independent state if it chooses. At best an existing state could have an obligation to establish a temporary procedure, e.g., a referendum, to assess the majority opinion of a nationalist group. But this would indicate only that members of a nationalist community have individually rights to form a collective political unity if a majority of them so choose.

Nevertheless, the contractualist doctrine tends to neglect features of nationalism which seem essential to the social and political life of individuals. In treating the contracting member only as an independent person with no politically relevant community ties apart from the social contract, the contractualist disregards the mode in which the cultural life and values of a person function to provide the person with an understanding of his social and political context and an awareness of his place in the national and international community. Indeed it might be suggested that such things as the nuances of a common language and traditions supply the individual with a kind of grammar through which he interprets his social and political ties.

It would, however, be going too far to suggest that persons cannot learn to communicate with members of different nationalities on matters of value and law. Members of all cultures, Asian, African, European etc. do this continually. What can never be shared are primarily the feelings of identity with a group which arise from a belief in common ancestry, from a common native language and from habitual contact and cooperation with other members. Nevertheless, these feelings can become restrictions on the social and political development of members of a national community unless they are balanced by a more reflective, rational understanding of human rights and justice.

But the contractualist, in regarding the state as based only on the consent of the independent person, neglects the element of *fraternity*, fundamental to nationalism, which is required for the cohesion of the members of a nation within the formal structure of state institutions. Fraternity seems to involve both the disposition to feel such things as loyalty to the community and the willingness, arising partly from this sentiment, to cooperate with other members of the community for the common good, even if doing so demands some sacrifice of the economic and cultural interests of groups within the nation. Fraternity then involves a subjective disposition which depends on the state actually pursuing a common good which includes the economic and cultural interests of all identifiable relevant interest groups. Should members of one national community acquire economic and/or political domination, members of another will tend to feel alienated from the political organization. As a result they will have less and less desire to cooperate for a conception of a common good which seems to exclude their interests.

The contractualist, then, by neglecting the nationalist feature of fraternity can overlook an important but informal factor relevant to the consent of the people. While contractualist theory supplies a general moral ground for political obligation and the duties of the state to the people, it does not give an account of why people would choose to belong to one state rather than another. This requires an account of how a particular state furthers the interests of its people through allowing and designing cooperative enterprises concerning especially economics, culture and welfare. Inasmuch as there is a pre-political content to culture, e.g., language and traditions, it seems that people would naturally choose to submit to a state only if it recognized their cultural interests.

Nationalist doctrine then gives an account of how membership in a national community provides persons with a natural basis for fraternity and thus for forming a political unity and consenting to a particular state. Nevertheless, common ancestry does not seem a necessary condition for the development of fraternity among the people governed by a state. There are states which seem to get along well even though their people lack this feature, e.g., the United Kingdom, Switzerland, and the United States. But also membership in a national community is not sufficient to produce fraternity. Economic and/or geographical factors can produce classes within a national community which have a sense of alienation from the political process inasmuch as it does not promote their interests. Interest groups, then, can overlap and criss-cross. Members of a national community might identify with workers of a distinct national community on some matters of class interest, but side with their own community on others.

3. There are, then, I suggest, two conditions which must be met in order for a state to have the consent of its people: 1) the state must secure the rights of the individual; 2) the state must further the common good of its people. The first condition may be regarded as a formal condition for the people to consent to any state at all. The second is a condition for consenting to the particular state in which a person is a citizen and is informal inasmuch as it is not possible to provide a criterion whereby it can be specified exactly when the interests of one national community, economic class, or geographical section of a country are furthered to the relative disadvantage of others. There are always borderline cases. Moreover, circumstances can produce periodicity in the furtherance of group interests, allowing one group to further its interests when the time is ripe in ways which will ultimately benefit the whole people. However, there can also be clear cases of violation of this condition, e.g., the treatment of the English working class in the nineteenth century or the treatment of the blacks in South Africa.

The first condition for consent has priority in cases where the rights of the individual are threatened by nationalist elitist interests. As such it establishes a negative restriction on state action. The second condition, however, requires that the state undertake positive action to further the common good. Often this requires delicate balancing of group interests. The aim of so doing, however, is to secure the consent of the people to remain in a cooperative relation to one another.

Now where the development of fraternity appears to be thwarted within a state as a result of the domination of members of one national community in an area which affects the economic and/or cultural interests of members of another, the willingness of the subordinate community to cooperate within the political unity cannot be assumed. As a result, inasmuch as the state's right over its people is based on consent, the state (i.e., the persons who exercise legislative authority) has a moral obligation to each individual member of the subordinate community to strive to correct the situation. This might be done through legislation and government policy. But should the situation be one which is perpetuated by the constitution, constitutional reform would be required.

If, however, the domination seems unresolvable, then the state has a moral obligation to determine whether members of the subordinate community would prefer to form a new political arrangement, such as the creation of a new state. Since the subordinate community has no political structure for making collective decisions, however, the state could determine whether a new state is wanted only by a referendum. Here, the conception of the indivisibility of sovereignty should not be seen as restricting the state from allowing a new state to emerge from its part. While a state cannot tolerate an institution within its jurisdiction which claims supreme authority in opposition to it, the state can coherently allow the formation of a new state from its part.

Inasmuch as a state cannot be expected to operate on the supposition that members of various interest groups might wish at any moment to form new states, there would have to be clear evidence of a continuing condition of unresolvable domination resulting in a breakdown of the desire to cooperate before the state would be justified in supposing that it lacked the consent of the members of a national community. Moreover, a state would violate its obligation to those of its members who are content with it (presumably the majority) if it were to destroy itself for the sake of a nationalist minority. Consequently, the state would be justified in postponing allowing a new state to be formed from it part until it is practically feasible to do so. This would not, however, entitle a state to postpone the formation of a new state for ever. But it would entitle a state to put it off if involved, say, in an economic crisis or a war. Moreover, a state has obligations to non-national minorities within a

nationalist community whose members propose to form a state. As a result, a state must have the right to secure to the extent possible that these minorities would not suffer in the new state. This would involve a right to negotiate the constitution of the new state.
4. Canada contains four distinct kinds of nationalist interest groups: native Indians and Eskimos; minorities of various national origins; persons of British origin and persons of French origin. Much concern should be given to the improvement of the condition of members of the first group on grounds of fraternity. Members of the second group come to Canada with an assumed awareness of the character of the nation. However, if they are not to become nationalist islands in the country, the pluralism of contractualism seems necessary for them to be at home in Canada and develop a sense of fraternity with other Canadians without sacrificing their traditions. Members of British origin along with those who have been assimilated into this group are the Canadians who are least threatened by cultural domination within Canada. However, their culture and economy are largely dominated from outside Canada especially by the United States. As a result, their nationalist aims require them to develop a national culture and economy whereby they can distinguish themselves from Americans in order to produce the sense of fraternity which furthers cooperation among members of Canada.

But the case of the francophone majority in Quebec poses a special problem. Not only is there in Quebec a large and distinct community emphasized by language, traditions, historical origin and territory, but also the political relation of Quebec to the rest of Canada arose from conquest rather than a natural course of settlement under the British flag. As a result of this conquest the political history of Quebec since 1763 has largely involved a struggle of the Québécois to preserve the French language and culture and overcome political and economic domination by anglophones. Accordingly, it is plausible for the francophone Québécois to maintain that political union with Canada has furthered his interests less than if he had been able to remain under the French flag and evolve toward independence through associations with a state which would further his language and culture.

There are then cultural, economic and political factors which suggest that members of the nationalist community of francophone Québécois cannot be assumed to consent to being governed by the Canadian state. There is then a case, based on the second condition for consent, for the Québécois to be allowed to choose whether to remain francophone Canadians. I suggest, moreover, that we cannot expect the Québécois to consent to be ruled by the Canadian state unless it secures French Canadian culture and language and, where necessary, provides means for the attainment of economic control by the francophone community. By virtue, then, of the special character of the nationalist community in Quebec and its relation to the rest of Canada, it would be justifiable on grounds of fraternity to create special legal and political provisions for the province of Quebec if its people choose to remain within Canada. Nevertheless, this would have to be done in a way which is compatible with the rational demand of pluralism which is also essential for the consent of the Canadian people.

THE NATIONAL RIGHT TO SELF-DETERMINATION*

D. GOLDSTICK

National self-determination comes into applied ethics as a question of *human rights* in the political sphere, in particular, a question of *collective* human rights.

In the present epoch, the primary collective human right in the political sphere is that of democracy, the people's right to self-rule. Its defence does not require maintaining that the people always know what is in their own best interests. It is sufficient that popular rule is likelier to further the people's interests, in the existing circumstances, than rule by any other feasible wielder of ultimate political authority. Moreover, at the collective just as at the individual level, self-rule is the practical meaning of *liberty*, people's right to which is a *right* to "make their own mistakes" — or, as the case may be, non-mistakes.

Just as every individual right involves a corresponding limitation upon the actions of other individuals, so every collective right similarly limits the actions both of individuals and of other collectivities. But the doctrinaire individualist counterposing of individual rights to collective rights bespeaks a callous disregard of the interests and concerns of these same individuals — provided, that is, that the consequentialist case for the recognition of those collective rights under current sociohistorical conditions can indeed be empirically made out.

The democratic right to collective political self-rule involves the right of appropriate collectivities to determine for themselves the character of their constitutional relations with one another, whether separated, "sovereignly associated", confederated, federated, or merged into a unitary state. How *could* anyone be a genuine democrat without acknowledging the right of such a collectivity to determine for itself its own form of government, including its governmental

* Portions of this paper appeared in W.R. Shea and J. King-Farlow, editors, *Contemporary Issues in Political Philosophy*. New York: Science History Publications, 1976. p.96ff. Editor.

relationships with other such collectivities? But to call this a right is not to call it an absolute right. As Lenin wrote in 1916, in the context of arguing *for* the recognition of such a right, against the views of other Marxist theorists, like Rosa Luxemburg, who were inclined to oppose it:

> The several demands of democracy, including self-determination, are not an absolute, but only a *small part* of the general-democratic (now: general-socialist) *world* movement. In individual concrete cases, the part may contradict the whole; if so, it must be rejected.[1]

A relatively non-controversial example of this may be found in the way Germany's right to national self-determination was quite properly set aside in May, 1945 in the higher interests of world peace, anti-fascism and the national rights of Germany's neighbours.

Some may find it strange to see Lenin speaking here of the world socialist movement as a continuation of the world democratic movement. In this, however, he just follows in the footsteps of Marx and Engels, who wrote in the *Communist Manifesto*:

> ...the first step in the revolution by the working class, is to raise the proletariat to the position of ruling class, to win the battle of democracy.[2]

If "democracy" means *rule by the people*, how can there be democracy in the economic sphere unless the people rule it; and how can the people rule it without owning it? And if economics is as sociologically basic as historical materialism claims, how can there be anything more than *formal* democracy in society at all without the social ownership of the materials and equipment used in production? That, at any rate, is how Marxists reason on the subject.

This is not the place to argue at length for the principle of *democracy*. Like other moral-political principles, it, too, is not eternal in the Marxist view, and only modern conditions have made it feasible. The existing productive technology and consequent social order in the European Middle Ages, for instance, clearly made a functioning democracy out of the question. But where it is practicable, government by the will of the governed seems obviously more likely to meet the governed people's needs than any alternative. In this connection, Marxists will readily endorse the words of Thomas Jefferson: "Sometimes it is said that man cannot be trusted with the government of himself. Can he, then, be trusted with the government of others?"[3]

To advocate a right of self-determination, though — or any other such right for that matter — it isn't necessary to be such an extreme deontologist as to insist on its inviolability regardless of consequences. Real application of the maxim "Fiat justitia, ruat coelum" in practice would be inhumanly callous. Indeed, the only rationale for *any* such right is of necessity along consequentialist lines. On the other hand, to affirm the right's justifiability only insofar as consequences warrant it does not necessitate denying it an independent moral authoritativeness capable of counter-balancing unfavourable consequences in all but extreme cases. For at the current stage of human history, the probable good consequences, on balance, of establishing it in positive morality as a principle to which conscience attaches weight independently of consequentialist considerations can in the long run amply justify such a political goal.

Perhaps the most persistent line of theoretical criticism of the right of nations to self-determination has centred on the problem of defining what a *nation* is. Since what is at issue here practically is the right of a part of a state to secede from its rule, there is no point in using the word "nation" in that sense which is relevant in the context of discussions on "international" law, for instance, where the word "nation" is simply another synonym for "state". We must use "nation", in this context, to stand for a sociological unit whose existence as a separate state would not be out of the question as a practical proposition if it were to choose such a separate existence and other nations did not interfere with its independence. We must use "nation" for a group of people whose political self-determination it would be reasonable to call it undemocratic to deny.

Doubtless the standard definition of the concept of a *nation* current in Marxist circles is still that of Stalin:

> A nation is a historically constituted, stable community of people, formed on the basis of a common language, territory, economic life, and psychological make-up manifested in a common culture.[4]

There are, indeed, points on which the definition apparently could benefit from some elaboration or amendment. For instance, a good case can be made for interpreting the "common culture" criterion for nationhood as including the requirement of a *national consciousness*, that is, some active sense on the part of a population that they jointly constitute a nation. Such a stipulation might seem unnecessary, since only populations which do possess such a sense of nationhood are going to demand the right of self-determination in any event, but the proviso will be of actual use in some cases in delimiting the boundaries between nations — that is, it is not always going to be clearcut what nation a population belongs to; and what nation it *thinks* it belongs to may sometimes be the deciding factor. It may seem that such a proviso must needs make the definition objectionably circular — and, certainly, someone who did not know what the word "nation" meant would hardly be enlightened sufficiently by being told it meant a group of people who, among other things, considered themselves to be a nation. We can avoid this difficulty here, however, by understanding "national consciousness" as a population's sense of possessing jointly a *right* to exist together as a separate country should they so choose.

A noteworthy feature of Stalin's definition is that in addition to ethnographic factors it expressly mentions two further criteria of nationhood: the necessity of a common territory and economic life. As far as territory is concerned, the point of including *it* is obvious. A population, such as Europe's gypsies, however cohesive otherwise, plainly cannot even be considered a candidate for existence as a separate country if it does not possess a common territory. It could not demand the right of self-determination in the name of democracy unless there were a territory which it occupied and in which it constituted the majority of the population. The same would clearly apply to the Jewish people living outside of Israel if they were more ethnographically homogeneous than they are. The requirement of a common economic life, however, is more debatable. Are North and South Korea two different nations just because (thanks to the U.S. military occupation of the South) the economic life of one of them is capitalist while the economic life of the other is socialist? Certainly no Korean, of whatever political stripe, will consent to the denial that Korea is a single nation. The requirement of a common economic life for any *nation* entitled to political self-determination as a unit should perhaps be amended to require only potential *economic viability* as a separate state. Even formulated like this, the economic requirement is probably still strong enough to exclude from nationhood the Inuit people of Northern Canada *at this time* although they do seem to qualify as a nation on most of the other counts. To protest against the injustice of their treatment by the Canadian government it is not necessary to demand formal recognition for them of a right of secession.

The French-Canadian people of Quebec are another story entirely. Here is a sociologically clear-cut case of nationhood, if ever there was one. Another such example is the population of Puerto Rico. It seems clear also, on the whole, that the Israelis now constitute a nation in the sense defined, as do the Arab Palestinians who live in the territory conquered by Israel in its 1967 attack.

But is Northern Ireland a separate nation? Southerners and Northern Catholics argue it is not, on the grounds that it has too much in common with the rest of Ireland, including an actual Catholic majority in much of the Six Counties which make up the Province of Northern Ireland. On that basis, it is not Northern Ireland which would have the right of self-determination as regards unity or otherwise with the Irish Republic, but rather the population of Ireland as a whole. By thc same token, the secessionist Confederacy in the southern United States in 1860 (even if we disregard the lack of support for it of the Black population which constituted a majority in large parts of its territory) was likewise no separate nation entitled to secession at will.

It is important to note here that to endorse the secession of any *part* of a nation that chooses to separate, however democratic such a principle can be made to appear, is actually undemocratic because it would in practice enable the interests of the majority of a nation to be adversely affected, perhaps gravely, by the actions of a minority, even if they do happen to be collected together territorially. If the territory in question should happen to be rich in oil or some other natural resource, it is very easy to imagine some imperialist power colluding with a local élite to break the territory away and deprive the majority of any democratic say over the development of that natural resource. That is more or less what Britain did with Kuwait before oil was discovered there, when port facilities were the issue at stake. That is what the U.S.A. did with Panama, which was part of Colombia until the Colombian government showed itself to be insufficiently co-operative with U.S. plans to dig a canal through its territory.

It seems plain that to allot a right of self-determination to any region or locality whatever, regardless of all ethnographic considerations, would turn out to be destructive of the real exercise of self-determination in practice and is thus a highly undemocratic idea in its actual tendency. For its actual tendency is evidently to subvert the democratic right of self-determination altogether. Indeed, one published objection to the principle of national self-determination is precisely that the nation is an *arbitrary* unit to exercise such a right, and, since *no* unit could be credited with such a right without denying it to other units, therefore no population whatsoever should be rcgarded as possessing any right of self-determination. This argument, however, proves too much. It shows precisely that the nation is *not* an arbitrary choice of unit to credit with a right of self-determination; for it shows that, unless some sociological unit such as that defined by

Stalin can be taken as entitled to determine its own political destiny, there can be no meaningful general claim of a right to self-determination at all; and yet, without self-determination at some level or other, there can be no real democracy. If we *start* from a position of commitment to a right of self-determination in the name of democracy, then *the nation*, as sociologically understood, will have to be the only reasonable candidate in sight to credit with such a right. It is not possible to reconcile any alternative position with the requirements of democracy.

Since the criteria of nationhood that are mentioned in the stated definition do all admit of variations in degree, it is not at all surprising that there should be plenty of bona fide *intermediate cases* in the real world of the present day. Is Scotland still a nation? Probably it is. Is Newfoundland still a nation? Possibly not. What about the Turkish Cypriots? Constituting less than one-fifth of the population of Cyprus, they were scattered about the island with no common territory until the 1974 invasion of the Turkish Army and the deliberate forcible resettlement of large numbers of Greek Cypriots. A persuasive case could no doubt be made for the nationhood of the Black population in those areas of the U.S. South where they constitute a majority, but for the demographic fact that the great majority of U.S. Blacks live outside of those areas, and but for the fact, as it appears, that the great majority even of those Blacks who do live in those areas actually consider themselves as belonging, together with their white compatriots, to a single people, of U.S. nationality. That in itself would arguably militate against their possessing a sufficiently separate "common culture" for distinct nationhood.

How does the principle of national self-determination apply to sub-Saharan Africa? Not very well in those areas where a tribal economy of hunting and gathering or self-sufficient peasant farming still prevails sufficiently to fragment the population and prevent the emergence, as yet, of fully-fledged cohesive *nations* in the sociological sense which we have been discussing. Does that mean that such populations should be ruled by others, by whites for example? Of course not. As this paper has argued, the role played by the self-determination principle is subordinate to the democratic principle. Where the subordinate principle breaks down, the more basic principle may still be directly applicable. It is still possible to differentiate among African regimes as more or as less democratic, as more or else less based on the will of the people, even in those areas where sociological conditions at present rule out full recourse to the principle of national self-determination. Only a superstitious reverence towards man-made principles will insist upon treating them as universal absolutes.

NOTES

1. V.I. Lenin, *Collected Works*, Volume 22 (Moscow, 1964), page 341.
2. Marx Engels, *Collected Works*, Volume 6 (New York, 1976), page 504.
3. First Inaugural Address as President of the United States, March 4, 1801; quoted in *Thomas Jefferson On Democracy*, edited by Saul K. Padover (New York, 1946), page 24.
4. J.V. Stalin, *Works*, Volume 2 (Moscow, 1953), page 307. How original with him his writings on the national question really were we need not inquire here.

LE CHOIX IDEOLOGIQUE DU QUEBEC

Guy LAFRANCE

Il importe de préciser au point de départ que le débat actuel sur l'avenir de la confédération canadienne est un débat de nature purement politique et qu'il porte sur la réalité politique "canadienne" en tout premier lieu. Cette réalité politique "canadienne" ne correspond pas à la réalité sociale et culturelle du Canada, laquelle réalité mise en rapport avec le débat politique actuel est reléguée au second rang. Tout au plus cette réalité sociale et culturelle intervient-elle dans le débat politique comme élément accessoire, parmi plusieurs autres, qui constituent la toile de fond de deux idéologies politiques assez nettement caractérisées et qui se font la lutte.

Dans ce débat politique où se trouvent véhiculés des concepts comme ceux de peuple, nation, pays, état, pouvoir politique, souveraineté, unité, etc..., mais avec des contenus et des significations fort différents, il me semble utile d'effectuer un travail de repérage idéologique sur le contenu et la signification des concepts utilisés.

Tout en reconnaissant la difficulté qu'il y a à bien percevoir et à interpréter le contenu idéologique de chacun des concepts utilisés par rapport à l'option idéologique première, je soumets néanmoins à la discussion la grille suivante d'interprétation des concepts utilisés par chacune des deux idéologies en présence.

Je commencerai par l'idéologie "fédéraliste", celle que j'appellerai volontiers l'idéologie du *pouvoir unificateur* fondée sur l'idée d'un pouvoir politique central et fort, voué à l'idéal de la *croissance économique,* qui suppose une certaine stabilité des prix, des profits, des salaires, de l'emploi, etc... Il s'agit en conséquence d'une idéologie de *l'unité*; elle présente l'unité sous des formes légèrement variées, mais toujours cette idée d'unité est maintenue et affirmée (rappelons-nous les expressions utilisées pour affirmer cette idée: "un pays", "une nation", "one Canada"; ou l'expression de compromis "deux peuples fondateurs, mais une nation et un Canada uni"). Paradoxallement, cette idéologie utilise tantôt le concept d'un pays unifié déjà existant et tantôt l'idée d'un pays à construire.

Il convient en passant de mentionner que l'idéologie fédéraliste a paru tenté pendant un certain temps dans la pensée de ses acteurs, par le concept de la société juste. Mais cette idée a été rapidement écartée lorsqu'à la suite de pressions de groupes d'intérêts, on y a vu une menace à l'option fondamentale de la croissance économique.

Cette idéologie de l'unité cherche logiquement à préserver par tous les moyens l'unité du pouvoir, concept très semblable à la conception Hobbienne de l'état et du pouvoir. Car cette idéologie de l'unité suppose que le pouvoir a été donné une fois pour toute; qu'il ne peut être négocié ou renégocié à aucune condition. Comme dans la logique du *Léviathan*, il n'y a de la part de ceux qui ont créé ce pouvoir, aucune possibilité de retirer leur adhésion, de reprendre leur droit premier, en se retirant du contrart pour retrouver leur condition première.

Cette idéologie fait aussi appel au concept de progrès, en ce sens qu'une plus grande unité conduit à un plus haut degré de compétitivité avec les grandes nations et contribue ainsi à faire du Canada un grand pays, une grande nation, dans le domaine économique surtout.

C'est pourquoi l'unité doit prévaloir si on veut atteindre l'objectif principal qui est la croissance économique. Voilà pourquoi le concept d'unité (unité nationale) apparaît comme un concept accessoire à la croissance économique. Bien sûr, pour bon nombre de personnes la relation entre ces deux concepts n'est pas évidente. Peut-être faut-il interpréter ainsi les résultats d'un récent sondage révélant que pour un grand nombre de Canadiens le concept d'unité nationale n'avait pas d'importance, que c'est même pour eux une question agaçante, tellement leur intérêt primordial va nettement du côté de leur situation économique, sans plus.

Il n'en reste pas moins que le concept d'unité est un élément essentiel de l'idéologie fédéraliste, du moins pour ceux qui la défendent, ceux qu'on appelle généralement les acteurs de l'idéologie. Sans doute convient-il de préciser que l'unité en question a une nature bien spécifique. Ce n'est certes pas l'unité spontanément exprimée par un vouloir vivre collectif, ce que Rousseau appelle "l'acte par lequel un peuple est un peuple"; il s'agit plutôt d'un concept politique d'unité animé par l'idée d'un pouvoir central fort en vue de faire tenir ensemble des intérêts différents, des tendances et des mentalités différentes.

La seconde idéologie, que j'appellerai l'idéologie de la souveraineté politique et représentée en l'occurrence par le mouvement nationaliste au Québec, est fondamentalement mue par les idées de fierté collective et de dignité collective qui sont présentées comme des attitudes normales de vie chez les nations adultes. Il s'ensuit que cette idéologie accorde une place importante au concept de *nation* qui, sans être clairement défini, semble correspondre à la définition suivante. La nation québécoise, ou le peuple québécois, est composé d'une forte majorité de gens qui parlent la même langue, qui partagent la même culture, la même histoire, les mêmes aspirations, les mêmes affinités psychologiques, et qui vivent sur un territoire clairement défini. En même temps, cette nation est présentée et perçue comme ayant déjà son propre pays. Ce *pays* n'est pas à bâtir; il est déjà là. En ce sens, cette idéologie se rattache à des faits et non à un projet.

En outre, l'idéologie de la souveraineté politique ne se préoccupe pas de la question de l'unité (de l'unité interne) parce qu'elle prend pour acquis que cette unité existe déjà en fait, et qu'elle se manifeste dans l'identification de la nation avec le pays. Plus encore, l'identification de la nation avec le pays est glorifiée. A titre d'exemple, c'est cette identification que les poètes et les artistes chantent et exhaltent. Rappelons-nous simplement, parmi plusieurs autres, les deux expressions significatives de Vigneault: "mon pays" et "gens du pays".

Comme première conséquence de ces postulats, cette idéologie revendique le droit pour la nation québécoise à la souveraineté politique, droit qui est identifié au droit généralement reconnu aux peuples et aux nations à l'autonomie ou à la souveraineté politique. Ce concept de souveraineté est présenté comme le droit et le devoir pour la nation ou le peuple de s'autodéterminer. La nation est aussi véritablement considérée comme ayant le pouvoir de décider; et le gouvernement ou l'Assemblé Nationale est perçue comme l'instrument de ce pouvoir décisionnel. Alors que dans l'actuel système politique fédéral du Canada la souveraineté repose entre les mains du parlement (en fait et non seulement en principe). Dès lors, l'idéologie de la souveraineté politique, propose un changement profond en ce qui regarde le concept de *pouvoir*. En proposant ce changement, elle propose un nouvel ordre politique.

En ce sens, elle est une idéologie d'agression qui combat l'idéologie dominante qui est présentée comme l'idéologie de l'aliénation. L'aliénation est dénoncée à plusieurs niveaux: au niveau culturel, au niveau linguistique, au niveau économique, aux niveaux politiques et sociologiques en termes de groupes proportionnels et de représentation politique désavantageux, au niveau psychologique (prenons comme exemple les expressions d'émancipation collective et nationale, l'invitation à surmonter les vieux sentiments de peur, de dépendance et d'infériorité, tous ces sentiments qui sont le partage des peuples colonisés).

Pour toutes ces raisons, l'idéologie de la souveraineté voit la nation placée devant les alternatives suivantes: ou bien continuer à jouer le rôle d'un groupe minoritaire engagé sur une voie qui mène à la disparition à plus ou moins longue échéance; ou bien devenir un groupe majoritaire, une nation indépendante et s'assurer ainsi de la survie et du développement.

Enfin, l'idéologie de la souveraineté tout comme l'idéologie du pouvoir unificateur, présente une conception particulière du pouvoir. Cette conception est de type républicain, en ce sens que pour l'idéologie de la souveraineté le peuple est considéré comme le détenteur du pouvoir (à titre d'exemples mentionnons les consultations populaires sur les bills et les mesures législatives importantes, l'ouverture des caisses électorales, le procédé référendaire comme tel, qui est à toute fin pratique inconnu de notre système politique actuel). Cette conception du pouvoir politique que l'idéologie de la souveraineté qualifie paradoxalement de démocratique, est toute proche de la conception Rousseauiste de l'état et du pouvoir tels qu'ils sont présentés dans *Le Contrat Social.* En poursuivant cette comparaison, je dirais que l'idéologie de la souveraineté politique oppose en quelque sorte Rousseau à Hobbes. Il semble même que cette opposition corresponde à la différence des cultures, des mentalités en présence.

Mentionnons enfin comme dernière caractéristique de l'idéologie de la souveraineté, son *aspect conciliateur.* Bien que l'unité interne ne soit pas considérée comme un problème, cette idéologie propose un nouveau type d'unité externe ou artificielle fondée sur des accords de réciprocité, des échanges principalement dans le domaine économique. Ce dernier type d'unité est appelé: *association économique.* Les deux idéologies utilisent donc le concept d'unité. Mais le contenu de ce concept est fort différent dans chacun des cas. L'une propose une unité du pouvoir politique ayant l'autorité pour contrôler, réglementer et promouvoir les échanges économiques; l'autre propose une union économique fondée sur des intérêts communs et des accords réciproques, mais en l'absence d'une autorité politique suprême.

C'est la perception de ces deux idéologies que je soumets à la discussion.

LES PARADIGMES IDEOLOGIQUES DES POSITIONS NATIONALISTES ET FEDERALISTES

Jean-Guy MEUNIER

C'est une attitude acceptée que de questionner de manière épistémologique une démarche scientifique pour en déceler le programme général de recherche et tenter d'y apporter les éléments critiques pertinents contribuant ainsi à l'avancement du questionnement. L'épistémologie, dans la mesure où elle considère la démarche scientifique comme un objet propre de réflexion, permet une attitude de distance vis-à-vis un discours qui, à cause du pouvoir institutionnel des savants, est reconnu comme vrai. L'identification, par exemple des paradigmes, c'est-à-dire les éléments structurant une science aide à mieux cerner l'étendue et la limite des thèses avancées dans une discipline donnée. Ainsi, par exemple, est-il plus facile de saisir le lieu de divergence de la psychologie behaviorale par rapport à la psychologie cognitive si l'on met en évidence la différence paradigmatique du cadre expérimentaliste statistique d'un versus le cadre formaliste/structural de l'autre.

La saisie de ces paradigmes permet de percevoir les lieux des différences des démarches scientifiques et surtout de montrer qu'elles sont, soit des traductions l'une de l'autre c'est-à-dire une même interrogation, mais dans un langage différent ou soit des théories incommensurables ou incompatibles n'ayant aucun lien en commun et donc ne permettant pas une traduction mutuelle. Dans le premier cas, le dialogue est rendu possible par la création d'un dictionnaire qui à la longue peut devenir commun dans l'autre cas, le dialogue est impossible à moins de remettre en question l'ensemble du programme de recherche. Ce qui n'est pas toujours prêt à être accepté par l'un ou l'autre partenaires de l'aventure scientifique.

Si l'on passe du domaine scientifique au domaine politique, il n'est pas de bon aloi ou du moins ce n'est pas dans la tradition que de questionner de manière épistémologique les avancés de nos politiciens. Cela fait trop académique.

Pourtant, si l'on y pense bien, les politiciens nous offrent des théories sur la réalité sociale. La matière de la théorie n'est certes pas physique ou psychologique mais organisationnelle, civile et économique. Leur discours n'est pas uniquement descriptif comme celui du sociologue mais prescriptif: "Etant donné telle situation de fait, nous disent-ils, voici ce que nous devrions faire collectivement".

Aussi nous a-t-il semblé important ici de tenter de sortir du débat politique lui-même, c'est-à-dire de discuter le point de vue de l'autre à partir de son propre terrain et d'attaquer le problème pour ce qu'il est, c'est-à-dire une théorie descriptive et prescriptive de la réalité sociale. De manière plus concrète, je considèrerai les deux interlocuteurs du débat sur la question canadienne comme présentant deux théories philosophiques sur la société. J'illustrerai, au passage ces positions par des exemples tirées des divers discours politiques et des programmes de parti et surtout de deux textes récents à savoir le livre blanc sur la culture produit par le gouvernement québécois et le rapport produit par la commission canadienne sur l'unité nationale et intitulé *se retrouver* et signé par MM. Pepin et Robarts. L'hypothèse d'analyse que je voudrais avancer dans les présentes réflexions est la suivante:

La question de l'unité canadienne et de la culture est présentée à travers des discours non pas contradictoires, mais incompatibles. C'est-à-dire qu'elle s'insère dans des vocabulaires spécifiques, intraduisibles, des raisonnements divergeants fondés sur des axiomes indépendants et différents et une sémantique incompatible en raison de l'incommensurabilité des définitions des univers de références. Bref, je tenterai de montrer que les paradigmes des discours fédéralistes et nationalistes ne permettent pas les mêmes programmes de recherches et par conséquent deviennent incompréhensibles aux interlocuteurs.

L'objectif que je poursuis en prenant cette distance n'est pas celle de l'aseptie politique, mais bien le désir de comprendre l'ordre des questions qui sont en jeu afin de mieux y participer. Il me semble que l'une des difficultés majeures de notre débat politique actuel est liée au fait que la présentation de la question elle-même traduit l'incompatibilité des questions et des solutions qui s'affrontent. Dès le point de départ, la question de la constitution ou de l'unité nationale, bien que légitime pour l'ensemble des canadiens, apparaît irrécevable aux québécois alors que la question culturelle et linguistique ne peut être posée comme prioritaire pour les tenants du fédéralisme. Il est évident, tant pour le Canada et le Québec, qu'il existe une crise au sein du pays. Cependant, une fois cette proposition avancée le désaccord apparaît sur la compréhension de cette crise et évidemment sur la solution proposée. Je tenterai d'analyser ici les divers niveaux d'incompatibilité de la compréhension de cette crise et de sa solution. Je distinguerai pour ce faire trois niveaux à savoir: celui de la description de la situation, celui de son explication et enfin celui de la justification. De cette manière, je tenterai de montrer la divergence radicale des idéologies qui s'affrontent.

2-*La spécificité des vocabulaires*

Au premier niveau, celui que j'appelle ici descriptif, se retrouve l'ensemble des concepts que les discours en jeu utilisent pour référer à la réalité dont ils parlent. Chaque discours présente un vocabulaire spécifique qui, par les définitions sémantiques, a pour fonction ultime de dénoter la réalité et donc ultimement de la décrire. Ce vocabulaire sert donc à déterminer le point d'ancrage du discours sur la réalité.

Or, si on lit bien les discours fédéralistes et nationalistes, on constatera déjà à ce niveau la divergence radicale des vocabulaires en jeu. Par exemple, l'un et l'autre n'identifient pas les mêmes points d'ancrage de la crise canadienne. Pour MM. Pépin et Robarts, la tension du pays tire son origine des "institutions publiques et politiques": "Les grands responsables de cette crise se trouvent dans les divers *'niveaux gouvernementaux'* et leurs *'institutions périphériques'.* Si l'économique et le culturel s'y inscrivent, ce n,est que par un défaut au niveau de l'organisation des divers paliers du système politique général."

Par contre, pour le *Livre Blanc* québécois, le problème vient de la différence radicale entre les "cultures"; concept qui tantôt reçoit une définition philosophique tel qu'un "milieu de vie", "une façon de concevoir pour les hommes leur existence de l'interpréter et de lui donner un avenir", et tantôt une définition sociologique telle que "des ensembles plus ou moins vastes de façons de parler, de penser, de vivre et en corrolaire à des langages et à des institutions".

Or, étant donné cette différence des cultures fondée ici sur la différence de la langue, il s'ensuit une différence des modes sociaux de réalisation et d'expression, donc des moyens financiers et politiques adéquats. Mais, les contrôles de ceux-ci sont entre d'autres mains, il faut donc les reprendre et être autonome.

La différence de vocabulaire entre les deux positions se retrouve dans plusieurs autres thèmes. Ainsi, par exemple, d'un côté le débat doit porter sur *l'unité* nationale et de l'autre, et sur *l'indépendance.* Ce point est intéressant à souligner, car il manifeste que la différence n'est pas celle d'une contradiction, mais bien d'une incompatibilité. Les nationalistes n'ont pas choisi de discuter du contraire de l'unité nationale, i.e. la désunion, mais bien de l'indépendance. Pour eux, il est pensable d'être indépendant et solidaire, souverain et associé. Parler de désunion et même de séparation serait poser le problème dans le langage de l'adversaire.

Il ne faut pas chercher longtemps pour trouver à quel discours appartient les concepts suivants: les *droits* de la majorité, et de la minorité, le *droit* à l'autodétermination, la *nation*, le *peuple*, la *volonté collective, l'ordre légal,* la *situation actuelle,* notre *avenir collectif,* etc.

Ainsi, à ce premier niveau, les démarches d'analyse s'éloignent. Il ne s'agit pas ici d'une différence lexicale, c'est-à-dire d'un simple désaccord sur la signification des termes. Bien au contraire, le désaccord se marque dans le choix même des concepts descriptifs, i.e. ce qui est mis en cause n'est pas identique. Sur le plan épistémologique il n'y a pas possibilité de traduire les termes d'une approche dans l'autre; les termes n'appartenant pas à une même manière de circonscrire la réalité. Il est curieux d'ailleurs de voir comment s'effectuent certaines incorporations mutuelles de concepts. Ce que les uns appellent la "culture", les autres l'appellent la "mentalité" ou ce qui est "l'institution" pour les uns devient les "décisions politiques" pour les autres.

Or, on serait tenté de dire qu'il n'y a là qu'une différence de termes; qu'une bonne définition préalable comme l'espérerait une démarche empirique résoudrait tout.

Sur un plan plus formel, la différence du vocabulaire révèle une différence sémantique au sens référentiel de cette expression. Les expressions sont différentes parce qu'elles dénotent une autre manière de désigner la réalité sociale. Même si l'on retrouve des expressions similaires tels les mots "état", "nation", "gouvernement", etc; celles-ci ne semblent pas référer aux mêmes réalités sociales. Leur mode de désignation ou leur sens est différent.

3- *Une différence des raisonnements*

Une divergence des choix d'un vocabulaire et des objets d'analyse ne constitue pas toujours une incompatibilité, si elle n'est que le reflet de préférences subjectives des analystes. Tout comme dans d'autres domaines on peut expliquer les divers choix de loisirs, de partenaires de vie par une préférence subjective. Il en est cependant tout autrement dans le cas qui nous intéresse. La divergence des points d'ancrage descriptifs repose non sur une préférence individuelle, mais sur une option méthodologique et une structure logique radicalement différente. En effet le choix des thèmes d'institutions, de rapports économiques, de droits, etc, versus une analyse culturelle nationale et linguistique n'est que la manifestation discursive d'une méthodologie d'analyse spécifique. Un concept comme celui d'institution ou de culture ne désigne une réalité concrète qu'à l'intérieur d'un discours qui en définit les critères de référence et d'usage; isolé, sans contexte, il perd toute signification. Ces concepts servent en l'occurrence de lieu privilégié de démonstration ou d'illustration pour une argumentation théorique sous-jacente et pas toujours consciente pour l'analyste ou le lecteur. Bref, comme je tenterai de le montrer brièvement la divergence descriptive repose sur une divergence encore plus importante, celle d'une divergence explicatrice c'est-à-dire d'une démarche du raisonnement déductif qui relie entre elles les propositions ou les thèses pour constituer à proprement parler la théorie politique que l'on soutient.

Si on lit attentivement les nombreux textes du fédéral ou rapports techniques soutenant la thèse de l'unité canadienne, on constatera la dominance d'une analyse fonctionnelle, c'est-à-dire d'une analyse explicatrice qui tente de circonscrire les problèmes en termes de rapports ou de relations de dépendance entre des parties constitutives d'un tout. Un pays, par exemple, est un organisme fonctionnel qui lie des *secteurs,* des *provinces* etc. Toute crise apparaît comme une disfonctionnalité à l'intérieur d'un *système.* Comme dit le rapport Pepin-Robarts:

> Il ne faut pas chercher l'origine du conflit actuel, ailleurs que dans la concurrence entre gouvernements central et provinciaux, pour la conduite des affaires que doit assumer un état moderne. (p.14)

Chaque partie à son tour est définie par une fonction (gestion, finance, contrôle etc.), qui souvent parce qu'elle présente une spécificité i.e. peut-être identifiée par des relations particulières, peut entrer en conflit avec un autre partie du système qui, elle, présente aussi ses caractéristiques propres. Ainsi y a-t-il possibilité de conflits entre les divers niveaux institutionnels, entre les technocrates et entre les citoyens.

Au niveau dynamique, ce modèle fonctionnel permet de comprendre les méchanismes de transformation comme une modification des fonctions ou des rapports à l'intérieur du tout. Ils affectent tant les relations entre les parties que la constitution même des parties. Ainsi dira-t-on que les changements technologiques et économiques modernes ont "encouragé la centralisation de la puissance bureaucratique et économique, l'homogénéisation de la vie sociale, l'intégration économique,"etc. Centralisation, homogénéisation, intégration sont évidemment des termes techniques qui qualifient une relation, relation qui à son tour a été souvent déterminée par une approche statistique de type corrélation, regression, factorisation, etc. Le rapport Pepin-Robarts utilise très bien d'ailleurs cette grille d'analyse:

"le noeud de la crise actuelle doit être cherché dans les conflits entrecroisés créés dans la société canadienne par deux types de clivage et par des institutions politiques qui les véhiculent ou leur servent de médiatrice". Clivage qu'il voit dans la dualité linguistique et le régionalisme. Ce sont là, pour lui, des *lignes de forces.*

La crise canadienne apparaît comme une *tension,* un *désiquilibre* à l'intérieur de ce tout. Elle brise la stabilité et l'efficacité des relations. Bref, elle brise un "tout harmonieux" et ainsi de suite.

Ainsi, ce n'est pas par hasard qu'on a porté le choix descriptif sur l'analyse institutionnel des rapports économiques. De tels concepts correspondent parfaitement à une analyse fonctionnaliste. Bien défini à l'intérieur d'une théorie sociologique ou économique, ils semblent assurer d'une définition correcte et donc d'une parfaite adéquation à la réalité. Qui, en effet, osera contester de tels concepts. Comment nier l'existence d'institutions politiques, de crise Québec-Canada? N'est-ce pas là, la preuve de la validité d'un tel discours?

Je ne voudrais pas ici répondre à ces questions qui nous entraîneraient loin dans le domaine de l'analyse des conditions de validité d'une démarche scientifique. Je me contenterai simplement de montrer que cette approche en est une parmi d'autres et qu'elle est relative.

En effet, analyser la réalité canadienne en termes de fonctions d'interdépendances institutionnelles, économiques et sociales est un choix parmi d'autres. Sa validité repose sur une tradition méthodologique bien établie et acceptée par l'institution scientifique. Elle est partagée par une population. Elle est limpide pour une majorité de personnes. Mais malgré cela, elle demeure un choix d'explication parmi d'autres. Pour démontrer cela, je me contenterai de présenter ici le choix effectué par d'autres, à savoir les tenants du nationalisme.

En effet on peut facilement percevoir à la lecture du programme politique du P.Q. et du Livre Blanc sur la Culture un schème d'explication radicalement différent. Ici le raisonnement qui lie les diverses propositions descriptives n'est plus fonctionnaliste mais interprétatif ou herméneutique. Je m'explique: Dans ces discours, le mode sous lequel est pensé la réalité sociale n'est pas celle d'une *organisation* mais plutôt de *l'organisme* et plus profondément de l'organisme humain personnel. La société est pensée comme une collectivité et la collectivité pensée sous le mode de la personne où la culture apparaît comme la conscience pratique de cette collectivité. Ainsi le corps social est pensé comme une personne collective. Et tout ce qu'on peut reconnaître comme propriété à un individu sera reconnue aussi comme propriété de cette collectivité.

une position épistémologique sur les conditions de vérité des thèses qu'une position morale sur le sens de ces thèses. En effet, la thèse fédéraliste est celle qui se présente comme la plus flexible, la plus adéquate, la plus expérimentée et donc la plus vraie par rapport à la complexité de la situation, mais où l'adéquation est mesurée en termes d'emprise sur la situation. En d'autres termes, c'est elle qui s'offre comme ayant le plus de chances de succès, parce que d'une part elle a été expérimentée et parce que d'autre part elle est un compromis institutionnel pratique i.e. "faisable".

Une telle philosophie répond à une tradition d'analyse et de comportement social bien déterminé et qui n'est pas partagé dans les circonstances uniquement par la tradition anglophone. En effet, de nombreux francophones marqués par ce courant de pensée partageront beaucoup plus facilement cette philosophie de l'existence et de la connaissance que celle du nationalisme. Le pragmatisme sous-jacent à la position fédéraliste est quoiqu'on en dise une position dominante dans le lieu historique américain de notre débat. Mais cela ne garantit pas davantage sa vérité, malgré qu'il ait ses paradigmes et sa cohérence propre. Sa force de conviction ne lui vient ultimement que de son acceptation générale par la tradition intellectuelle dominante en Amérique. Pour sa part, la position nationaliste est, malgré l'aversion qu'on peut avoir pour cette expression, une position morale, c'est-à-dire un ensemble de propositions qui visent à instaurer un nouvel ordre de choses eu égard à une situation non acceptable. En ce sens, elle n'est pas pragmatique au sens technique de ce terme. Sa visée relève d'un idéal poursuivi et non d'une situation concrète à laquelle on doit s'adapter. Elle véhicule plus un discours de "valeurs", qu'un discours de "faits".

Cette visée est, par ailleurs, déterminée à l'intérieur d'une philosophie de ce que j'ai tenté d'appeler un humanisme culturel, c'est-à-dire une philosophie qui considère la société comme une personne morale ayant des modes d'expression culturelle qu'elle veut et désire marquer par des droits et des institutions.

En ce sens, l'option nationaliste est une transposition au niveau social par le biais de la culture de l'humanisme classique qui a marqué depuis trois siècle la tradition européenne. Encore là, cette conception est relative. Sa force de conviction ne lui vient, comme dans l'autre cas, que par le partage qu'une collectivité a eu pendant plusieurs siècles avec une tradition intellectuelle différente. Ainsi les paradigmes idéologiques des positions fédéralistes et nationalistes se marquent-ils en termes philosophiques de pragmatisme et d'humanisme culturel. Malgré l'allure de généralité que peut prendre un tel type de caractérisation, il permet, je crois, de mettre en évidence un des lieux dominant de l'incompatibilité des positions politiques en jeu.

En effet, la divergence radicale qui surgit ne vient pas du fait que les deux partenaires ne s'entendent pas i.e. qu'on ne réussit pas à traduire les problèmes de l'un dans le langage de l'autre. Au contraire, il est pensable qu'un tel travail se fasse, mais cela ne changerait guère le débat. Car le véritable foyer de la divergence réside dans l'attitude, dirais-je, psychologique ou épistémologique qu'impliquent ces positions.

L'un voit un problème et veut y trouver non une solution idéale mais pratique i.e. "harmonieuse" fondé sur le compromis et le fair play. L'autre n'accepte pas de voir le problème ainsi posé et l'inscrit à l'intérieur d'un désir d'une situation meilleure calquée sur une philosophie de l'homme libre.

Certes, il n'y a pas contradiction, jamais les fédéralistes nieront la liberté et les nationalistes les solutions pratiques. Mais l'un et l'autre les placeront à l'intérieur de leurs options. Il faut, diront les uns, un système qui permet la libre expression. Les autres affirmeront que la solution la plus pratique est celle de l'indépendance. Ainsi posée ces deux positions expliquent bien pourquoi il est simpliste de dire que le débat politique actuel en est un de simple différence linguistique. La thèse que j'ai avancée est qu'il y a deux options philosophiques différentes qui s'affrontent et que celles-ci sont partagées autant par des francophones que des anglophones.

En conclusion je dirais donc que tant et aussi longtemps que le débat politique actuel sera traduit dans les termes où il et posé présentement, l'incompatibilité demeurera. Mais le sera-t-il toujours ainsi posé? Sur le plan théorique, les deux positions sont indiscutablement stables. Elles présentent leur propre critère de validité et de cohérence. Elles chemineront ainsi isolées et fermées. Idéalement parlant, on doit penser qu'il doit en être ainsi pour une conscience critique et une richesse culturelle. Pourtant en pratique on peut se demander si une position recevant de plus en plus d'adhérents n'amènera pas la désuétude de l'autre. Ce point est important car il met en lumière le véritable problème que doit affronter la communauté québécoise à savoir, que ce qui la menace n'est pas avant tout d'ordre linguistique mais oserais-je dire philosophique ou ce qui est traduit de manière générale par culture et mentalité. C'est en gros sa "manière de penser la réalité" qui est menacée. Reste à savoir si la langue est le moyen privilégié de la protéger?

Pourtant analyser le problème ainsi c'est-à-dire en termes de deux conceptions qui s'affrontent, n'est-ce pas parler le langage même de cet humanisme culturel? Je crois que oui. Au lieu de deux volontés qui s'affrontent nous avons traduit le débat en termes de deux consciences ou rationalités. Mais parler ainsi c'est manifester sa propre différence. Peut-être la seule valeur qui s'y rattache est celle d'en être conscient si jamais une telle attitude peut-être valorisée!

UNE SCIENCE DE LA NATION, DE L'ETAT, DE LA SOUVERAINETE ET DE L'AUTODETERMINATION?

Vincent LEMIEUX

Au praticien de la science politique ces notions apparaissent suspectes. Elles sont plus utiles pour décrire l'univers des idéologies et des institutions que pour décrire l'univers des comportements. Dans les termes de Lévi-Strauss, elles appartiennent aux ordres conçus davantage qu'aux ordres vécus. Leur caractère mobilisateur et polémique les rend plus obscures que claires à ceux qui cherchent à les réduire à des concepts scientifiques.

Le constat de Durkheim, établi à la fin du siècle dernier, demeure actuel. Dans *Les Règles de la méthode sociologique,* publiées en 1895, il écrivait:

> Dans l'état actuel de nos connaissances, nous ne savons pas avec certitude ce que c'est que l'Etat, la souveraineté, la liberté politique, la démocratie, le socialisme, le communisme, etc., la méthode voudrait donc que l'on s'interdit tout usage de ces concepts, tant qu'ils ne sont pas scientifiquement constitués. Et cependant les mots qui les expriment reviennent sans cesse dans les discussions des sociologues. On les emploie couramment et avec assurance comme s'ils correspondaient à des choses bien connues et définies, alors qu'ils ne réveillent en nous que des notions confuses, mélanges indistincts d'impressions vagues, de préjugés et de passions. (pp. 22-23)

Depuis que ces lignes ont été écrites les anthropologues, sociologues et politologues ont essayé sans beaucoup de succès de donner une définition scientifique de la nation, de l'Etat, de la souveraineté, etc. Ainsi Mauss, neveu et disciple de Durkheim, dans un ouvrage inachevé sur la nation, distinguait celle-ci de formes politiques plus primitives et la définissait comme "une société matériellement et moralement intégrée, à pouvoir central stable, permanent, à frontières déterminées, à relative unité morale, mentale et culturelle des habitants qui adhèrent consciemment à l'Etat et à ses lois" (Marcel Mauss, *Oeuvres,* tome 3, Paris, Les Editions de Minuit, 1969, p.584).

Mauss n'est pas resté célèbre pour cette définition de la nation, qui n'a d'ailleurs pas été reprise après lui. Parmi les courants intéressants qui se sont dessinés depuis, on peut signaler celui dont Karl Deutsch fut l'instigateur. Il consiste à définir la nation en termes de communications (voir de cet auteur, *Nationalism and Social Communication*, New York, Wiley, 1953). Mais ce courant de pensée est loin de faire l'unanimité, car aux dires de certains il néglige des dimensions importantes de la nation.

De même les débats autour de la notion d'Etat n'ont pas dégagé un quelconque consensus. Certains prétendent que l'Etat correspond à une forme historique qui s'est développée en Occident et qu'on ne peut appliquer, sans distorsion, à d'autres civilisations. D'autres y voient une forme plus universelle d'organisation politique, avec des traits récurrents: des frontières précises, un appareil administratif, la réussite dans l'utilisation légitime de la force physique. Mais ces traits sont débattus et il n'y a pas de définition minimale qui soit acceptée par une proportion significative des anthropologues, sociologues ou politologues.

Toutes ces tentatives me semblent engagées sur de fausses voies. Il vaut mieux, me semble-t-il, commencer par une science critique qui fasse éclater ces notions idéologiques et institutionnelles, plus utiles aux combats politiques qu'aux débats scientifiques, pour les remplacer par des concepts élémentaires, plus appropriés aux phénomèmes collectifs auxquels ils renvoient. A partir de ces concepts élémentaires on pourra ensuite construire des approximations, sans plus, de ce qui est généralement désigné comme nation, Etat, souveraineté, autodétermination.

D'un point de vue critique ces notions ont au moins deux défauts majeurs: leur caractère globalisant ou totalisant qui cherche à voiler une complexité gênante pour leurs défenseurs, et plus fondamentalement la confusion, "intéressée" elle aussi, des types logiques sur lesquels elles reposent.

L'Etat n'est pas la société, c'est plutôt un appareil ou un ensemble d'appareils qui cherchent tant bien que mal à réguler la société. La nation n'est pas une: elle est faite d'organisations et de classes dont les relations sont aussi conflictuelles que coopératives. On veut nous faire croire que la souveraineté est une qualité qu'on a ou qu'on n'a pas, à une époque où, comme le remarque Stanley Hoffman, "il y a des fuites dans le réseau de la souveraineté". La prétendue autodétermination d'un peuple n'est souvent en fait que le privilège d'une classe restreinte de gouvernants.

Toutes ces notions renvoient à des types logiques supérieurs à ceux des individus et de leurs actions, mais on fait comme si c'étaient des propriétés individuelles. Comme le dit Gregory Bateson, la classe des éléphants n'a pas de trompe. De même faut-il voir que ces grandes classes que sont l'Etat et la nation n'ont pas de volonté — alors que les individus qui les composent en ont peut-être une. La souveraineté et l'autodétermination sont (peut-être...) à un individu ce que la trompe est à un éléphant, mais c'est une erreur logique que de les attribuer à ces classes d'individus que sont la nation et l'Etat. Evidemment les politiciens ont intérêt à perpétuer ces erreurs logiques.

La nation et l'Etat recouvrent des groupes et des organisations qui se recoupent plus ou moins et où s'exercent des relations de pouvoir où des acteurs et des coalitions d'acteurs cherchent à rendre leurs préférences efficaces en utilisant à leur avantage ces atouts parmi d'autres que sont les idéologies et les règles institutionnelles du jeu. L'Etat et la nation apparaissent alors comme des symboles dont se parent ceux qui ont le dernier mot, qu'il soit d'eux-mêmes ou de ceux qui le leur ont mis dans la bouche. La souveraineté et l'autodétermination qu'ils magnifient ou réclament, c'est la leur, plus ou moins contrainte par les préférences exprimées ou pressenties de ceux qu'ils gouvernent.

Peut-être qu'une société ne peut pas tenir ensemble sans ces notions mystificatrices, mais la science commence quand elle fait tomber les masques et s'interroge sur leurs fonctions.

THE ISSUE IS EQUALITY

Stanley Bréhaut RYERSON

The crisis of Canadian federalism is a composite one. Its main components involve the federal/provincial state structure and the relationships of French and English (francophones and anglophones). In a long-range sense this is a crisis of the ordering of Canadian and Québec society, in their external context of dependency and in the persistent internal undertone of tensions of social class. At the heart of the malaise growing through the 1960s and '70s are issues of equality within a nationally plural state. They found expression in Lester Pearson's concern for an "equal partnership" of peoples; in the B & B Commission's findings on socio-economic as well as cultural-linguistic inequalities, and in its allusion to the pertinence of the dimension of political equality which is "that of self-determination". One recalls Pearson's earlier comment, that "Quebec is in a sense the homeland of a people".[1]

Two particular and long-standing difficulties bedevil our understanding of the current crisis. One is the extreme complexity of the historical evolution of the Canadian state, of the plurality of nation-communities that are its components, and of the emergence of a staple-based corporate capitalism tied successively to British colonial and U.S. "multinational" empire (an evolution "from colony to nation to colony", as Innis put it). There resulted the setting up of the 1867 federal-provincial structure that is neither coterminous with the bi-national communities (French/English), nor constitutionally amenable, or even accessible, to negotiation of their relationship. Similar is the case of the vast marginal "territories" alloted to colonialist neglect and humiliating subordination of the native peoples.

There results the triple entanglement of competing regionalisms, provincial vs. federal powers, and the "national question". Regional identities and interests transcend provincial boundaries (Prairie, Maritime, Northern-Ontario, etc.). The nation-community of the francophone Québécois (and the Acadians) is asserting an identity and making demands that cannot be resolved as a matter of "provincial rights", a simplistic assumption that recurs constantly in English Canada with the suggestion that the "Quebec question" can be met by some across-the-board granting of increased autonomy to the ten provinces.

Our second difficulty is a sort of institutionalized conceptual unclarity regarding the phenomenon of the "nation".[2] The word, of course, has *two* possible meanings, in French as in English. (I) juridical, an independent sovereign state: as in "Canada, colony to nation". (II) social and cultural, a community of people, who may or may not be in possession of a state of their own; thus the Poles, partitioned in 1772 among Prussia, Austria and Russia, or the Kurds today, intersected by the boundaries of four adjoining states. Sense (I) speaks of a country, sense (II) of a people; the former is a "nation-state", the latter a "nation-community". Thus to assert, "Canada is a nation" makes sense in sense (I); to deny that the francophone Québécois constitute a nation, or to wonder whether the Canadians whose common tongue is English *are* a nation, are discussions invoking sense (II). But to point to the *lack* of a state as proof that a people are not a nation, is to play one sense of the term against the other, in order to evade the issue of self-determination, the demand of a nation-community to acquire its own state. Another facet of the same confusion is to claim that "Québec constitutes a nation", which is accurate in neither of the two senses. The provincial sub-state is not a sovereign entity (or nation-state). And the nation-community are the francophone Québécois. Province and nation-community are not coterminous; the Québec anglo-minority are part of the English-speaking nation in Canada. Should the Province become a sovereign state, with its present borders, the non-francophones within it would become in fact the minority that has been largely unacknowledged thanks to a "majoritarian" status-image bestowed by membership in predominantly "English" Canada. Moreover, were an independent Québec ever to emerge, the process might be given an assist by the faint (and fiercely disputed) element of national quasi-statehood accorded in 1791 to Lower Canada and resumed, after the post-1837 obliteration of identity during the Union, in the form of Québec as a province within Confederation. The distinction between state-form and nation-communities is essential to an understanding of this contorted and ever-ambiguous evolution of British North America.

For their part, the vast majority of non-francophones scattered "from sea to sea" tend to see themselves simply as Canadians. The awkward and unsatisfactory designations, "English-Canadian", "English-speaking (or Anglo-) Canadian" have use-value mainly as a demarcation from "the other", from "French Canada". Politically, for such Canadians the position of dominance dating from the Conquest makes the question of possession of a state of their own as a desideratum to be striven for, a non-issue: they already have it. Anxiety in this area focuses rather on the U.S. take-over. But now, the hankering of French Québec for a changed relationship with the anglo-majority does call in question the historic pattern of dominance and subordination. The bogy of "separatism" is compelling a whole new look at the fundamentals of Canadian and Québec identity.

Here, confusion and uncertainty and ambivalence contend with a stubbornly resistant complacency of the dominant nation. Assumed, but rarely acknowledged explicitly, the status of dominance is the precondition of national inequality of the "other". The insecurity lived by the latter community, constrained to permanent minority status (state-political, military, cultural, socio-economic) has at last in the post World War II de-colonization context, given rise to a nationalism that is no longer clerical-traditionalist but charged with social radicalism. No longer confined to the issue of survival as a "cultural-linguistic group", it is a national-popular movement of state-political assertion. In one sense or another, implicit in it is the right of self-determination; and the movement extends to, and is headed by the Government of Québec.

Yet nationalism is *not* identical with "separatism". The pretence that it is, underpins the ruling Anglo-Canadian élite's strategy and ideology of "national unity". Like the October 1970 hoax of "apprehended insurrection", the current demagogy serves as a smokescreen for preservation of a status quo founded on national inequality. The ballyhoo over "separatism" needs to be seen in the context of the six opinion polls since 1977, showing about 16% of Quebec electors favoring outright independence, a minority support for the status quo (made up 1/3 of francophones but 2/3 of anglophones), and a majority in favor of change whether as restructured federalism or sovereignty-association (44% as of April '79). The dimension of "Canadianism" in Québécois sentiment is not to be ignored. It is interwoven with the sense of insecurity as well as with historical tradition (one is still asked, "Etes-vous anglais — ou canadien?").

The ambivalence of those who are Canadian (in English) is of a rather different order: an uncertain identity, born of British and American mixed dominance, not yet outgrown, a heterogeneity of origins and mother tongue (that of 13%, in 1971, was other than

English or French); yet in response particularly to United States expansionism, a Canadian consciousness and will to survive has asserted itself. "Canada First" of the 1870s was its precursor: by developing a bitterly anti-French stance, it made itself an appendage of imperialism. A democratic nationalism, to be effective, will have to find common ground with Québec's demand for national equality, for a new relationship "d'égal à égal", a footing of equality.

From yet another quarter the Canadian structure is being challenged: after long suffering in silence an appalling poverty and deprivation, the northern native peoples (the Dènè nation of the Mackenzie, the Cree and Montagnais of James Bay, the Inuit people), are beginning to seek self-government within Canada. The Malouf and Berger findings testify to the resonance of the protest. The far North may yet be restructured and democratized. If the power of the multinational corporations can be broken...

Which brings us, finally, to the question of the ontological status of the entities of nation-community and social class. The prevailing view is that they are no more than ideological fictions. Or purely subjective phenomena. A neo-Marxist-structuralist view of the nation reduces it to a side-effect of the CMP (capitalist mode of production), imaginary as well as ideological.[3] This approach is paralyzing any positive, constructive intervention of the left on the issues of national equality and self-determination, playing straight into the hands of the right. But denial of the national fact falsifies historical reality. The imbrication of nation-community with social class structures is the fundamental fact of the past two centuries of our history. From the British military-mercantile conquest (with its characteristically asymmetric images in the present social memory of the two peoples), the "deal" of the Quebec Act of 1774, still operative between the élites, the Britain-based Industrial Revolution and the imperial design, Confederation and the creeping U.S. take-over, down to Ottawa's so-called "over-reaction" to the October Crisis, nerve-tremor at the centre of power: what else is this but an evolving socio-historical reality? The findings of Book III of the B & B Commission on the intersecting, in the "work world", of ethnic and socio-economic inequalities, echo the judgment and warning of Tocqueville and Durham almost a century and a half ago: "Il est facile de voir que les Français sont le peuple vaincu. Les classes riches appartiennent pour la plupart à la race anglaise... Les entreprises commerciales sont presque toutes entre leurs mains. C'est véritablement la classe dirigeante au Canada..." [4]

The greater part of them...labourers in the employ of English capitalists...it would appear that the great mass of the French Canadians are doomed, in some measure, to occupy an inferior position, and to be dependent on the English for employment. The evils of poverty and dependence would merely be aggravated in a tenfold degree, by a spirit of jealous and resentful nationality, which should separate the working class of the community from the possessors of wealth and employers of labour.[5]

NOTES

1. *B & B Commission Report,* General Introduction, sec. 82-84; Pearson speech, Jan. 5, 1964 in P. Stursberg, *Lester Pearson and the Dream of Unity* (1978), 198.

2. "L'histoire sociale est portée à reconnaître la réalité des classes sociales (au sens de groupements distincts, différenciés par la situation qu'ils occupent dans un système de production, de rapports de travail, de propriété, de pouvoir) et de la *nation* (au sens d'une communauté possédant sa propre langue et sa culture, occupant un territoire donné, liée par une économie commune, tendant à chercher ou à affirmer une expression politico-étatique qui lui soit propre). Loin de nier le rôle des individus, des *sujets* individuels ou collectifs, une telle reconnaissance permet de la rendre explicable, en faisant ressortir le contexte social réel au sein duquel leur vie, leur action, se déroulent". S.B.R., *Capitalisme et Confédération* (1978), 322. (French edition of Unequal Union, 1968).

3. Cf. the critique of the position of Gilles Bourque by Nicole Laurin-Frenette, *Production de l'Etat et Formes de la Nation,* (1978); and polemic with Eric Hobsbawm, in Jacques Mascotto et Pierre-Yves Soucy, *Sociologie politique de la question nationale* (1979).

4. Alexis de Tocqueville, *Voyages en Sicile et aux Etats-Unis,* Note du 25 août 1831.

5. Lord Durham, Report (1839), Lucas ed., vol. 2, p.293.

NATION, STATE AND HISTORY

Bruce HUNTER

In one of his many attacks on Canadian and French Canadian nationalism, Prime Minister Trudeau claimed that the proper function of a political society is not "the glorification of a 'national fact' (in its ethnic sense)" and that the territorial state, if it is to fulfil its proper function, "must seek the welfare of all of its citizens, regardless of sex, colour, race, religious beliefs or ethnic origin".[1] I have no desire to dispute these claims, but they, like the reflections of a good many philosophers on the purpose and basis of political society, strike me as unduly limited.

Territorial states arise in a number of ways. Usually one group of people has the power, typically military, by itself or with the help of neighbours, to establish authority over a given territory and its population. Sometimes groups of people form states, unitary or federal, assigning sovereign powers in various ways, in order to satisfy common and diverse interests and protect them from others (e.g., Swiss cantons and the Hapsburgs). However states which have little chance of survival are not worth creating or struggling to preserve, unless the harm risked by other options is sufficiently great. The energy spent maintaining such political associations is usually at the expense of serious attention to education, social and economic reform, and the general welfare of the population. The form a political association takes should reflect, among other things, its chances of survival and the ease with which it can be changed without neglecting the general welfare of the population.

Why do territorial states last for any length of time? (1) Some territorial states last because a dynasty or ruling elite has the power, typically military, to enforce its authority over the population of a territory for some considerable length of time. Sometimes such states last beyond the power of a dynasty or ruling elite because there is no special reason for some part of the territorial state to change the *status quo* and such states continue to last until there is such a reason. (2) Some territorial states last because they are needed as buffer states between hostile, more powerful neighbours. (3) So far nothing has been said about the *undoubted* role of economic interests in the persistence of states. However, the long term economic benefits for any region of a territorial state and for territorial states in their current territorial form are difficult to assess by historical agents and play little direct role in historical events. At times in the history of most territorial states, the short and middle term material interests of some regions would be best served, or at least not harmed and possibly better served, by separation or incorporation into another state. Change in territorial state is not an option adopted or seriously considered only insofar as regions are bound to the territorial state by some other factor, e.g., a dynasty's or ruling elite's military power, or great power politics. There are other factors, nowadays perhaps more important factors, which involve the desires of a population more directly.

(4) Some territorial states last because a sufficiently large part of the population of a territory share an ideology, typically a religion, which it does not share with neighbouring populations. An ideology may consist of secular ideals. (Trudeau once offered us bilingualism and pluralism from sea to sea.) (5) Some territorial states last because a sufficiently large part of the population sufficiently share a sense of history to strive to maintain traditional political associations. Shared senses of history are a matter of degree. A shared sense of history is chiefly a matter of a shared interpretation of history, in particular of common emotional responses to historical events involving the ancestors of the population. Thus people share a sense of history to the extent they feel similarly intense pride, shame, resentment or joy about the same historical events, including mythical, putative historical events, and do not conflict in their feelings about these events. People may share a sense of history without being all members of one linguistic or ethnic group and without being virtually all the members of a linguistic or ethnic group. Usually groups with a highly shared sense of history share a language or ethnic origin. However, a shared sense of history is a more important factor in the persistence of states than common ethnic origin or language although these often explain, in part, why people share a sense of history.

People who share a sense of history have common sympathies with the past. Shared pride tends to give people a sense of what must be maintained or upheld, shared shame or resentment, a sense of what must be changed or rectified, thus providing a framework for persisting common political life. When the first three factors are not strong, mutual sympathies amongst the members of a community are needed for the continued existence of a political society centred around the community. In the absence of a strongly shared ideology, common sympathies with the past must support mutual sympathies and, normally, they do. Nonetheless, people may share a sense of history without that fact being recognized by some of them. Some may believe that others can't share a sense of history with them because they have different ethnic or ideological origins. This was the tragic situation of 'assimilated' Jews in Weimar Germany. Thus some German nationalists incorrectly believed that Jews could not share a sense of history with them in any significant way and thereby limited the scope of mutual sympathies. According to them, Jews must have 'Jewish' sympathies which conflict with Germans' sense of history. (I remember a Swiss Nazi complaint about Jews at Bayreuth because, according to him, Jews could not properly understand or appreciate the Germanic significance of Wagner's work.)

Some territorial states may survive as a result of several of these factors — either present together with varying strength throughout the history of a state or present successively at different periods in the history of a state. (Armenia is a fine example of the second, fourth, and fifth factors, and even the first to a lesser extent.) Any territorial state which is not bound by any of the first two or the last two factors has little hope for a harmonious future and will be constantly subject to centrifugal forces. The first two factors have no relevance for the contemporary Canadian situation and the fourth little relevance. The fifth is of great significance.

Shared senses of history can be created by clever distortions of a population's common history. Even without deliberate distortion, shared senses of history are frequently as much the product of common ignorance as of common knowledge. This is one reason why intellectuals are often alienated from their communities. Sometimes the more one knows about what really happened in the history of one's society the more difficult it is to share a sense of that history with others. Nevertheless a population may come to share its perception of the past by moral suasion as well, and by correcting past wrongs to part of the population in the hope that conflicting perceptions of distant common history are overridden by shared perceptions of more recent history. There is nothing objectionable as such in the creation or maintainence of a shared sense of history. Indeed it is incumbent upon a state, if it is to serve its function for its subjects, to create or preserve a shared sense of history in the least objectionable way, especially if a distinct shared ideology can be imposed or preserved with any chance of success only in a morally objectionable way. (This seems to be the point of the Trudeau government's otherwise inane concern with changing the names of government ministries and state holidays, e.g., "Dominion Day" to "Canada Day".) To the extent that this is what glorification of the 'national fact' amounts to, philosophers should not view it with distaste.

The concept of a nation is important in history and in modern politics, but it seems less fundamental for historical understanding and political theory than the notion of a shared sense of history. A nation must be a group of people with a highly and firmly shared sense of history, strong enough to support a firm, persisting desire to create or maintain *some* sort of state (with *some* sovereign powers) centred around the group. What about the ethnographic and geographic factors we associate with nations? Must a nation have a common language? I'm inclined to think so. If we do think so, however, we must say that Israeli Jews were not a nation until very recently, if even now, since diaspora Jews, when gathered in Israel, did not share a language. Must a nation have sufficient population and common territory to make a national state feasible? I'm inclined to think not. The feasibility of a state is, in part, a matter of its ability to survive the slings and arrows of fortune for any length of time. Since this is a matter of degree, how much a nation a people is would depend on how strong and aggressive its neighbours are, how hilly its territory is, how much great powers need buffer states, etc. We should have to say that Estonians are less of a nation than Lithuanians, Kurds less of a nation than Afghans. Though nationhood is a matter of degree, I find these judgments counter-intuitive or at least not very obvious. These factors affect nationhood, not directly by being a condition of nationhood, but insofar as they affect the degree to which a population develops and maintains a shared sense of history and the consequent strength of its desire to form or maintain a national state. A territorially disparate people is less likely to develop or maintain a highly shared sense of history of much intensity because it will tend to have less history in common, and more history in common with other groups with which it is interspersed. The smaller a group of people the more it will tend to associate with other groups, and the less likely it will develop or maintain a distinct shared sense of history. Of course distinct ethnographic features, e.g., distinct language, as well as the character of the group's relations with others, e.g., discrimination, persecution, etc. may override these tendencies, and geographic isolation may override the latter tendency.

Moreover sufficient population and common territory affect a nation's right to self-determination, not by being a condition of nationhood, but insofar as a nation's right to self-determination may be overriden by considerations of the feasibility of a nation state. In this respect, nations do not have any special group right to self-determination. A religious community with a shared ideology and a consequent desire to create or maintain some sort of state has a right to create or maintain such a state. A population with a shared sense of history and a consequent desire to create or maintain some sort of state centred around the group has a right to do so, even if it lacks a common language and thus is not a nation. For that matter, any group with a stable desire to create or maintain some sort of state centred around the group has a right to do so. However a group's right to create or maintain a state may be overridden by considerations of cost to others — especially important when a group is territorially disparate or shares its territory with other groups. Just as important is the cost to future generations of inheriting a state inherently subject to centrifugal forces. The right of nations to self-determination is especially strong because of their shared senses of history.

Although a shared sense of history can be created with time, we cannot bank on it. Sometimes love may arise during marriage, but this is usually unlikely, at best difficult to predict, and is an irrational basis for entering marriage or continuing it when the issue arises. Better to seek the most advantageous looser form of association available. The relative economic merits of federalism and sovereignty/association for Quebec as a whole, though not for parts of its middle classes, are unclear. The upcoming referendum will reflect the extent to which Quebeckers share a sense of history with the rest of Canada. If Quebeckers vote for sovereignty/association, the rest of Canada should seek the most advantageous economic association and concentrate its efforts on badly needed social and economic reform. In any case, the West, despite its economic grievances, won't seek sovereignty/association or even seriously consider it. Why? Its shared sense of history with the rest of Canada.

NOTE

1. Trudeau, P.E. *Federalism and the French Canadians.* Toronto, 1968, p.4.

THE SEPARATION OF CULTURE AND STATE (AN ABSTRACT)

Robert BINKLEY

Basically, what I want to do is promote the theme of separation of Culture and State, by analogy with separation of Church and State.

The State is for boring things like sewers and mine safety regulation and international trade. If individuals are not to suffer, it is well for them to belong to States that are big enough not to be pushed around by multi-national corporations and other states. Canada-size seems about right, at least for the North American context. So I'm for federalism and strong central government on State affairs.

Culture is the space in which the individual finds the non-boring and important goods of life (once we get beyond the necessities of material existence). Such things must be voluntary. A culture will survive if individuals want it to; if they don't let it die.

One of the two main threats to Canadian federation is the wish to enlist the State in support of Culture. (The other threat is regional greed, which I won't discuss.)

The wish to have the State back a Culture is, I submit, irrational, and rests upon primitive emotions which it is the task of civilization to bring under control. Loyalty to Culture is not in itself a bad emotion, but it should be kept at the level of amiable sentimentality and not allowed to become an important political force.

This problem, of course, is not uniquely Canadian, but arises all over the world. Often it is associated with issues of injustice, but in Canada the injustices have been fairly trivial, at least when measured against world standards of injustice.

What to do? Basically, the cure to problems of emotional disturbance is psycho-therapy. Here the therapy must be orchestrated by politicians (that is their *job)*, and must be done on a coast-to-coast basis, perhaps along the lines prescribed by Pepin-Robarts, and perhaps including an element of constitutional psycho-drama. But I am not myself prepared to make detailed recommendations in this area. The important point, for philosophers, is to locate the problem where it belongs, in the realm of psychiatry.

This is where I find my thoughts drifting, influenced to some extent by Russell's *Principles of Social Reconstruction.*

NATION, STATE, SOVEREIGNTY AND SELF-DETERMINATION (AN ABSTRACT)

Léon THIRY

The above-mentioned concepts are continuously being used in the debates concerning Canadian federalism. It is therefore imperative that we use them univocally in order to avoid discussing at cross-purposes. Yet these concepts seem to resist definition. In my paper I defend the position that "nation" must be distinguished from "state"; nation being a community, state a society. The concept of "nation-state" is a misnomer as there are almost no states actually on the map that are nationally homogeneous; the multinational state is the rule. A union of two or more nationalities in one body politic often serves best the interests of all concerned.

The concept of sovereignty is obsolete, to say the least; in a sense it is even contradictory.

The right to national self-determination is not an ethical absolute. It can justifiably be advocated in certain circumstances, as for example after a war, when changes on the political map have become necessary, or also when a national minority is being deprived of its natural rights. Otherwise a minority has no right to break up a country that offers all its citizens without discrimination the means to better their conditions of life.

NATIONAL SELF-DETERMINATION AND FREEDOM (AN ABSTRACT)

J. WUBNIG

The emotional appeal of slogans for a 'free ——— ', as in De Gaulle's 'Vive le Québec libre!', depends on confusing the political independence of people within certain geographical boundaries with the liberty of the individual. To be free is to be able to do what you want, and everyone wants to do what he wants to do. If freedom in this sense is good it does not follow that the political independence of a given geographical territory is also good.

Political self-government is what is called 'democratic' government, and it may well be essential for individual freedom. It is a procedure for making decisions in which all citizens have some voice. There is, however, no necessary connection between living in an area which is politically independent and democracy or any particular kind of government.

Different areas may have different population subgroups, so that if an area becomes politically independent the majorities on different issues may be different from what they would have been in the former state. Those whose view might have been in the minority in the former state may be in the majority in the new one. Having a view you support prevail means that you will be 'free' to do what you have supported, like requiring people to speak French, if that is what you want, or driving on the right-hand side of the road instead of the left-hand side if that is what you want. This kind of 'freedom' to do a particular thing is not, however, the same as political self-government, which is procedural.

SELF-DETERMINATION AND CANADIAN FEDERALISM (AN ABSTRACT)

Sheldon RICHMOND

'Nation', 'state', 'sovereignty', and 'self-determination' are dangerous political abstractions. They disguise the fundamental realities of political activity: individuals and institutions. It is individuals who bleed and suffer on the battlefields of national liberation movements. It is the institutions of family, education, and civil society that are transformed or obliterated in attempts to gain national sovereignty. The basic question we must put to those who urge vast social and political change is, who will gain and who will lose?

The basic facts of human history are fallibility and change. We cannot confront those facts by polaristic thinking: dividing people and social forms of living into Good and Evil. Nor can we face those facts by reificationist thinking: pretending that cherished concepts such as 'nation' or 'right' denote transhistorical realities. The best antidote to those misleading patterns of thinking is to keep in mind that social changes affect the lives of individual people, and that social changes have consequences which are beyond our knowledge and control. The best means for articulating and confronting the key political problem that faces Canada — how can the francophones form a community centered on the language of their choice without increasing but rather decreasing human suffering? — is within the context of the theory and practice of the experimental federal state.

In the experimental state: individuals are legally given the right to form communities of their own choosing as controlled experiments in social living. The function of the federal government, apart from developing techniques for arbitrating conflicts among the various communities, is to minimize the risks and harms of failed social experiments.

If francophone individuals in Quebec wish to form a "sovereign" state, then they should do so under a federal experimental system of government. The federal government must retain one unilateral coercive power: the power to protect dissenting individuals. The new nation of Quebec would have the power to employ French as the language of commerce, education, communication, and government. The forms of government, forms of economic life, and civil life that would be established in Quebec would be dependent upon the decisions of the members of the new nation. The forms of association between the new Quebec and the experimental state (federal government) can be developed through trial and adjustment, as opposed to being set up once and for all *a priori.*

FORMS of ASSOCIATION, SOCIAL CONTRACT and CONSTITUTION

FORMES d'ASSOCIATION, CONTRAT SOCIAL et CONSTITUTION

PARTICIPANTS

LESLIE ARMOUR
Philosophy, University of Ottawa

GERARD BERGERON
Philosophie, Université Laval

NATHAN BRETT
Philosophy, University of Toronto

ANDREW BROOK
Philosophy, Carleton University

WILLIAM CHRISTIAN
Political Studies, University of Guelph

DAVID GAUTHIER
Philosophy, University of Toronto

CHRISTOPHER GRAY
Philosophy, Concordia University

CLAUDE LAGADEC
Philosophie, Université de Montréal

GEORGES LEGAULT
Philosophie, Collège Bois de Boulogne

ALISTAIR MACLEOD
Philosophy, Queen's University

WILLIAM MATHIE
Politics, Brock University

ARTHUR MONAHAN
Philosophy, Saint Mary's University

JAN NARVESON
Philosophy, University of Waterloo

VINCENT DI NORCIA
Philosophy, University of Sudbury

JOSEPH PESTIEAU
Philosophie, Collège Saint-Laurent

SERGE ROBERT
Philosophie, Université du Québec à Montréal

JEAN-LOUIS ROY
Etudes canadiennes-françaises, McGill University

RICHARD SIMEON
Political Studies, Queen's University

DONALD SMILEY
Political Science, York University

JACK STEVENSON
Philosophy, University of Toronto

ROBERT WARE
Philosophy, University of Calgary

WORKSHOP II REPORT

ATELIER II RAPPORT

Le sujet de l'atelier était la forme (ou les formes) d'association souhaitable entre les nations (groupes, régions) qui composent le Canada. Parce que le débat était assez complexe, nous avons organisé la matière sous deux rubriques, l'une temporelle et l'autre logique, dont la dernière sera dominante.

In the morning session each participant gave a short summary of his views and was questioned briefly on them. The chairman (Arthur Monahan) in his summary detected four issues which had excited the most interest, presented them to us, and suggested two of them as foci for the afternoon's debate. The four were:

(a) whether the debate on forms of association should be a rational one, and if so, what the forms of rationality would be;

(b) whether the notion of special status is logically and politically coherent;

(c) whether the term "empire" is an appropriate and enlightening one to describe the Canadian state;

(d) whether the contractarian approach to the confederation issue is valid and if so whether, and under what conditions, one of the parties could abrogate the contract.

The afternoon's debate centred on the special status and contractarian issues, but all the other issues arose again during the course of it. We have taken the liberty of exposing what we perceive to be the underlying five-level structure of the afternoon's discussion:

(1) the level of moral principles and the question of rationality;

(2) the level of the application of these principles to concrete situations and proposals;

(3) the level of descriptive political analysis and theory;

(4) the level of political process, its forms and modalities;

(5) a return to the first, or ideal, level in a new form.
We will report on these *seriatim.*

(1) At the highest level of abstract moral principles there was little disagreement. For example, there was no clear, discernible opposition to the principle that individuals and peoples have some sort of right to self-determination, or that some form of autonomy is an important property for a human being to have, or that freedom is desirable, or that the debate should be a rational one.

(2) It was the application and specification of these principles which engendered disagreement.

Thus three forms of rationality were appealed to by different philosophers: (i) that form of rationality which insists on sharp distinctions, explicit definitions, the formulation of general principles and the deduction of consequences from them; (ii) that form of rationality which defines rational behaviour as the behaviour of 'economic man' — the person who uses instrumental reason to maximize utilities relative to her/his preference structure; and (iii) the rationality of the 'reasonable man' who, in cognitive matters, follows canons of scientific evidence additional to those determining consistency and who, in practical matters, follows complex principles of 'practical reason', 'right reason' or 'the good' which are difficult to formalize. For the first, philosophy's contribution to the forms of association question appears to end once definitions are clearly stated and formal consistency is achieved. Thus, the philosophical problem is merely to define the term "special status" and to determine its internal coherence and external consistency with other concepts and principles. For the second, rationality requires that we go a step further to appeal to matters of fact (especially causes) in order to determine whether chosen means are conducive to given ends. Although basic interests (preferences, ends, etc.) are nonrational, there are secondary interests (means) which are objective (rational) interests provided they are effective means to our ends. Thus we can ask whether a contract is rationally binding: Did the contract serve the interests of the contracting parties? For the third, rationality requires that we go further still: the rational person will strive not only for clarity and logical consistency, not only for a consistent, i.e., effective will, in the light of the facts in the real world; but also will ask, for example, whether ends are themselves reasonable or good, indeed whether they will comport well with the 'common good'. Thus we can ask whether a form of association, special status or compact is reasonable: Is it feasible? What good(s) does it serve? Is it fair? Will it be really effective? Some of the disagreements of the afternoon session reflected, we believe, an underlying disagreement about the limits of reason.

The specification of other generally accepted principles also produced some disagreement.

For example, the specification of the right to self-determination and the desirability of liberty led a minority of two to question the legitimacy of the state altogether and one to advocate something approaching individualistic anarchism under which all forms of association would be voluntary ones amongst individuals.

The Pepin-Robarts rejection of 'special status' for Quebec was criticized on logical grounds: the notion is really a coherent one and was actually rejected by the Task Force only because of its unacceptable political and emotional associations. There was general agreement on the logical point, but several objections were raised against the application of the 'special status' solution: it would produce an asymmetry or inequality with respect to sovereign powers; it would lead to loss of French culture outside Quebec; it would fail to deal adequately with the minority native and immigrant cultures, and thus would prevent the development of a new dynamic of self-determination for all peoples comprising Canada. One participant then noted an apparent paradox: a large percentage of Canadians accept a right to self-determination but reject its practical application, especially as regards concrete suggestions for special status by functions. He suggested that we give up a sterile "juggling with concepts" in favour of a search for a reasonable modality for negotiations amongst the politicians who would have to decide the issues.

Finally, a 'contractarian' version of the traditional 'compact theory of Confederation' was presented and engendered much debate. It was argued that there had been a contract, that it was a rational one (i.e., in the interests of the contracting parties), and that since it was still binding it could not be unilaterally abrogated. Amongst the objections raised were the following. An essential element in a valid contract is the capacity (autonomy) of the parties; it is doubtful that this element was present; hence the contract may not be valid. If, as is plausible, one of the interests involved in the contract was an interest in the development of autonomy, the contract would be self-limiting and would have a natural termination when that development had occurred. Contracts are based not only on self-interest but also on such considerations as benefits to others and fairness; these must be taken into account when assessing the validity of a contract. Questions about the transitivity of the contractual obligation and the nature of the parties were raised. The original contractors and beneficiaries are all dead. Is there no limit to the binding force of the contract, regardless of the length of the chain of 'heirs' to it and regardless of the changing circumstances and interests of these 'heirs'? "A contract without the sword is worthless"; the current unenforcibility of the contract invalidates it. The doubtful historicity of the original contract and the necessity of appeals to hypothetical, retroactive justifications of its current binding force show that this application of contractarianism is a mere ideological rationalization of the *status quo.* Although no one questioned the principles that some contracts create obligations, and much of the debate took place within the contractarian framework, there was some general scepticism about the applicability of contractarianism to questions in political philosophy.

(3) En opposition à l'approche philosophique des principes moraux et de leur application à l'étude des contrats ou du "statut particulier", une analyse en termes de théorie politique s'est aussi manifestée. La question plus spécifique consistait à déterminer si le Canada constitue ou non un Empire. Sur ce sujet, deux points de vue se sont opposés: un point de vue à tendance marxiste considérait que des déterminations économiques influencent profondément les systèmes politiques et qu'en ce sens l'économie politique interne du Canada était nettement celle d'un Empire centralisateur sur ses différentes régions. A cela s'opposait une conception plus politique de l'Etat, selon laquelle le Canada serait davantage une fédération de provinces associées pour résister à un impérialisme qui ne s'exercerait que de l'extérieur, en l'occurrence l'impérialisme américain. A cette occasion, on a rappelé que l'origine du Canada est elle-même dépendante de la lutte entre les Empires français et britannique pour la conquête de colonies, et que c'est la victoire de l'Empire britannique qui a pu assurer la domination de la communauté anglophone sur la communauté francophone.

La thèse selon laquelle le Canada fonctionnerait comme un Empire a servi à soutenir la volonté d'un remaniement de la constitution dans le sens d'une décentralisation considérable du pouvoir, qui serait favorable à la souveraineté-association. Contre cette thèse, une autre analyse tentait de montrer que dans les sociétés industrielles avancées le capitalisme tend précisément à exercer ses pouvoirs à travers une filière décentralisatrice et qu'alors la décentralisation est peut-être le meilleur moyen de rendre l'impérialisme plus efficace.

(4) La conception plus politique de l'Etat a préféré aux théories sur l'impérialisme une analyse pragmatique qui est issue d'une volonté

d'éviter les crises violentes au profit d'une constitution plus satisfaisante pour tous. A ce niveau, le thème qui a retenu l'attention est l'étude du procès de négociation de cette nouvelle constitution, de façon à créer les conditions matérielles permettant d'arriver à des solutions pouvant satisfaire les parties. Mais, dès lors, on a soulevé une question épineuse, à savoir quelles seront les parties? Le problème majeur étant la difficulté de déterminer, par un critère précis, les parties ayant le droit de négocier.

(5) Le débat est finalement revenu plusieurs fois au niveau des principes fondamentaux, non pas en ce qui a trait à la question de la rationalité ou des principes moraux, mais plutôt à travers le concept d'utopie. Une approche normative de l'utopie a posé le principe du droit à l'auto-détermination comme étant un droit que devraient avoir non seulement les sociétés mais aussi tout groupe social, et même les individus. Cette thèse aboutit alors à un anarchisme basé sur le volontarisme, et pour lequel tout gouvernement est une acceptation de vivre par l'autre et un instrument de répression.

Un autre discours a aussi été tenu sur l'utopie, à travers une tentative d'analyse de ses effets politiques. Dans cette perspective, le discours nationaliste québécois a été qualifié d'utopique, mais on a fait remarquer que, puisque le pouvoir réprime les idées contestataires, toute entreprise de changement politique d'importance ne peut se faire sans une prise de conscience qui fait appel aux sentiments à travers un discours utopique. En dépassant le réalisable, l'utopie serait un stimulant nécessaire à réaliser la partie faisable de ses aspirations.

En résumé, on pourrait classifier les différentes orientations qu'a pris l'atelier sur les *formes d'association* à partir des trois couples d'oppositions conceptuelles suivants: le philosophique et le politique, le théorique et le pratique, le descriptif et le normatif. Si on suit les cinq niveaux de discussion selon leur ordre: les principes moraux concernant le droit à l'auto-détermination et l'appel à la rationalité, du niveau (1), sont de l'ordre de la prescription philosophique théorique; le niveau (2) porte sur les conséquences pratiques de ces prescriptions; le niveau (3) relève de la théorie politique quant à la controverse sur l'impérialisme; les préoccupations du niveau (4) sont de l'ordre de la pratique politique quand elles traitent du procès de négociation, mais elles reviennent à des questions théoriques et philosophiques lorsqu'elles posent le problème de l'identification des parties impliquées. Enfin, au niveau (5), toute la réflexion est de nature philosophique: l'anarchisme utopiste est de l'ordre de la prescription et la conception de l'utopie comme moteur du changement est de l'ordre de la description.

Voilà donc autant de problèmes que nous pouvons identifier comme ayant été traités à l'atelier sur les *formes d'association.*

Serge ROBERT et J.T. STEVENSON

CONFEDERATION, CONTRACT, AND CONSTITUTION

David GAUTHIER

1. Confederation established a union of the provinces of British North America. In a normative and hypothetical analysis we may, however, ignore this clear historical reality, and treat Confederation rather as an agreement among parties defined by their interests, to whom Confederation might have appeared to afford fair mutual advantage. This will enable us to bring the resources of contractarian moral-political theory to bear on the specific issue of our constitutional future.

It then seems reasonable to identify three parties, or if you prefer three interests, as the hypothetical contractors. The first I shall call the capitalist interest, the interest of the bankers, merchants, and businessmen, the commercial class of the Canadas. These persons were largely English-speaking which I shall abbreviate as "English", even though the group in question was more Scots in composition than anything else. The second I shall call the French interest, the interest of the French-speaking clerical and professional classes, but also to some extent the interest of the ordinary *habitant,* in maintaining the French fact, the pre-revolutionary French way of life in British North America. The third I shall call the Imperial interest, the interest, widespread among the English inhabitants of British North America, in retaining the tie with Britain and with British institutions to counteract the pull, economic, political, and cultural, of the United States.

The consequences of the Act of Union of 1840, which established the united province of the Canadas with parity representation for its two constituent parts, were profoundly dissatisfying to each of the first two parties. On the one hand, the English capitalists found the Union government an unwieldy instrument with which to support their commercial designs, since they were faced with the necessity of securing the support of French Canadians at best uninterested in, at worst hostile to, those designs. On the other hand, the French Canadians found themselves deprived of a government which they could control, and which would take as its prime concerns the protection of their religion and society. Although assured parity by the Act of Union, Lower Canada, or Canada East as it became known, was uncomfortably aware that it was losing the population race, and that sooner or later the cries from the Grits of Canada West for "Rep by Pop" would be heard, and would submerge even more the French interest in the government of the united Canadas.

Adding to the frustration of the first, capitalist interest was awareness of the potential of the new technology offered by the railroad, which made possible the extension of the empire of the St Lawrence both eastward and westward. The railroad would permit the development of the Atlantic and Western regions which were under the British flag, not from the geographically nearer and apparently more natural points in the United States, but from Canada, and so *by* the English Canadian capitalist class. But this would be possible only if the barriers existing among the British North American provinces were removed, in favour of a single barrier against the expansionist designs of the United States.

And these designs threatened the third, Imperial interest. The rapid emergence of American power in the Civil War threatened the security of the fragmented colonies to the north. Only a single country could hope to exercise control over the extensive but thinly populated lands under the British flag.

2. Confederation, then, was the logical and natural answer to the demands made by these three interests. The separation of the Canadas, and the recreation of the province of Québec, would afford to the French interest the possibility of maintaining the distinctive institutions dear to it, without fear of being overwhelmed by an ever-increasing English majority. The creation of a federal government for British North America, with a secure English majority in Parliament, would permit effective support for the commercial designs of the capitalist class, and in particular, would provide public backing for the development of the railways needed to make Montréal and Toronto, rather than Boston and Chicago, the centres for the development of the eastern and western hinterlands of the continent. The same federal government would be the effective guarantor of the Imperial tie against the traditional enemy to the south.

The payoffs from Confederation corresponded roughly to what might reasonably have been expected. Each interest received fair satisfaction. The federal government provided the guarantees necessary for the construction of the Intercolonial and Canadian Pacific Railways, and in Macdonald's National Policy, provided the tariff needed for the development of Canadian manufactures to serve the needs of the new country — for without this barrier, American imports would have undercut the higher-cost Canadian producers. It is worth noting that the decision to develop Canada on an East-West basis, to extend the empire of the St. Lawrence to the entire continent through the use of the railroads and the tariff, determined the emergence of the Canadian economy as a miniature replica of larger-scale economies — providing the full range of goods and services needed in modern society but on a sub-optimal basis — and led ultimately to the branch-plant character of the Canadian economy today, as takeover bids from American and multinational corporations made possible by indirect means the foreign penetration of the Canadian market which was directly precluded by the tariff. This historical legacy is one of our main problems today, but it is not clear that it could have been avoided, given the interests of Canadian capitalists which Confederation was intended to advance.

Equally, the French interest was advanced. If there are those today who complain that the French Canadian has been exploited by his English Canadian brother, and excluded from the development of the hinterland, they should be asked what alternative realistically existed. The price of a separate French province was made very clear in the destruction of the widespread but thin quasi-French society in western Canada; Confederation doomed Riel and the Métis. But only the full assimilation of the French people into a dominant English society could have retained for them, as individuals, a part in the process of development. And this price would not have been paid by the French clerical and professional classes who dominated, and indeed largely constituted, French Canadian society.

One can imagine other scenarios for Québec. Suppose that in 1867 it had been annexed by the United States; then the French Canadian people would have joined their relatives in New England and Louisiana in the American melting pot. There would be no real French society in North America today. Had instead Québec been launched into independence in 1867, then the model of the Latin American republics is available — economic control would have rested firmly in the hands of American, rather than English Canadian, capitalists, who would have had even less interest in what for them would have been a mere foreign backwater. The present arrangement represents a reasonable return, both in maintaining control over one's own way of life, and in promoting material progress. A second Louisiana might have enjoyed a higher standard of living; a second Mexico might have been culturally and politically more separate. Would either have been a more reasonable choice?

What I have called the Imperial interest has also received its due — no doubt to a continually decreasing extent, but only as the concern among English Canadians to look to Britain rather than to America has correspondingly diminished. To the extent to which the Imperial interest has been abandoned in contemporary Canada, we have abandoned it willingly.

At this point no doubt a word about the groups so far neglected in this analysis is in order. The average English Canadian, except insofar as he has shared the Imperial interest, has not gained significantly from those institutions which have protected him against the economic and political forces to the south. But this is simply the price of not being American. Take it away, and little cause for complaint remains. The disgruntled Maritimer should reflect that his ills stem from the end of the age of sail, and that had his destinies not been decided in Montréal, they would have been decided in Boston. In any event, the men who actually made the decisions were disproportionately themselves Maritimers, bankers and politicans who moved to the new head offices. The disgruntled Westerner, whose hatred of Toronto has been imbibed with his mother's milk, would equally have hated Chicago, had the cookie crumbled differently. And in any event, there are cities, and even corporation headquarters, in Alberta, but not in Montana or the Dakotas; in some ways — though admittedly not in weather — Alberta shares characteristics with the American sunbelt which it would hardly have developed under the Stars and Stripes.

3. This exercise in hypothetical analysis leads me to conclude that Confederation has been a reasonably good and fair deal, in terms of the interests which it was brought into being to serve, and that those interests it has not served would not have been served by any realistic alternative. But there is a problem with any good deal which exists over an extended period of time — the problem of continued compliance. One of the parties may conclude that it has reaped its gains, and so — to change the metaphor — may seek to pick up its marbles and leave, while other parties still look to the deal as a source of benefits. This is, I suggest, what is currently happening among the French Canadian separatists. They claim — falsely — that the French interest has been ill served by Confederation, but more important, they claim — whether truly or falsely — that Confederation no longer serves the French interest. So they seek unilaterally to abrogate the hypothetical bargain which Confederation represents.

There is nothing atypical or surprising about this move. But there is not the slightest reason why the rest of us, who consider that we still have much to gain from the Canadian bargain, should feel obliged in any way to accommodate it. Suppose that you and I agree that this week we shall bring in my crops and next week we shall bring in yours. So this week we bring in my crops, and next week I demand to renegotiate — I have what I want from our deal, so either I want out or I want better terms to continue. You will, rightly, insist that I honor our arrangement — and if I refuse, then, although you may not consider it worth your while to try to *compel* me by *force* to honor it, you will certainly in future make sure that your advantage is guaranteed before you enter into any dealings with me. And this, I suggest, is precisely the message we should convey to the French separatists. If you go, we should say, you will go on whatever terms we find most advantageous from our point of view, given the extent of our power to enforce terms. And thenceforth we shall deal with you, as we should deal with any foreign group, on the basis of strict self-interest.

4. It will be said that this approach overlooks the possibility that renegotiation might be mutually advantageous. So let us consider this possibility — or in other words, let us consider replacing the British North America Act with a new constitution.

Contractarian theory will lead us to suppose that a constitution, considered as an agreed and not as an imposed arrangement of political affairs, must reflect a convergence of interests on some outcome which affords each party a satisfaction greater than it finds in the status quo situation, since otherwise, voluntary agreement on the new constitution could not be expected.

It is hardly a profound observation on the present situation in Canada to suggest that such a convergence is not to be found. The most striking feature of the interminable federal-provincial conferences which have addressed the constitutional issue is that any significant departure from the existing state of affairs is rejected by the spokesmen of some significant interest as undesirable.

But there is more. The clamour for change comes primarily from those who seek a greater decentralization of powers than exists in our present system. Now such a decentralization would almost certainly be destabilizing, and ultimately destructive to our national existence, and this for two reasons. In the first place, the decentralists argue that by increasing the powers of the provinces we can accommodate the desires of the French separatists. On this point I am of one mind with M. Levesque: "The appetite grows with eating." Decentralization of powers from Ottawa to Québec would almost certainly result in an increased concentration of French Canadian politicians and civil servants in the provincial, rather than the federal sphere. Nothing could be better calculated to intensify demands for a yet further devolution of powers. For as French Canadians come to see Québec and not Ottawa as the focal point of their political activity and participation, then the retention, even of lesser powers, by Ottawa, a government perceived increasingly as foreign, must intensify resentment and rejection. Only a federal government with powers sufficiently extensive that French Canadians have a strong stake in its character, can expect to attract significant French participation, and so offset the dynamics of the separatist appeal.

But this is only one consideration. The decentralists also forget that prime purpose of Confederation which was represented in 1867 by what I have called the Imperial interest, and which today takes the form of resistance to complete economic and cultural domination by our southern neighbour. The federal government has certainly proved itself a weak reed, but it is nevertheless the only reed we, as Canadians, have.

Now I am not one of those who considers the United States intrinsically evil, or Canada intrinsically good. The value in preserving our ways arises, not from their intrinsic superiority over the ways of others, but simply from the fact that they are *our ways.* We want to be, and to continue to be, ourselves. Or so I suppose. For it is just possible that we do not care about our survival as a people apart — if only a little apart.

But Canada — our national existence — is predicated on the assumption that we do care. And if we care, then we need institutions to preserve our little apartness. The decentralists would proceed to continue the work of the Imperial Privy Council, in eroding those powers exercised by and at the centre, and would thereby facilitate the quite unconscious absorptive activity of that country which is both our closest friend and, in terms of our national existence, the historic enemy. The Fathers of Confederation intended Canada to be a union; learning from the problems which erupted in the American Civil War they intended that the power of the provincial units would be clearly established in limited spheres of local concern, but that they would be generally secondary and subordinate to the overriding powers of the Dominion. We forget that condition of our national existence at our peril.

The British North America Act is, I suggest, the best constitution we should expect. In a time when we lack a clear sense of common objectives — a time when the forces which divide us threaten to overcome the forces which unite us — it divides us least, for it represents, to paraphrase Hume, the present established practice of the age. Whatever may be its abstract merits or demerits, its familiarity makes it salient for us. And it has, for better of for worse, for richer or for poorer, provided the basis of our national existence, our little apartness, for more than a century.

The future of Confederation is to make no radical break with the past. There are times in the affairs of nations for radical breaks — but such times arise only when either matters are not settled by agreement, but by the imposed will of one interest overriding all others, or when a true convergence of interests gives a new direction to the affairs of a people. The first we do not want; the second we do not have. These are not inspiring times for Canadians, but rather times for soldiering on. More than a decade ago, when our sense of purpose was clearer, we agreed to soldier on under a new flag. Reflection on the costs of that exercise should make very clear why today we do not want to embark on the quest for a new constitution.

ON SELF-DETERMINATION FOR THE PEOPLE OF QUEBEC

Robert WARE

Among the many factors that are relevant to the forms of association that Canada might assume is the self-determination that might be exercised by the people of Quebec. Many have already taken up a variety of positions on the issue of self-determination by the people of Quebec, ranging from the claim that they have an absolute right of self-determination to the denial of any such right and the threat of retaliation at any attempt to exercise self-determination. I shall argue for a claim made by the Task Force on Canadian Unity — one that I consider minimal but basic. They claim that in "a community of the size and character of Quebec society...the clearly expressed will of the population must prevail, and that it would be...ethically questionable to deny or thwart it."[1] Their answer to the moral question of whether Quebecers would be justified in exercising self-determination is that they would be justified in doing so. I agree with this claim, although I have some minor qualifications to add.

The claim is not vitiated nor should the issues be confused by any further claims that there are other matters which are more important to the outcome of the "Confederation crisis". Certainly "bargaining for power positions" will be crucial,[2] and I agree with the Task Force that "principles and rights are usually subordinate to political events and to the hard facts of success or failure."[3] But this is not to deny (nor have they denied it) that principles and rights are involved. I am merely claiming that self-determination for the people of Quebec is morally justified and that this is one factor in the dispute and one that is likely to have an effect on the outcome. The ongoing debate about a right to self-determination corroborates this judgement. I shall turn to some arguments about self-determination before considering its status as a right or as founded on other moral considerations.

It is not uncommon to try to establish the legitimacy of the present political structures on the basis of a contract or compact. Although I think this approach is unpromising, it is instructive to consider the question of self-determination in terms of contract theory. It seems to me that the case for self-determination by the people of Quebec is most easily made within a contract theory. Assuming for the moment that contract theory does provide justification for the present political arrangements, we can note that much of the persuasive force of the theory comes from the arrangements being contracted between virtually all of the participants. Although some contractarians would consider the contract to be between groups of one kind or another (and thus the participants to be groups rather than individuals), it is more common to regard individuals as the contracting participants. The political arrangements are thus claimed to be the result of decisions by the participating individuals, at least their voluntary consent.

It is well known by now that this consent has not been and is not explicit. There is no point in looking for any manuscripts or tapes that record such a contract explicitly contracted. Much less will we find any terms of contract or dates of expiry that have been recognized by explicit consent. Some find it plausible, however, to say that participants have given and do give implicit consent to the political structures of their society. There are various ways in which it might be established that someone has given implicit or tacit consent. If a particular arrangement is in a person's self-recognized interest, we might assume that consent has been and/or is given. What makes the assumption plausible is that people often do accept arrangements that are in their own interest. Much of the plausibility is lost, however, if it is known that the person does not recognize the arrangement as being in his or her interest. Nevertheless, there is nothing contradictory about someone acting in a way or consenting to an arrangement contrary to his or her interest, even where the interest is correctly recognized as such by the person. We can voluntarily act, and contract, in the interests of others, and in fact I think people should do so more often. But since people often do correctly perceive their interests and act in their interests, it is often reasonable to assume that arrangements have the implicit consent of the participants.

No matter how reasonable it might be for a person to act in his or her own interest on a particular occasion, the person might still want to do something else not in their best interest. What we most want, are most interested in, is not necessarily what is in our best interest. We have to distinguish what interests us and what is in our interest. It is what interests us (whether it be our own interests, those of others or some combination) that more often moves us to action, including to consent and agreement. Even so, what interests us cannot be the sole factor that moves us to action, consent or agreement. What we finally do voluntarily can be the result of inertia, emotional attraction, duty, friendliness or feelings of solidarity. It is our voluntary action, and in particular our voluntary consent or agreement, that gives a contract theory plausibility in legitimating a social arrangement. The arrangement is legitimate if it is the result of the participants willingly participating in the sense of voluntarily accepting the arrangement.

There is no reason to object to consent or acceptance that is implicit. Implicit consent is still consent. Moreover, consent does not have to be restricted to an agreement or bargain that is concluded on a particular occasion. Silence can be consent when you take my keys as well as when you continue to play my piano. My tolerating a situation that I could otherwise stop or object to is a good indication that I implicitly consent to or accept the situation. I may not have bargained for it or made a deal, but it still gains some legitimacy from me.

The plausibility of the theory does require my willingly consenting, no matter how implicitly. If I positively object or disapprove, then the situation is rather different. What were formerly good reasons to believe that I have given implicit consent suddenly lose their strength. Someone might still be able to make out a case for saying that there is implicit consent even in the face of explicit objection. But the case for accepting the word of a third person over the word of the first person usually has to be pretty strong. The onus is certainly on the third person to show that a bargain has been made or that a deal is on. If anything, that is an understatement.

Since even implicit consent seems to fly in the face of the facts of modern society and governments, it is now common to depend upon a notion of hypothetical consent.[4] If the hypothetical nature is that I would have consented if I had been asked or if I had been there, then this is something to be established on some of the same grounds on which implicit consent would be established. But in any case, it assumes that consent has not been given and some of the original plausibility of the contract theory as a foundation for legitimacy is lost. It is not something that I have voluntarily accepted. The case is weakened even more if the hypothetical nature is that someone in a particular situation, not I, would have consented to the arrangement. In order not to be countered by a participant's explicit objection, the hypothetical consent must hypothesize a situation that the participant cannot enter and then voice objections. Of course it could be said that the arrangement is one to which I would consent if I were fully rational or a self-interested bargainer, but the point is that by hypothesis I am not and thus by hypothesis I would not necessarily give consent even if I should. Wherever the dispute leads us about the hypothesizer's ideal bargainers, real people are not them. I have to conclude with Dworkin, "A hypothetical contract is not simply a pale form of an actual contract; it is no contract at all." [5]

To make decisions for real people on the basis of what ideal bargainers would do is one way to take the decision away from real people. Government by the people would then have to be kissed goodbye, and there would be little left for a democratic theory. It could still be argued that a particular arrangement is a good arrangement on the basis of promoting the interests of the participants, but, to repeat, it would not be legitimized as their decision. (Similarly, a utilitarian would justify an arrangement on the basis of the promotion of the greatest utility, but not on the basis of the participants' consent.) Of course, it is not enough to show that the participants have benefited from the arrangement in the past, because even in this kind of 'justification' it must be shown that the arrangement will continue to be in the interest of the participants. No doubt the people of Quebec have benefited from the Canadian confederation (although I am not willing to bet that they would not have benefited more from another possible arrangement), but what is sorely lacking is any good case that the present confederation or any confederation with a single sovereign Canadian state will continue to be in the interest of the people of Quebec considering the reasonable alternatives that might be agreed upon. It might just be that if a good case were made, Quebecers would consent to the preferred arrangement.

The point has been that if a social arrangement is to be legitimated by the participants' consent then it is their decision whether or not to continue as participants in the arrangement. It does not even have to be shown that they have been ill-treated or that the present arrangement is or will be against their interest. They may just want to get out. Moreover, they may want to get out even though the other participants would benefit more by their staying in. Someone is not under an obligation to stay merely for someone else's benefit. So if Quebecers want to get out of the present arrangement, even to the point of forming a separate state, then they ought to be allowed to do so without any interference from other people in Canada. At least that seems to be what a contract theory warrants, with a couple of minor conditions to be added.

Although I have already indicated my suspicions about the plausibility of contract theories, I shall briefly continue to assume that a contract theory can provide some legitimacy for confederation. There are still lessons to be learnt. It certainly has to be granted that if there is a contract I cannot just get out at will without doing what I contracted to do. I cannot just ignore my agreement to do something. So to take an example from Gauthier,[6] if we agree to bring in my crops this week and yours next week I cannot try to get out of the deal immediately after my crops are in. I am morally obligated to honour our arrangement, and you are morally permitted to interfere if I do not honour it. I might ask to renegotiate the arrangement immediately after reaping my benefits, and the negotiations might even be carried out on terms that satisfy you. My offense at backing out of the agreement would not be so great if we had agreed to bring in twenty crops each and I backed out after my twentieth and your nineteenth, but I would still agree that there was an offense. The offense would also be diminished if I were to back out of an agreement to bring in two crops each after bringing in only one crop each. If, however, we were returning favors and we had lost count of how many good turns each had done the other, I do not see how it could vitiate a renegotiation or reconsideration of the arrangement.

Rather than making a deal for a particular period of time or a particular number of benefits, we might agree to, accept or acquiesce in a continuing arrangement. We might come to legitimately expect each other's aid, but we cannot legitimately require that aid for the rest of our lives. My commitment might be continuing, but it cannot be perpetual and independent of my will. Human arrangements should allow for a way of changing the provisions, even to the point of getting out. I see no argument for it being morally required that I continue in an arrangement against my will because I have agreed to the arrangement up to now. Commitments for a particular period of time may be different, but I see no reason to believe that Quebecers have made a commitment for a definite period of time nor do I know any who have made a lifetime commitment. Some may think that if it could be argued that the arrangement is no longer mutually beneficial then the party that is not benefiting may renegotiate or get out of the arrangement that has continued to get agreement. But this is only reason to expect renegotiation, while continuing benefits to a party would only explain the lack of interest in renegotiation. The benefits alone do not bind one, and our agreements are not for irreversible lifetime commitments. Certainly you have no right to restrain me just because I have reaped some benefits in the past.

There is one further condition to my renegotiation or getting out of an arrangement that might be mentioned. If we are involved in a mutual effort that, for example, involved your standing on my shoulders to get the loot in the upper shelf, then even if I have agreed to it so far, I can back out, but not when and as I like. I cannot suddenly abandon a project without giving you warning and perhaps also without giving you some compensation or help in finding an adequate alternative. Human arrangements can be changed but not without regard to the temporary necessities that require short term mandatory participation. The people of Quebec should be able to get out but with the minimal conditions that they have fulfilled their share of temporary deals and that they have given sufficient warning. This is a qualification that I would put on Milner's claim that Quebec has an "unassailable right to decide its future when and how it wishes".[7] The moral permissibility of a participant getting out has to be qualified, but it cannot be qualified out of existence.

After all, this seems to be in the spirit of most social contract theory. A contract is not made so that a collective can proceed to ignore the will of the individual. The contract was presumably made to preserve the individual's independence and autonomy even if it is done by establishing a sovereign. The arrangement would certainly be restrictive and the individuals restricted if they are not permitted to determine their future within the arrangement if they support it and are otherwise outside it. Individuals are not protected or respected by taking away their autonomy. The social contract may establish sovereignty but it should not take away autonomy, which should be promoted for its own sake.

I have already suggested that a contract provides no explanation for the establishment of sovereign states. States are not established on the basis of universal individual consent or even continuing acceptance. Groups of people and communities have been conquered and ruled from outside but for those of us who support self rule we seek a government established by and representative of the group itself or the community. It is not for another community to decide the nature of the state in our community. As long as there are states, this is at least a minimal condition on them. It seems to me that social contract theory has failed to explain and to justify the role of communities in establishing the way in which they are governed and administered. It has also failed to see the importance of social behaviour and the formation of communities.[8]

I think there is reason to see a community as a focus of interests and the subject of decisions, but I shall not try to argue here whether or not these are reducible to individual interests and decisions. A community is the kind of group that can decide about its own government and establish a state. I agree with the Task Force that in "a community of the size and character of Quebec society...the clearly expressed will of the population must prevail."[9] The important point is that a distinct society should be permitted to form its own state, and among the relevant factors are "history, language, law, common origins, feelings and politics — which, together with others, have led to the development of a distinct society in modern Quebec."[10] These factors are among the same factors that are used to distinguish nations. I have no serious quarrel with the Task Force's characterization of a nation. According to them,[11]

> A nation is a community of persons bound together by a sense of solidarity and wishing to perpetuate this solidarity through some political means. Contributing to this solidarity are common "objective" factors such as history, territory, race, ethnicity, culture, language, religion and customs and common "subjective" factors such as the consciousness of a distinct identity, an awareness of common interests and a consequent willingness to live together. Because of the existence of such factors, there is a special relationship among members of a nation which enables them to cooperate politically more easily among themselves than with outsiders.

An important addition, in the characterization of a nation, is that the people live in a common territory, which allows the establishment of a state.

It is useful to use Ryerson's terminology of a nation-state and a nation-community,[12] since there is a difference between the nations that join the United Nations or harbour multinational corporations and nations that form binational or multinational states. Nation-states are established and formed while nation-communities evolve and develop. It is nation-communities that account for the duality in Canada that the Task Force discusses. What the Task Force does not say is that Quebec is a nation, which would make the conditions for being a self-determining group even stronger. It appears to be enough for them that there is a distinct society for the will of the people to prevail. I agree, but the conditions for being a nation are even stronger and thus are likely to make the reasons for self-determination even stronger.

A nation-community involves a cohesiveness that develops and fosters feelings of identity through a common language and culture and through living and working together. The resulting community and community feelings are factors in explaining social behaviour. It is such factors that I have accused contract theories of ignoring. Nation-communities are not the only source of fostering legitimate collective behaviour, but they are one source often ignored in both theory and practice. The Task Force itself ignores the nature of nations in Canada when it speaks of the duality that exists in Quebec.[13] This is comparable to confusing nations and neighborhoods. There are nationals, people of a different nationality, but one can be a national without participating in one's original nation-community. Recognizing a nation-community is more than just recognizing folk dances and a different language. It also involves recognizing cohesive interaction and communal cooperation. It is the economic and political participation as well as the cultural participation in a community that provides much of the justification and explanation of social behaviour. It is on this basis that self-determination is reasonable and legitimate. Economic and political factors also allow the participation of other nationals despite the lack of a common culture or even a common language.

There is no reason that each separate nation-community has to have its own separate state to administer its own affairs, but if any community is justified in forming its own state then a nation-community would certainly seem to be one. If Canada is justified in being a nation-state independent of the United States, then the people of Quebec are equally justified in forming an independent nation-state. The people of Quebec form an equally cohesive and viable community to justify their self-determination to the point of forming an independent state. It is not only nation-communities that are justified in forming a nation-state, but they certainly count among the groups of people who are so justified.

It is sometimes feared that the legitimation of self-determination on the part of nation-communities carries with it the threat of chauvinism and discrimination against those who are not members of the nation-community. Apart from the fact that this is so hypocritical whenever it comes from societies that already practice discrimination against a nation, it is also irrelevant to the legitimacy of self-determination. Of course such discrimination against other nationals is wrong, and it should be criticized. Certainly that there might be discrimination is no reason to deny self-determination, and in any case there is no reason to think that an independent Quebec would be as discriminatory as an independent Canada. It is even more peculiar to hear that Quebec should not become independent because of the threat to francophone Albertans. Such a claim is little better than a threat in itself.

I have argued we should recognize a nation of Quebecers and that at least on this basis we should also recognize the legitimacy of their forming an independent nation-state. In other words they have the power of self-determination, which they are justified in exercising. I have so far studiously avoided speaking of a right to self-determination, although I think it is a right the the people of Quebec have. Whether the legitimacy of this self-determination is based on right or some other ground is a larger question than can be dealt with here, except for a few comments. Certainly a right to self-determination cannot be denied by arguing against absolute rights[14] or abstract a priori universal rights.[15] Rights can be restricted, overridded by other rights, compensated and qualified, and they do not have to be absolute or a priori. If the legitimacy of self-determination for Quebecers is based on a right, then that right can be restricted or qualified along the lines that I have argued above. Few who have claimed a right of self-determination for Quebecers would contest this. They can have such a right without it being absolute, although a case will have to be made for any particular restrictions or qualifications.

If the people of Quebec do have a right of self-determination, then I think it is important to recognize that right, particularly when so many are so quick to deny them that right. Some have claimed that to speak of rights is to muddy the waters by using unclear moral concepts and to introduce an unnecessary mood of confrontation.[16] The notion of a right is certainly not clear, but then there are few moral notions that are, and a confrontation is certainly not to be avoided by ignoring any rights of the people of Quebec. If Canadians ignore or disregard their rights, then it is only to be expected that their interests will be ignored or disregarded as well. If there are any moral considerations in the justification of self-determination, then they are considerations that should be argued for and respected. Assuming that self-determination is not based on a right, would there be any less of a confrontation once the moral positions are developed? I would suggest that any confrontation that there is comes from very different sources. In any case, the problem will not be clarified by ignoring the moral issues. If we are to respect the people of Quebec we must also respect their moral interests and rights. It may be that the people of Quebec will not choose independence, but they will have even more reason to do so as long as the legitimacy of their determining their own destiny is denied or faced with threats. On the other hand, it may be that if we respect their right to self-determination we will strengthen their role as an ally in our aspirations and endeavors.

NOTES

1. The Task Force on Canadian Unity, *A Future Together* (Hull: Canadian Government Publishing Centre, 1979), Chapter 8, pp. 113-114.

2. See Reginald Whitaker, "Competition for Power", *Canadian Forum*, Jan.-Feb., 1979, p. 8.
3. *A Future Together*, p. 113.
4. Much of what I say here comes from and is discussed further in L. W. Sumner's "Rawls and the Contract Theory of Civil Disobedience" in *New Essays on Contract Theory* (K. Nielsen and R. A. Shiner, eds.) (*Canadian Journal of Philosophy*, Supp. Vol. III, 1977), esp. pp. 41-48.
5. Ronald Dworkin, "The Original Position" as in Norman Daniels, ed., *Reading Rawls* (New York: Basic Books, 1974), p. 18.
6. From David Gauthier's contribution to this conference.
7. Henry Milner, *Politics in the New Quebec* (Toronto: McClelland & Stewart, 1978), p. 250. This is a small amendment to Milner's interesting and substantive contribution.
8. This is a larger issue than I can pursue here, but there is an interesting discussion of it by Elizabeth Rapaport in "Classical Liberalism and Rawlsian Revisionism" in *New Essays on Contract Theory.*
9. *A Future Together*, p. 113.
10. *Ibid.*, p. 23.
11. *The Task Force on Canadian Unity, Coming to Terms* (Hull: Canadian Government Publishing Centre, 1979), p. 6.
12. See Stanley Ryerson's "Quebec: Concepts of Class and Nation" in Gary Teeple, ed., *Capitalism and the National Question in Canada* (Toronto: Univ. of Toronto Press, 1972), p. 212.
13. See *A Future Together*, p. 31.
14. See David Cameron, *Nationalism, Self-Determination and the Quebec Question* (Macmillan of Canada, 1974), pp. 143-157.
15. See Whitaker, "Competition for Power" , p. 8.
16. See Cameron, *Nationalism, Self-Determination and the Quebec Question*, p. 148 and David Braybrooke's contribution to this conference.

IS CONFEDERATION A FAIR BARGAIN?

Michael McDONALD

Gauthier's strongly affirmative answer to this question might be challenged on two levels. First on the factual level, it can be argued that even within a contractarian framework Canada's record and prospects cannot support the fair bargain conclusion. Second on the philosophical level, doubts can be raised both about the *applicability* of contractarian theory and its *moral soundness*. Now it is these two philosophical issues that will mainly concern me in what follows.

But before beginning, I should say that Gauthier's paper is an admirable response to the challenge laid down by the organisers of the Montreal Conference on Confederation, viz. to have philosophers respond to Canada's crisis as philosophers and not as, say, amateur political economists or constitutionalists. Gauthier's paper shows us how a philosopher can illuminate Canadian problems, and this is something all of us welcome. Gauthier's paper is particularly interesting in that it draws on his extensive previous work on contractarianism. And, indeed, when read in the light of that work, it is clear that even if one rejects his conclusions his arguments must be taken very seriously. Now to my critical comments.

I **Applicability.** Here I want to pick out problems in determining how contractarian theory is to be applied to practical situations and in particular the Canadian situation. What I want to suggest is not just that we can answer the fair bargaining question differently than Gauthier, but more importantly, that contract theory may be such that we cannot ascertain the correct answer.

I will start with some simple questions about determining who is party to the bargain Confederation is supposed to represent. The two main continuing parties or interests are the French and the English. (The Imperial interest becomes with time an interest of the English and, possibly, the French.) Where this leaves third parties — ethnic minorities and, more significantly, native peoples — is unclear; perhaps they are meant to have interests in common with one or both of the francophone and anglophone communities, although such commonalities (in my view) are hard to find in the case of native peoples.

Ignoring these third parties for the moment, there still remain questions about treating the francophone and anglophone *communities* as parties to the social contract. Each of these two main communities is made up of sub-communities and individuals whose interests may themselves conflict. Indeed, as Gauthier observes, there are conflicts within each community along class lines. Now it might be suggested that at best Gauthier has given us a reason for thinking that from a contractarian point of view Confederation provides satisfactory 'elite accommodation' (to use Jack Stevenson's terminology). There is not much in his paper to convince us that those in each community who are not members of the elite gain from Confederation, but then this fits in well with one of the main historic functions of Canadian nationalism, viz. preserving the dominance of our domestic elites. The main question here (as in the case of native peoples) is whether or not there are contractarian characterisations of the francophone and anglophone communities such that the putative fair bargain struck between the French and English communities does not rest on unfair (from a contractarian point of view) internal arrangements in each community. Later I will argue that there is a contractarian answer to this question of internal fairness but it is one that is morally dubious.

The second sort of applicability problem concerns the contractarian content of Confederation. Gauthier argues that Quebec's separating from the rest of Canada would be unfair, and he illustrates this with the following:

> Suppose that you and I agree that this week we shall bring in my crops, and next week I demand to renegotiate — I have what I want from our deal, so either I want out or I want better terms to continue. You will, rightly, insist that I honour our agreement...(p. 197)

The example suggests that if I were to help you take in your crops (in exchange for your previous help taking in mine) then we have each done our part; accordingly, there would seem to be no reason for moral criticism of me if I were to decide that next year I won't help you. If the social contract justifying Confederation is thus dischargable, then presumably at some point Quebec would not violate anyone's rights by opting out or demanding new terms.

But I do not see how a hypothetical contract could be dischargable given that nothing has changed in the relations of the two parties other than a desire not to continue the current arrangement. If, however, the contract is not dischargable and is more like a standing duty (e.g. to tell the truth), then undue prominence and permanence is given the political status quo.

Gauthier's illustration and his analysis of historic factors illuminates an oddness in his application of contractarianism. To make his theory apply to the French now in Quebec he has to suppose that the current benefit the French receive from Confederation is the preservation of their distinctness. Since Gauthier admits that Quebec could go it alone and retain or even enhance its distinctness (which is, after all, what he says would be unfair), then presumably present day Quebecois have a kind of historically based indebtedness for now being a distinct people. Gauthier seems to be saying that they couldn't today be a distinct people unless there were Confederation. Now if I am right about this being a *Crito*-like argument, then the debt in question is a strange one for a contractarian to admit. For the debt is not just for what one *has* (i.e. one's possessions) but for what one *is*, i.e. for the cultural and linguistic components of one's identity. It will be recalled that Locke made much out of the inheritance of wealth as a basis for tacit consent; Locke, however, never went so far as Gauthier does in making the components of one's identity a basis of political obligation. Moreover, I do not see why this argument can't be used to establish a historic indebtedness of the English to the French for preserving English Canada's 'little apartness', in which case the two debts might well cancel each other out.

There is yet another problem in determining what in fact the social contract requires. In real life contracts, other things being equal, it is wrong to try to get out of the contract; to contemplate doing so is to have what I will call 'immoral second thoughts'. Now Gauthier argues in effect that the Pequistes are having immoral second thoughts when they contemplate upsetting Canada's current constitutional arrangements.

But it is not at all clear how to characterise the Pequistes' drive for sovereignty-association: is it a case of 'immoral second thoughts' or instead a case of the 'moral first thoughts of an ideal contractor'? To understand the latter, consider a Rawlsian sort of Original Position. In such a position each contractor must be able to judge any proposed agreement by two standards: (a) whether it is likely to be in his general (if not specific) interests; and (b) whether he and others will as non-ideal, i.e. real, people be able to keep the agreement. These two, (a) desirability and (b) tenability, mark necessary conditions for generating a fair hypothetical contract from the original position. These contractarian judgements about desirability and tenability are to be imagined as being made with a degree of foresight and reflectiveness lacking in real life deliberations. Our best efforts yield, accordingly, somewhat inaccurate approximations to these ideal judgements.

Now it seems to me that a contractarian Pequiste could characterise his demands for a new deal as evidence that questions of (a) desirability and/or (b) tenability must now be negatively answered. Thus, for example, he might say that unlike his clerical and professional predecessors he can see that cultural and linguistic distinctiveness is not possible without political and economic autonomy. Now if our moral standard were simply 'to keep promises made', then we could rightly argue that his predecessor's lack of foresight is morally irrelevant; however, our standard is an ideal contract, so that an ideal contractor would not have put himself or his descendents in a situation which they will find (a) undesirable or (b) untenable. In real life, yesterday's good deal can turn out to be today's or tomorrow's bad deal. In contractarian theory there are no temporally grounded misjudgements, so today's bad deal is no deal at all.

This raises a third problem of applicability: how do we know if Gauthier has found the correct historical base line (or state of nature) in terms of which he judges Confederation a bargain for all parties concerned? He picks what seems at first glance to be the natural time, viz. the period immediately preceeding Confederation 1840-1867. Now it is with reference to this period that Confederation represents an improvement. But can we now apply the contractarian standard to this period, and, perhaps, in the light of a previous period (e.g. pre-Conquest) decide that 1840-1867 involved the violation of a fair bargain (e.g. to share North America between France and England)? Can we build justice on a foundation of injustice?

II **Moral Soundness.** Now I think there is a contractarian answer to this and other questions I have raised concerning applicability, including questions about native peoples and elite accommodation, but it is an answer which I find morally disquieting. To show this, I ask you to consider what constitutes a 'fair' as opposed to an 'unfair' social contract or bargain. A fair bargain must improve the situation of each party to it with respect to *its* situation in the state of nature. As Gauthier's criticism of Rawls made clear, it is essential to realise that while a fair bargain will improve one's situation relative to the state of nature, it will not improve it relative to the other parties involved; relative inequalities are not erased by the social contract, but everyone who is party to the contract is better off in absolute terms than he was before in the state of nature.

Now to this extent Gauthier's description of the three 'parties' involved as three 'interests' is somewhat misleading, for it suggests that an ideally fair bargain involves each party having its best interests met. But no such thing is involved, for each party receives satisfaction according to its power and the ability of other parties to satisfy its interests. Weaker parties — regardless of need, size, intensity of desire and the like — can then perforce expect to get less because they have less to give. Now very weak parties, like the native peoples, can expect very little indeed compared to much stronger parties, like the white immigrants to Canada. Little more is owed them than life and liberty in exchange for political obedience; and this in fact is all Hobbes requires for establishing an obligation of obedience by force of arms ('Sovereignty by Acquisition'). In an unpublished paper, Gauthier makes clear that the little more necessary for extinguishing native rights — thus, satisfying Locke's requirement of 'enough and as good' — is simply access to a Western technology and economy.

Stronger, but still weaker relative to the English majority, bargainers such as the French in North America cannot realistically expect much more than they have in Confederation. This is fair in virtue of their relative weakness compared to the English majority. (And the same, I contend, holds true of the internal arrangements permitting elite dominance in the francophone and anglophone communities.) This, I suppose, also applies within Quebec to the English minority there with regard to education rights and the like. In fact, it seems to follow that if English Canadians did not want to preserve their little apartness from the U.S. (for which a bilingual Canada is to them useful), French Canadians would have little to offer in return for the institutions necessary for the preservation of a French fact in North America. In this case, the only alternatives might be somewhat worse than a 'second Louisiana' or 'second Mexico' — perhaps a second Nicaragua or a second Peru.

Now I find it disquieting to settle moral questions solely in terms of relative, albeit contractarianly 'fair', uses of bargaining power. By comparison, theories which are mainly interest-based, such as utilitarianism, are more morally attractive. But maximisation theories like utilitarianism seem to ignore important distributive questions that a contractarian at least tries to address. May there not be room here for a moral theory that captures the best of both contractarianism and utilitarianism: what I have in mind here is a kind of contractarianism that is interest- rather than power-based (although, of course, power considerations would be relevant in determining what 'could' be done; I am not sure that I am suggesting more than just an alternative, though perhaps more appealing, characterisation of utilitarianism).

In any event, I think this has some bearing on our current crisis. A contractarian approach, like other rights-based approaches, is likely to aggravate rather than alleviate our problems. Each side will produce its own version of a social contract, which version will justify its demands. Thus, the French, as I argued, will claim that they have paid their dues to Canada and can now opt out; the English, as Gauthier argues, will claim that they haven't. And, as I have indicated, it is not at all clear which version is most plausible. What we need here is a moral theory that requires more sympathy to the needs and aspirations of the two founding nations of Canada as well as its diverse regions (and ultimately its people) than does contractarianism, which has as its paradigm, as Maitland observed, 'the greediest of legal categories'.

THE EMPIRE STRUCTURES OF THE CANADIAN STATE

Vincent DI NORCIA

> "A self-governing dependency is a contradiction in terms. If the government of the dominant country substantially govern the dependency, the representative body cannot substantially govern it; and conversely." Sir George Lewis, 1841[1]

Sir George has given us an excellent statement of the imperial philosophy which prevented the British Colonial Secretary of the day from granting responsible government to a rebellious Canada. The rulers of empire well understood the contradiction between empire and democracy (that is, in the dependencies). This conflict, in my view, lies at the heart of Canada's political order, which rests on force and authority rather than on consent and contract.[2] In this essay I wish to show the substantive extent to which Canada's political economy has been defined by a threefold empire structure, political, economic, and cultural. In consequence, I maintain, Canada is not "substantially" a federation, a nation, or a democracy, and is presently undergoing a profound crisis.

Empire, as used here, refers to one society's dominion over another society in a different territory. It is classically expressed in the political rule by the empire society's state over that of the colonized society(ies). But empire typically extends beyond the political realm into economic and cultural forms of dominion.[3] Almost by definition empire involves the territorial expansionism of the empire society and state and a refusal to tolerate any competitors to the unity of its rule. Like any form of dominion, however, empire breeds resistance in forms appropriate to the structures of its rule. Just as empire entails 'alienated government', government by another opposed to a society's collective self, so its opposite is democracy or self-government, in its myriad forms. And democracy has taken many forms in Canada, from hinterland protest and rebellions, to demands for representative government and national or provincial autonomy.

The creation of North America in and through the rivalry of foreign European states, especially Britain and France, offers us a classic expression of the political structures of empire. Almost simultaneously with the British conquest of Quebec, moreover, the United States emerged as a new imperial rival with British North America for the control of the vast transcontinental territories of the northwest. From 1793 to 1903 she pursued her Manifest expansionist Destiny, with Britain repeatedly handing over great sections of territory to America, to the ultimate and immeasurable cost of her northern colonies.

Confederation itself was spurred by the American threat. In 1858 Alexander Galt argued that Canada "should assume the responsibility of occupying that great empire" in the northwest, since "otherwise the Americans would go there first... Half a continent is ours if we do not keep quarrelling among ourselves."[4] The American civil war, its imperial policies and unpunished raids into Canada, all affected the internal political structure of the union of the British North American colonies, as MacDonald himself acknowledged in proposing an almost unitary federal system. For, the Canadian conservatives argued in their meetings with the Maritime governments, only a strong Canadian state could simultaneously withstand the American threat and develop the northwest. Thus a conservative central statism characterised Canada's origin; it served to impose a central Canadian "neo-imperium" over its vast hinterlands.[5]

The Canadian union was imperial in form and content. The process of making the decision to unite was imperial. Coercive pressure for union from the Colonial Office was constant in the Maritimes. The centralised scheme was itself brought from the centre to the governments of the maritime margin in 1864. The actual decision process was a foretaste of the federal-provincial conference: secret discussions among imperial and provincial state regimes on the nature of *their* relations.

Legislatures, opposition parties, and the people themselves were excluded from the process. Democratic sentiment nonetheless found many ways to express its disapproval. In the Maritimes the scheme was repeatedly labelled as "Canadian perfidy". Many worried about the loss of local autonomy. Many French and a few English liberals in the Canadas criticised the scheme for being the work of politicians, not having been demanded by the people, for being unfederal and illiberal in content.[6]

In its substance the scheme indeed represented an imperial centralism rather than a voluntary pact to create a decentralised federation. The former relation between London and the colonies is internally replicated in that between the central government, Ottawa, and the provinces. The division of powers itself is not unlike the former division of jurisdiction between London and each colonial government. All the great powers of state and all residual powers, moreover, were allotted to the central state. To it in addition was given the old imperial mandate to "make laws for the peace, order and good government of Canada" (BNA 91). All executive authority is invested in the Crown, not the people. The provincial executives and legislatures are moreover subordinate to the central, which can unconditionally disallow any act of a provincial government. The central state alone appoints the Supreme Court, Senators, and the provincial Lieutenant Governors. In fine, as J.R. Mallory observes, "the principle of absolute central control governs the Canadian Constitution".[7] These are not dead letters, moreover, for Ottawa's repeated intrusions into provincial jurisdiction have increased since the forties, not lessened. And constitutional discussions have yet to seriously broach the matter of the division of powers. The result is paradoxical, an imperial federalism. Like all empires it has an imperial ideology of its own, that of a powerful, centralised Canadian nation state.

This state centralism has bred democratic political responses, from the 1837 rebellion for responsible government to the 1887 conference, convened by Ontario, to protest the central state's disallowance powers. A motion to secede from the union was passed by the Nova Scotia legislature in 1886, and tabled in Quebec's in 1917. And, of course, the last twenty-five years have seen the rise of provincial demands for autonomy.

Imperial economic structures have defined Canada from the beginning, when its territory was the battleground of European states seeking control first of the cod fishery, then of the fur trade. The imperially chartered monopoly trading companies, like the Hudson's Bay, were themselves almost private governments. The trade's penetration of the interior ultimately destroyed the native economies, making them dependent on the European. British merchants later took over the burgeoning economy of Quebec.[8]

The weak economic infrastructure of colonial British North America, followed by America's unilateral termination of free trade in 1864, were major economic causes of the union of 1867. That union represented, in Creighton's phrase, the victory of the commercial empire of the St. Lawrence, which "has inspired generations of Canadians to build a great territorial empire, both commercial and political, in the western interior of the continent. The prime feature of this imperial drive is western expansion... The West, it was believed, would make Canada a nation, and the east-west axis would be its backbone".[9]

The post-confederation era saw the rise of a pan-Canadian economic nationalism, led by the state. But American corporations ultimately jumped the border and established branch plants within Canada. More recently their multinational corporations have acquired so extensive a control of major sectors of our economy that it has itself become an economic dependency. The American empire has beaten its old northern rival.

State and economic centralism have been the classic remedies suggested for the problem of foreign economic domination, first by conservatives and then, from the twenties forward, by socialists. However that centralism has succeeded internally in creating an internal economic empire of the central Canadian metropolis over its eastern, northern, and western hinterlands.[10] The rise of economic nationalism in the provinces, such as Ontario in the 1900's, the west in the thirties, and Quebec and Alberta more recently, is a direct anti-imperial response to this centralism. It is another expression of the empire/democracy dialectic.

Finally, the empire structure of Canada has a cultural form. This is implicit in the fact that empire is constituted by one *society's* dominion over another *society*. Political and economic structures are means whereby that dominion is secured. Culture is not an institution but a deep collective structure which determines the whole of social life. To the extent that the cultures of the empire and colony societies are different, such differences contribute both to the empire's rule and, through nationalism, to the colony's resistance to empire.

Canada began in some European societies' conquest of the north America, which was the habitat of many indigenous tribal societies profoundly different from Britain or France. European economic exploitativeness, statism, arrogance, missionary Christianity, and military force all combined to create here what George Manuel has termed "the fourth world situation".[11] In it the natives of a territory are robbed by foreign invaders of their own rights and powers to control their lives, maintain their own languages and cultures. They become strangers in their own lands. European societies, for example, imposed the state form of government with its precise territorial limits, in indifference to the actual and more variable habitats of nomadic peoples. Innis' work on the fur trade shows clearly how it was based on European penetration and control of the interior and the resultant destruction of native cultures.

Canada itself was created as a European state in and through the struggles of British and French, not by its native cultures. The ultimate victory of Britain over France created British North America. It was built on the double cultural dominion of European over native and British over French societies. Its primary result has been the natural French response of seeking to maintain its culture and developing various forms of nationalism to this end. This cultural-imperial relationship has persisted down to this day. It has meant that Canada itself can never culturally be one nation. Indeed even to hold this view is to promote a culturally assimilatory ideology, Canadianism.[12]

The Confederation scheme recognized this unresolved problem explicitly in granting special powers to Quebec as a French province, with its own state, however colonial, and protecting the English minority within Quebec. The assimilation intent of the English, visible since the 1830's, and reinforced by Durham, was confirmed in a series of violations of French rights from the northwest rebellions, Manitoban and Ontarian unilingualism, to the 1917 conscription law. The *canadien* response to these violations of the federal *entente* was swift: a conservative religious nationalism movement promoting Quebec as the only homeland of the *canadiens* grew rapidly. Quebec was to be their nation state, the government which alone would protect their culture and nation and their economy, as Quebec liberals argued in the 1900's. From the election of Honoré Mercier in 1886 after Riel's execution, to Duplessis' demands that the provincial jurisdiction be respected, to the Quiet Revolution, and finally to the PQ's independentism there is a continuous line. Federalism, it holds, is based on a pact between English and French. The English have violated that pact and reasserted their traditional assimilatory intent, the central expression of their cultural empire. Bilingualism is too little too late. Since Quebec alone is the government which can be trusted to protect the French Canadian nation, Quebec's powers must be increased. Since Quebec's existence is based on a pact or *entente*, and since it is a national state, it has the right to determine its own form of government if that nation is threatened.[13]

In the last twenty-five years two other levels of cultural empire have emerged in Canadian politics: the American threat to Canada's continued existence as a distinctive society (which it is), and the resurgence of the forgotten cultures of our indigenous tribes. The latter issue has come to a head in the recent surge of Indian demands for recognition of their treaty rights, land claims, sovereignty where no treaty was ever signed, and national status in the North. The Berger report has recognized the justice of many of their claims and, in principle, their right to self-determination. Again, empire in the realm of culture has bred a democratic counter-response, nationalism.

Few Canadians need to be told of the American threat to Canada's existence as a distinctive society. It meets them everywhere: in the mass media, radio, TV, print, in the products they use, and more disturbingly in the quiet takeover of most sectors of our economy by American multinational corporations. The degree of American control and penetration of our society is astounding. That it involves the cultural form of empire is apparent in our literally collective ignorance of ourselves, continued distortion of our own society by interpreting it in terms of alien symbols and mythologies from the Presidency to free enterprise, and in a sense of inferiority so deep that to be pro-Canadian is often termed as irrational because anti-American. That one could give rational grounds for opposing American policies, practices, and culture — and Canadians repeatedly have argued their case — is assumed to be beyond question.

That an imperial federalism exists in Canada is apparent in the strength of the national unity ideology, in the increasing treatment of ethnic immigrant minorities as if they were equivalent in numbers and importance to the French, and in the growth of independentism in Quebec and nationalism in Alberta. I conclude that Canada is not a nation, nor a federation, nor a democracy in the substantive sense of these terms.

In corollary, I suggest, only democratic mechanisms can resolve our problem, such as a constitutional convention and referendum. Three major options confront us: greater economic centralism (to meet the American threat), a bi-centralist association of Quebec and Canada, and a truly federal, democratically decentralised Canada based on the free federal union of its component regional and cultural collectivities. This is proposed in the spirit of the federalist visions of Durham in 1840, Dorion in 1865, of theorists as disparate as George Woodcock and Fernand Dumont, of the cooperative ideals of Quebec, Nova Scotia, and Saskatchewan, and of the federal principles enunciated in Quebec's 1954 *Tremblay Report*, according to which federalism "stems from social life as it exists and admits it in all its variety and complexity. Its purpose is not to enslave but to co-ordinate, to conserve for social life its freedom and vitality... Because it rests entirely on the principle of association, and because it sees society as a vast network of associations, it can only oppose any single dictatorship, even that of the state".[14]

NOTES

1. S. Ryerson, *Unequal Union* (Toronto, 1968), p. 139. See also W.L.M. Kennedy, *The Constitution of Canada* (Oxford, 1922), pp. 5f, 117f, 150, 162f, 215, 230f, 234.

2. Three points on contract theory. First, Canada's constitution is based on the authority of the crown and the sovereignty of parliament and the Crown, but not of the people. In no way does it express a contract. Second, if the 1867 union is termed a contract, then it was a very imperial and statist one indeed; such an interpretation would cast doubt on the democratic value of contract theory. Third, with Hume and in the precise fashion of contract theorists themselves, I maintain that contract means what it seems to mean: a mutually binding voluntary pact, listing specific mutually known and agreed-to conditions and modes of amending or renegotiating the contract. Accordingly, no social contract seems to exist anywhere. If one did, unilateral violations would void it. Moreover it could not bind any party to anything unethical. Rather, one must revert to substantive ethical norms of democracy, justice, freedom, equality, mutual aid, participation, etc. to assess the ethically binding force of any contract. Thus no contract could bind to *Leviathan.* Moreover, contracts are but *one* mechanism for constituting a democratic regime. Social contracts, I conclude, are neither a sufficient nor a necessary condition of either democratic or legitimate government.

   Contract theory, then, seems to serve three purposes: (1) of retroactively legitimating unworthy regimes, like Canada's, (2) of a scientific ideal type for studying forms of government, or (3) the ethical purpose of evaluating the degree of democracy and ethical soundness of any political system. This last is the kernel of truth in the theory, in my view, especially as applied to ourselves.

3. On these themes see: G. Lichtheim, *Imperialism* (New York, 1971); G. Balandier, *Political Anthropology* (New York, 1970) and Harold Innis, *Empire and Communications* (Toronto, 1972).

4. In Kennedy, p. 284-5; see also Galt's, MacDonald's and McGee's speeches in *The Confederation Debates in the Province of Canada 1865* (Toronto, 1963). On U.S. expansionism see J. Morchain, *Sharing a Continent* (Toronto, 1973).

5. Thomas Hockin, *Government in Canada* (Toronto, 1976), p.70; see Whitaker's essay in L. Panitch, ed. *The Canadian State* (Toronto, 1977).

6. See P.B. Waite, *The Life and Times of Confederation* (Toronto, 1962); Dorion's speech in *The Confederation Debates; Lord Durham's Report* (Toronto, 1973), pp. 105-24; and C. Howell's essay in D. Bercuson, ed., *Canada and the Burden of Unity* (Toronto, 1977).

7. In his *Social Credit and the Federal Power in Canada* (Toronto, 1977), p. 8; cf. also Kennedy, pp. 166-181, chs. XVIII, XIX.; and E. Black, *Divided Loyalties* (Montreal, 1975), ch. 2.

8. See the "Conclusion" of Harold Innis' *The Fur Trade in Canada* (Toronto, 1975); and ch. 1 of G.F.G. Stanley's *Short Constitutional History of Canada* (Toronto, 1969).

9. In *Towards the Discovery of Canada* (Toronto, 1972), p. 60-61 and parts II and IV; also *The Empire of the St. Lawrence* (Toronto, 1956); see also the CCF's statement, *Social Planning for Canada* (Toronto, 1975), ch. XXI; and F.R. Scott's essays on centralism in his *Essays on the Constitution* (Toronto, 1977).

10. See W.L. Morton and J.M.S. Careless's essays in C. Berger, ed., *The Approaches to Canadian History* (Toronto, 1967); and chs. 2, 10, and 11 of Berger's *The Writing of Canadian History* (Toronto, 1976); also A.R. Davis's essay in R. Ossenberg, ed., *Canadian Society, Pluralism, Change, and Conflict* (Scarborough, 1971): and Bercuson's "Introduction".

11. In *The Fourth World,* (Galt, 1974), pp. 214f, 192; see also Judge Thos. Berger, *Northern Frontier, Northern Homeland,* vol. I (Ottawa, 1977), and J.S. Frideres, *Canada's Indians: Contemporary Conflicts* (Scarborough, 1974), chs. 5-8.

12. See M. Brunet, *Canadians et canadiens* (Ottawa, 1954), pp. 17-32; and his *La présence anglaise et les canadiens* (Montreal, 1968), pp. 167-90.

13. See Black, chs 4-7; C. Morin, *Quebec vs. Ottawa* (Toronto, 1976); P.E. Trudeau, *Federalism and the French Canadians* (Toronto, 1968), pp. 32, 162; M. Rioux, *Quebec in Question* (Toronto, 1977); on Alberta see Pratt's essay in Panitch; on Ontario see H.V. Nelles, *The Politics of Development* (Toronto, 1974); and Hockin, ch.2 on the provinces.

14. (Toronto, 1973), pp. 90-91; see also G. Woodcock, "A Plea for the Anti-Nation" , *Can. Forum,* (April, 1972); F. Dumont, *A Vigil for Quebec* (Toronto, 1976), pp. 59-63; and L. Dion, *The Unfinished Revolution* (Montreal, 1976), pp. 2, 199.

CONFEDERATION AND THE IDEA OF SOVEREIGNTY

Leslie ARMOUR

The justification of any proposed structure of government depends upon the location of a source of legitimate authority. It thus becomes the problem of sovereignty. That problem is, I shall argue, tractable or intractable depending upon the questions which give rise to it and I shall try to use the Canadian experience in searching for the right questions.

It is common in our time and has been since the enlightenment to say that the crucial questions are: how does one man or group of men come to have the right (or the justified power) to make decisions for others? and how are limitations rightly established when such decision-makers confront one another in situations such as that of a United Nations meeting or within a political federation?

I shall suggest that these questions are mistaken, misleading and simplistic. The questions are individualistic in assumption and in form and, if they are allowed to stand, the issue becomes one about the justification which one man has for compelling the behaviour of another. On the strictest reading, any possible answer would deny or threaten moral autonomy. At best, one might respond that such a right could come about only through agreement. But even that would threaten moral autonomy since it at most allows one to be autonomous only when one makes the agreement or at intervals when the agreement may be reconsidered. Any political order must be stable through some span of time and, in the case of the most basic features of that order, that span will have to be fairly long. Agreement cannot account for those who have morally acceptable reasons for changing their minds at shorter intervals.

Threats to the moral autonomy of rational agents are, evidently, objectionable. The strongest case one could logically make for compelling the behaviour of another would be that one had a moral theory which was demonstrably complete and true, and that that theory necessitated an action resisted by the agent who was to be compelled. But such a theory, if rationally demonstrable, must be demonstrable to any rational agent. One's case would have to be that the agent to whom it was not demonstrable was not rational. But if he were not rational he would not have the duties of rational agents which the theory prescribes. Alternatively, one could argue that someone must decide which potential acts were instances of wrong acts and which were instances of permissible acts. If the theory were really complete and demonstrable, any rational agent should be able to make the determination. Failure to allow someone to make a given decision would be an inhibition upon a right act.

That is essentially the case for individualist anarchism. (Canadians are familiar with another sort of anarchism, communitarian anarchism. I shall refer later to this theory which is, I think, held by people like George Woodcock.)

One might be persuaded to waive the strictest reading on the ground that men must be content to make decisions at intervals or give up living in groups. We could then accept decision by mutual consent. If we accept that, it looks at first glance as if the system can be quickly expanded to allow for something like a legitimate modern state. For we can add second-order agreements. If agreements are acceptable, then agreements to make agreements can function at a more distant level. The political arrangement can be that some men have power to decide, on condition that they constantly do their utmost to seek agreements, and act in a provisional way when they fail. If everyone agrees to this, one has a kind of social contract which makes a real but minimal inroad into moral autonomy. (This, indeed, was Mackenzie King's theory of government.)

It is not so evident, however, that such a notion can be extended to the idea of a federal state and this may cause one to doubt the whole arrangement. There are two different notions about divisions of power in a federal system: according to one, each of the component political entities has a specified set of powers and has these powers absolutely, so that, though provincial and federal government have different powers, they are equals. According to the second view, different component entities have different powers, but one or more of the components have general supervisory powers. In fact, in every such system, there will be some (often judicial) supervisory authority which decides how powers are to be determined and what happens in cases of conflict.

On the individualist view, however, the *ultimate* supervisory power will rest with the individuals within the system. And this leads to two insoluble problems. The first is that it appears that no decisions can be made by one of the component groups without some interference with the moral autonomy of the others. For a decision by one group, say, to secede from the union changes the relations — rights, duties, and responsibilities — of the others. The moral decisions which are open to the members change with the range of things about which agreement is to be reached or put in question. The second problem is that one must, in any case, ask in such a situation how assents are to be assembled.

First of all, who is to decide, say, if Quebec has a right to leave? Everyone in Canada? Those who reside in Quebec? Those who reside in Quebec together with those who were born there and would have a right of return even if Quebec were independent? The question is not more easily settled if one takes one view or the other about whether the arrangement is one between equals or is hierarchical. If only Albertans are to decide the future of Alberta, everyone may have his life changed without his consent, while, if all of us may decide about Alberta, Albertans may be subjected to a regime to which they do not assent.

If one takes into account actual cultural diversity, the situation grows considerably more complex. One has two cultures if one has two identifiable groups the members of each of which customarily (and without deliberate reflection) attach different meanings to a significant range of human acts. If one has two or several cultures assents may not be equivalent, for the same assertion may describe two or more different acts. (If this is so, we cannot expect that, if everyone in Canada is allowed to decide whether Quebec should remain in confederation, these decisions can be amalgamated and we cannot, equally, suppose Quebeckers can decide. For the cultures run across the lines of any possible political boundary.)

It is reasonable to suppose that there are at least two cultures in Canada and that assents to political questions are apt to have different meanings in the two cultures. One can well exaggerate the "two solitudes" thesis but there is little doubt that, historically, there has been a different weight given to the political, economic and cultural components of political organizations and, even more evidently, that a different sense of relative identity prevails in the two cultures so that assent to its breakup will mean one thing in one culture and another in the other.

But to talk in this way is to begin to raise the question of the relation of the individual to the community. The argument against assembling intents becomes very puzzling.

Under what conditions in fact do two assents have the same meaning? It is tempting to say that they do so when there are two agents, each of whom is adequately rational and both of whom face the same proposition. But the question is really: under what conditions does either of them know whether or not he faces the same proposition as the other? The answer is, I suppose, that that knowledge is possible if and only if they both belong to the same community of meaning and know that they do. Language is important in these matters because it forms part of the base of the community of meaning though, in reality, it is only one factor and can sometimes be a minor one. But it is one of the devices which make individuation possible.

The important issue arises from the fact that social individuation admits of degree, that it depends to a large extent upon the joint ability to share in the common pool of experience and to distinguish oneself within it. In a society which provides only the bare means of survival and which does so under conditions which are onerous, the range of individual experiences might be relatively small if for no better reason than that most of the time of most people must be devoted to survival and most people must devote themselves to the same tasks. But the mere fact of the existence of language — a possession which no organized group of men lacks — permits anyone to share a significant part of the experiences of anyone else and anything we do to enlarge on that base is probably — in relation to that gain — relatively trivial. Notice, however, that, since men do not differ much in genetic structure or sheer physiological capacity, the differentiation of experience which makes possible genuine individuality is a social matter. One is individuated within a community and one's assents and dissents have their meaning in relation to that community. One knows that one belongs exactly because one's assents and dissents bring about the anticipated responses, because they are the kinds of responses for which, evidently, the rules were intended.

This suggests that, on one level, individuals are related to one another within a community and, on another, that communities are related to one another so that the question between communities is one of the assent or dissent of the community and not that of individuals. Such communities are not necessarily political entities. They are necessarily cultures — systems within which common meanings are given to identifiable human acts — but beyond that almost any structure is possible. This makes it tempting to suppose that the relation must be between the two (or more) *cultures* in the sense of communities of meaning. This is no doubt partly true but needs to be treated with caution.

The notion that the crucial relations are those between cultures draws strength from the fact that a feature of the Canadian problem is that those who belong to a culture which forms a numerical minority in a given place are, on some questions, disenfranchised. Representation is determined by counting individuals within a geographical area. French speakers in British Columbia, for instance, cannot really be said to have a "voice" in the question of what language should be the language of official business there.

But to say this without qualification is to slip into the curious error of supposing that two cultures can have nothing in common or that everyone or nearly everyone belongs univocally to one culture. Neither proposition is true. Three large groups influential in the formation of Canada — the French, the highland Scots, and the United Empire Loyalists — formed cultures which either rejected or were not greatly influenced by the more exaggerated forms of enlightenment individualism. Thus our history has been marked by a communitarian bias and by a certain clannishness. This gives rise to a common culture which influences institutions such as public broadcasting, transportation, and health services. It seems inevitable, for instance, that an independent Quebec would have many institutions which remained recognizably and uniquely Canadian. The form though not the specific content of them is generally agreed upon by English and French Canadians. Equally, however, Canadians have been influenced by patterns of industrialization and tastes in consumer goods which are North American. There is enough commonality to assemble decisions and, inevitably, enough misunderstandings of rival cultural forces to create tension.

Within Canada, it should be evident that communities play a part in making assent intelligible. One cannot assemble individual assents because of the problem of different meanings. But the individual assents, on this thesis, come to have their meanings within the communities. Can one then assemble the assents of the communities?

If we see that there are many strata of the communities of meaning, and realize that many human activities — the contemplative activities of science, philosophy and literary criticism along with the practical concerns of technology, religion, and commerce — tend to create communities which are more general and sometimes tend toward universality, then we may be able to see possible answers.

The answer is "yes" we *can* assemble assents of communities if it is true that there are levels on which there exists a common community and if the system of stratification of governments can be made to match the distinctions of culture and to provide for the necessary spheres of communal autonomy.

The justification of sovereignty depends upon the assembly of the assents of those communities which define the meanings of the assents of the individuals who compose them. Insofar as we share common meanings, we have a community whose protection is necessary to the protection of our own individuality. This justifies the claim to a right of common action. If my community is dissolved, I enter a community within which new meanings may be assigned to my acts, and my identity may change.

But one must not suppose that this reconceptualization somehow legitimizes the surrender of the individual's moral autonomy to the community. It may provide a route to the justification of sovereignty, but it cannot evade the moral point which emerges clearly when the questions are posed in an individualist way. I have suggested that the individual's duty to the community derives from the fact that he is individuated only by and through that community and so would not possess the conditions for individuality without it. Its protection is therefore a necessary condition for a situation within which the questions of individual right can be raised.

But this does not wholly answer the objection. True, it is logically possible that morality is only possible against the background of a situation itself immoral — a community which sustains itself by violating the conditions of moral autonomy. But I find this implausible. It suggests what I think is not finally possible, a separation of the individual and the community. The better conclusion, I think, is that what is demanded as an ideal is a kind of communitarian anarchism.

The communitarian anarchist suggests that an ideal community would assign meanings to acts and assemble common meanings so that there could be no need for a state. Anything less is to be judged a measure of moral failure for it invokes the name of the community which does not really exist. The community which would justify sovereignty would be the community in which the component members were ultimately completely individuated and aware of their individuality in its social context and of their dependence upon it. In order to be so individuated and to be aware of their social situation in that way they would have to have a degree of rationality which would seem to make coercion unnecessary.

But of course that condition does not apply in any society we presently know. How, then, is the state to be justified? Just as we might agree to work through as much agreement as we can muster, so we might properly accept the proposition that existing organizations are to be replaced only when it is clear that there is another possibility more likely to lead to the ultimate ideal community and that existing communities are to be developed and not obliterated. It is clear, that is, that we may work within communities to reach levels of understanding which transcend their peculiarities but also that these higher levels are only attainable so long as a community exists. Its justification is thus provisional and relative to the prospects of its own transcendence.

The Canadian case is instructive. Evidently, it does provide a framework within which individual communities have been preserved and have provided opportunities for forms of human community which go beyond their particularities. In a sense it is a set of arrangements which might in principle be universalized. But it also has had its darker side. In creating allegiances which have gone beyond the particularities of the original founding communities it has also put those communities in peril in a way which threatens the whole purpose. If for example a francophone finds his language and culture in peril he also stands in danger of losing the very base from which he seeks to participate in the larger communities. But since it is the duality of cultures, in part, which opens to all Canadians the possibility of a larger, more human community, the threat of secession by one of the founding communities also imperils the prospects of the other.

These notions can be given more concrete intelligibility if they are put in the form of actual proposals for the organization of the community as it now exists.

Suppose that:

1. We define levels of government so as to provide services for culturally homogeneous groups and to give adequate powers to existing governments. The government of Quebec might be given the power and resources to provide certain kinds of services for francophones everywhere in Canada. Groups, such as Doukhobors, might be given a limited range of powers and revenues to provide special services;

2. We assign some property permanently to groups rather than individuals or governments. Royalty payments for clean air, sunlight, rainfall and other common resources might be vested in perpetuity in ethnic and cultural groups with rules prohibiting their reassignment to individuals;

3. We rigorously protect individual rights. When legal status is given to ethnic or cultural groups, the right of individuals to affiliate themselves with groups of their choice must be secured. (At present, a citizen may, in several provinces, declare himself a public or separate school supporter and this principle will have to be clarified and extended.);
4. We restructure the political order so some representation is by place, and some by culture (allowing francophones and others a united voice).

In these ways, we might move toward the provisional justification of sovereignty. We would, that is, have preserved the processes of community transcendence while protecting the structures of existing communities and providing additional protection for whatever degree of individuality we have been able to achieve.

We must accept, however, that the justification is *provisional.* And this seems to evade the question which springs to mind. Do we have the right to protect the system by force if we have clearly established a justified sovereign state?

On the theory I have been using, I think nothing justifies the use of violence to facilitate a political decision. This follows from the fact that the justification derives from the continuity of agreement, whether of communities or by individuals. A political decision I take to be one which is proper within the context of a given constitution, but not morally necessary. If one accepts this, the question becomes complicated. If a separation can be effected in a way which allows the individuals to be maintained as the same individuals and the communities to be retained intact, no issue arises. For there is no moral wrong of the sort for which communities are responsible.

But if the severance threatens the personal identities of the participants, they have no choice but to use whatever minimum force is necessary to repel the threat. To be forced to stay in a union which poses the same threat entails the same right — the right to whatever force is needed to sustain what is then a justified revolt. But to say this is merely to underline the fact that separation must take place, if at all, through understanding, not to say that it cannot take place. Failure to reach such an understanding would itself be immoral since it would lead to the use of force as a substitute for agreement. Surely if we can understand what is at issue, we can avoid that.

LIBERALISM, NATIONALISM AND COMMUNITY

William MATHIE

The issue of national unity generated or manifested by the election of the Parti Quebecois is whether those of us related to one another under the British North America Act as fellow citizens should continue so. What is it that constitutes a political community, or connects its members to one another by mutual claims and duties distinct from those claims and duties men have to other men as merely human? Ancient political science seems to suggest that this question might best be resolved "politically" through the community's acceptance of an autochtonous account of its origin.[1] To the extent that it was compelled, or wished, to search out an account of the unity or identity of the political community apart from the myth of autochtony, ancient political science looked to the end or purpose of each community as expressed in its common pursuit of some particular way of life.[2] The crisis of Confederation takes place within a politics and political understanding which rejects both the account of politics as guided towards some comprehensive and common human good and the necessity of the mythic account of an autochtonous origin;[3] the crisis occurs within and tests the account of community furnished by liberal contractualism.[4]

Liberal contractualism teaches us that state and government must be founded on the consent of individuals understood as equal and independent by nature, and they are established for the securing of the liberty or rights of those individuals.[5] To arrive at a true account of the proper aims and nature of government we must look to "the state of nature"; we find there dissociated individuals pursuing their own essentially private interests. Liberal contractualism proceeds from the denial that man is by nature a political being — the state must rather be understood to furnish conditions within which essentially individual goods are pursued.[6] It would seem that the individual of liberal contractualism would be by nature no more the member of a nation than a political being, that liberal contractualism must be at best indifferent to the claims of nationalism understood as the opinion that good politics has as its necessary, or even sufficient condition, the coincidence of state and nation.[7] Indeed, liberalism continues frequently to deplore the existence of nationalism as a "retrograde concept", an obstacle to the progress of mankind towards ever wider communal loyalities.[8] Yet the relation between liberal contractualism and nationalism is not one of simple hostility. Nationalism has followed liberalism into the world and has seemed, even to one of its most persistent and articulate critics, to remedy, at least provisionally, a defect of the contractualist account of community.[9] If liberal contractualism dissociated men so as to affirm their natural freedom and equality as independent sources of a binding consent to political authority, nationalism furnished "a new glue" that would bind men together on a durable basis. Liberal contractualism supposed that rationally calculated self-interest proceeding above all from the passionate desire for self-preservation might provide, or take the place of, dedication to the common good. The emergence and vigour of nationalism makes that supposition doubtful. If dedication to the common good cannot be dispensed with, or supplied through the rational calculation of individuals pursuing their own interests, nationalism may not be regarded as a mere remnant of a pre-liberal tradition that may finally be overcome by the progress of liberalism.

Liberal contractualism must then war with nationalism as the latter denies the moral primacy of individual rights and liberty while continuing to rely upon it as a source of commitment to the common good. Further, there is even a sense in which contractual liberalism can barely express a coherent objection in principle to the nationalist claim. Thus the priority and fundamental importance of consent within liberalism must justify the principle of nationalities so long as "the sentiment of nationality exists in any force" ; even J.S. Mill held there to be "a *prima facie* case for uniting all the members of nationality under the same government, and a government to themselves apart" whenever this was so.[10] Nationalism and liberalism agree that politics and government serve something prepolitical or nonpolitical in character while disagreeing as to whether this nonpolitical end of politics is to be found in the rationally conceived interests of individuals or the consciousness by members of groups of linguistic or cultural similarities they share. If liberal politics is, like reason, a hand-maiden of the passions, the liberal objection to nationalism loses much of its force. This difficulty is illustrated by Lord Acton's "anti-nationalist" remark, much admired by contemporary foes of nationalism, that "a state which is incompetent to satisfy different races condemns itself"; what is to be noted here is that the satisfaction of races remains at least implicitly a purpose of politics.[11]

If contractual liberalism needs, or cannot refute, nationalism, might Canadian unity be preserved through a reconciliation of these two accounts of community? The suggestion that Canadian unity might be established through an entrenched bill of rights which treats language as an individual right seems to attempt one form of this reconciliation.[12] Can language rights be understood to belong to the rights of the individual as ordinarily understood? Certainly, an affirmation of rights like these which require governmental action and expenditure for their realization should not be confused with a constitutional declaration of such rights as require for their protection only that governments *not* act. If the problem here may be reduced by distinguishing the linguistic from the cultural concerns of nationalists and interpreting the former as narrowly as possible it should still be noted that the more restrictive the interpretation of these rights the less likely is national unity to be obtained by their guarantee. It is at least doubtful whether a genuine synthesis of liberalism and nationalism is possible through the reinterpretation of those kinds of similarity that are the bonds of nationality as the rights of individuals, or citizens of a polyethnic state.

We have accepted here the argument of a leading Canadian opponent of nationalism that nationalism may be seen to furnish bonds of community not supplied by liberal contractualism. We have also noted the great difficulty for liberal contractualism as a politics of consent in stating coherently its critique of nationalism; if politics exists only to serve the subjective preferences or expressions of will of the governed, one can do little more than regret the fact that the governed choose to express a will located in their linguistic or cultural identity rather than their real or economic interests. It was perhaps a reasonable if brutal view that supposed the complete success of liberal contractualism in Canada would require the destruction of these identities.

In order to move beyond the present impasse it may be necessary to view the claim of nationalism within a perspective wider than that of liberal contractualism. Nationalism correctly recognizes the need for a bond among men that can summon commitment to the common good but fails itself to provide a coherent account of community. Nationalism, at least as it approaches the claim that it is a sufficient condition of a good political order that state and nation coincide, sees the community as political only to the extent that politics might be used to preserve or strengthen the (linguistic, ethnic, or cultural) basis of the community. Apart from the difficulties and dangers that may surround the effort to secure a coincidence of nation and state, the reasonableness of the nationalist belief may be questioned because it would seem to attach much greater weight to the demand that a particular group be ruled together than to the question of how that group is to be ruled or to the ends to be accomplished through that rule.

Within a perspective that locates the purpose of the political community in the common pursuit of some shared account of human happiness or excellence, the partial truth and partial falsehood of nationalism begin to emerge. If, as seems likely, this kind of pursuit is possible within a community of limited, or human, dimensions, nationalism may be justified as the effort to obtain and preserve the necessary conditions of such a policy. Indeed, as nationalism sometimes intends the preservation not only of nonpolitical similarities of race or language but also of an existing way of life it may perhaps see itself and be seen in just this way. Nationalism ceases to be justified, on the other hand, when it equates the necessary and sufficient conditions of such a politics. Proceeding to this equation nationalism identifies the good with what is one's own; we recognize the partial truth of nationalism and the limits of this truth as we consider the extent to which our love of what is our own enters into our very learning of the (political) good.[14]

If nationalism could be partly true and justified as the effort to secure the necessary conditions of a political order directed to a common good outside the terms of liberal contractualism, the question for us becomes whether such a pursuit is possible within the arrangements of federalism. Federalism was once seen by a great critic of liberal contractualism as a way of combining "the external power of a great people with ... the good order of a small state" ; more recently the Tremblay Report saw federalism as a principle that puts "man's moral forces and spiritual values to work, through a social and political education effected in and by the communities which surround ... man, and primarily in and by those which touch him most closely, which are made to his size ...." [15] Yet even if the partial truth of nationalism might be expressed within some kind of federal organization this is not to say that it can be so expressed within our present understanding and practice of federalism. For us, for the framers of Confederation, and for the architects of the American constitution who fashioned the modern account of federalism, federalism has not been a framework within which the partial truth of nationalism might become the basis for a more adequate political community so much as a half-hearted concession to local interests which, it was hoped, would eventually be dissolved in the progress towards a wider human community.[16] In the Canadian case it remains uncertain whether this expectation was justified.

NOTES

1. Plato *Republic* 414C-D, Aristotle *Politics* 1275b25; see also J-J. Rousseau, "A la Republique de Genève", *Discours sur l'origine de l'inégalité parmi les hommes* (Classiques Garnier) pp. 26-27.
2. Aristotle *Politics* 1276b1-15.
3. Hobbes *Leviathan* 1.11, Locke, *Essay* II.XXI.56, John Rawls, *A Theory of Justice* (Cambridge: Harvard, 1971) II.15, pp. 93-94.
4. I do not assume the equivalence of liberalism and contractualism but do suppose that the liberal account of community is furnished by contractualism, e.g., it seems to be dubious whether utilitarianism has any (alternative) account of political unity.
5. Locke *Second Treatise* 2.4; *Declaration of Independence.*
6. Hobbes, *De Cive* 1.1.2.
7. This definition of nationalism is given by Anne Cohler, *Rousseau and Nationalism* (NY: Basic Books, 1970) p. 4.
8. P.E. Trudeau, *Federalism and the French Canadians* (Toronto: Macmillan, 1968), p. 4. For a more thorough treatment of Trudeau's analysis and policies as of other issues in this paper see my "Political Community and the Canadian Experience", *Canadian Journal of Political Science* (March 1979).
9. Trudeau, *Federalism*, p. 188.
10. *Utilitarianism, Liberty and Representative Government* (N.Y.: Dutton, 1951), p. 486.
11. Elie Kedourie, *Nationalism* (London: Hutchinson, 1960), p. 133. See also Cohler, *Rousseau...*, pp. 7-11, from whom I derive this point.
12. Trudeau, *Federalism...*, p. 54.
13. Cohler, *Rousseau*
14. George Grant, *Technology and Empire* (Toronto: Anansi, 1969), p. 73.
15. Rousseau, *Du Contrat Social* (Classiques Garnier), p. 303; D. Kwavnick, ed., *The Tremblay Report* (Toronto: McClelland and Stewart, 1973), p. 104.
16. Madison, Hamilton, Jay, *The Federalist Papers*, #27, 39; Trudeau, *Federalism...*, pp. 194-196.

POURQUOI CETTE TENDANCE A LA SOUVERAINETE AU QUEBEC?

Serge ROBERT

Pour esquisser une réponse à cette question, il faut faire un double détour, d'une part théorique, et d'autre part historique.

1. La détermination du politique par l'économique

Au lieu de considérer l'organisation politique de la société comme un contrat social librement consenti entre individus rationnels, il m'apparaît plus fertile de penser que les décisions politiques sont déterminées par des contraintes économiques. Ainsi, dans les sociétés pré-capitalistes, l'organisation politique vise surtout à l'appropriation du surplus social par la classe dominante. L'exploitation du travailleur est alors indépendante du procès économique de production, et doit lui être imposée par l'appareil politique. C'est de cette façon que le seigneur impose une corvée ou un champart au paysan, ou que le roi collecte des impôts en déléguant des percepteurs auprès des producteurs.

En société capitaliste, l'accaparement du surplus se fait de façon nettement différente, puisque, par la plus-value que rapporte le capital, il s'intègre au processus de production. L'organisation politique change par conséquent de fonction: au lieu de réaliser l'exploitation des travailleurs, elle travaille à intégrer cette exploitation dans la production. La fonction de l'appareil politique est donc changée et ses décisions sont plus subtilement déterminées par des intérêts économiques. C'est ce qui permet aux idéologies, non plus de justifier une exploitation manifeste, mais de nier une exploitation cachée. Cette négation idéologique, c'est elle qui s'exprime dans la croyance au libre contrat social et à l'autonomie du politique relativement à l'économique.

2. Les deux phases du capitalisme

A partir de la distinction classique entre deux phases de développement du capitalisme, à savoir la manufacture et la grande industrie, on peut distinguer les deux modes successifs de l'intégration politique de l'exploitation dans le procès de production. D'abord, en tant que transition au capitalisme, la phase manufacturière entame cette intégration, à travers une politique de centralisation du pouvoir. C'est ainsi qu'à partir du XVIe et du XVIIe siècle, se sont constitués les grands Etats européens, par le contrôle centralisateur du bourgeois sur les ouvriers, de la ville sur la campagne, de l'Etat sur les citoyens, de la capitale sur la colonie.

C'est ensuite l'avènement de la révolution industrielle qui, à partir du XIXe siècle, amènera l'achèvement du capitalisme. Pour réaliser l'intégration totale de l'exploitation dans la production, une nouvelle orientation politique devra être prise: la décentralisation du pouvoir. Cette décentralisation servira d'intermédiaire pour assurer une meilleure centralisation du capital. A ce stade la détermination du politique par l'économique devient encore plus subtile et plus abstraite, au point que le politique semble viser des buts inverses de ceux qu'il sert effectivement. Cette fonction politique paradoxale est confirmée par l'intervention des sciences de l'homme dans l'organisation sociale. L'ouvrier est mieux exploité, par le fait qu'on prétend le consulter par l'intermédiaire de son syndicat; la campagne est mieux asservie au capital urbain par l'aménagement régional et la protection de l'environnement; le citoyen est mieux soumis par l'Etat aux intérêts des grandes entreprises capitalistes, à travers la consultation qu'on fait auprès de lui; la colonie acquiert son indépendance politique par l'appui d'une métropole qui, en retour, l'intègre dans son empire économique.

3. Les rapports de la France et de l'Angleterre à leurs colonies

La constitution du capitalisme ne s'est pas faite de la même manière en France et en Angleterre, et cela a entraîné des répercussions importantes sur leurs rapports respectifs à leurs colonies. En France, la montée de la bourgeoisie commerçante a été ralentie par la constitution, dans le bas Moyen Age, d'un royaume féodal fortement structuré et assurant la concentration des surplus agricoles autour du roi et de ses proches. En Angleterre, il n'y a pas eu de royaume aussi puissant et, de cette façon, la bourgeoisie n'a pas été freinée, de même qu'il n'y a pas eu de distinction nette et de lutte révolutionnaire entre bourgeoisie et noblesse. Après avoir été un grand royaume de la transition au capitalisme (XVIIe et XVIIIe siècle), à travers un partage de la richesse et du pouvoir entre la bourgeoisie et la noblesse, la France a dû voir ces deux classes s'affronter dans la Révolution. Prisonnière de structures féodales, la bourgeoisie victorieuse a dû ensuite être sclérosée dans son développement, par un appareil politique trop rigide, trop hiérarchique et trop bureaucratique. Inversement, la bourgeoisie anglaise a pu, à travers un parlementarisme souple, sur lequel elle a eu un contrôle total, se développer un empire économique prospère. A partir de cette différence majeure entre les développements économiques et politiques de la France et de l'Angleterre, on peut comprendre les relations différentes qu'elles ont eues avec leurs colonies. La France a subordonné ses colonies à son empire politique rigide, pour les déposséder de leurs matières premières, en vue d'enrichir le roi et de faire fonctionner les manufactures. De cette façon, la plupart de ses colonies se sont révoltées contre elle et ont dû acquérir leur indépendance au moyen de guerres violentes; la France a alors perdu tout contrôle économique sur elles (cf. l'Afrique et le sud-est asiatique). C'est ce même rapport aux colonies qui explique que quand ces dernières sont entrées en guerre avec d'autres nations, comme ce fut le cas pour la Nouvelle-France, la France ne leur a apporté aucun support. Par contre, l'Angleterre a beaucoup plus facilement concédé la souveraineté politique à ses colonies (cf. les U.S.A.), parce que son intérêt était de se constituer, en douceur, un empire économique (cf. le Commonwealth). Avec ses colonies, l'Angleterre a toujours entretenu un échange bilatéral: achat de matières premières et vente de produits finis. De cette façon, elle a mieux su profiter de ses colonies et y a permis la constitution de bourgeoisies locales. Sur la base de cette politique coloniale, l'Angleterre a défendu son marché en soutenant ses colonies contre les agresseurs étrangers. On comprend ainsi comment la Nouvelle-France a pu être conquise par les Anglais et comment une bourgeoisie anglaise a pu se constituer en Amérique britannique du Nord, pour donner naissance au Canada, Etat où une bourgeoisie anglaise pourra exploiter une nation française. En ce sens l'avènement de la confédération canadienne est la constitution d'un Etat centralisateur nécessaire à une organisation capitaliste de la production.

4. Nation, Etat et classes sociales

Pour mieux comprendre la tendance à la souveraineté politique des nations, il s'avère intéressant de penser les rapports de la nation à l'Etat et aux classes sociales. Le concept de nation est précisément apparu en Europe à l'époque de la transition au capitalisme. Le nationalisme a alors été l'idéologie qui a permis à la bourgeoisie de s'associer le peuple dans une lutte contre l'aristocratie féodale. Ainsi, le concept de nation a joué un rôle déterminant dans la Révolution française. On voit tout de suite que la nation comprend une dimension sociale et une dimension idéologique. Plus précisément, la nation est apparue historiquement comme le regroupement d'un ou de plusieurs groupe(s) ethnique(s) occupant un même territoire. Ce regroupement se réalise à travers une idéologie qui permet aux individus de se donner un sentiment d'appartenance à une même collectivité. Le sentiment fondateur de l'appartenance à la collectivité nationale s'exprime comme sentiment d'exploitation par une même classe ou, plus généralement, comme réaction de peur devant une menace commune. On voit donc que le nationalisme ne se définit que par opposition à un pouvoir, que par relation conflictuelle à un adversaire.

La nation est donc une entité socio-idéologique qui permet à une classe montante de s'allier d'autres classes sociales pour renverser la classe au pouvoir. De la même façon que la bourgeoisie française, le prolétariat et la paysannerie s'unissaient dans la Révolution pour renverser l'aristocratie féodale et instaurer l'Etat bourgeois, c'est aujourd'hui la bourgeoisie canadienne-française qui s'associe le peuple québécois pour rivaliser avec la bourgeoisie canadienne-anglaise et constituer un Etat québécois francophone. Comment le nationalisme réussit-il à réaliser cette alliance de classes? Par une prémisse cachée qui en constitue le fondement et qui prétend que l'intérêt d'une classe est l'intérêt de tous. En ce sens l'idéologie de la nation n'a d'efficace que si elle s'acharne à nier le concept de classe.

5. Les idéologies fédéralistes et nationalistes

En promouvant un nouvel Etat, l'idéologie nationaliste active les idéologies conservatrices du pouvoir établi. C'est ainsi qu'actuellement le Canada est tiraillé, dans le débat idéologique, entre le nationalisme et le fédéralisme. L'analyse épistémologique de cette lutte idéologique révèle des points de vue totalement différents. L'idéologie conservatrice du pouvoir central à une approche individualiste de la question: on fait appel aux intérêts et aux droits des individus. Quand on parle des groupes ou des collectivités, ils sont considérés comme une simple juxtaposition d'individus. L'approche est plus précisément utilitariste: plus que les individus, ce sont les intérêts pratiques des individus qui comptent. Devant l'opposition nationaliste, l'Etat cherche alors un accommodement récupérateur qui pourrait calmer cette opposition sans changer le pouvoir. C'est, par exemple, le sens du "What does Quebec want?". L'individualisme utilitariste s'explique par des fondements politiques: c'est pour mieux se maintenir que le pouvoir isole l'individu du tissu social, en faisant un inventaire élogieux des conditions d'existence que le régime en place lui a procurées.

Inversement, l'idéologie nationaliste oppose un point de vue collectiviste et aprioriste à l'individualisme utilitariste. L'enjeu est vu sous l'angle de la collectivité que constitue la nation. Les individus, de même que leurs intérêts personnels et leurs biens matériels, ne doivent pas trop entrer en ligne de compte: ils ne sont que les éléments d'une nation qui se définit par des caractères propres trans-individuels. Comme la nation n'existe qu'à travers une idéologie nationale, elle appuie son argumentation sur des principes idéologiques et des valeurs morales, comme le respect, la dignité, la réalisation collective. C'est là que son apriorisme s'oppose à l'utilitarisme. Ici, il ne s'agit pas d'être pratique ou rationnel, mais bien d'être utopiste et sensible. Pour constituer une force apte à renverser l'ancien régime, le nationalisme doit rassembler le plus d'individus possible, en les contraignant à l'abnégation par une obnubilation de leurs intérêts matériels. On comprend ainsi pourquoi le nationalisme oppose un refus systématique et entêté au nom de principes irréductibles, à toute tentative pratique de récupération. Entre fédéralistes et nationalistes, il y a non seulement conflit politique et idéologique, mais aussi une relative incommunicabilité épistémologique.

Comme les idéologies nationalistes sont l'expression d'une réaction collective face à une menace commune, on peut comprendre comment le nationalisme canadien-français anti-anglophone remonte à la conquête anglaise sur la Nouvelle-France (1760). Mais quand ce nationalisme aboutit, grâce à la montée d'une bourgeoisie canadienne-française, à l'élection d'un gouvernement nationaliste au Québec (1976), la partie n'est plus la même. Ce sont les Canadiens-Anglais et les fédéralistes francophones qui sentent à leur tour une menace, celle de voir leur pays démembré. Il est alors étonnant de voir leur nationalisme pan-canadien réveillé et de prendre, eux aussi, un ton passionné qui fait appel à la morale, au sentiment et à la collectivité. Dès lors, le Canada ne peut plus se maintenir dans sa forme actuelle, puisqu'il constitue un seul Etat avec deux nations.

6. Le nationalisme et la décentralisation du pouvoir

Aujourd'hui, après la subordination de l'économie canadienne à l'empire économique américain, la tendance à la décentralisation du pouvoir devient une nécessité pour l'achèvement de l'organisation capitaliste de la production canadienne. Le nationalisme québécois s'inscrit dans une tendance actuellement répandue dans le monde: la lutte pour la décentralisation du pouvoir politique, lutte qui, à l'insu de ses protagonistes, s'inscrit dans les intérêts économiques des grands monopoles capitalistes internationaux. C'est en ce sens que le projet péquiste se précise comme souveraineté-association: la souveraineté, c'est la décentralisation du pouvoir, que l'on retrouve dans l'aménagement régional, les sommets économiques, les commissions d'enquête ou le rôle accru des parents à l'école; tandis que ce qu'on appelle l'association, c'est un meilleur soutien aux entreprises capitalistes qu'assurerait la souveraineté, à travers l'encouragement pour les investisseurs étrangers, l'association économique au Canada anglais et les subventions aux seules entreprises capitalistes rentables.

7. Conclusion: l'avenir du Canada

En ce qui concerne la constitution canadienne, le statu quo est donc impensable, en tant qu'il assure un pouvoir centralisateur qui correspond à un capitalisme périmé. C'est ce qui fait que le trudeauisme pert de plus en plus de popularité. Quant à l'indépendance politique et économique totale pour le Québec, ce n'est plus que le vieux rêve de quelques québécois utopistes, qui auraient voulu repartir à zéro, en faisant fi de l'histoire et des dépendances économiques auxquelles elle nous lie. Le Parti Québécois a d'ailleurs vite compris qu'une telle option ne l'aurait jamais porté au pouvoir. Entre ces deux extrêmes, l'état actuel de développement du capitalisme exige un pouvoir relativement décentralisé, c'est-à-dire, aussi décentralisé que la centralisation du capital le permet. Il y aura donc, au nom de la prospérité économique, une constitution remaniée dans le sens d'une plus grande autonomie des provinces. Des premiers ministres de provinces riches et freinées par le pouvoir central, comme Lougheed et Blakeney, l'ont d'ailleurs déjà clairement compris. Sur cette base, le Québec réussira à négocier une relative souveraineté-association, qui ne sera pas aussi radicale que certains idéalistes ou affolés peuvent le croire. C'est alors que le Parti Québécois devra, pour se maintenir au pouvoir, faire croire que la relative souveraineté obtenue est bien celle qu'il souhaitait. C'est pourquoi les questions les plus litigieuses et les plus délicates de la négociation ne seront pas les questions économiques fondamentales, mais, comme c'est souvent le cas en politique, les questions qui ont le plus d'impact idéologique sur l'électeur, celles qui, plus spécifiquement, vont définir jusqu'où ira l'autonomie des provinces en ce qui concerne la langue, le drapeau, l'hymne national et la couleur des passeports...

CONSOCIATIONALIST MODELS FOR CANADA

J.T. STEVENSON

1. **Introduction.** The question addressed concerns forms of association amongst the entities comprising Canada. It is therefore a question of comparative political typology, a matter of alternative political models. These models have both a descriptive, analytical, explanatory use and a normative, prescriptive one; they may be used both by political scientists and political philosophers. Although these uses are not identical, there is a close relation between them in my approach. I am concerned with what is practically desirable in a concrete, historical situation, rather than what might be ultimately desirable in an ideal one. An accurate descriptive model provides one element in the feasibility constraints for a practical normative one and provides the understanding required for sound prescription.

An influential, contemporary typology concerned with both forms of democracy and regime stability is that of Almond. He distinguishes four types of political system: (1) *Anglo-American* (characterized by a homogenous, secular culture, highly differentiated role structure, many cross-cutting cleavages, two-party system and stability); (2) *Continental European* (characterized by fragmentation into political subcultures, social/political roles imbedded in the subcultures, and instability or immobilism); (3) *Pre-industrial* (3rd world, developing nations); (4) *Totalitarian* (2nd world, communist bloc). There is a strong, widespread tendency to take the first of these as prescriptively normative — and to suppose that Canada should avoid (2) by becoming (1). It is assumed that:

> Social homogeneity and political consensus are prerequisites for, or factors strongly conducive to, stable democracy. Conversely, the deep social divisions and political differences within plural societies are held responsible for instability and breakdown in democracies. (Lijphart)

This typology and its normative use have been criticized as inadequate and ethnocentric. In particular, Austria, Switzerland, Belgium and the Netherlands are relatively stable, yet lack the supposed 'functional requisites' of stability: they are bi or polylinguistic, polyethnic, ideologically split or culturally fragmented social systems; their deep splits are not cross-cutting; their discontinuities are institutionalized in the political system through devices such as federalism, proportionality and rotation. Indeed, virtually no modern state fits the first model, not even the paradigm cases — Britain has its four nationalities; the U.S. has its racial and regional minorities. Further, the commonplace notion that there is a world tendency towards an isomorphism between states and homogenous societies (nations, tribes, races, etc.) is a complete myth, as any empirical survey quickly shows.

Thus the rise of a consociationalist model: first devised to fit the four deeply segmented European states, it has become an important engine of analysis in world comparative politics, and since the late sixties has been applied to Canada by some political scientists.

2. **Essentials of Consociationalism.** Arend Lijphart, the leader of the school, distinguishes four types of democracy:

STRUCTURE OF SOCIETY

ELITE BEHAVIOUR	Homogenous	Plural
Coalescent	A Depoliticized Democracy	C Consociational Democracy
Adversarial	B Centripetal Democracy	D Centrifugal Democracy

Our concern here is with cells C and D. Some preliminary definitions: (a) "democracy" means Dahl's polyarchy, i.e., only some approximation to a democratic ideal; (b) by "plural society" is meant one in which political divisions, functions and social institutions follow or concern salient segmental cleavages whether linguistic, religious, ideological, cultural, racial, socio-economic, or regional; (c) "stability" means regime continuity and the maintenance of civil order, legitimacy and effectiveness.

Like many political concepts, "consociationalism" is not sharply defined in practice. The core concept seems to have two individually necessary and jointly sufficient conditions:

(i) that the democracy be pluralistic, i.e., segmental as defined;

(ii) that there be certain restrictions on, or deviations from, majority rule.

But, in the literature, a specification of (ii) has been dominant and elite accommodation is taken as a hallmark of consociationalism:

(iii) that there be an overarching cooperation at the elite level with the deliberate aim of counteracting disintegrative tendencies in the system.

Other salient conditions sometimes cited in some form are:

(iv) that there be a variety of formal or informal arrangements such as coalition cabinets, grand councils, rotation of office holders, mutual vetoes or double majorities, proportionality in voting systems or government jobs or segment autonomy in the form of areal, personal or functional federalism;

(v) that the elites share a normative consensus sufficient to transcend cleavages at the subcultural level and sufficient to yield a commitment to the survival of the regime;

(vi) that the elite memberships come from closely related socio-economic classes; that there be personal interaction amongst them and circulation of elites or role interchange;

(vii) that, psychologically, the elites believe in their efficacy, need the dividends of power and deference, accept their place in the upper echelons of the social hierarchy — all of this being based on an elitist education and socialization;

(viii) that there be only a moderate level of nationalism;

(ix) that there be an external threat affecting the interests of a large proportion of both elites and masses;

(x) that there be sufficient segmental isolation to encourage reliance on elite negotiation to achieve stability;

(xi) that there be particular historical precedents for elite accommodation.

3. **Descriptive Application to Canada.** There is a fair amount of agreement that consociationalism offers an approximate descriptive model for Canada. S.J.R. Noel says, "What it offers is a way of viewing the Canadian political process which accounts for its successful maintenance yet requires no dubious assumptions about the role of political parties and posits no chimerical notion of an 'underlying' national identity." Presthus thinks Canada "fits nicely"

into the consociationalist category. On the other hand, McRae thinks it is but an "imperfect example of consociationalist democracy" and Lijphart says it "fits approximately in between centrifugal and consociationalist types". I would argue that the Canadian regime, from 1867 until quite recently, has been an approximation to consociationalism.

The salient cleavages are religious (mainly Catholic/Protestant), linguistic (Francophone/Anglophone), racial (European/Aboriginal, Métis), and regional (Atlantic/Lower Canada/Upper Canada/West/North). The main accommodation has been, historically, between the Catholic-Francophone axis and the Protestant-Anglophone axis, although some accommodations have been made along the other axes.

Canadian political culture has been conducive to elite accommodation. The following are four, well-substantiated, general features of Canadian political culture.

Government and the Economy. The early dominance of mercantilism in Canada (Quebec historians now, too, say that New France was as much mercantilist as feudal) has had persistent effects which, together with a "staples economy" and metropole/hinterland relations, have prevented the formation of industrial, laissez-faire, high capitalism. To simplify, we have gone from mercantilist to Keynesian economics with very little in between, and thus have always allowed the state an important economic role. Our political, business and external elites have always worked closely together.

Collectivism. We have had some tendency to accept an organic view of society in which collective aspirations or the notion of a common good have priority over the claims of individualism. The corporatist form derives from Catholic social philosophy and survives in attempts at economic tripartitism. Moreover, the idealist philosophies of John Watson *et. al.*, the relative dominance of Catholic and Anglican over Calvinistic churches, prairie populism, the community spirit of isolated towns, villages and farms, and the 'primitive' communism of the aboriginal and métis peoples, all have contributed to collectivist tendencies. Even the individualism of the presbyterian and methodist capitalists of the 'commercial empire of the St. Lawrence' was tempered by the general economic framework outlined above. This collectivism gives rise to the notion of collective rights which can be negotiated by elites.

Deference. In Canada there is a history of traditional and deferential patterns of authority — in Weberian terms, charismatic and elite leadership rather than legal-rational authority. This social structure is grounded in the remnants of a monarchical and quasi-feudal past, some forms of the aforementioned collectivism, the ascriptive status attached to inherited wealth and an elitist and confessional educational system.

Political Passivity. Canadian political culture has been described as 'quasi-participative' or 'spectator-participative'. Surveys show a low level of trust, interest, knowledge and participation in the political process. There is also a low level of participation in voluntary cross-cutting associations. Party organizations are only large and active at election time. Most Canadians participate directly only by voting — a process of deciding between the 'ins' and 'outs' of the parliamentary elites.

Finally, there has been an historical trend towards consociationalism. The precursor regime of 1841 provided a seedbed with its double majorities, dual ministries, rotating capitals, etc. The regime of 1867 has evolved to provide formal and informal mechanisms of accommodation. On the formal side, 28 amendments to the BNA Act have modified it from what is, legally, a highly centralist federal document to one giving some functional quasi-sovereignty to the provinces and thus one closer to an areal confederationalist constitution. On the less formal, non-constitutional side of the regime, in the high tide of Pearsonian 'cooperative federalism', we have a plethora of councils, commissions, boards, conferences, etc., involving tacit forms of proportionality. The rotation principle is applied to certain posts, e.g., Governor-General, leader of the dominant Liberal party, certain Crown Corporations, etc. The bilingual policy tends to reserve key posts for 'accommodationist' mandarins and provides a form of *de facto* proportionality.

The satisfaction of the two major and several subsidiary conditions shows that Canada fits the consociationalist model.

However, the signal failures of consociationalism in certain cases have created the tendency to centrifugal democracy or left festering sores on our polity. First, there has been a persistent repression and exploitation of aboriginal and métis peoples in all provinces. Second, there have been assimilationist pressures against the Acadian minority in Atlantic Canada. Third, there was the breakdown of consociationalist arrangements regarding language and education in Manitoba and the West in the 1880-90's, and during WWI in Ontario. There were the conscription crises of the two world wars. There have been flaws in taxation powers leading to fiscal crisis and confrontation. And there have been gross economic inequalities, regionally and by groups, as revealed by Lorenz curves which have remained stable over several decades in spite of substantial transfer payments. These are historic grounds for the centrifugal tendencies which are now in the ascendency. But, more important, massive recent changes have made the old arrangements unworkable.

The former dominant cleavage, religion, has lost its importance with the decline of religious bigotry and the secularization of educational, health and social services. Language now takes precedence over religion. There have been significant demographic changes concerning birth rates, immigration and urbanization. Multiculturalism and the mosaic theory have threatened to give Québécois culture the status of one *folklorique* culture among many others. Rising education levels, increased government services, the growing importance of science, technology and economics have produced a new, middle class, technocratic elite gradually infiltrating business and government and, in Quebec, dramatically displacing the older elite. A population explosion amongst aboriginal and métis peoples, the total economic inadequacy of the reserves, and the pressures of development have produced a new impoverished, demoralized urban proletariat. Economically we must note: the high proportion of the GNP now controlled by provincial governments; the westward shift of the financial centre in the direction Montreal to Toronto to Calgary; the threat posed to primary staples industries, especially nonferrous metals and forest products by third world countries under the aegis of multinational corporations, and the consequent shift in economic importance from central Canadian staples to western (grains, fossil fuel) and eastern (fish) ones; but most important, the massive foreign control of major sectors of the economy leading to a process of de-industrialization, particularly in branch plant Ontario, and to a chronic, growing balance of payments deficit caused largely, and for the long term, by transfers of the profits, dividends, royalties, etc. associated with direct investment.

This welter of new forces has shifted us from a consociationalist to a centrifugal state. The question is now normative: within the bounds of the feasible, what new form of association is desirable for the future?

4. **Normative Implications.** Gérard Bergeron poses the problem in this way:

> L'indépendance du Québec réussit, ou échoue, ou n'est pas essayée. La troisième hypothèse ne bonifierait pas le fédéralisme canadien: quelques parures de circonstance ajouteraient a l'ornementation de ce musée des horreurs. Si l'indépendance

réussit, il faudra négocier une réassociation. Si elle échoue, il faudra procéder a une réintegration. Dans les trois hypothèses, comment pourrait être relancée la chose Canada?

Whether or not federalism in Canada is a "museum of horrors", all major political parties and most political thinkers are agreed (a) that the independence option must be tried, e.g., put to the test of a referendum, and (b) that some changes must be made in Confederation. We can, then, eliminate the third hypothesis. Assimilation of the Francophone heartland has not worked and will not work. Even the horror of a civil war has, eventually, to lead to a negotiated peace settlement. The PQ policy is to negotiate a form of association. It would be totally unrealistic, given our tangled affairs, to maintain — except perhaps as an initial bargaining position — that there would be no association of any form between an 'independent' Quebec and the rest of the country. Therefore, Bergeron is essentially correct: there will be some form of association and it will be a negotiated one.

I believe the new arrangement should be a type of consociationalism, both as regards its substance and as regards the procedures for arriving at and maintaining it. That is, we will need major modifications on strict majority rule and will need a process of elite accommodation to arrive at and maintain the new arrangement.

As McRae so aptly put it, majoritarianism is the "*damnosa hereditas* of Anglo-American democracy" and "the Achilles heel of the Canadian political system". English-Canadian majoritarianism has driven the Québécois into a majoritarianism of their own — and there is no logical limit to the process of minorities seeking divisions which turn their situations into majority ones. Under all plausible scenarios we will need a variety of deviations — bills of rights, rotation, proportionality, etc. — from majority rule in order to protect the vital interests of linguistic and other minorities. On the other hand, certain gross deviations from majority rule will not work. For example, an internal anglophone minority controlling all the major economic institutions of Quebec is unacceptable. Likewise, the flaw in a sovereign Quebec controlling, in exact numerical equality with all the rest of Canada combined, a common monetary system and certain other joint enterprises is that it would be rejected as unacceptable by the other provinces. One of the attractions of Émile Colas' *troisième voie* is that it provides for five roughly equal partners with protections for internal minorities. I think this is the direction in which we can and should move, although I am not sanguine that we can or will do so in some neat legalistic fashion. This change might be achieved *de facto* by an evolutionary process without, for example, a *de jure* union of the Atlantic provinces and a *de jure* union of the prairie provinces. Gérard Bergeron's 'Canadian Commonwealth canadien' is another alternative worth consideration. Within the general framework of consociationalism I can see no *a priori* way of determining detailed arrangements. They must be consonant with the socio-economic exigencies of our situation, but their substantial fairness will, in large measure, be a consequence of the fairness and effectiveness of the procedures for arriving at them. (In the absence of an exactly fair, e.g., equal division of a pie, we fall back on a fair method of division and choice.) I expect a decade of complex manoeuvering and negotiation before we arrive at the new equilibrium point we need.

Although referenda and general elections may give some indication of the general sentiments of the populations involved, the detailed issues are so complex and technical that the new arrangements will have to be negotiated amongst salient elites and, I am afraid, will have to accommodate their vital interests. These elites are: the political and parliamentary, the mandarinates both provincial and federal, the technocratic and indigenous middle management, the indigenous capitalist and financial, and the critically important foreign, i.e. U.S. elite. Cross-cutting these will be the regional elites. That elites should play a key role is offensive to egalitarians, but a dominant role for them is anakastically necessary and hence relatively desirable, i.e., desirable *faute de mieux*, given the complexities of the division of powers, rights and functions, whether political, legal, economic or fiscal, that is required.

Some qualifications are now in order. The great danger in elitist consociationalism is that its negotiations can lead to an *accommodation rentable* for the elites alone without any concern for the common good. *We* need *them* to have a normative consensus requiring them to pay at least some attention to the common good. Thus it would be highly desirable to have a modern philosophical analysis of the notion of the 'common good', consonant with our organicist background and based on the concepts of *vital interests* or *basic needs* rather than on the essentially sceptical 'preference structures' of utilitarianism or 'interests' of American analytic pluralism. Second, some groups are not adequately represented in the corridors of power. In particular, a fundamental cleavage, socio-economic class, has not been accommodated in our past structures. The obvious vehicle for the representation of the working class is the labour movement and its political arm, a social democratic party. Both should be greatly expanded and strengthened. We need, and rising education levels permit, the formation of many *groupes intermédiaires* and forms of participatory democracy in the work place and in local communities — where the daily lives of most citizens are most directly affected and where they have the knowledge and interest to be effective. Finally, all working Canadians as well as the political, mandarin, technocractic, intellectual and management elites have a common interest in the building of a strong, modern economy in which the staples exploitation chains and hinterland/metropole relations are, for the first time in our history, fundamentally changed.

SELECTED REFERENCES

1. Arend Lijphart, *Democracy in Plural Societies* (New Haven: Yale University Press, 1977).
2. Kenneth D. McRae, *Consociational Democracy: Political Accommodation in Segmented Societies* (Toronto: McClelland & Stewart, 1974).
3. Robert Presthus, *Elite Accommodation in Canadian Politics* (Toronto: MacMillan of Canada, 1973).
4. John Porter, *The Vertical Mosaic* (Toronto: The University of Toronto Press, 1965).
5. Wallace Clement, *The Canadian Corporate Elite* (Toronto: McClelland & Stewart, 1975).
6. Pierre Fournier, *The Quebec Establishment* (Montreal: Black Rose Books, 1976).
7. Gary Teeple, ed., *Capitalism and the National Question* (Toronto: University of Toronto Press, 1972).
8. W.T. Easterbrook and M.H. Watkins, *Approaches to Canadian Economic History* (Toronto: McClelland & Stewart, 1967).
9. Emile Colas, *La Troisième Voie* (Montréal: Les Editions de l'homme, 1978).
10. Denis Moniere, *Le développment des idéologies au Québec* (Montreal: Editions Québec/Amerique, 1977).
11. Gérard Bergeron, *Ce Jour-là...le referendum* (Montréal: Les Editions Quinze, 1978).
12. Jean-Yves Desrosiers et Luc-Normand Tellier, *Qui decide au Québec? les centres de décision de l'économie québécoise* (Montréal: Les Editions Quinze, 1978).

UTOPIE ET POLITIQUE NATIONALISTES

Joseph PESTIEAU

Une utopie correspond à un idéal que l'on rêve de réaliser tel quel. En même temps qu'elle refuse les compromis et l'adaptation au réel, l'utopie est volontiers totalitaire ou, à tout le moins, unilatérale et sourde aux valeurs qui ne sont pas les siennes. Mais, précisément, parce qu'elle se définit sans tenir compte du rapport des forces politiques en présence et des mentalités timides qui végètent à l'ombre de l'ordre établi, elle permet de prospecter des possibilités neuves et d'amorcer éventuellement un réalignement des forces avec une certaine indépendance vis-à-vis des idées reçues et des partis établis. L'utopie peut être un catalyseur politique plutôt qu'une évasion consolatrice si elle réussit à dénoncer les idéologies en place, tire au clair des aspirations latentes, accuse des manques auxquels on s'habituait, prépare une nouvelle vision des choses et un ralliement autour de celle-ci. Mais alors il ne s'agit plus d'une utopie ou plutôt elle est devenue un programme politique réaliste après avoir bouleversé ce qui semblait réaliste.

L'idée d'indépendance nationale au Québec n'a-t-elle pas eu quelques-uns des traits que je prête à l'utopie qui réussit? Unilatérale, dénoncée comme simpliste et irréaliste, elle a cependant fini par provoquer une redistribution des forces et des enjeux politiques. Plus précisément, cette idée a mobilisé des effectifs nombreux parce qu'elle était à la fois:

- simple et claire, promettant une sécurité culturelle, garantissant la permanence de la nation canadienne-française, correspondant à une aspiration enracinée et cultivée dans la mémoire des Canadiens-Français;
- programme d'action énergique, pris en charge par une équipe qui semblait faire preuve d'efficacité;
- identifiée à une force imposante, donnant à ses adhérents le sentiment de compter sur la scène du monde.

Notons que le nationalisme du Parti Québécois n'est pas ou n'est plus utopique, mais il a dû compter sur des attentes apparemment utopiques pour rassembler une force politique et devenir un programme réalisable. D'autre part, les détracteurs du P.Q. retiennent ce qu'il y a d'unilatéral et de simpliste dans certains aspects de son nationalisme pour discréditer le P.Q. et défendre d'autres simplismes.

Il est sans doute inhérent au nationalisme québécois de soulever des attentes excessives, de soulever ce que des opposants perçoivent comme du fanatisme. On ne transforme pas à moindre frais le cadre, les présupposés et les habitudes d'une tradition politique. Il faut bien remarquer que, dans une démocratie libérale, on accepte facilement de remettre en cause les programmes de gouvernement et les hommes politiques. Il est déjà plus difficile de changer le régime constitutionnel. (Les choses peuvent se compliquer si les mécanismes de révision constitutionnelle ne sont pas prévus.) Mais c'est une tout autre histoire que de soulever la question de la légitimité du peuple, source de toute légitimité. La question de l'unité de ce peuple (ou de l'intégrité nationale) paraît à peine légitime. A ce dernier point de vue, le Canada a été obligé d'être relativement tolérant. L'unité du peuple canadien n'a jamais été de soi. Néanmoins, la thèse des deux nations ne va pas non plus de soi. Pour ébranler les assurances des fédéralistes (non renouvelés) comme pour dépasser les timidités d'une nation minoritaire dans l'ensemble canadien, infériorisée, qui n'ose s'affirmer, qui hésite entre un statu quo insatisfaisant et des récrimentions sans espoir, il faut une stratégie audacieuse et une mobilisation qui peut paraître théâtrale.

Il y a dans le nationalisme québécois des motifs émotionnels très puissants, mais pas toujours clairs (à gauche, comme à droite, on est embarrassé de reconnaître des aspirations et des besoins ne correspondant pas à des intérêts matériels) ni raisonnables. En voici quelques-uns: l'identification à un gouvernement unique, protecteur et redresseur de torts; l'allégeance à une société nationale qui prédomine sur toutes les autres allégeances et solidarités, parfois contradictoires, que connaissent tous les citoyens du monde industrialisé; refus des complexités et tergiversations qui vont avec le partage des pouvoirs; faire d'Ottawa, ou d'une classe dominante plus ou moins mythique, les boucs émissaires de toutes ses insuffisances, est aussi une tentation facile. Comme le P.Q. désire gérer la province prudemment, il est plutôt embarrassé par des espoirs excessifs et des attentes saugrenues qui lui ont pourtant valu des soutiens nécessaires. Heureusement, les sondages ont souligné les risques d'une position maximaliste, ont assagi bien des radicaux et aidé le premier ministre à garder une ligne modérée. Il reste que la raison d'être du P.Q. est de susciter une volonté collective (exprimée par un certain pourcentage des oui à une certaine question lors du référendum) en vue d'aborder en position de force la (re)négociation d'une union du Québec avec le reste du Canada. Sans une volonté nationale québécoise clairement exprimée lors du référendum, les propositions du rapport Pepin-Robarts et les prétentions de tous les partis du Québec (prétention à l'autonomie, à l'égalité, au statut particulier) sont chimériques. Cela dit, je ne nie pas la difficulté de constituer une union économique pan-canadienne après avoir "défait" le pays.

Concluons. Le P.Q. veut la renégociation d'une union canadienne à partir d'une affirmation de la souveraineté québécoise. Ce qu'il veut peut être considéré comme une révision constitutionnelle en vue de rendre le Canada viable ou comme un bris dramatique de ce pays. Ces deux vues ont chacune leur part de vérité. Selon le P.Q., le Québec ne peut sauvegarder les intérêts de la nation canadienne-française (qu'il représente moins mal que tout autre Etat) qu'en prenant son indépendance et en obligeant le reste du Canada à la reconnaître. Or, ceci exige une mobilisation assez passionnelle des Québécois et provoque bien du ressentiment dans toutes les provinces. Le Québec court le risque de ne plus pouvoir s'entendre avec un Canada qu'il aura bousculé. Cependant, ceux qui seront indisposés le seront moins par les procédés du P.Q. que par l'obligation de reconnaitre la réalité nationale québécoise. Remarquez le sort réservé au rapport Pepin-Robarts hors du Québec. Ne fût-ce que pour faire accepter ce rapport par le Canada, il faudrait une victoire de la thèse souverainiste au Québec.

* * * *

The P.Q. wants to renegotiate the Canadian union starting from an affirmation of Quebec's sovereignty. Its goal can be seen as a reform of the constitution aimed at making Canada viable or as a dramatic break-up of the country. Both interpretations are partially true. According to the P.Q., Quebec can only safeguard the interests of the French Canadian nation by assuming its independance and forcing the rest of Canada to acknowledge it. Yet this step requires rather an emotional mobilization of Quebecers at the same time as it provokes considerable resentment in the rest of the country. Quebec runs the risk of no longer being able to get together with a Canada that it has shaken up in this manner. However, those who are upset will be so in the last resort not on account of the P.Q.'s strategy but on account of the national reality of Quebec. We have only to look at the reception given to the Pepin-Robarts Task Force Report outside Quebec. A "souverainiste" victory in Quebec may be necessary if only to get the Report accepted by the rest of Canada.

DEFINIR LA CRISE DE L'UNITE CANADIENNE POUR CHOISIR LA FORME D'ASSOCIATION

Georges A. LEGAULT

La Commission de l'unité canadienne a publié deux documents que je considère importants dans le débat actuel: *Se retrouver, observations et recommandations* et *Définir pour choisir.* Ces documents poursuivent un même but, présenter le plus clairement possible: 1) l'état de la crise de la Confédération; 2) le terrain de discussion; 3) les grands principes de la solution de la crise. En voulant clarifier les termes du débat, la Commission s'inscrit déjà dans une démarche conceptuelle. Si nous voulons poursuivre plus à fond cette démarche, nous pouvons regarder la réalité canadienne en cherchant à déterminer:

1. En quels termes présenter la crise de l'unité canadienne?

1.1 Quels mots, quels arguments utiliser pour que la présentation de la crise soit comprise?

1.2 Quels mots, quels arguments utiliser pour que la présentation de la crise soit acceptée?

2. Quels est la meilleure solution à la crise?

2.1 Quels mots, quels arguments utiliser pour que la solution soit comprise comme la meilleure?

2.2 Quels mots, quels arguments utiliser pour que la solution soit acceptée comme la meilleure?

La qualité du débat sur l'unité canadienne dépend, à mes yeux, de la réponse qu'on donnera à ces questions. De plus, les réponses doivent aussi suivre l'ordre indiqué car la meilleure forme d'association pour les canadiens n'est pensable qu'en fonction d'une solution globale de la crise. Or l'analyse exige qu'on distingue deux niveaux d'étude, le descriptif et le normatif (morale et droit). La confusion des deux niveaux explique souvent l'infécondité des débats et particulièrement l'infécondité du débat sur la crise canadienne. Ainsi, les réponses à la question ci-haut 1, "En quels termes présenter la crise de l'unité canadienne?'', doivent refléter la distinction entre les mots, arguments descriptifs et les mots, arguments normatifs.

La Commission a choisi de présenter la crise canadienne à partir de deux clivages qui s'institutionnalisent dans la pratique parlementaire et dans les discussions autour de la constitution: la dualité et le régionalisme. Il s'agit dans un premier temps de vérifier si la Commission a raison de dire que ces deux clivages constituent le noeud de la crise de l'unité canadienne. Afin de vérifier cette prétention, nous devons étudier les définitions de dualité et de régionalisme telles qu'elles sont présentées dans les deux rapports.

Dans *Définir pour choisir* les commissaires précisent les sens de dualité et de dualisme en rapport avec la situation canadienne. Ainsi ils affirment:

> Le terme dualité est fréquemment utilisé au Canada pour décrire la présence de deux communautés principales, l'anglophone et la francophone. Chacune de ces communautés possède ses propres institutions et on considère donc qu'elles forment deux sociétés distinctes dans la société canadienne. Ces deux sociétés partagent également un grand nombre d'institutions communes publiques et privées, de nature culturelle, juridique, économique et politique. ... Comme principe, la dualité ou le *dualisme* s'appuie sur l'évidence démographique et sur un certain nombre de concepts historiques, juridiques et politiques, comme 'les deux peuples fondateurs', 'le pacte confédératif', 'les deux nations' et 'le principe d'égalité'. (p.10)

Plus loin dans ce texte, les commissaires avouent que le mot 'dualité' est très controversé dans l'actuel débat sur l'avenir du Canada. Bien qu'ils illustrent cette controverse à l'aide d'exemples, ils confondent la contestation du principe de dualité et la critique de la désignation de ce terme. Or, l'analyse conceptuelle exige de distinguer les deux et d'établir, s'il existe, le lien entre le principe et la désignation de ce terme.

Dans le rapport *Se retrouver...* les commissaires utilisent le terme 'dualité' dans un sens descriptif. Dans ce texte, le mot 'dualité' désigne la 'dualité francophonie-anglophonie'. (p.22) Essayant de définir ce terme, les commissaires soutiennent que les thèses des deux peuples fondateurs, des deux nations, du pacte confédératif, des deux langues ou celle de la distinction Québec-Canada en sont des définitions multiples qui ne font pas l'unanimité.

Ce rappel de l'utilisation du terme 'dualité' par les commissaires, montre au moins la difficulté qu'ont les commissaires 1) de préciser exactement quelle réalité est désignée par ce terme; 2) de formuler le principe du dualisme; 3) d'établir les liens entre la réalité désignée et le principe et de montrer dans quelle mesure le fait justifie le principe. Pourtant, leur point de départ est juste, on ne peut décrire la crise canadienne sans le concept de dualité. Par contre, il faut corriger l'orientation de la commission. Ainsi, pour répondre à la question 1, "En quels termes présenter la crise de l'unité canadienne?", nous devons étudier le terme de dualité, établir son sens descriptif, établir son sens normatif (principe) et déterminer les liens entre ces deux sens. Pour accomplir 1.1 nous devons nous demander "Que désigne l'expression 'dualité francophonie-anglophonie'" ou "Comment faire partie de la dualité francophonie-anglophonie?"

1.1. Quels mots, quels arguments utiliser pour que la présentation de la crise canadienne soit comprise?

1.1.1. Que désigne l'expression 'dualité francophonie-anglophonie' ou comment faire partie de la dualité anglophonie-francophonie?

Lorsqu'on utilise le terme de dualité on présuppose au moins l'existence de deux ensembles qualifiés par une caractéristique propre aux éléments de l'ensemble. On présuppose aussi que ces ensembles sont exclusifs, par exemple la dualité homme-femme. La caractéristique propre à l'ensemble est l'élément déterminant de la classification. Elle donne le sens de la classification et elle détermine la valeur opératoire de cette dualité, comme expression descriptive d'une réalité. Lorsqu'on parle de dualité anglophonie-francophonie au Canada on devrait donc distinguer deux ensembles exclusifs. Comment déterminer à quel ensemble un individu appartient? Voilà le problème du critère.

1.1.1.1. Ce n'est pas 'posséder une langue' parce que ce critère est 1) insuffisant pour distinguer deux groupes, une dualité, 2) incomplet car qu'est-ce que posséder une langue? (indéterminable)

Etre anglophone ou francophone peut être considéré comme un fait individuel, une caractéristique d'un individu. Selon cette hypothèse, est anglophone celui qui possède la langue anglaise et francophone, celui qui possède la langue française. On retrouve cette conception dans le rapport *Se retrouver...* grâce aux expressions 'populations francophones', 'le tiers de la population y étant de langue française'. (p.22-23)

'Posséder une langue' n'apparaît pas un critère suffisant pour distinguer la dualité francophonie-anglophonie au Canada, parce qu'il ne peut à lui seul déterminer deux groupes distincts. Dans la mesure où 'posséder une langue' est une caractéristique individuelle désignant les opérations langagières qu'un individu peut effecter, cette caractéristique est insuffisante pour distinguer deux groupes. Que faire de l'ensemble des individus qui possèdent deux langues? Comment les considérer dans la dualité?

De plus, cette hypothèse présuppose que 'posséder une langue' est déterminable, identifiable grâce à une série de critères bien définis. Qu'est-ce que posséder une langue? Retenons comme critères:

1. le fait de comprendre cette langue maintenant
2. le fait de parler cette langue maintenant
3. le fait de lire quelque chose d'écrit dans cette langue, maintenant
4. le fait d'écrire quelque chose dans cette langue, maintenant
5. la catégorie d'un, deux ou de trois de ces critères précédents (1 à 4)
6. tous ces éléments ensembles (1 à 4)

Il y a donc des niveaux de possession d'une langue. "Il y a posséder et posséder" diront certains. Cependant, combien de ces critères devons-nous retenir? Voilà la première difficulté. Advenant une entente sur les critères, il n'en demeure pas moins que ceux-ci présentent des difficultés particulières car le grand conflit réside dans l'évaluation de chaque opération. Suffit-il de comprendre, parler, lire ou écrire n'importe comment le français pour "posséder la langue française"? Toute la question est là. Comparons des franco-manitobains, des franco-ontariens, des franco-américains et des franco-québécois. Bien que tous se disent 'francophones' la différence au niveau de la qualité de la langue existe. Quel niveau de qualité de langue doit-on considérer comme essentiel pour posséder une langue?

Plus les critères pour distinguer la possession d'une langue sont nombreux et exigeants au niveau de la qualité moins il y aura de canadiens possédant l'une ou l'autre des langues. La dualité francophonie-anglophonie au Canada ne peut donc pas se saisir à partir de l'idée de deux groupes possédant leur langue.

1.1.1.2. Ce n'est pas être membre d'une communauté parce qu'au Canada, il faut reconnaître l'existence d'une pluralité de communautés (pluralité ethnique).

Le terme de dualité renvoie donc à deux groupes, la francophonie et l'anglophonie. Plutôt que des groupes d'individus parlant une même langue, pourquoi ne s'agirait-il pas de communautés? Ainsi serait francophone celui qui fait partie de la communauté francophone et anglophone, celui qui fait partie de la communauté anglophone. C'est ce qu'affirme le rapport *Définir pour choisir.* "Le terme dualité est souvent utilisé au Canada pour décrire la présence de deux communautés principales, l'anglophone et la francophone". (p.10) On retrouve la même idée dans *Un temps pour parler:* "Si l'on s'arrête au seul facteur ethnique, on constate que le Canada est composé essentiellement de deux communautés principales: la communauté française et la communauté anglaise, souvent désignées comme 'les peuples fondateurs'. Le chapitre 1 est consacré à cette dualité." (T.3 p.1)

On s'aperçoit, en regardant de près les mots utilisés par les commissaires que le seul terme de communauté est insuffisant pour décrire la dualité canadienne puisqu'il faut ajouter le qualificatif de 'principales'. Les deux communautés francophone et anglophone ne regroupent pas tous les individus sur le territoire du Canada. Il faut donc admettre l'existence d'autres communautés, par exemple, les autochtones (T.3 p.1), les Ukrainiens, les Italiens, les Grecs. "Par ailleurs, le Canada compte un grand nombre de communautés et de groupes ethno-culturels distincts — les Ukrainiens, les Italiens, les Grecs, pour n'en nommer que quelques-uns". (T.2 p.9)

En présentant la dualité en terme de communautés principales, on situe des groupes de personnes à l'extérieur de la question canadienne. (cf. T.3 p.8) Ces autres communautés ont donc l'impression de ne pas faire partie du débat, de la dualité. De plus, ils s'opposent au fait qu'on réduise le Canada à une dualité de communautés et ils revendiquent, par leur présence, la reconnaissance d'un Canada 'pluraliste'. Le Canada, pays pluraliste, où chaque communauté a le droit de vivre, d'exiger le respect des autres communautés et le soutien de l'Etat.

1.1.1.3 Selon le rapport *Se retrouver...* c'est faire partie d'une société, la société francophone ou la société anglophone.

Selon cette dernière hypothèse, serait anglophone celui qui fait partie de la société anglophone et serait francophone, celui qui fait partie de la société francophone. "Chacune de ces communautés possède ses propres institutions et on considère donc qu'elles forment deux sociétés distinctes dans la société canadienne." (T.2 p.10) Le terme de société est important. En effet, si on avait seulement utilisé celui de communauté, on aurait du admettre la pluralité canadienne plutôt que la dualité. La pluralité des communautés ethniques est reconnue puisque la population canadienne n'est pas uniquement formée d'individus dont les ascendants sont soit français soit anglais. Cependant, bien qu'il y ait plusieurs communautés, elles s'intègrent nécessairement dans les deux sociétés francophone et anglophone. Le concept de société permet de distinguer deux catégories exclusives au Canada, catégories qui regroupent tous les citoyens. La distinction entre société et communauté devient donc capitale. Selon le rapport,

> Une communauté est un groupe de personnes unies par la *conscience* de certaines caractéristiques qu'elles ont en commun (par exemple, l'ethnicité, la culture, la langue, la race, la religion, le territoire) et de certains intérêts (sociaux, économiques ou politiques) qu'elles partagent. Tous ces facteurs d'unité ne se rencontrent pas obligatoirement dans chaque communauté, mais chacune en comprend habituellement plus d'un, par exemple l'ethnicité et la langue. (T.2 p.3)

La société se définit ainsi,

> Une communauté qui réussit à établir un réseau suffisamment vaste et cohérent d'institutions acquiert par le fait même la direction de ses activités et peut alors être considérée comme une société distincte. . . Une société se définit surtout par des structures alors que c'est plutôt par un esprit et un sentiment collectifs que se définit une communauté. (T.2 p.3)

Le critère essentiel qui permet de distinguer une société d'une communauté est celui de structure. Ces structures peuvent être sociales, culturelles, économiques et politiques. Mais comment savoir si un individu entre dans la catégorie des membres de la société francophone ou de la société anglophone? De plus, y a-t-il plusieurs sociétés anglophones au Canada? Combien de sociétés francophones?

Les explications du rapport sont très peu explicites. Fait intéressant, les exemples sont toujours ceux du Canada-français. Par exemple, les commissaires maintiennent:

> Un québécois de langue française participe simultanément à quatre sociétés au moins: la société francophone du Québec, la société du Québec comme province, la société canadien-nefrançaise dans son ensemble et la société canadienne globale fondée sur des institutions, des rapports et des activités existant à l'échelle du pays. (T.2 p.4)

Si cela est vrai, et que la dualité existe au Canada, on devra dire que "Un québécois de langue anglaise participe simultanément à quatre sociétés au moins: la société anglaise du Québec, la société du Québec comme province, la société canadienne-anglaise dans son ensemble et la société canadienne globale fondée sur des institutions, des rapports et des activités existant à l'échelle du pays".

L'exemple donné ne clarifie pas le sens de 'société' et ne permet pas de distinguer une société d'une communauté. En effet, cet exemple des commissaires, prend comme point de départ, "un québécois de langue française" comme si on savait déjà ce qu'est 'un québécois' et ce qu'est 'être de langue française'. Qu'est-ce qu'un Québécois? Certains pourraient soutenir qu'il s'agit d'un individu habitant le territoire du Québec, d'autres diront qu'il s'agit d'un individu membre de la société francophone du Québec, d'autres, qu'il suffit d'habiter le territoire, enfin certains admettront qu'on peut habiter dans une autre province et demeurer Québécois puisqu'on y est né. De plus, le point de départ suppose qu'on sait reconnaître un québécois de langue française. Or nous ne pouvons utiliser cette expression, 'de langue française' sans évoquer toutes les difficultés mentionnées plus haut concernant le critère de 'posséder une langue'.(cf. 1.1.1.1) Enfin, on peut se demander ce qu'il advient d'un Québécois de langue italienne? Est-ce qu'il participe seulement à la société du Québec comme province et à la société canadienne dans son ensemble? Est-il hors de la dualité?

L'exemple des commissaires suppose l'existence d'une société canadienne distincte de la société canadienne-française et de la société canadienne-anglaise, une société provinciale anglaise. Doit-on aussi admettre le même phénomène pour toutes les provinces du Canada? Est-ce qu'il existe effectivement, une société canadienne, une société canadienne-française, une société canadienne-anglaise, dix sociétés provinciales, dix sociétés provinciales françaises, dix sociétés provinciales anglaises, une société territoriale, une société territoriale française et une société territoriale anglaise? Pour établir leur existence, il faudrait entre autre déterminer quelles sont les structures qui font qu'une société se distingue de l'autre.

Si nous conservons le sens donné à société, celui de communauté qui établit "un réseau suffisamment vaste et cohérent d'institutions", nous pouvons facilement admettre que la société francophone du Québec existe. L'expression 'un québécois' est souvent utilisé pour désigner un membre de cette société francophone du Québec. Si la société francophone du Québec existe, ne doit-on pas reconnaître aussi la société francophone ontarienne, etc. De plus, doit-on reconnaître une société francophone hors-Québec, et une société francophone canadienne? De telles sociétés n'existent pas car il n'y a pas comme l'exige la définition, de réseau suffisamment vaste et cohérent d'institutions sociales, économiques ou politiques. On ne peut pas parler de la communauté canadienne-française comme d'une société. Si le terme de 'société' s'applique à toutes les entités que mentionne le rapport sur l'unité canadienne, il devient dès lors synonyme de communauté.

Il est étonnant de constater que les commissaires expliquent le concept de dualité à partir du Québec. Dans la section réservée à la dualité, il y a une seule sous-section, intitulée *Le Québec*. Pourquoi n'y a-t-il pas de sous-section réservée à la société anglophone? Voici l'explication des commissaires.

> Prenant de la réalité une vue dualiste ils ont parfois tendance à percevoir le Canada anglais comme un bloc monolithique. Il n'en est rien. Le Canada anglophone est bien loin d'être aussi homogène que bien des Québécois semblent le croire; il est infiniment plus divers et compliqué. . . . On est même fondé à affirmer que le caractère régionaliste du Canada anglophone complique à son tour la vue qu'il prend du Canada français, exactement comme le caractère homogène et concentré de la société québécoise complique l'opinion qu'il peut avoir du reste du pays. (T.1 p.26)

Il est difficile ici de suivre la logique des commisaires. D'une part, ils soutiennent qu'on ne peut comprendre la crise de l'unité canadienne sans utiliser le concept de dualité. D'autre part, ils refusent les conséquences de ce concept, l'obligation de concevoir deux groupes, deux blocs monolitiques. Par contre, dans les définitions, ils reconnaissent que la société canadienne est formée d'une société canadienne-française et d'une société canadienne-anglaise. S'il faut admettre le caractère régionaliste du Canada anglophone, ne faut-il pas l'admettre aussi pour le Canada francophone? S'il n'y a pas de société canadienne-anglaise, pourquoi y aurait-il une société canadienne-française? Le caractère régionaliste du Canada français est aussi évident sinon plus que le caractère régionaliste du Canada anglais. Les franco-ontariens se distinguent des franco-manitobains, des Acadiens et des Québécois.

1.1.1.4. L'expression 'dualité francophonie-anglophonie' désigne en fait la réalité suivante: Au Canada, les gens vivent quotidiennement la langue française ou la langue anglaise.

A première vue, il n'est pas évident que 'vivre sa langue' soit préférable à 'posséder une langue' et j'entends déjà les commentaires associant cette idée de vivre sa langue à la publicité faite au Québec "On vie en français". Cependant, si on adopte un instant la position d'une personne qui immigre au Canada, on s'aperçoit qu'elle est obligée de faire un choix de vie. Dans quelle langue communiquera-t-elle au travail, avec ses amis, avec ses voisins, à l'école pour ses enfants?

La dualité canadienne désigne donc ce fait, "Au Canada, les gens vivent quotidiennement la langue française ou la langue anglaise".

Nous pouvons choisir de vivre une langue ou l'autre. Evidemment il se parle beaucoup de langues au Canada. D'ailleurs certains immigrants d'un âge avancé ne parlent que leur langue nationale. Ne pourrait-on pas dire que ces gens vivent aussi leur langue? Non, puisque vivre sa langue n'est pas uniquement parler sa langue dans un seul contexte déterminé. Vivre sa langue, renvoie à tous les contextes sociaux. C'est pourquoi nous pouvons déterminer les critères de vérification de la façon suivante: Vivre sa langue se mesure d'abord en terme de pourcentage d'utilisation d'un niveau de langue et par le nombre de niveaux de langue pratiqués (l'utilisation signifie plus que 0%).

Niveaux de langue:

1. la langue familiale: avec le conjoint
   avec les enfants
   avec les parents
   avec la parenté
2. langue du voisinage: voisinage immédiat de la résidence
   amis et relations personnelles
3. la langue scolaire:
   1. primaire
   2. secondaire
   3. professionnel ou pré-universitaire
   4. universitaire: premier cycle
      deuxième cycle
4. la langue des médias de communication utilisés: radio, télévision, presse écrite, revues....
5. la langue de travail: parlée
   écrite: 1. à lire
   2. à écrire
6. la langue des loisirs: cinéma, théâtre
7. la langue des services publics:
   1. transports en commun
   2. affichage public
   3. magasins
   4. administration municipale
   5. administration scolaire
   6. administration provinciale
   7. administration fédérale

Si on demandait à tous les canadiens d'indiquer quel pourcentage d'utilisation ils font de l'anglais, du français et de toute autre langue qu'ils connaissent, nous aurions une mesure précise de notre réalité canadienne. Comparativement aux autres provinces, je me demande combien de Québécois réponderaient 100% à tous les niveaux.

L'étude des résultats nous montrerait avec beaucoup de précision les régions du Canada ou l'on vit tous les niveaux en français et en anglais, en d'autres mots, la dualité canadienne. De plus on verrait les régions ou le français n'est plus vécu régionalement qu'une autre langue, l'allemand par exemple. Grâce à ces critères nous pouvons donc distinguer le pluralisme des langues et la dualité canadienne, de même que vérifier, le régionalisme que prend cette dualité dans toutes les provinces du Canada.

C'est seulement à partir de ce concept de dualité canadienne qu'on peut espérer décrire un des éléments de la crise de la Confédération. Grâce à cette description de la dualité on peut maintenant formuler le principe de la dualité et les différents arguments qui justifient la revendication de vivre sa langue. L'analyse du premier point: En quels termes présenter la crise canadienne est loin d'être terminée. Nous devrions au moins: (1.1.2.) définir le principe de dualité (le dualisme) et (1.1.3.) montrer les liens entre la dualité (description) et le dualisme (principe).

CONSTITUTIONAL SYMMETRY AND THE QUESTION OF SPECIAL STATUS FOR QUEBEC

Alistair M. MACLEOD

Quebec is the only province in Canada in which there is a distinctive linguistic and cultural community which constitutes a majority of the population. It is a threat to the very survival of their language and culture, deeply felt by the members of this community, which is the most important source of the present constitutional crisis. Despite persistent demands in recent years for substantial enlargement of the powers, both legislative and executive, of the provincial government in Quebec — demands motivated largely, even if not exclusively, by a desire to deal with this threat — most defenders of a federal system in Canada have been opposed to any move in the direction of conferment of special constitutional status upon Quebec. I want in this paper to assess one recurrent objection to the so-called special status solution to the Quebec problem.

It is convenient to view the special status proposal, in the form in which I wish to consider it in this paper, as incorporating at least four claims. These should not be regarded, however, as providing an exhaustive definition of the proposal. Several of them cannot even be taken to be *essential* ingredients in a special status approach. Strictly speaking, it is only the second claim to which any serious defender of such an approach must commit himself. First, preservation of the language and culture of the Francophone majority in Quebec is a desirable objective of public policy for reasons which go beyond the stake Canadians have in preventing the break-up of Canada. There are, of course, more ways than one in which this objective might be vindicated if the need to do so were to arise. The simplest would be to note that preservation of their cultural heritage is something in fact desired, and desired intensely, by the members of the Francophone community. Alternatively, and more ambitiously, attainment of this objective might be shown to be a necessary condition of personal fulfilment for members of the Francophone community.

Second, conferment of additional legislative and executive powers upon the province of Quebec is an important part — although no doubt no more than a part — of the strategy which must be adopted if the objective of preserving the Quebecois cultural heritage is to be achieved. This contention is open to challenge from two quite different quarters: on the one hand, from those who think the powers already possessed by the federal and provincial governments would suffice to meet, and meet fully, the cultural aspirations of the Francophone majority in Quebec; on the other hand, from those who maintain that nothing short of complete independence for Quebec can ensure the preservation of the Quebecois cultural heritage. An intermediate position on this issue is presented in the powerfully-argued parts of the Pepin-Robarts report dealing with the problem of the threatened Francophone culture in Quebec, even though, for reasons which (as I shall suggest below) are quite inadequate, they back away in the event from a special status approach to the Quebec problem.

Third, the question whether constitutional change in the form of expanded provincial jurisdiction is a condition of preservation of the French language and culture in Quebec is not to be answered by trying to determine how far the members of the community in fact want or desire such change. On the contrary, provided the objective presumptively served by such constitutional adjustments can be shown to be desirable, what means to its achievement are indispensable is a technical question of fact quite distinct from, and independent of, the question whether all (or most) French-speaking Canadians — or Canadians in general, for that matter — actually wish such means to be adopted. There is room in this context for appeal to the Kantian maxim 'Who so wills the end wills the means' in response to any determined advocacy of referendum-style settlement of the question whether this or that determinate constitutional proposal is acceptable.

Fourth, any acceptable case for conferment of additional powers upon the province of Quebec for the purpose of preserving the language and culture of the Francophone majority must be consistent with adequate protection of the interests and needs of individuals and groups outside the Francophone community. It is clearly as essential that the linguistic and cultural rights of non-Francophone Quebec residents be afforded constitutional protection as it is that the rights of Francophone minorities in the rest of Canada be guaranteed.

The primary objection among advocates of a federal solution to the Quebec problem to the so-called special status option springs from the belief that conferment of additional powers on the province of Quebec would introduce an unacceptable asymmetry into the Canadian constitution. In the words of the Task Force on Canadian

Unity, "Many Canadians ... find the notion of 'special status' for one province, with its connotation of 'privileged' and favoured treatment, repugnant to their belief that all Canadians should be equal under the constitution." *(A Future Together*, p.87). I want in this paper to argue that when it is seen in the light of the limited purpose it is designed to serve, the conferment of special legislative and executive powers upon the provincial government in Quebec would be wholly consistent with the requirement that all provinces within a just federal system must be treated with equal respect. The constitutional asymmetry which such an arrangement for Quebec involves is consequently, in my judgment, a benign asymmetry. Crucial to my argument is the recognition that once the powers to be conferred on Quebec under the special status proposal are seen as powers needed for the preservation of the language and culture of the Quebecois, it would be a misdescription of the proposal to say, or imply, that under it Quebec had been given the kind of special deal which might well be made available to other provinces as well. The explanation is obvious. No other province has the problem faced by Quebec. Consequently there is a sense in which no other province can — logically — lay claim to powers of the kind contemplated for the province of Quebec under the special status proposal.

A distinction must be drawn between two ways in which constitutional arrangements within a federal system might be asymmetrical. (1) Two provinces, A and B, with identical needs and aspirations, might be dealt with differently by the drafters of a new constitution, with ampler powers being conferred upon A than upon B. (2) Alternatively, two provinces, C and D, might be assigned different powers precisely because of differences in their needs and aspirations. In both cases, different powers would be being assigned the provinces in question, so in one obvious sense the constitutional arrangements would be asymmetrical. Yet it is only in the case of (1) that it would be reasonable to complain that preferential treatment was being accorded one of the provinces. In (2), by contrast, differences in the powers allocated to C and D would be readily explicable in terms of differences in their needs, and it would consequently be unreasonable to complain that the special treatment accorded C is inconsistent with the enjoyment by C and D of equal status as provinces. A son cannot reasonably tax his parents with favouritism *simply* because they spend more on his sister than on him. If the explanation is that she requires expensive orthodontal treatment (for more than merely cosmetic reasons, let us suppose), he can hardly claim that he ought in fairness to be helped to buy, say, a sports car. On any acceptable version of the principle of equality, it requires not that all cases be treated alike but only that *relevantly similar* cases be treated alike.

Now if the conferment of special powers on Quebec for the express purpose of dealing with a problem unique to Quebec is consistent with the kind of constitutional symmetry demanded by the principle that provinces must enjoy equality of status within a just federal system, it is a mistake to try to undercut opposition to the granting of such powers to Quebec by making available "similar" powers to all the other provinces in the way recommended by the Task Force on Canadian Unity. "The preferable approach", they write, "is to allot to all provinces powers in the areas needed by Quebec to maintain its distinctive culture and heritage, but to do so in a manner which would enable the other provinces, if they so wished, not to exercise these responsibilities and instead leave them to Ottawa." (*Our Future Together*, page 87.)

This particular Task Force recommendation is open to objection not so much because the transfer of additional powers to the provinces would unduly weaken the federal government in areas in which its powers must be maintained — though this objection, a standard one from the standpoint of those who are fearful of any movement in the direction of substantial decentralisation of authority within the system, may have some force — but rather because it would introduce an undesirable asymmetry into the constitution. For as we have seen, when the powers to be conferred upon Quebec under the special status proposal are circumspectly characterized — or (perhaps better) when the limited purpose they are designed to serve is borne in mind — it becomes clear that they cannot be made available to all the other provinces. In a merely formal way, of course, these powers might perhaps be put on offer to all the provinces, but this would be an idle gesture given the knowledge that none of the provinces except Quebec is in a position to accept the proffered powers. Consequently, any serious constitutional offer made to the provinces under the Task Force proposal would have to be one for which these provinces, given their circumstances and needs, could qualify. Yet this means that the powers in question would have to be either different powers from those envisaged under the special status proposal or — if there should be an objection to defining constitutional powers in terms of the purposes they are designed to serve — powers serving ends quite different from that to be served by the conferment of special status on Quebec. Despite appearances, it is the Task Force proposal, and not the so-called special status proposal, which would introduce an unacceptable asymmetry into constitutional arrangements.

The animus against an asymmetrical solution to the constitution problem, at any rate of the sort exemplified by the special status proposal, is also partly responsible for the rejection by many Quebecers of the idea that adequate protection of their language and culture can in principle be provided within a restructured federal system. Pessimistic about the prospects of securing the sort of restructured federal system which would provide a reasonable guarantee of the preservation of their cultural heritage, they have in recent years opted in increasing numbers either for a radically independentist strategy (as 'separatists' properly so-called have done) or they have come to advocate 'sovereignty-association'. While there are no doubt some advocates of independence for Quebec who believe that political independence is itself an absolutely necessary condition of the adequate protection of the traditions they value, it seems likely that many more have found themselves supporting the independence strategy because of increasing signs that no federal solution to the constitutional problem is being seriously entertained which would allocate to the province of Quebec powers substantial enough to protect the language and culture of the Francophone majority. As for the so-called sovereignty-association option, it seems likely that it too would have gained fewer adherents had a special status version of the federalist position been championed more vigorously. Indeed, on some interpretations of the sovereignty-association model, it is difficult to draw any very sharp principled distinction between it and the special status proposal, which suggests that at least some advocates of sovereignty-association might well be brought to favour a federalist solution to the constitutional problem were it not for doctrinaire opposition to the kind of asymmetry in constitutional matters which is demanded by the special status approach.

The demand for a symmetrical constitution — out of loyalty to a confused version of the principle that all provinces in a just federal system must have equal status — has thus had three unfortunate effects on debate about the future relations between Quebec and Canada. In the first place, it has encouraged some federalists, in rejecting the idea of special status for Quebec, to refuse to entertain constitutional proposals far-reaching enough to accommodate satisfactorily the cultural aspirations of French-speaking Quebecers. Secondly, it has encouraged those federalists who see that a break-up of Canada is inevitable if the cultural distinctiveness of Quebec is not given adequate recognition in a revised constitution to recommend that the powers Quebec needs be made available to all the other provinces as well. Thirdly, it has given an undeserved fillip both to the view that nothing short of political independence will suffice for the preservation of the French cultural heritage in Quebec and to the view that sovereignty-association (as a sort of non-federalist special status solution!) is what must be striven for.

Although I have been critical of the strand in the Task Force Report which connects the case for enlargement of the jurisdiction of the provinces with the need to come to terms with the special problem Quebec faces, it should go without saying that proposals substantially similar to those favoured by the Task Force on the question of division of powers may deserve support for reasons unrelated to the supposedly objectionable asymmetry a special status solution to the Quebec problem would introduce into the constitution. There might, for example, be a case for conferring certain additional powers upon the provinces to enable them to develop their natural resources more effectively. But it is a case which must be examined – and which must stand or fall – wholly independently of the case for special constitutional status for Quebec. That Quebec needs certain powers in order to preserve its cultural heritage is not an argument for giving Alberta the powers it might require for the promotion of its Heritage Fund.

MUST QUEBEC NATIONALISM BE RACIST? DELOS AND *LA NATION*

Christopher Berry GRAY

The problem posed by the title implies that (1) Quebec nationalism is racist, (2) nationalism tends to be racist, (3) Quebec nationalism tends peculiarly to be so. This paper seeks (4) a solution distinctively *québécois*, so as by its very presence to refute the assumptions factually as well as theoretically. The solution offered is J.T. Delos'; its terms will be used also to focus the problem, and (5) rebuttal to critiques of it will give it contemporaneity.

1. Quebec nationalism is racist, or at least is so perceived by its opponents or victims, which is all that can be said of any accusation of racism. (1.1) Despite C.S.N's resolutions to the contrary, the francophone Conférence Afro-Canada considers Quebec a *société bloquée*, a nationalism founded on race and biological vigour.[1] (1.2) Despite Camille Laurin's urging in the green paper on culture that "Laissons les racistes à leur mépris, c'est d'une fraternité de la culture qu'il s'agit",[2] his original definition of *québécois* as francophone in the *Charte de la langue française* belied it for many,[3] as does his *postulat incontestable* in the green paper that French is the pole for convergence of cultural differences into a principal culture because francophones there are strongest, when added to its *suite logique* that "common language" induces a systematized daily *vie d'un ensemble*. One of those for whom it did so was P.E. Trudeau, who in response disclaimed nation as an ethnic group — linguistic, racial or religious — on his 1977 France visit. (1.3) Nor is this novelty. Lionel Groulx, modern "father of Quebec nationalism", plumbed its feelings in *L'appel de la race* of 1922, whose bent led him to publish it as "Alonié de Lestres" until its final fifth edition in 1956.[4] His later demurrer prefacing a second edition of *La naissance d'une race*, that he meant only "a variety of the French family" and not an anthropological meaning, did little to counter the bent.

2. Nationalism tends towards racism because it situates a grouping upon particular factors. The least contestably particular qualities of humans are their genetically determined ones.

3. Quebec nationalist racism is distinctive, and thereby itself a feature of the nationalism, because of its dual direction: from heredity towards culture; and from culture towards politics. A group of people, not autochthonous, established itself on a territory; its descendents are francophone, as their forebearers; their identity is to be francophone descendents; their well-being is ensured by others on that territory being francophone; but it is the descendents' well-being and identity which is being assured, not the others'; the good of that grouping in turn, must be couched in political terms, for the only claim to locate francophone heredity as their identity on this territory must lie in a claim to their sovereignty over that territory, since they are not autochthonous and thereby attached to or upon territory.

4. Philosophically, the response to Quebec nationalist racism is not to effect individual or social metanoia but to locate a doctrinal basis which (4.1) does counteract the racism because of its factual influence, and (4.2) can perform this role because of its rational rigour.

4.1 Joseph Thomas Delos' political philosophy had an influence recognized as counter to the Montreal Jesuit ideology of Groulx, and continues to have that influence, though not in a manner well recognized. Delos taught sociology in l'Ecole des sciences sociales at l'Université Laval at its opening in the early forties. Delos had an acknowledged formative influence upon the School's influential founder, George-Henri Lévesque. Delos published, while in Quebec, several texts of his courses which are of highest relevance to our problem. Delos' and later Lévesque's disciples are prominent influences upon Quebec's recent and current ideology.[5]

4.2 Delos' recommendations have a methodological appearance, but substantial results. Sociology has a distinctive object: phenomena of life together, which while scientifically available, are moral and not necessitated phenomena, and which while personal are not political.[6] Social phenomena are neither biological nor political: race is not a legitimate object for sociology, nor is the state. Nation is. The remedy to the problems of nationalism is to distinguish nation from state, for their confusion works in one direction: to assimilate state to nation, and nation to biological phenomena. This is the assimilation that is prominent in the Quebec nationalism referred to above at (3). In the main text, *La nation*,[7] the problem is posed in terms of rights: (4.2.1) rights of man are basic, of which (4.2.2) rights of citizens and (4.2.3) rights of nationals are forms; on this basis, (4.2.4) rights of nations and of states diminish in importance, and (4.2.5) relations of nation and state are appreciable apart from a nation-state.

4.2.1 Man alone bears rights. For rights are the reflection of a moral judgment made about a particular kind of nature, and are not just the matter of fact that something exists, whether individual or solidary. The aspect of man's nature which elicits moral judgment is that he is a whole, and not just a part. The sense in which man is such and absolute is that he appropriates the universe rather than being simply contained by it; his knowledge and love "comprehend" and "embrace" the world. The term 'rights' refers to relationships between such absolutes.

4.2.2 For rights to become exercisable, the relationships with others must be ascertainable in terms common to both. An organization whose role is none other than to be common to both is rational; rights which are ascertained by reference to it are declarations of the conditions under which human rights can be realized at a particular point. These rights of citizens, or civil liberties, are no more particularized than is man's nature to one or another.

4.2.3 Men, however, live dependent upon time and space as well, divided from each other by a particular history and country. "Le national est l'homme marqué par un particularisme qui voile sa personnalité sous des traits ethniques." Or, elsewhere,[8] nationality is "un ensemble de 'formes' physiques et psychologiques qui détermine les sentiments, les pensées et l'agir humains". Only in space and time can men become really existent; but the value of national particularities is solely their relation to human nature, "a use of time for ends which go beyond time". Nonetheless, man is embodied in nationality; national traits are not means in a sense only extrinsic and instrumental.

> Les liens nationaux et les caractères qu'ils impriment ne sont pas plus un moyen d'accéder à la vie civilisée que, dans l'ordre individuel, le corps et les dispositions du tempéra-

> ment ne sont un moyen qui permet de vivre en homme: ils sont de l'homme même. Ainsi, être français, espagnol ou anglais n'est pas un moyen de devenir un homme, c'est une manière d'être. ... Les nuances . . . ne sont pas pour Racine des moyens d'exprimer ses sentiments: ce sont ses sentiments mêmes, et la forme qui les qualifie français, . . . pas un moyen de devenir un homme cultivé, mais une façon de l'être.

So social facts which initially appear mechanistic are, so far as social, reintegrated into human wholeness: as for the influence of racial characteristics upon social relations, "la cause du fait social est ici un élément psychique: une répulsion ou un attrait, un préjugé ou un jugement moral, politique ou religieux, bref, toujours une 'représentation'";[9] the alleged "contagion" by opinion is in reality the development of a continuingly intellectual event — "la raison d'aujourd'hui, opinion de demain, et tradition de l'après-demain".[10]

4.2.4 Men as nationals bear the rights of nationality. The nation, on the other hand, is a community structured out of communities, always characterized by their contingency, indeterminacy and potentiality; it is a matter of fact, not a subject of right. State nonetheless, regards the rights of citizens founded absolutely in human nature, rights not subject to any functional limitation. It can, therefore, achieve the moral personality required to act as a subject of right.[11] In order for those rights to be exercised, however, they must be directed at some end, one determined by nature and not the state. Their end limits the rights both of individual and of state. State protects these rights, but only insofar as these rights constitute the common good, and not insofar as they are personal absolutes.

4.2.5 The relation between state and nation, or between political order and national order, is harmonious in that both serve the same end. They cannot be rival autonomies, because neither is autonomous. Their distinction is best achieved by detailing the different strata which make up the social patrimony that is the nation — cultural, economic, familial, religious, . . . — for then one after another of the possible confusions is dispelled. Carrying out this sociological research is to develop "the fundamental law of human societies: the law of differentiation and organization"; indeed, it constitutes their very progress.[11]

> *Le progrès de la vie sociale* consiste à distinguer et séparer les groupes et les sociétés selon leur but spécifique, et à

> différencier et organiser les fonctions selon leur objet. . . spécialisés, si l'on peut dire, dans la recherche de leur objet mais rapprochés et ordonnés entre eux par la pensée de l'homme et la hiérarchie de ses besoins.

Lacking a principle of limitation by finality, rights would have to be unconditional and unlimited, all have one single foundation, whether national or political rights. The state's rights, too, are unlimited; only isolated individuals face state, and for any cohesion at all among them the state must look to the nation. In turn, nation looks to state as its personification; and those not part of the nation are excluded from state's protection, and must seek a separated state for their nation. Parallel to such internal splintering is the nation-state's external voracity, or imperialism: the nation is closed upon its own characteristics, the state is open upon men's complete humanity, the nation-state derives a universal appetite to make all into its particular characteristics.

If state is identified with nation, and especially if nation is identified by characteristics linked to ancestry, the separation of a new nation-state is of no avail; the older nation-state's worm is transmitted with it. If nation is distinguished from state, and on the other side from race, then even imperial state is no threat to nation. Nonetheless, the best fit for nations is the federal state, whose identity is none other than to mold the face of its component groups, whether nations or states. Even here, however, identity is never achieved, and the stress to preserve the tension between man's transcendence and man's situatedness endures; "renewed federalism" is, for Delos, constant.

5. Given human transcendence and immanence, the solution via distinction of state and nation follows. But the former frankly depends upon essentialist footings, viz., a common human nature. And in a Canada less advanced in its escape from positivist assumptions than its anglophone sister cultures, that is unpalatable before even tasting. Cochran's rephrasing of another Dominican's political philosophy may make it less so.[12] Faculties to "comprehend" and "embrace" all being are less bizarre when simply called "common good" which, while still objectionable, is still more pointed in its critiques. Rejection of analysis by common good because it ignores the existence of conflict among interests is answered by separating common good from the sum of interests. "A common good . . . is so not because the happinesses of users may be summed in a fashion which increases total individual happiness. Rather, it is a

common good because each may use it . . . and, in so using it, enhance the common intercourse." It is not subject to critiques of sums of private interests, because it is simply something else.

This is just what the "end" of Delos' rights is: the common good.

> Le bien commun est d'abord un bien de l'homme. . . . Non pas quand plusieurs individus en jouissent simultanément, ou possèdent un droit indivis à en jouir. Pas davantage quand il est susceptible d'être partagé. . . . Un bien est commun dans la mesure où, par sa nature, il est apte à satisfaire les besoins d'un nombre indéterminé d'individus. Il est alors commun, non parce qu'une pluralité d'individus en bénéficie, mais parce qu'il est naturellement apte à satisfaire les besoins d'une collectivité, d'un nombre indéterminé d'individus. . . . L'objet est un bien commun parce qu'il va au devant d'un besoin de la nature de l'homme, . . . un besoin humain, un besoin de tous les hommes, un besoin qui vient aux individus de leur nature même et non de leurs particularités individuelles. . . . Or, qu'y a-t-il de commun entre tous ces êtres? Précisément ceci que . . . tous ont une même fin, un même bien temporel et spirituel à atteindre.

The alternative to determining common good according to man and his nature is to do so by reference to race on the one side or state on the other,[13] which, as has been shown, tend to merge. What, in particular, constitutes such common good?

> La sécurité de la vie privée sur la base du droit est en effet le bien le plus général. L'ordre social qui institue le règne du droit — l'ordre de droit lui-même — tel est vraiment le bien commun auquel tous ont part, car les rapports les plus généraux des hommes sont des rapports juridiques: la seule chose vraiment commune à tous les hommes, c'est leur nature, c'est le fait d'être une personne, et la personnalité se manifeste par la qualité de sujet de droit. ...[14]

The apparent equivocation on the word *droit* is no more or less decisive than appeal to the discourse of "common good" and "human nature". Whether law *(droit)* is or is not a matter of moral considerations *(droit)*, i.e., what rights *(droit)* mean, is equally a matter of vaster legal philosophy and indeed metaphysics than is permissible here. At any rate, it is neither tarred nor hallowed in the mere saying of it.

What is of note, however, are several points. Contemporary solutions are at hand to resolve the problems of this doctrine. The doctrine itself is worked out in a way that is open to evaluation. And, most of all, this doctrine — worthy or not — is authentically *québécoise.* Nothing could be more foolish than to ignore a Quebec solution to Quebec problems because it has had currency only among those who struck the institutions only of Quebec. Especially when it is less racist, and thereby less separatist.

NOTES

1. *Le Devoir* (30 mars 1979)
2. Ministre d'Etat au Développement culturel, *La politique québécoise du développement culturel*, Québec, Editeur officiel, 1978, p.47.
3. L.Q., 1977, c., "Préambule", Para. 1 (Bill 101), at 1st Reading (as Bill 1).
4. See: M. Descôteaux, "Les problèmes du pseudonyme",*Phizero*6, no 2 *(La question du nationalisme*, mars 1978), U. Montréal, Dép. de philosophie.
5. On the Jesuit-Dominican split here, see: "Passé défini: les origines de la révolution tranquille; l'université au pouvoir", film of Explo-mundo, Montreal, 1976; G.H. Lévesque, "Notes nouvelles sur d'anciens instruments: La révolution tranquille au Québec", paper at Canadian Historical Society, 55th Congress, Laval, 3 June 1976; R. Parisé, *Georges-Henri Lévesque, père de la Renaissance québécoise*, Montréal, A. Stanké, 1976.On the Delos-Lévesque influence, see: G.H. Lévesque, "Itinéraire sociologique," *Recherches Sociographiques* 15 (1974), 202, p.211. Lévesque in personal conversation has said: "If you are looking for Delos' influences, take me!" Delos, says Lévesque, brought him into E. Mounier's founding meeting of *Esprit:* Mounier recalls the meeting in *Oeuvres* IV, Paris, Seuil, 1963, p.499, and praises the personalism of Delos' predecessors in "Institutionalism", M. Hauriou and G. Renard, at p.465 and I, 459. See: *The French Institutionalists*, ed. a. Broderick, Harvard, 1970.On the influence by Delos and Lévesque: Lévesque's 1979 nomination to the Order of Canada mentions as disciples Jean Marchand, Marcel Pépin, Maurice Lamontagne, Louis Robichaud; Lévesque, *loc.cit.,* mentions J.Ch. Falardeau, Léon Dion, Fernand Dumont (architect of the cultural green paper), G. Bergeron, G. Rocher, Y. Martin, G. Fortin, M.A. Tremblay; various correspondents mention D. Lussier, L. Lortie, J.P. Gaboury; the Laval classlist for Delos includes also R. Cliche, G. and R. Dion, J.P. Geoffroy.
6. J.T. Delos, "L'objet de la sociologie," *Vie intellectuelle* 7 (10 mai 1930), tr. in Broderick; derived from M. Hauriou, *La science sociale traditionnelle*, Paris, Larose, 1899, tr. C.B. Gray, *Tradition in Social Science*, Philosophy Research Archives, 1980. See: C.B. Gray, *Methodology of Maurice Hauriou*, C.U.A., 1970, ch.5.
7. *Le problème de la civilisation: La nation*, 2v., Montréal, Arbre, 1944.
8. *La société internationale et les principes de droit public*, 2 éd., 1950 (1 éd., 1929), p.16.
9. "La notion de race en sociologie et le génétique," *Bulletin des études françaises* 3 (sep., 1941), Montréal, Collège Stanislas.

10. *L'opinion, le gouvernement d'opinion, le gouvernement de foule*, Québec, Université Laval, Ecole des Sciences sociales, 1943. See also Hauriou, *Tradition,* above.

11. Again, Hauriou's hand appears in the law of progress and in the social tissues, the two parts of *Tradition;* and in the stages of the process of institutionalization for groups - from factual organization through objective individuality to subjective moral personality and legal personality - by ever deepening awareness and pursuit of *l'idée de l'institution,* in "La théorie de l'institution et de la fondation", tr. Broderick, esp. p.99.

12. Clarke E. Cochran, "Yves R. Simon and 'The Common Good': A Note on the Concept," *Ethics* 88, no.3 (April, 1978), 229, p.233.

13. Le bien commun, base du monde d'après-guerre, *"La nouvelle relève"* (sep., 1943), 524.

14. *La nation*, II, p.190.

CONFEDERATION AND THE WAR MEASURES ACT (AN ABSTRACT)

Nathan BRETT

The War Measures Act confers such extraordinary powers that it changes the nature of confederation. One would expect important changes under emergency conditions, but (i) determining when such conditions exist is problematic; and (ii) it is important to realize that some emergency measures have been in effect for more than one-third of the time since 1914, when the Act became law.

I. Powers assumed under the WMA:

   1. The cabinet can introduce such regulations as are deemed (a) necessary for defence, or (b) advisable for the welfare of Canada.

   2. There is no limitation on the kinds of activity that can be subject to regulation. Jurisdiction extends to what is normally controlled by the provinces.

   3. Enforcement procedures are also indefinitely alterable; hence "due process" can be set aside. (E.g., people can be, have been, dealt with under secret provisions, arrested for acts legal at the time they were done, presumed guilty.)

      (a) Penalties under the WMA are limited (5 years); but detentions can be indefinite.

      (b) The Bill of Rights (1960) contained ammendments to the WMA which automatically cancel its own operation under these measures.

II. Evidence of War: The WMA confers power "in the event of war, invasion or insurrection", but

   1. Catch-22: "conclusive evidence" of war is the invocation of the WMA itself. This suggests that the proclamation should be analyzed as a performative, that is, as a *declaration* of war.

2. Catch 22a: the emergency need not be "real".

3. Dilemma: If the WMA is interpreted in such a way that its invocation excludes judicial review then either

   (a) it is *ultra vires*, or

   (b) it somehow takes precedence over the BNA Act and confederation is not what it appears to be.

   Courts have held that they are not competent to rule on the question of whether emergency exists (or existed).

III. Concluding remarks:

1. It is to be expected that such broad powers would be abused; they have been.

2. The desire to dissociate from a form of government underwritten by this power is not unreasonable, hence

3. This Act is an impediment to the unity of Canada.

4. (An indication of the quality of thought behind the document from which all this power derives is that it ends (redundantly) with a provision for appointing "scouts and boys" to the RCMP.)

INDIVIDUAL, COLLECTIVE and MINORITY RIGHTS

DROITS DE L'INDIVIDU, DROITS de la COLLECTIVITE et DROITS des MINORITES

PARTICIPANTS

MARYANN AYIM
Philosophy, University of Western Ontario

BRENDA BAKER
Philosophy, University of Calgary

DAVID BRAYBROOKE
Philosophy, Dalhousie University

STEVEN BURNS
Philosophy, Dalhousie University

STEVEN DAVIS
Philosophy, Simon Fraser University

MARSHA HANEN
Philosophy, University of Calgary

NICOLAS KAUFMANN
Philosophie, Université du Québec à Trois-Rivières

MICHAEL McDONALD
Philosophy, University of Waterloo

VIRGINIA McDONALD
Political Science, York University

ALASTAIR McKINNON
Philosophy, McGill University

SERGE MORIN
Philosophie, Université de Moncton

WORKSHOP III REPORT

ATELIER III RAPPORT

Workshop III was addressed to questions concerning rights — individual, collective and minority. Ably, not to say firmly, chaired by David Braybrooke, and operating with the advantage of relatively small numbers, we began with brief summaries of the abstracts prepared by all participants, and by the time of the morning coffee break a structure had emerged within which the rest of the day's discussion could be carried on.

I **Three members had addressed themselves to the question of the rights of collectivities and how these are to be assigned, and we took this as the first focus of our discussion. In some way prior to this question were two others: the problem of what is a collectivity, and what are rights.**

(a) The first of these — the nature of collectivities — is obviously in part a question about the sorts of entities that can be the bearers of rights. It was suggested that rights are held by metaphysical individuals — persons, groups, corporations, governments, countries — and that there are various sorts of relationships that can obtain between the group and individuals that compose it so that we needn't say the rights of the group are really derivative from those of its members. Not all groups, of course, are rights bearers. One suggestion was that groups that were would have within them a significant number of shared interests, though there were counter examples such as the case of a jury where the interests served are not significantly those of jury members. Some members stressed the importance of subjective criteria of group identity, but these were not thought to be sufficient. Indeed it appeared there was a variety of criteria, though for purposes of the confederation debate we needed to be concerned with, among others, historical communities possessing a subjective sense of identity.

(b) On the question of the nature of rights, we began with the following characterization. We might say: *S* has a right to *X* with respect to *H* which gives rise to a duty of *H* to *Y*. It was suggested that the easiest cases are those where rights are already enshrined in law and are also endorsed morally; more difficult are those cases of legal rights which are not morally endorsed; and still harder are those cases of rights morally endorsed that are *not* embodied in law. (Some of the latter, of course, we would not want to embody in law, often for reasons of expediency.) But even rights embodied in law frequently receive no de facto recognition: indeed it was suggested that if we need to insist on particular rights this is a sign that they are not being acted upon.

The notions of interests and of needs were both suggested as bases for rights, and we thought it useful to distinguish between autonomy rights and dignity rights — the latter sometimes referred to as declaration rights. The former seem to appear earlier historically and to be connected with liberty and security, involving largely rights not to be interfered with in certain ways. These coincide in large measure with what some have called negative rights. But we seem to require also rights to self-respect, dignity and to certain kinds of benefits of a more positive nature. The two kinds of rights can sometimes conflict or be in tension with one another, as in the case of taxation.

(c) There were four ways suggested for looking at the rights of collectivities: (1) by analogy with those of individuals, (2) as arising from obligations, (3) as a device for the exercise of power and arising from interests, or (4) as emerging from contracts. We tried to explore the question whether one of these is the best way to look at the rights of collectivities, or whether several or even all are appropriate in some measure. As a touchstone for our views on this matter we tried to bear in mind the problem of sociological minorities. There is an important difference between situations where the majority changes from issue to issue and those where it is the same on every issue, for in the latter case, the rationale of majority rule is thwarted. It was pointed out that minorities such as Acadians, Franco-Ontarians and native peoples lack status, always having to look over their shoulders and be conscious of their position. Here what seems needed is some form of humanizing struggle so that the majority begins to feel obligations toward minorities.

(1) and (2): There was considerable discussion of and some disagreement over the question whether autonomy is fundamental and collective rights are to be seen as based on those of individuals. On the one hand autonomy and self-mastery were seen as fundamental to what it is to be human; on the other, there was a worry that this leads to the view that autonomy is inalienable and unwaivable, even if

it becomes burdensome. Here the suggestion was made that it is always possible that we might trade off any right for a greater good: to defend autonomy as fundamental and absolute may lead to an impasse. This theme of accommodation and of its being unwise in our current situation to be too absolutistic about rights was one to which we returned several times. Towards such an accommodation, the autonomy position was viewed as holding that it is important not to be dependent on the *arbitrary* will of others, and this was taken to be bound up with a particular cultural and historical context. Much of the disagreement having been resolved, there still seemed to be two distinct emphases: one on *who* is to make the decisions, the other on *what* is the right decision, and here interests played a large role.

(3): The view that rights are to be grounded on duties, and that duty claims are based on the natural needs of people was thought to be compatible with the interests view, though with greater emphasis on needs and less on preferences. What emerged was that it was not clear that these views had significantly different implications for the problems of confederation, for the point about the importance of detaching the minority from its anomalous position can be made without reference to rights at all, to say nothing of without reference to any particular view of how they are grounded.

(4): Questions about how rights arise through contract led us to problems with which we hoped members of other workshops could help us. There are difficulties about what the contract is supposed to be, whether it is explicit in the BNA Act, in which case it may no longer reflect the realities with which we live, or whether it is implicit only, in which case we have a less than clear understanding of its provisions. The problem seems to be one of defining who are the contractors and what the contract says. English Canadians, it was thought, tend to hold that the rights holders are individuals, or sometimes provinces, whereas francophones are more likely to speak of collective rights or of rights as belonging to peoples or nations, and to view the parties to the contract as two founding nations. Thus we have the insistence in Quebec that other groups define themselves in terms of collectivities if they wish to make claims to have rights protected. The fact that Quebec had a dominant English minority for a long time, of course, plays a considerable role in this sort of position.

With respect to the problem of contract we tried also to consider whether in general parties to contracts had an obligation — consider the example of a marriage — to consult one another if they wanted to exit from the contract. Most members thought there was at least some sort of moral obligation in this situation.

II **The problem of contract raises questions about other sorts of rights in confederation. The discussion had turned largely on problems connected with language and education, but there were concerns as well about resources and the question of whether these should be held by some sort of collectivity and, if so, which one.**

Some general claims about provincial rights to set economic policy and the growing importance of the provinces in some areas were touched upon, but to no very definite conclusion.

With respect to rights not primarily of an economic sort it emerged that there were various confusions about when we are speaking of minorities, which along with individuals, have traditionally been the focus of rights talk. We explored briefly the question of whether there might be interesting analogies between questions about women's rights and those we were considering, for clearly there has been in recent years some move on the part of women, not themselves a numerical minority, to view themselves as some sort of collectivity. But there were problems with this from the point of view of some members of our group, for women's lives are deeply bound up in the mainstream culture, and they have no easy means for identifying themselves regionally or in any of the other clear ways defined by the Task Force on Canadian Unity. Of the two models for achieving women's rights — equality of status with men, or special status — the consensus seemed to be that the former was practically preferable, at least in our present situation.

III **This question of rights, focussed on groups that are not minorities, led us to notice that, when we speak of collective rights of the French in Quebec we are not speaking of minority rights at all, though we are when we attend to the rights of francophones in other parts of Canada. Some thought that, if we value perpetuating francophone culture in Canada in general, then this might be better accomplished with Quebec a part of the whole than otherwise.**

But the whole perspective of minorities and majorities seemed to turn the discussion in inappropriate directions, a point that Serge Morin discussed more fully.

IV **In sum, then, we thought that both persons and various collectivities could be rights holders, and that the collectivities involved would usually be coherent cultural communities the boundaries of which would not in general coincide with provincial boundaries. But we found ourselves puzzled by questions about contract and constitution and whether the contract gives rise to**

rights, on which topic we hoped for enlightenment from members of other workshops. Related to this is the question of what rights are rights *to* — to autonomy, or culture, or language, or economic power or the self-determination of nations, or all of these.

The difficulty of settling these questions, and the fact of conflict of rights (for those of interest in the Confederation debate are by their very nature not absolute) led us also to suggest that it may be unwise in our current situation to focus too heavily on rights. For one thing, to grant that people *have* rights is not yet to see that they are implemented and the corresponding powers given free reign; for another, rights are the sorts of things people are inclined to insist on and to refuse to allow to be compromised, so that there may be a tendency in the Confederation debate to become involved too quickly in stances of confrontation and hostility.

Marsha HANEN

DROITS DES MINORITES, UNE IMPASSE

J.N. KAUFMANN

L'analyse (à la von Wright) d'une règle de droit retient généralement deux moments: le moment de la permission pour X de faire *a*, et corrélativement le moment de l'obligation pour Y de faire *b* ou celui de la prohibition pour Y d'empêcher X de faire *a*. Quand il est question de droits d'une minorité, X représente un ensemble d'individus répondant en tant qu'ensemble à certaines conditions, et Y représente un autre ensemble d'individus, à savoir la majorité.

D'après la règle de la majorité qu'ont adoptée les démocraties occidentales, ce n'est pas la minorité qui décide quels sont les droits qu'elle peut exercer et qui doivent lui être reconnus; (dans le cas contraire nous devrons ou bien traiter cette minorité comme souveraine et il ne pourra plus être question de minorité sous le même aspect; ou bien nous devrons la considérer comme une minorité dominante et nous n'aurons plus affaire à une démocratie électorale, mais, par exemple, à une oligarchie). D'après cette règle c'est la majorité qui décide et qui est censée exprimer la volonté collective.

Or il y a minorité (au sens sociologique) dans la mesure où un sous-ensemble invariable d'une population ou d'une collectivité se définit à partir des traits à la fois objectifs (langue, histoire, culture, institutions sociales), subjectifs (conscience commune, conscience de coappartenance) et volontaristes ("vouloir vivre ensemble", "vouloir maintenir son identité") que partagent les membres, comme différent par rapport à la majorité à laquelle il est incorporé, et s'oppose traditionnellement par ces traits distinctifs à cette majorité. Il y a minorité précisément dans la mesure où le sous-ensemble sociologiquement identifié *décide* de persévérer collectivement dans la différence tout en acceptant le verdict de la majorité sans cependant s'identifier en ce qui concerne des points précis à la volonté collective que la majorité est supposée exprimer.

Les querelles à propos de l'identification des minorités sociologiques en vue de leur accorder le statut de minorité juridique à laquelle la société internationale reconnaît des droits spéciaux et en fournit la garantie, ont toujours porté sur les critères à retenir et sur la manière de les appliquer de sorte que l'on ne confonde pas une minorité authentique avec une minorité factice. Il faut en effet qu'une minorité se manifeste comme différente sur un ensemble de caractéristiques qui constituent les ou certaines des fonctions vitales du système social que forme cette minorité. Des "minorités" formées par des individus ayant un QI > 160, ou un revenu > $200 000, ou formées par des homosexuels (?) ne seront probablement pas des candidates appropriées. Mais cela ne fait que poser l'épineux problème des lignes à tracer d'une part entre une minorité authentique et une minorité artificielle, entre une simple minorité et une minorité nationale qui constitue un peuple avec le droit à l'auto-détermination. C'est sans doute pour pallier à l'éventualité que se créent des minorités factices et pour lever l'ambiguïté concernant les minorités nationales que le droit international a remplacé les droits des minorités par les "droits de l'homme" garantissant les droits fondamentaux pour des *individus* et reconnaissant les droits des *peuples*, entre autres, de disposer d'eux-mêmes. (Cf. la déclaration de 1948 et celle de 1966 de l'O.N.U.)

A l'occasion des décisions collectives qui affectent directement ou indirectement l'identité de la minorité, qui atteignent celle-ci dans ce qui fait sa différence — et les critères généralement retenus pour déterminer une minorité sociologique montrant que l'éventail des décisions de cette nature peut être très large — les rapports entre la majorité et la minorité (sociologique) constituent une situation où la majorité et la minorité sont polarisées de telle sorte que la majorité est toujours gagnante et la minorité toujours perdante. (Cette affirmation n'est pas tautologique.)

Le fait que les membres d'une minorité se savent d'avance perdants sur des questions qui concernent leur *identité* est une atteinte sérieuse à la vie démocratique. Dans la situation normale, les membres minoritaires lors des votations sont supposés se redistribuer périodiquement, condition qui en principe n'est pas satisfaite quand on a affaire *à des minorités sociologiques* qui ne sont pas simplement des minorités d'opinion. N'est-ce pas devant les absurdités qu'a engendrées la redistribution de la carte géo-politique à l'occasion du traité de Versailles, où des empires furent amputés, des états bricolés de toute pièce, et des peuples littéralement ballottés dans leur réaffectation, que la question des droits spéciaux pour des minorités (de toutes sortes) est devenue brûlante, que des droits particuliers ont dû être accordés pour fournir un semblant de garantie pour la viabilité de ces nouvelles entités politiques. Bien que des minorités sociologiques aient probablement toujours existé, c'est l'histoire récente seulement qui les a promues minorités juridiques.[1] Et c'est l'histoire plus récente encore qui paraît avoir renoncé à la protection des minorités en mettant l'accent sur les garanties générales des libertés fondamentales des individus. Est-ce parce qu'on a dû admettre que la situation dans laquelle se trouvent les minorités est strictement insoutenable parce qu'elle constitue une impasse, une dénégation de l'idéal démocratique?

Pour sortir de l'impasse, il suffirait d'écarter la règle de la majorité pour toute question ayant trait à ce qu'on pourrait appeler "identité collective", "identité de la minorité". Cela me paraît être la motivation principale pour l'adoption d'une constitution confédérale où majorité et minorité ne s'opposent plus sous des rapports numériques, mais se séparent en tant que deux entités distinctes pour lesquelles il existe des droits en autant qu'ils procèdent à partir d'une reconnaissance mutuelle. Cette reconnaissance mutuelle n'est pas une affaire de droit et n'est pas garantie par des droits, parce qu'elle est la condition même de l'exercice des droits à la fois sur le plan des rapports entre individus et sur le plan des rapports entre des nations et des peuples.

NOTE

1. Il serait intéressant d'examiner chaque cas de minorité juridique pour voir quelles alternations la reconnaissance de droits spéciaux a pu faciliter: l'assimilation (Alsace, Tyrol, Schleswig-Holstein), l'indépendance (Algérie) ou le statut quo.

TAKING LANGUAGE RIGHTS SERIOUSLY*

Marsha HANEN

Introduction

In this paper I address the question whether, in our attempts to resolve the issues of language rights in Canada, we have anything to learn from current philosophical work on legal and political rights. For convenience, I concentrate on the rights theory of Ronald Dworkin, in the light of which I look at some claims about language rights in Canada, and actions taken or proposed in response to them, both by the federal and Quebec governments. What I want to consider is whether there is any reason to suppose that treating the problem about the claims of linguistic groups as a problem about rights is especially helpful, either from a conceptual or a practical point of view.

Dworkin's Theory

Recall Dworkin's fundamental distinction between two bases for the justification of political or legal decisions. Arguments of *policy* justify a political decision by showing that it advances or protects some collective goal of the community as a whole. Arguments of *principle* justify a decision by showing that it respects or secures some individual or group right.[1]

According to Dworkin,

> some state of affairs is a *goal* within a particular political theory if it counts in favor of a political act, within that theory, that the act will advance or preserve that state of affairs, and counts against an act that it will retard or threaten it.[2]

On the other hand

> an individual has a *right* to a particular political act, within a political theory, if the failure to provide that act, when he calls for it, would be unjustified within that theory even if the goals of the theory would, in the balance, be disserviced by that act.[3]

Rights may be less than absolute, and may in some cases be

* I wish to thank my research assistant, Janet Keeping, for invaluable help with many aspects of this paper.

outweighed by other rights or even by goals. The weight of a right is defined as its power to withstand the competition of other rights or goals, although by definition, a right cannot be outweighed by all social goals. But whether a political aim is a right or a goal

> depends upon its place and function within a single political theory. The same phrase might describe a right within one theory and a goal within another, or a right that is absolute or powerful within one theory but relatively weak within another.[4]

Thus what we say about language rights depends upon their place in the political theory we take to underlie our association. For example, it may be that what we think of as language rights function more like goals than like rights (in Dworkin's terminology) within the theory that best justifies the claims we make about them. But if this were to turn out to be so, would it matter? Would it be any less important to preserve language "rights" if they turned out to be goals rather than genuine rights? And is there any reason to think that chances of working out reasonable principles on which to base a renewed confederation would be reduced in such a case? I want to suggest that they would not — indeed that they might even be enhanced. But, to do this we shall need to look at some of the claims that have been made about language "rights".

Federal and Provincial Claims

A. The federal government has put forward proposals that, if adopted, would entrench a Canadian Charter of Rights and Freedoms[5] in an amended constitution. The rights so entrenched would be political, legal, egalitarian and linguistic but not economic, for the latter are thought to be better treated as goals to be accomplished through ordinary legislation rather than through a statement as constitutional rights. On the other hand, the values that become guaranteed rights are those that are "identified as warranting the protection which flows from constitutional entrenchment" [6] Thus we have another distinction between rights and goals, though this one is drawn somewhat differently from the way in which Dworkin draws his, and indeed the basis for the distinction in the *Charter* is none too clear. It seems, however, at least in part to be grounded on policy considerations, such as the issue of how the values in question can best be protected. The rights-goals distinction is also found in some of the international instruments adopted by the United Nations,[7] but none of these is thought to provide a clear basis for a distinction applicable in the Canadian context.

Of the four broad categories of rights to be entrenched in a constitution, the only ones apparently needing special justification are linguistic rights: the importance of political, legal, and egalitarian rights is perhaps thought to be sufficiently widely accepted already. As regards linguistic rights, the justifications given are

(a) that Canadian institutions must exist to help both the English-speaking and French-speaking groups to prosper; and

(b) that the federation will fall apart unless the equality of our two official languages is recognized and guaranteed. This is said to be a political reality whose practical implications must be accepted.

The second of these is put in an obviously goal-oriented way, suggesting as it does that the federal government is interested in protecting linguistic preferences in order to serve the goal of national unity. But the first justification is perhaps more rights-oriented. Still, even that one is quite unlike the reasons usually given for protecting other basic rights, such as the claim that they are fundamental to human dignity or freedom. Interestingly, too, no appeal is made to the right of freedom of expression, which some have thought to be the deeper right underlying claims about language rights in Canada.[8]

According to S.21(1) of the *Charter*, fundamental rights are designed to protect minorities, for majorities "have the power of the ballot to protect their interests" . But which minorities? The choice of English or French language instruction for children, for example, is to be limited to parents who are Canadian citizens: it will not be available to landed immigrants. Why should we accept this particular restriction? Is there something about the difference between those who have the status of citizens and those who are merely landed immigrants that makes it appropriate to extend the right to this particular choice to the former but not the latter? We begin to see how differently the Charter views linguistic rights from other basic rights, for suppose the right in question were to, say, freedom of religion. In that case, would the approach of treating citizens and landed immigrants differently be tolerated? It is said that an extension of the right to choice of language of instruction to landed immigrants might unduly restrict certain rights of provinces, so it appears that linguistic rights give way rather easily in the face of certain forms of competition. Provinces, it was thought, should have the right to determine the language of education for those who immigrate from outside Canada. In particular, this obviously will be important for Quebec, whose "government obviously wishes immigrants who will adopt the francophone culture".[9] This freedom of choice that applies to parents who are Canadian citizens would be extended to immigrant parents once they have become citizens; and it should prevail in Quebec as well as the rest of Canada "both because the French language was now adequately secure and because choice of language of education was a basic human right" .[10] One cannot help wondering whether, had French not been deemed to be sufficiently secure, this "basic human right" might not have been outweighed by the obvious policy consideration of protecting the French language in Canada. One can but speculate, but both of the two clear policy alternatives — of denying to Quebec citizens a right granted to citizens of other provinces, or of denying the right altogether for the sake of uniformity — seem anomalous.

The problem whether the rights to be entrenched are rights of individuals or of collectivities is hard to sort out; and the question whether the notion of collective rights makes sense is not even addressed. Various rights are categorized in the Charter as belonging to individuals or groups, but these classifications display a number of confusions. In the first place, certain language rights (such as those respecting government services) are said to be individual rights, yet some are made available only where a substantial number of the population uses the minority language. Not every individual, then, is in a position to claim these rights. More fundamentally, what sense does it make to say of a Ukranian- or German-speaking Albertan that the Charter would entrench a basic human right (a new one!) in providing for a choice between English and French as her main language of instruction? The response that in theory language rights needn't be confined to French and English, but that in practice anything else would be unworkable, won't do, for there *are* substantial communities of speakers of other languages, unquestionably large enough to support a school or school system. Pretty clearly, the basic "rights" with respect to language supposedly being embodied by the legislation can't be individual rights: they must be group rights, if they are rights at all. And we must ask what features a group must have in order to qualify for having these rights protected. Resort here, one supposes, must ultimately be to some such concept as that of two founding nations or peoples, especially if we are seeking a justification based on principle rather than policy. The latter kind of justification, of course, might simply point to a concern that without guarantees of such rights for francophones, Canadian unity would be in dire jeopardy.

B. The situation of linguistic guarantees in Quebec is somewhat different, for the protection of the French language through the provisions of Quebec's Bill 101 is fairly obviously goal-oriented, being seen as a means to another end — the "articulation of identity" and support of Quebecois culture. The French language is even described as the "instrument by which..." these ends will be achieved.[11]

The position of the French language in Quebec, then, is seen as subserving certain important societal goals. The notion of rights is perhaps more applicable to such provisions of Bill 101 as those of Section 73 respecting the receipt of instruction in English, and such provisions can appropriately be viewed as entrenching minority rights. Thus there is a kind of parallel between the purposes of the proposed federal legislation and the Quebec legislation, though the protections granted in the latter case for English speakers seem considerably more limited than what the federal government would propose. There is, however, also another sense in which legislation such as Bill 101 is directed toward achieving a political situation that protects rights — in particular certain rights of individual members of the majority group. These rights have presumably in the past frequently been infringed, and it could be claimed that what is sought now is a righting of the balance which can only be achieved by some form of reverse discrimination.[12]

Reverse Discrimination

A crucial question for affirmative action or reverse discrimination programs is what rights individual citizens have that might defeat programs aimed at important economic and social policies, including the social policy of improving equality overall, where such programs have the consequence of denying to some individual, on grounds that he is not a member of the group being advanced, something for which he is otherwise qualified. The kinds of cases usually considered have been preferential hiring cases, or cases having to do with admission to educational programs.[13] Dworkin has offered the following set of conditions that must be fulfilled if affirmative action in this sense is to be justified:

1) The denial of equal treatment to an individual must not make it unlikely that person will lead a useful life.

2) There must be no other course of action that would yield roughly the same gain without providing comparable disadvantages.

3) The overall gain must exceed the overall loss.

4) The action taken must serve a proper policy.[14]

How do such considerations relate to selected policies regarding language rights proposed and in some cases implemented by the federal and Quebec governments?

A. Within the affirmative action program of the federal government, clear preference has been given to bilingual candidates in certain civil service jobs. One might assume that most bilingual Canadians have French as their first language, so that this policy results in a higher proportion of francophones in the civil service (and perhaps a higher proportion at higher ranks) than might otherwise be the case. Presumably the policy being served is that of strengthening national unity by arranging for greater francophone participation in the federal government, and a resulting greater stake for them in that government. And surely it is at least arguable that pursuing national unity is a proper policy for the federal government. Thus the fourth of Dworkin's conditions seems to be satisfied.

It is hard to say whether unilingual (especially anglophone) Canadians are prevented by this policy from leading useful lives, but one would suppose not, on the whole, and if this is so, then Dworkin's first condition is also satisfied. Whether the overall gain exceeds the overall loss, and whether any alternative policy would achieve the same results with less infringment of principles of equal treatment is of course debatable; but an unequivocal answer to these questions might help us to answer the question whether certain federal bilingualism policies are justified. (I leave aside here the question as to whether these policies accomplish their goal at all. But this is a question that should be discussed, especially in light of the recent reports of the task force on Canadian unity.)[15]

B. One could raise similar questions about various provisions of Quebec's Bill 101, such as those regarding the language of instruction, or Section 35, concerning the issuing of permits by professional corporations only to French speakers. These provisions come closer to providing for what is usually thought of as reverse discrimination than do the federal government's bilingualism policies with respect to the civil service. The latter policies, indeed, are more akin to the usual notion of affirmative action, if such a distinction can be maintained. If one were to quarrel with provisions such as those of Bill 101 to which I have referred, it would be not so much on grounds of the policy served, but on grounds that one might accomplish the same result with less harm overall, and on grounds that whole categories of positions will be denied to anglophone Quebeckers, and this may very well systematically exclude them from the possibility of leading useful lives. If so, this would be a reason against the provisions, even if we could be sure that the overall gain exceeds the overall loss, and there is no other way to achieve the gain without at least equivalent disadvantages. But such considerations are not at all decisive. We need to ask to what extent it is permissible to discriminate against certain individuals in order to right certain past wrongs, or in order to provide large numbers of appropriate models. And of course it must be remembered that the feature with respect to which the discrimination is occurring is not an unalterable feature of an individual's constitution such as sex or skin color: one can, after all, learn another language, or at least one's children can.

Right-based vs. Goal-based Theories

It remains to say a few words about the classification of political theories as rights-based or goal-based. Rights-based theories place the individual at the centre and are

> concerned with the independence rather than the conformity of individual action. Goal-based theories are concerned with the welfare of any particular individual only insofar as this contributes to some state of affairs stipulated as good quite apart from his choice of that state of affairs.[16]

The distinction is by no means sharp, but it does appear that much of the language policy of the present Quebec government derives from a goal-based theory. And this fits with Dworkin's suggestion that goal-based theories seem especially compatible with societies "at least temporarily united by an urgent, overriding goal, like self-defense or economic expansion".[17] The concern to be faced is, of course, how to ensure that the rights (or perhaps claims or legitimate interests) of minorities that conflict with the goals of the majority are at least given due weight. On the federal side, the rhetoric has been more clearly rights-based, even if fairly obviously motivated by certain goals. And here the complaint from the majority has usually been either that too much has been conceded to the minority, or, more recently, that the policies chosen are not proper means to the end of promoting national unity. This may be so, and surely needs discussing, but we should at least be clear that we can consider abandoning such policies only if we also abandon or modify the view that there are genuine minority language *rights.*

But perhaps such a step is not utterly unthinkable. No doubt we should not be prepared to give up speaking of certain fundamental democratic, political, legal and egalitarian rights as genuine rights, for it is hard to see how we could regard equal protection of the law, due process, freedom of thought, conscience and religion, or freedom from discrimination on grounds of race or colour, national or ethnic origin, religion, or sex (to name but a few) as anything else. But this does not settle the question whether what we have wanted to accomplish by speaking of language rights might not be as well or better accomplished in some other way.

Should we take language rights seriously?

How important, then, is it that we view the language question as a question about rights? The received view has been that

> claims of right are argumentatively powerful. The rhetoric of rights raises the moral stakes and obliges one's opponent to discredit one's claim or else provide strong arguments to outweigh it. One's right is not a mere desire, interest, or preference.[18]

Rights are, on this sort of view, thought to be closely associated with justice, and to focus on what is due one as due *as of right* is often alleged to be more likely to yield both procedural and substantive justice, than would alternative approaches. On the other hand, though no one could deny that an appeal to rights carries considerable emotive force, it is not clear that substantive results are different under such an appeal from what they would be under an appeal to goals. Furthermore, result-orientation need not be unprincipled, and may be far more politically workable than an insistence on adhering to abstract principles. Indeed, this way of putting the matter points to three worries I have about an overemphasis on rights in the context of the language debate.

The first is that such an emphasis carries with it the danger of solidifying positions, thus promoting conflict where compromise is needed, for if one believes oneself to be appealing to a genuine right, one will not (and probably should not) easily accept the suggestion that it is outweighed in the circumstances by some other consideration. Yet precisely this sort of spirit of compromise seems to be what is required in our present political situation. In addition, I think that appealing to rights in this context carries with it the risk of clinging to untenable arguments, thus weakening the whole position, as in the case of the reasons offered against entrenching the language rights of minority groups other than French-speaking and English-speaking. My second concern relates to the first. If rights conflict, it's just not clear that, within a political theory that makes them paramount, we have any mechanism for resolving them, or any court of further appeal. This of course depends upon how absolute the rights in question are supposed to be, but calling them rights at all certainly suggests they are supposed to withstand the competition of a wide range of other considerations. One might claim that there is some fundamental right, such as the right to respect and treatment as an equal, from which all others are derived. But it's not obvious that appealing to such a right will settle difficult disputes, for this fundamental right might well be thought by different interest groups to have different implications for some actual controversy. And when we recall that in some cases the individual rights of some will conflict with the collective rights of others, a rights-based solution is even harder to see. Thirdly, and again relatedly, there is the epistemological problem concerning how we know what rights we have, and how we are to settle disagreements on this matter. To claim that legal and political disputes are to be settled by an appeal to the rights of the parties is of no help without some way of deciding what these rights are. This, I suppose, is an especially difficult problem in our political context given that we can hardly expect much agreement on the question of what political theory a philosopher-politician-judge with the qualifications of Dworkin's Hercules would find underlying our confederation. And the kinds of rights invoked in the language debate are of a rather specific nature, which compounds the problem. If I am right about all this, then perhaps the time is ripe for us to turn away from an insistence on inviolable rights, and to find ways of achieving some reasonable and workable compromise of competing claims concerning language usage in Canada.

NOTES

1. Ronald Dworkin, *Taking Rights Seriously,* Harvard University Press, 1977, chapter 4. Hereinafter, references to Dworkin's book are given as *TRS.*
2. *TRS,* p.169.
3. *TRS,* p.169.
4. *TRS,* p.92.
5. "The Canadian Charter of Rights and Freedoms", Division III of the Constitutional Amendment Bill (1978), hereinafter referred to as "Charter". Just what will be the fate of documents such as this under the new federal government is, of course, unclear.
6. *Charter,* p.2.
7. The Charter cites the Universal Declaration of Human Rights (1948), the International Convention of Elimination of All Forms of Racial Discrimination (1965), the International Covenant on Civil and Political Rights (1966) and the International Covenant on Economic, Social and Cultural Rights (1966).
8. See, for example: W.R. Lederman, "Securing Human Rights in a Renewed Confederation", in Richard Simeon, ed., *Must Canada Fail?*, McGill-Queen's University Press, 1977, pp. 281-290.
9. *Charter,* p.14.
10. *Charter,* p.14.
11. Bill 101, Charter of the French Language, Assemblée Nationale du Québec, (assented to on 26 Aug. 1970).

12. I use this term in spite of its controversial and, some would say, even prejudicial connotations because the usual more positive term — "affirmative action" — seems not, in the Canadian context, to carry all of the desired implications.

13. See, for example: *Sweatt* v. *Painter,* 339 U.S. 629, 70 S.C. 848; *DeFunis* v. *Odegaard,* 94 S. Ct. 1704; *Regents of the University of California* v. *Bakke,* United States Supreme Court, 1978.

14. See *TRS,* chapter 9.

15. See "Coming to Terms, The Words of the Debate" and "A Future Together, Observations and Recommendations", Reports of the Task Force on Canadian Unity, Ministry of Supply and Services, Canada, 1979.

16. *TRS,* p.172.

17. *TRS,* p.173.

18. D. Lyons, *Rights,* Wadsworth Publishing Company, 1979, p.4.

WOULD THE CRISIS IN CONFEDERATION BE RESOLVED MORE EASILY WITH LESS TALK ABOUT RIGHTS?

David BRAYBROOKE

Attacks on the recently released initial report of the Pepin-Robarts Task Force on Canadian Unity have concentrated on its recommendation that for the time being the treatment of linguistic minorities, English-speaking and French-speaking, be left to the provinces, largely without the protection of rights entrenched in the federal constitution.

The special status for the English language in the legislature and the courts of Quebec imposed on the government of Quebec by Section 133 of the British North America Act would be revoked, if the recommendation were followed, and no equivalent federal constitutional guarantees would be imposed in respect to the French language on provincial governments elsewhere. Rights in the federal constitution would give Canadians throughout the country access to federal services in both official languages so far as practical. The Task Force recommends further protection of the two languages by rights respecting criminal trials, education, and health and social services; but for the time being, the Task Force would have these rights legislated by the provinces.

Noting the consideration offered English-speakers in the recent language legislation of Quebec and the progress made in Ontario and elsewhere toward provincial practices favorable to the use of French, Pepin-Robarts look forward to these practices evolving in the direction of a consensus among the provinces. When, sometime in the future, that consensus has been achieved, the time will have come, in the view of the Task Force, to entrench further language rights in the federal constitution.

Pointing to the delinquent record of the provinces in respect to past practices — and surely with the English-speaking provinces in mind — Prime Minister Trudeau has denounced this part of the report as "naive". Claude Ryan, leader of the Quebec Liberal Party, has joined Trudeau in this judgment. So has Paul Comeau, president of the Federation of Francophones Outside Quebec, who has cried out that

Pepin-Robarts would set the cause of his people back and indeed "throw us to the wolves".

I do not exactly want to pit my judgment of the history and politics of Canada against Comeau's or Ryan's or Trudeau's. Some adjustment of the Task Force recommendation in the direction of entrenching more rights in the federal constitution may be advisable. However, before the issue is settled, I want to point out that the recommendation does open up another approach to resolving the crisis in Confederation. It is an approach that, compared to others, does less to insist upon rights and does more to encourage initiatives of good faith. Some use can be made of this approach, one may hope, if its virtues are recognized, even should the recommendation in the end not be followed.

I shall discuss those virtues on the negative side, where they have to do with avoiding to a degree the disadvantages of carrying on the discussion in terms of rights. The Pepin-Robarts report illustrates the virtues at several crucial points, not only in its recommendation about language rights.

In making that recommendation, Pepin-Robarts take the view that reliance on rights involves too much "confrontation". Have they not, with this word, identified one of the main disadvantages of the concept? No one, least of all me, wants to see anyone's rights denied; but as soon as the concept has been invoked, both freedom of discussion and chances of compromise sharply diminish. For how can there be any compromise about rights? Rights do not even conflict, then get compromised; for what appears to be a compromise revising given rights amounts really to discovering that those rights did not exist as they seemed to be given. Even to ask for a compromise respecting rights, when they really are rights, is to ask for something unjustified. So rights draw lines that in principle cannot be budged.

Moreover, when one group asserts a right against another group that has hitherto not heeded the right, the two groups, on either side of the line, are immediately cast into fixed postures — the victims, who have been denied their rights until now; opposing them, the villains, who have been so insensitive and conscienceless as to do the denying. We might privately agree that the history of the treatment of the French-speaking people of Canada fits this picture all too well — yet consider, with Pepin-Robarts, that it does not help toward a cooperative solution to insist upon the picture.

Another crucial point in the Task Force report at which their reliance on the concept of rights is remarkably muted is in their reference to the possibility of secession by Quebec. The Task Force acknowledges "Quebec's right to settle upon its own destiny", but comments, "So far as self-determination is concerned, principles and rights are usually subordinate to political events and to the hard facts of success or failure. People who succeed in establishing themselves as distinct political communities will generally secure appropriate international recognition in due course". If in fact, Quebec should decide to secede, it is a community with a size and character capable of establishing itself in independence; and it would be unwise of the rest of Canada to oppose secession in the face of the decision.

Does not this judgment of the Task Force that the issue of secession "is not a question of deciding in the abstract whether Quebec possesses a right of self-determination" reflect some awareness of how strained and inconclusive the case for such a right must be? This is the second great drawback — a whole family of drawbacks — to using the concept of rights centrally in the debate about Confederation.

There are arguments, set forth for instance by Professor Stanley French and before him by Abraham Lincoln,[1] that, to say the least, shake the claim by any state or province to a right to secede. If a state or province can claim such a right against the federal government, why cannot a county claim it against a state or province, or a city against a county? Moreover, why should a majority vote in a state or province be sacrosanct as an expression of popular will? There is not only the question, which voting rule to choose, but also the question, which jurisdiction to follow. Does a majority or two-thirds majority in the province deserve all respect, and the majority in the whole country, or in one region of the province, none? The right to secede is not readily limited to any jurisdiction; but if it is generalized, then it sanctions anarchy. Any minority with local supremacy could secede, whenever it disliked a law passed in larger jurisdiction.

Lincoln offers another general argument, which applies to our situation in this way: suppose Quebec wanted to stay in Confederation and the other nine provinces asserted the right to drive her out. Would that not be thought very unjust by Quebec and her friends? Yet what is the asserted right, redescribed, but the right of "seceding of the others from that one"? If, however, they, the majority of provinces, do not have that right, can it be the case that Quebec, as a minority of one, has the right to secede, that is to say the right to drive the others out?

It may be objected that none of these arguments is conclusive. I am quite willing to agree, so long as it is accepted that their refutations are not conclusive either. To invoke a right to secede invites a combative response in the same terms. It may call forth in opposition a right to block secession.

Of course, if the right to secede is just an implication of a resolve on both sides to arrive at a peaceful solution, with secession as one alternative, it does no harm. Even then, is it not better — more productive — debating tactics to begin with an agreement to keep the peace whatever happens than to take a stand on rights and risk the sort of quarrel such a stand may provoke?

Another drawback about rights brings together the right to secede with the problem about leaving language rights to the provinces. It is difficult, as students of the subject have pointed out, and the Task Force has evidently had prominently in mind, to reconcile overarching guarantees of language rights with greater provincial automony — with what the Quebec government is demanding as of right, and in the end may demand involving a right to secede. That is a consistent way out of the dilemma, but it implies, in the end, that Quebec's historic claim to offer cultural leadership to the whole of French Canada will ring hollow, since it will be abandoning the French-speaking minorities outside Quebec.

The Task Force is calling for giving those minorities another chance to enjoy that wider leadership. At the same time, it is posing a challenge to the other provinces. Forget about rights for a moment; think about opportunities. Suppose the other provinces take seriously Quebec's claim to offer cultural leadership for French-speaking people throughout Canada. If it is not to be resented among other French-speaking people, that leadership will have to be exercised with tact and discretion; still, there is no doubt of the difference that participating in a vital French-speaking culture centered in Quebec can make to invigorating the cultural life of the minorities outside. How can the other provinces show that they value the difference? Is it not by doing, at last, what they can to enable their French-speaking minorities to flourish? They would do so, just as Pepin-Robarts are asking, by demonstrating practical support for the use of French in education, in the delivery of public services, and even, locally at least, in the language of work.

A sincere and vigorous effort of this kind will certainly attract Quebec more, and be more difficult for Quebec to disregard, than a set of rights imposed from above on unwilling or half-hearted provincial governments. Not everyone in Quebec will, it is true, be moved to rally to Confederation by such an effort, taken by itself, or taken in combination with the other things that the Task Force recommends. But not everyone in Quebec has to be. A large number of French-speaking Quebeckers are already more favorably disposed toward keeping Canada going than the Parti Québécois relishes. The actions and undertakings of the other provincial governments could have a decisive impact upon them.

Will cooperating with Quebec to give the French-speaking minorities outside the best chance of surviving not have this impact even if eventually the effort fails? Forces making for assimilation are very powerful in the other provinces. As the Task Force notes, demographic trends are unfavorable; sociological predictions are gloomy. Some people in the Parti Québécois have written off the minorities outside already. But is that not premature? The effort that Pepin-Robarts call for — a continuing demonstration of practical good faith — would at least put off the event of failure. Meanwhile — for several generations more — it would give Quebec a larger and culturally richer community to lead directly. It would also allow its activity to reverberate more widely at points of contact with English-speaking Canada. Even failure, then, has some glory to offer; and failure is by no means certain.

NOTE

1. S.G. French, "Droit à la sécession", in M. Gagnon, ed., *Philosophie et Droit* (Montréal: Bellarmin et Desclée, 1979). P.M. Angle, ed., *Abraham Lincoln's Speeches and Letters, 1832-1865* (London: Everyman's Library, Dent, 1907, 1957).

LANGUAGE AND HUMAN RIGHTS

Steven DAVIS

Language, some believe, is the mark of the human. It is that which distinguishes us from the lower animals. Others hold, however, that animals as well have language. Whether language or some other characteristic of ours, such as our ability to tell jokes, do card tricks, or be ironical is the essential characteristic which marks us off from other creatures, language itself, at many times in history and in many places of the globe, has aroused human passions. The reason this should be so is not mysterious. The language people speak is often the touchstone of their cultural identity. Their language is not just a means of communication which could be changed without changing other aspects of their culture. And culture infuses language with particular phrases, words, expressions, *etc.* which embody various cultural artifacts. Moreover, through a common language people are able to understand one another or at least to think they do. But the lack of a common language sets up an enormous barrier to understanding among people.

In Canada there is a long history of acts and laws which bear on questions of language from the *Quebec Act* of 1774 enacted by the British Parliament to *Bill 101* of 1977 enacted by the Quebec National Assembly. *Bill 101* passed by the Levesque government is not the first law governing language in Quebec. There were others, the most notable of which was Bill 22 passed by the Liberal government of Bourassa in 1974. Its purpose was to protect French within Quebec and its most controversial provision provided criteria to determine the language of instruction for school children in Quebec. Admission to an English school was determined on the basis of whether a child could pass a test which was supposed to determine whether his home language was English.

Bill 101 does not change the thrust of the education provision of *Bill 22.* Rather it changes the criterion for admission to English schools. The reason for the change is that the tests administered under *Bill 22* were thought unfair and special schools were set up to teach people whose home language was not English to pass the tests, thus subverting the intent of the Bill. The criterion of admission in *Bill 101* has the merit of being clear and simpler to administer. The basic provision is that a child is permitted to have English as his language of instruction, if one of his parents received his or her elementary education in English in Quebec. The law permits children already enrolled in English schools to continue in these schools and allows any of their siblings to enter an English school. A provision is made also to allow reciprocity agreements between Quebec and other provinces. The consequence of the Bill is that landed immigrants, regardless of country of origin, must send their children to French schools. As well, Canadian citizens from outside the province who move into the province after the Bill was passed must, also, send their children to French schools. The loudest outcry against the Bill has come from landed immigrants who claim that a basic right is being violated by virtue of their being denied access to public education in English.

Rights are a very serious business; at least they have been taken very seriously in North America at least for the last 25 years. Rights have been claimed for racial minorities, linguistic minorities, linguistic majorities, women, men, veterans, unionists, native people, the unborn, children and even animals. A claim to a right is emotionally charged, for we believe that if rights are being violated, then something reprehensible is being done. And a right is the sort of thing that people can demand be respected; they can stand on their rights.

Moreover, on must people's conception of the function of government, it is part of its function, if not its most important function, to protect people from having their rights violated. In addition any government which, as a matter of policy, systematically violates people's rights is considered to be a repressive government. The question I wish to raise in this paper is whether the education provisions of *Bill 101* are a violation of people's rights. Given the past history of Canada and Quebec, there are some who would regard raising the question to be insulting. But the issue has been raised in public debate and I believe it is better to take up such questions about which passions have been inflamed and attempt to settle them by reason, if at all possible. I shall begin by making certain distinctions between rights.[1]

Let us begin with a distinction between legal and moral rights. The former are rights the justification for which is contained in the law; the latter are rights the justification for which is given by moral principle or theory. There are legal rights which are not moral rights, for example my right to take certain deductions in computing my income tax. And there are moral rights which are not embodied in our system of laws. A child, I suppose, has a moral right to be loved equally with his siblings, but if his parents love another more, there is no law which is being broken.

There should be a connection between legal rights and moral rights in a body of laws we regard to be just. Our fundamental moral rights should be protected as legal rights. However, even in a just system of laws, if some right is a legal, but not a moral right, then it is within the power of the duly constituted authorities to change the law modifying it or removing it as one of our rights. Moreover, if the authorities empowered with such responsibilities make changes in accordance with the laws governing their authority, then they cannot be charged with violating anyone's rights. For example, the tax laws could be changed either modifying or even disallowing my right to certain deductions. It should be emphasized that it does not follow from such changes not being violations of rights, that they are not open to criticism, including moral criticism. Tax laws designed to promote general welfare need not do so and, thus, can be judged to be bad laws.

I take all rights to have the following structure: *S* has a right to *X* with respect to *H* which gives rise to a duty of *H* to *Y*. *S* is the right holder; *H* is the duty holder; *X* is the object of the right; and *Y* is the duty required by the right. Rights can be classified on the basis of the range of *S*, *H*, *X*, and *Y*. Let us begin with right holders. Right holders can be either persons or collectives, such as states, nations, tribes or corporations. The corresponding right is either a personal or collective right. An example of a personal right is the right to be free from bodily harm, and of a collective right, the right of the Canadian parliament to declare war.

Rights give rise to claims against others, that is against duty holders. The claim can be either specific or general. The former are *in personnem* rights and the latter *in rem* rights. An example of the former is the right I have against someone who owes me money, and of the latter, the right I have against everyone that they not do me bodily harm. Rights give rise to duties which can be either positive or negative. A positive right is a right against others that they perform some action, and a negative right is the right against others that they forbear from interfering. An example of a positive right is the right against my debtor to pay me the money owed, and of a negative right, the right against everyone that they not do me bodily harm.

The object of a right can be either active or passive. An active right is the right of the right-holder to perform some action and a passive right is a right of the right-holder to be secure in certain of his possessions. Examples of the former are the rights of free speech and movement, and of the latter, the right to be secure in possession of one's reputation and of one's property. Both active and passive rights are negative rights against others, since they lay claim against them not to interfere.

There is a special class of rights which arises from certain sorts of needs. The United Nations 1948 Universal Declaration of Human Rights includes the following sort of rights: the right to work, to food, to clothing, to rest and leisure, to education, to enjoy the arts, and to share in scientific advancement and its benefits. These rights are rights to benefits which supposedly are necessary for a person to be able to have a happy life with dignity. Hence, these rights are a positive personal right which places a requirement on the duty-holder to provide certain goods and services to people. The one difference between these and other positive rights is that they do not arise because of any actions or properties of the duty-holder. They do not have their source, for example, in the duty-holder's having contractually obligated himself to the right-holder to provide some goods or services. Rather, they appear to arise because of our view that the right-holder is a particular sort of creature, a person, and it is by virture of this that these sorts of rights accrue to him. To distinguish these from other sorts of rights I shall call them *declaration rights.*

Rights can be restricted in various ways. First, the set of right-holders can be limited. For example, the right to vote in Canada in federal elections is restricted to citizens of voting age. Second, the range of actions which fall under the object of the right can be limited. For instance, voters in Canada can vote for members of parliament, but not for senators. Lastly, an important restriction on rights arises when there is a conflict between competing rights. I have the *prima facie* right to move about freely, but I cannot walk into your home uninvited. Your property rights to your house take precedence over my right of free movement.

Not only can rights be restricted, but they can be overridden because of general public utility. My right to my property can be overridden, if it is thought to be in the public interest to build a road on my property. And even my rights of free speech and movement can be curtailed, if a draft for a military service is instituted and I am drafted. However, some rights, the most basic ones, cannot be overridden by reasons of public utility. I cannot justifiably be tortured, made a slave, or be tried unfairly, even if it would serve the public interest to do so.

Lastly, some rights depend upon other rights for their justification. For example, in Canada, defendants charged with a crime have the right to call and question witnesses, the right to a speedy trial, and the right to refuse to answer questions which might tend to be self-incriminating. The justification for these rights is based upon the right a defendant has to a fair trial. We shall say that if some right, A, depends for its justification on another right, B, then A is a *dependent right* and further it is *dependent with respect* to B. In turn, this gives us a way of defining another notion of *basic right*, which is distinct from the sense in which a right is said to be basic if it cannot be overridden. In the new sense, a right is said to be basic in case it is not dependent with respect to any other right. There is no clear test for determining whether some right is a dependent or basic right, but perhaps some evidence that a right is dependent is contained in the object of the right. If the object of a right, A, contains some specific activity or state to which the right-holder has a right, then there is probably some other right, B, with a more general object such that A is dependent with respect to B.

Let us turn to the education provision of *Bill 101*. There has been a good deal of opposition to the restriction which prevents newcomers to Quebec from sending their children to English schools. It has been claimed that since there is a public school system in which instruction is given in English, parents have the right to send their children to these schools. Do parents have such a right? Since the putative right to send one's children to an anglophone school has a very specific object, we can take it to be a dependent right. What more basic right justifies it? There are, I believe, two such rights which might serve this purpose: the right to an education and the right parents have to do what they hold to be in the best interests of their children. It might be questioned whether these are rights, but they are generally so regarded and consequently I shall take them to be rights.

The right to an education is a declaration right in which the duty-holder is the government which has jurisdiction over education and the right-holders are the students who fall under this jurisdiction. In Canada, the provinces are the duty-holders and the residents of school age, citizen and non-citizen, are the right-holders. A problem with declaration rights is that it is difficult to determine the requirements of duty of the right. There are several sources of this difficulty. First, it is not always obvious what is in the best interest of the right-holder with respect to the right. There has been much controversy in recent years about the best form of education for students. Second, the particular requirements of duty of declaration rights seem to depend upon the ability of the duty-holder to fulfil the requirement. It is not thought that poor countries violate anyone's rights if they do not provide comprehensive secondary level education. Lastly, the activities or institutions required by declaration rights are often justified not only by an appeal to rights, but also by considerations of public utility. Public education is justified not only because a student has a right to an education, but, also, because a greater economic, social, and political good is achieved by having it. However, the problem is that these two sources of justification can conflict and it is, then, difficult to adjudicate between them.

In the last fifteen years there has been a great deal of debate about the best educational system for students. Should their education be primarily concerned with preparing them for a job or should its main aim be to make them well-adjusted, broadly educated citizens of a democratic society? Another issue that has arisen at universities is whether students should be allowed maximum choice on determining their own programmes or should their programmes, especially in the first two years, be highly structured leaving little room for individual choice? There is honest disagreement about these sorts of questions, and hence, disagreement about what sort of education best serves the interests of students.

Let us turn to a consideration of cases in which there is a conflict between a student's interests and the more general interests of society. I shall consider two examples. Recently, in Quebec, some students claimed that they had a right to a greater share in the province's tax resources to support their post-secondary education. Undoubtedly, it would have been in the students' interests to give them what they asked for. But the provincial government decided that it was not in the public interest to do so. Another case in which a conflict can arise between a student's and society's interests is in the limited admissions granted to medical school. Since the medical profession is a high status and remunerative profession, there are many students who seek admittance to medical school. But because it is believed that only highly qualified students will make good doctors, admissions to medical schools are restricted. In both these cases the interests of some students have been overridden and by doing so their educational opportunities have been decreased. But in neither case would it be thought that the students' rights have been violated. The Quebec Government did not violate the students' rights by refusing to grant them an increase in public funds. Nor does a student's not being admitted to medical school violate his or her rights.

To show that an educational policy violates the right to an education, I believe the following must be established: first, the policy is clearly contrary to the interests of the students, or second, if it is contrary to their interests, there is no public interest being served which overrides their interests. French is now the official language of Quebec which means that all government and most business activity must be carried on in French. Moreover, since 80% of the citizens in the province are francophones, a good deal of the cultural life takes place in French. Consequently, to hold a job in government or business, or to participate in a great deal of the cultural life of Quebec, it is necessary not only to be verbally fluent in French, but to have writing skills in the language and to know about the cultural and intellectual history of the province. It would seem that under such circumstances it is in the best interests of students in Quebec to be educated in French. However, against this, it might be argued that since Quebec is surrounded by an English speaking sea, that a student's best interests are served if he or she is educated in English. But it can hardly be the responsibility of the province of Quebec to provide an education for its students so that they can take jobs and participate in cultural life outside the province, although it can be argued that it is the responsibility of the province to make available programmes of high quality which make students fluent in English. In addition, there is a public interest served by educating newcomers in French. Eighty percent of the population is francophone and their interests are protected by providing them with services in government and business in French; and this requires that those who serve the public be fluent in French. Moreover, given present demographic trends in Quebec, if newcomers to the province were permitted to have an education in English, an increasing number of people in the province and perhaps a majority in the Montreal area would be non-French speakers. It is clearly not in the interests of the overwhelming majority of the people of Quebec that they come to feel like foreigners in the largest city in their province. Consequently, the right to an education does not justify the putative right for newcomers to Quebec to have access to anglophone schools.

Does the right parents have to do what they regard to be in the best interest of their children justify this putative right? Parents' rights vis-à-vis their children are greatly restricted. When parents do what is clearly inimical to the welfare of their children, the state has the responsibility to prevent them from doing it. In Canada, parents, for example, must send their children to school. And if they do not, the provinces can force them to do so. Moreover, there are many activities formerly the responsibility of parents which are now responsibilities of the state. The most notable of these is in education where the parents' rights are greatly restricted. An individual parent, or even a sizable group of parents, does not have the right to determine educational policy for their children. Consequently, although a number of parents regard an education in English to be in the best interests of their children, they do not have the right to have them provided with such an education at public expense. The views of parents, of course, should not be disregarded, but that they desire to have a certain policy followed does not give them a right to have it followed. Moreover, I have argued that it is in the interests of newcomers to Quebec to have their children educated in French. Hence, a parent's right to do what is in the best interests of their children does not establish that they have a right to a public education for their children in English.

I have shown that neither the right to an education nor the rights of parents to do what they regard to be in the best interests of their children establishes the putative right of newcomers to Quebec to have their children educated in English. This does not show that no such right can be established, but those who make a claim that there is such a right must offer arguments to establish it as a right. Until such arguments are forthcoming, I believe we can take it that the education provisions of *Bill 101* do not violate anyone's rights.

NOTE

1. Most of the distinctions among different sorts of rights are drawn from Feinberg, Joel, *Social Philosophy*, (Englewood Cliffs, Prentice Hall), 1973, pp. 55-97.

A LIBERAL DEMOCRATIC RESPONSE TO THE CANADIAN CRISIS

Virginia McDONALD

In Dion's analysis of the "new consciousness" in Quebec society, with its stress on the demand for a participatory society in which individuals feel they are masters of their own destiny; in his historical sketch of Quebec nationalism in its conservative, liberal, social democratic and socialist garb, as a commitment to the principle "maître chez nous", those of us of the liberal democratic persuasion should feel at home. To trace the historical development of that principle is to trace the historical development of liberal man. If Macpherson is right that in liberal theory all roads lead to property, he fails to grasp the significance of that "property". "Self-propriety" is the clue to the possessiveness of liberal man.

> To every Individual in nature is given an individual property by nature, not to be invaded or usurped by any other; for everyone as he is himself, so he hath a self-propriety, else could not be himself. . . ...Every man by nature being a King, Priest and Prophet in his own natural circuit and compasse...[1]

Isaiah Berlin has movingly captured the sense of self-propriety or self-mastery:

> I wish my life and decisions to depend on myself, not on external forces of whatever kind. I wish to be the instrument of my own, not of other men's, acts of will. I wish to be a subject, not an object; to be moved by reasons, by conscious purposes which are my own, not by causes which affect me, as it were, from outside. I wish to be somebody, not nobody; a doer-deciding, not being decided for, self-directed and not acted upon by external nature or by other men as if I were a thing, or an animal, or a slave incapable of playing a human role, that is, of conceiving goals and policies of my own and realizing them.[2]

The first claim to such self-determination was made by the religious man of the Protestant Reformation whose tender conscience could not brook the intrusion of any intermediary between him and his God. This claim to such religious liberty led in turn to the claim to political liberty. Only liberty from the state and liberty to control the state would assure man of his protection of that essential human right. For Hobbes the cacophonous din of the moral disputations of such religious men signified nothing but sound and fury. For a liberal these disputations were evidence of the birth of a new man — the masterless man.

Examination of the origins of the liberal democratic movement reveals a dawning realisation that "every man hath a life to lead", that "all men are equal", that they are first and foremost persons, of intrinsic worth simply because they are human beings. Men came to recognise that to be fully human they must be masters of themselves, not dependent on the arbitrary will of any other. Over a span of some four centuries men have sought to peal off layer upon layer of such tyrannical sway, of relations of superior/inferior, master/servant, dominance/subjection, and to build relations of trust, consent, cooperation, community, and accountability in political, social, and economic relationships.

In their search for self-mastery, men probed into the very meaning of 'human being', evolving a normative conception of men as 'persons', capable of choice, entitled to be treated as equals instead of being treated as non-human, as cattle, commodities, or property. To be a person was to be a self-conscious, self-objectifying, rational being. To be self-conscious was to be capable of critical self-examination, refusing to assent to the truth of a proposition or to consent to a political rule except after searching examination of the grounds of both. To be self-objectifying was to express oneself in the outer world as productive, creative beings in works of art, in social, economic, and political relationships. To be rational was to deliberate thoughtfully on the basis of accessible and reliable information.

One became a person by being recognised by government and one's fellow men as entitled to certain rights: the right to be free, the right to have one's interests heard, considered, and satisfied, the right to self-development. Both negative and positive freedom were needed: freedom from arbitrary coercive interference and freedom to act to develop one's powers both as a private and a public self. It came to be realised that to actualise such freedom men needed to participate significantly in their political and social worlds to guarantee their right to self-protection and to self-development — leading thus to the demand for political participation as a right to a control over one's environment, over the allocation of resources in that environment, and a right to a share in those resources.

The right to be left alone was not enough. Without access to certain basic necessities and resources one was unable to develop one's potentialities as a person. For "Without a command of certain elementary arts and knowledge, thc individual in modern society is as effectively crippled as by the loss of a limb or a broken constitution. He is not free to develop his faculties."[3] Such access gives one the power to use one's liberty to participate in the political and social worlds and to develop one's potentialities. The right to know, the right of access to information, would enable onc to withstand the subtle pressures of ideological indoctrination and to deliberate sensibly on substantive issues and plans of action.

Participation in political, social and economic institutions was seen to be a key element in becoming a person. Through such participation one would grow in self-character, self-discipline, self-reliance and one would grow as a citizen, broadening one's perspective.

This awakening of men is, as Dion points out, now being exhibited in Quebec society by individuals and groups determined to be "masters of their own destiny" — demanding a participatory society and government as evidence of such self-mastery. This stirring by formerly inarticulate and unaware individuals is being paralleled by the stirring of the nationalist fervour of the Quebec society as a whole. Their sense of "we-ness", of collective solidarity, their nationalist commitment, is wearing new garb in the form of liberal, social democratic and socialist ideologies which are so redefining what in fact that "we-ness" requires for its self-realization that it is tearing apart the very fabric of the Canadian political system.

This brief sketch of the historical and logical development of the concept of self-propriety or self-mastery has addressed itself to this concept in relation both to the individual and to the collectivity. I would argue that the distinction between pcrsonality and territoriality may in fact be a false one inasmuch as thc personality of the individual only develops through its relation to a specific cultural, social and political milieu. Culture as part of individual personality is not evident to English-speaking Canadians because they wear that culture comfortably around their shoulders wherever they move. They cannot 'see' or 'feel' it because it is as natural to them as breathing the air. Only for the minority English-speaking community of Quebec is the importance of such culture brought sharply to their attention as they are seeing its erosion and their denial of access to it in the recent language and other cultural legislation of the PQ government.

Elsewhere[4] I have argued for the need for significant participation for significant publics, i.e. the provinces in relation to the federal government — for the stability of the Canadian political system. That analysis recognised what the Pepin-Robarts Task Force has brought so graphically to our attention — the importance of regional communities and the duality of our society. I have argued that provinces locked out of national decision-making — in particular a province such as Quebec in which are concentrated all the criteria of a "nation" — will resort to less legitimate forms of participation by reactions in the form of alienation, obstructionism, and possibly even secession.

This brief survey of the contemporary crisis of Confederation has addressed itself to the rights of individuals and collectivities. I have argued that the rights of individuals have historically been claimed as the necessary entitlement for self-mastery and self-development. Such rights are not seen as liberties to do as one lists but as rights of recipience, addressed by and to "selves" as essential preconditions for the actualisation of such selves. Such rights may legitimately be invoked by collectivities which, on the basis of subjective and objective criteria, can be said to be "selves". Self-mastery or self-determination need not be seen and historically have not been seen by liberal theorists as total independence of other selves, individual or collective, but as a condition of non-dependence on the arbitrary will of other men and collectivities.

The rights we have been considering are what have been called inalienable, natural, native, human rights. They are not conceived as liberties to do as I list; as powers to use my resources to preserve myself even to the point of subduing, overwhelming and injuring others. These rights are conceived as moral entitlements of man qua man, of self qua self, to act, to be, to have, and invoked as claims for protection by social and political institutions and as claims against society and state when in fact such protection is denied or ineffectually assured. Being moral claims or entitlements of myself as human being addressed to other human beings, their validity exists irrespective of their recognition by society or state but their efficacy does rest upon such recognition. Being moral claims advanced by human beings they imply similar rights in all other human beings and correlative duties on my part and theirs to acknowledge such rights in all other human beings.

We have considered these rights in relation to selves — individual selves who are self-conscious, self-objectifying beings, seeking to be masters of their own destiny. I have argued that we can legitimately speak of collectivities in this sense. Subjective and objective criteria have been advanced for determining collective selves. Subjectively, the collectivity must see itself as a totality, a "we-ness"; objectively, its totality and "we-ness" must be evidenced in a cluster of criteria —

territorial, historical, racial, religious, etc. All the criteria which are usually invoked assigning selfhood to particular collectivities apply to Quebec. This selfhood of Quebec is acknowledged by the Pepin-Robarts Task Force, the B and B Commission, as a legitimate claim. Such acknowledgement pervades Dion's analysis and that of other English and French Canadian sociologists and intellectuals.

We have considered these rights in terms of self-mastery or self-determination. The right to self-mastery has historically been advanced by individuals as in part the right to political participation. It has also been advanced as the right to emigrate, the right to establish a political society, and the right to resist. The latter demands were not advanced if in fact effective political participation was available within one's society. Similarly, the right to self-determination of a collective self need not lead to the claim to the right to secede if in fact political participation is effectively realised within one's political nationality.

Political organisation has been seen historically and philosophically by liberal theorists to rest on a social compact for "...every particular and individual man and woman...(being) all equal and alike in power, dignity, authority, and majesty, none of them (has) (by nature) any authority, dominion, or magisterial power, one over or above another...but merely by...mutual agreement or consent...for the good benefit and comfort of each other..."[5] Such a view, first articulated in the 17th century, foreshadowed the development of the concept of the state as "a specifically legal association created by the sentiment and action of the national society, and based on the constitution which is of the nature of a contract."[6] Political obligation was seen to arise from the commitment to come together as a community to do things together now and in the future. Such commitment is evidenced in the founding of Canada. As Professor Smiley has observed: "Those who state their claims on Confederation in terms of a continuing compact are asserting the reality of a Canadian political community...The concept of a Canadian political community — or nationality — means that Canadians as such have reciprocal moral and legal claims upon one another that have no precise counterparts in their relations with others..."[7]

Lévesque's claim to the right to self-determination is not being advanced as a Hobbesian right to unilateral action. There is a tacit acknowledgement of a tacit moral compact between Quebec and the other partners in Confederation. While Quebec might argue that in fact that compact was violated by acts of omission and commission by English-speaking Canadians in the form of exploitation and colonisation and hence English Canadians have forfeited the right to be consulted, in fact the PQ has not adopted that posture. While under international law it may be feasible for Quebec to appeal to the arguments of remedial secession or to the rights of an awakened collectivity to fulfill itself most effectively on its own, Quebec has resorted to neither of these options. Her right to self-determination is in fact being invoked in terms of a Lockean moral claim and not in terms of an Hobbesian amoral liberty to do as she lists. Negotiation and consultation are being acknowledged. What still requires explicit acknowledgement by Quebec is her moral obligation to consider the impact of her proposals on the rest of the country and the world society as a whole. What still requires explicit acknowledgement by the rest of Canada is the moral obligation to consider the implications of the question Smiley posed in relation to a social compact: "Because (the) matters deemed crucial to the integrity of French Canadian culture were entrusted to the provinces by Confederation, does it follow that provincial powers should extend to other matters later deemed necessary to this culture by Quebec?"[8]

And, finally, it is particularly incumbent upon English Canadians to acknowledge that if a clear and unequivocal voice for independence is heard from Quebec we do not ourselves resort to an Hobbesian liberty to maintain the Canadian political nationality by any means — a position which would be both morally unacceptable and pragmatically senseless. Out of the crisis of seeking to find a humane and revised conception of our liberal/egalitarian concept of equality as applied to the needs of a self-conscious minority whose status as a permanent minority is proving a denial of its chance to be heard within the wider majoritarian context, Canadians face yet a further test of their commitment to traditional beliefs. Our sobering brush with terrorism in Quebec in 1970 brought with it the temporary withdrawal of constitutional order with the invocation of the War Measures Act. Given the very real possibility a decade later of Quebec's decision to leave Canada, we have as philosophers and citizens not only to assess the legitimacy of that decision but the legitimacy — if such it be — for yet another and more permanent invocation of the War Measures Act in an attempt to prevent Quebec's secession. We would be advised to ponder well the assessment of the Pepin-Robarts Task Force: If, in the course of the next few years, Quebecers decided, definitely and democratically, to secede, ought that decision to be respected and accepted by the rest of Canada?

To that question we answer an unequivocal Yes. Our response is a virtual corollary of our acceptance of the democratic process. Given a community of the size and character of Quebec society, we believe that the clearly expressed will of the population must prevail and that it would be both unwise and ethically questionable to deny or thwart it. Practically speaking, this means the renunciation of the use of force to maintain the integrity of the Canadian state and commitment to construct political institutions which reflect the will and aspirations of the citizens concerned. We believe most Canadians and virtually all the country's political leaders would share our view.[9]

NOTES

1. R. Overton, *An Arrow against all Tyrants*, quoted in C.B. Macpherson, *The Political Theory of Possessive Individualism: Hobbes and Locke* (Oxford, 1962), pp.140-141.
2. I. Berlin, "Two Concepts of Liberty", quoted in C.B. Macpherson, *Democratic Theory: Essays in Retrieval* (Oxford, 1973), p.105.
3. T.H. Green, "Liberal Legislation and Freedom of Contract", in J.R. Rodman (ed.)., *The Political Theory of T.H. Green* (New York), p.55.
4. V. McDonald, "Participation in the Canadian Context", *Queen's Quarterly*, v. 84, no.3, Autumn 1977.
5. J. Lilburne, *Freemans Freedom Vindicated*, in T.C. Pease, *The Leveller Movement* (reprinted, Gloucester, 1965), p.137.
6. E. Barker, *Principles of Social and Political Thought* (Oxford, 1965), p.205.
7. D. Smiley, *The Canadian Political Nationality* (Toronto, 1967), p.30-1.
8. *Ibid.*, p.23-4.
9. J.L. Pepin and J.P. Robarts, *A Future Together: Observations and Recommendations*, The Task Force on Canadian Unity, Jan. 1959., p.113.

THE RIGHTS OF PEOPLE AND THE RIGHTS OF A PEOPLE

Michael McDONALD

If individual people can have rights, could a collection of them into 'a people' have rights in some non-derivative sense? That is the question I wish to address to this workshop; its relevance to this Conference's topic — the future of Canada and Québec — is in part immediately present. And I hope less obvious implications of this question for Canada's future will become clearer as I proceed. I intend to address this question by dividing it into what I take to be two clearer questions: (1) can collectivities like individuals be right-holders (i.e. claim, exercise, waive, and in general have rights)? and (2), can collectivities like individuals be the concernees (beneficiaries) of rights? In treating these two questions I shall assume for the sake of argument that individual persons can have rights of various sorts — legal, moral, and customary. My purpose will be to see if on the model of individual rights there can be collective rights.

However, I will be writing against the background of a traditional view of rights that allows only individual rights and denies the possibility of collective rights. This view or tradition could be identified as 'liberal-contractarian'; it begins roughly with Hobbes and Locke and finds its contemporary exponents in philosophers as diverse as Rawls, Nozick, Dworkin, and Gauthier. A view that is common to many but not all of those in this tradition is that the central (and, perhaps, only) cases of moral rights are civil liberties. It would be natural for one who shares the main views and assumptions made in this tradition to construe claims about collective rights to claims about individual rights of members of the collectivity in question; that is, a liberal-contractarian would reduce claims about collective rights to claims about individual rights. My enterprise is to resist this reductionism where I can. I also hope in the process to relate what I say to the Confederation question.

(1) Can collectivities like a people be right-holders? Here we might imagine the liberal-contractarian arguing that a people cannot hold

rights though the people who make up that people can. He might argue as follows. "When we say that an individual has a particular right we mean that he meets certain criteria, e.g. one has a right to supplement old-age benefits if one is over 65 and has an income less than a certain amount. To talk about a collective right of the aged to income supplementation is simply to talk 'compendiously' about the rights of all those individuals who satisfy these criteria."

But this is not, I believe, what is meant by talking about a collective right. The example misses the point. The collectivity in question — the aged — cannot exercise, waive, claim, etc. the right in question; only individual aged persons can do this. For a collectivity to have a right, it must be the case that it has that right in a way that its members do not. Think, for example, of a jury's right to convict or acquit in a criminal proceeding. No member of the jury can on his own claim or exercise the right; only the jurors acting together can exercise this right by following the rules in question, usually by unanimous agreement. Many of the examples of collective rights are like the one just cited — examples of *institutional* (in this case legal) rights. Of course, not all such claims to collective rights involve an appeal to existing institutions; they may well involve an appeal to changed institutions, e.g. the claim of the Ayotollah on behalf of his followers to establish an Islamic Republic of Iran. We can also imagine non-institutional collective rights which do not in any way involve a formal decision procedure but rather involve a 'sense of the collectivity' in question being clearly shown. We do this when we get a 'sense of the meeting' without taking a formal vote. Peoples do this when over a fairly long period of time they establish certain customs and expectations of each other; thus, we don't vote on customs, manners, and the like, but we know what they are and often believe that they ground individual and collective rights. So I want to say that in a clear sense collectivities including peoples can be holders of rights.

And here I would contend that Canadian experience politically, legally, and socially has centered on collective rather than on individual rights. This stands in sharp contrast to the American experience. Certainly, the present crisis of Confederation is in a large part a result of assertions of conflicting collective rights — French and English, provincial and federal. Some of these conflicts appeal to existing institutions (such as the BNA) others to institutions that do not yet exist (a sovereign state of Québec or even of Acadia). Some are non-institutional, concerning the protection of established ways of life (e.g. non-Québec French). To substantiate the priority of collective over individual rights in Canada, other examples from our present and our past could be cited, e.g. native rights, rights to tax supported sectarian education, rights of religious minorities such as the Mennonites, Hutterites, and Doukhobors. In these and many other disputes there have been claims to rights that only the collectivities in question can exercise.

This view that in Canada collective rights have been most important is consistent with the widely held (and, I think, accurate) opinion that by and large the French and English communities in Canada have conflicting perceptions of which rights are most important. Thus, in the Pepin-Robarts' *Report's* definition of 'rights' it is noted that

> Generally speaking, while white anglo-saxon Canadians have tended to think primarily of individual rights, French-Canadians and some ethnic minorities have also stressed the importance of collective rights.[1]

While there are these different perceptions, I maintain that in fact our political and legal history has been one in which collective and not individual rights have been functionally predominant. Thus, for example, consider how *un*important in the Canadian legal system is the Canadian Bill of Rights. Consider, too, the institutionalisation of collective rights in federal-provincial conferences.

(2) But can collectivities be the concernees (beneficiaries) of rights? This is the more basic question of the two. Indeed, I can imagine the liberal-contractarian agreeing with my answer to (1), at least with respect to legal rights, but refusing to give an affirmative answer to (2), for this raises the question of the ground or justification of rights claims in a way that (1) does not. Thus (2) is about the point or purpose of rights claims.

Now, one way of trying to provide an affirmative answer to (2) I want to quickly dismiss as likely to be unprofitable: this is an appeal to the dignity of the collectivity in question where that dignity is unpacked *solely* in terms of that collectivity's freedom (i.e. unpacked in a Kantian way). Even though such appeals, e.g. to national honour, are common, I am inclined to think that of themselves they are baseless. And baseless for the same reasons as appeals to human dignity as a basis for individual rights where that dignity is unpacked solely in terms of individual freedom. I do not find a 'respect-for-the autonomy-of-nations' view any more convincing than a 'respect-for-the autonomy-of-individuals' view. The question, "Why should I or all of us care about my own or my people's freedom or autonomy?"

demands an answer; the 'respect-for' views I reject say that no such answer can or should be given.[2]

A much more useful approach in my view is to look at the interests rights are meant to serve. Consider one of the rights of children, viz. a right to adequate nurture. The contention that children have this individual right requires that both the following be true: (a) that it is desirable for children to receive such nurture, and (b) that it is desirable for there to be a mechanism to ensure the provision of such nurture (perhaps through the legal compulsion of parents).[3] The first is a statement about the interests (not the preferences) of children in general. If it were the case that (a) is true but that a particular child not be better off having such nurture provided, there would be raised also a question about the wisdom of exercising that right. The second (b) could be false though the first is true, e.g. it might not be better to compel the parents to provide such nurture.

The question (2) of whether or not there are collective concernees (beneficiaries) of rights might be answered in the same way as we answered the question (1) about there being collective right-holders.[4] This is because we can easily find examples of collectives benefiting though their members do not. Thus, a state might be wealthy even though and, perhaps, because its citizens are poor. And this may be even though the state's rulers are not lining their pockets at the expense of the citizenry. But I think that we find such situations morally objectionable (even though fraud, force, and corruption are ruled out). We could not morally defend a right whose purpose is to benefit a collectivity as such (e.g. the state) but not to benefit the individual members of the collectivity (in this case that state's citizens). And the reason why this right couldn't be defended is along the lines of (a) above; it is that a collectivity does not in the relevant sense have interests independently of its members, even though, as I have admitted, the collectivity can be the concernee of a right. For what constitutes having an interest is having certain sorts of experiences, viz. hedonic or affective reactions, and only individuals can be said to have experiences. Now sometimes we talk as if collectivities have experiences (e.g. "the French-Canadian experience of English domination" or "the black experience in the U.S."), but such talk is ultimately about the experiences of individual French-Canadians or blacks — perhaps as shared sympathetically over time. That is, I cannot accept as morally justified what might be termed 'Hegelian' (or should I say, 'fascist'?) 'collectivism'.

But this does not prevent me from endorsing a welfare-oriented collectivism, where the welfares in question are those in and affected by the collectivity. This might be described as 'utilitarian' or 'socialist' collectivism. So I do not see why we should insist on unpacking collective rights in terms of an irreducibly collective experience. Rather, we should think of the interests on which collective rights rest for justification as being shared individual interests, in particular interests in being in a certain kind of community with definite other people who share and sympathetically join in what can broadly be described as 'a way of life'. If enough people in a given area share such interests, then this may well be enough to answer affirmatively (a) and (b) even though this is at the expense of a minority or of specific individuals (assuming that, alas, compatible arrangements are impossible). In such situations there may well be equally well-grounded claims to rights that are in deep conflict, and thus force a collectivity to decide which of the conflicting rights to respect or even implement. How we should settle such deep conflicts may not be a matter of rights but a matter of weighing conflicting interests. (It is worth remembering here that not all internal divisions occur in collectivities. Some occur within a given individual.)

Now this will no doubt displease liberal-contractarians. I cannot anticipate all the arguments against what I have just claimed, but I do want to comment on one, viz. that to ground collective rights I mistakenly counted external, especially associational, preferences of individuals, (say) wanting to be with their own kind.[5] Now I count such preferences, insofar as they reflect interests, for two reasons. First, in practice (e.g. in a vote or opinion poll) it is next to impossible to sort out external from personal preferences either inter-, or even more strikingly, intra-personally. Secondly, even though this may seem to let in bigotry as well as fellow-feeling (though it need not let in the former if we only count non-maleficent desires), it still is the case that people in fact care about such matters as their homelands as much or even more than about more individual matters such as personal freedoms or civil liberties. My suggestion is that if in fact people care or could care about such matters there is a possible basis for collective rights, not just in the exercise sense (1) of collective right-holding, but in the beneficiary sense (2) of securing certain public (not private) goods to individuals in virtue of their felt commonality.

Finally what I have said here on the second question (2) does, I believe, shed some light on our present situation. On my view legislation such as that embodied in what is popularly known as 'Bill 101' could conceivably be justified as an assertion of a morally legitimate collective right. This question would have to be settled on whether Bill 101 meets (a) and (b) listed above. Similarly my view would let us consider minority rights inside and outside Québec, i.e. we could look at the collectivities that are meant to benefit (in the persons of their members) by such rights. Moreover, I think separating the question (a) about the beneficiaries of such rights from the question (b) about the desirability of providing a mechanism to provide such benefits lets us bring out an important point. While the issues may be separable conceptually, they may not be separable in fact; those who control the mechanisms — political, economic, legal, etc. — that protect rights are in a position to shape the interests of those whose rights are meant to be protected. Moreover, in providing a specific mechanism they can thereby change what is regarded as the interest there to be protected. The realization of this interconnexion between interests and the mechanisms for their protection is what gives so much importance to the PQ victory in November 1976.

At the end I would add my hope that this gathering of philosophers from across Canada might help show that there can be a coalescence of interests along other than purely national lines — that Canadians have intellectual and creative interests that may serve to unite rather than divide us.

NOTES

1. From page 17 of *Coming to Terms: The Words of the Debate* the second part of the *Report of the Task Force on Canadian Unity*, (Ottawa, 1979). The same point is made in more detail by Ramsay Cook in *Canada and the French-Canadian Question*, (Toronto, 1966) pp. 146-147. Cook percipiently describes English-Canadians as 'Lockean' and French-Canadians as 'Rousseauian' in their political outlooks.

2. It was clear at the Conference that this is a point on which I and other philosophers, in particular Charles Taylor, disagree. This is not the place for me to spell out my own position even though I believe the issue is not only philosophically basic but also crucial to our current concerns with what is widely perceived as Québec's 'drive for autonomy'. The basis of my view is set out in my article "Autarchy and Interest" in the *Australasian Journal of Philosophy* v. 53 (1978). I would only add here that in its collective forms the search for autonomy seems to go through two stages: (i) seeking equal status with one's 'oppressors' and following that (ii) trying to acquire the specific exercise-rights necessary to achieve the collectivity's main goals. On hearing Professor Ayim's paper on women's rights, it struck me that women are by and large at state (i), whereas Québec is now at state (ii). I still am of the opinion (despite counter-arguments by Professor Virginia McDonald) that the moral value of autonomy must be established by reference to the interests of those who seek autonomy. Thus, I would ask if women would on the whole be better off having actual equal status in specified regards with men or if Québec would be better off having certain specified exercise-rights. That I, as my opponents would, likely

answer these questions in the affirmative, does not commit me to denying my claim that autonomy has only instrumental value.

3. The account of rights provided in (a) and (b) is based on Kurt Baier's "The Right to Life" which is, as far as I know, not yet published.

4. My colleague Professor Haworth pointed out this similarity.

5. I have Dworkin in mind here. See *Taking Rights Seriously,* (London 1977) p. 275; also his "Liberalism" in Hampshire's (ed) *Public and Private Morality,* (Cambridge, 1978) p. 134.

BIBLIOGRAPHY

Baier, Kurt. "Moral Obligation", *American Philosophical Quarterly.* v. 3 (1966)."The Right to Life". Not yet published.

Dworkin, Ronald. *Taking Rights Seriously.* London, 1977. Chapters 7, 9, and 12.

"Liberalism", *Public and Private Morality.* Stuart Hampshire. Cambridge, 1978.

Feinberg, Joel. *"Duties, Rights and Claims", American Philosophical Quarterly.* v. 3 (1966).

French, Stanley and Gutman, Andres. "The Principle of National Self-determination", in Held, Morgenbesser, and Nagel (eds.) *Philosophy, Morality, and International Affairs.* Oxford, 1974. pp. 138-153.

Lyons, David. "Rights, Claimants and Beneficiaries", *American Philosophical Quarterly.* v. 6 (1969).

Mackie, J.L. "The Law of the Jungle", *Philosophy.* v. 53 (1978).

McDonald, Michael. "Autarchy and Interest", *Australasian Journal of Philosophy.* v. 53 (1978).

RIGHTS AND COLLECTIVITIES (AN ABSTRACT)

Steven BURNS

Simone Weil offers three reasons for the conclusion that obligations are prior to rights. Although in rhetoric we speak of a conflict between the right to education for one's child in the (founding) language of one's choice, and the right of the collectivity to preserve its language, it is not clear where these rights come from. Also, the mentality of the authors and supporters of Bill 101 in Québec is better represented in Weil's terms than in the language of rights.

The argument of greatest impact is that a right does not exist except viewed in the third person. Weil claims:

> Un homme, considéré en lui-même, a seulement des devoirs, parmi lesquelles se trouvent certains devoirs envers lui-même. Les autres, considérés de son point de vue, ont seulement des droits. Il a des droits à son tour quand il est considéré du point de vue des autres, qui se reconnaissent des obligations envers lui. Un homme qui serait seul dans l'univers n'aurait aucun droit, mais il aurait des obligations. (*l'Enracinement*, p. 2)

One can think of a person or collectivity as a bearer of rights only on the prior basis of other persons who bear obligations toward them. These obligations are grounded in turn on certain needs of people for which a proper collectivity can uniquely provide. Spiritual and cultural connections with past and future generations are not least among these needs.

It is merely abstract to think that a collectivity *per se* has a right to self-preservation, and naive to claim that *simply* because French is a great language anyone should be happy to have a child educated in it. Weil shows much more profoundly why we have an obligation to support a collectivity such as francophone Canada and the Québec which is its fundamental political embodiment.

A COMPARISON OF WOMEN'S RIGHTS AND MINORITY GROUP RIGHTS WITHIN THE FRAMEWORK OF THE CONFEDERATION DEBATE

Maryann AYIM

The egalitarian versus special status controversy continues to rage in feminist and minority group literature. Many advocates of both positions tend not to distinguish between minority groups and women, but to argue across the board for either egalitarianism or special status. It is difficult to assess whether current writing on the issue of confederation also collapses the case of women with that of minority groups, for the simple reason that women as a group are not considered in this writing. In the report of the Task Force on Canadian Unity, for example, women come up for *mention* a grand total of four times! The report suggests twice (once in the form of an actual recommendation) that among native Canadians the conditions for acquiring and losing status should be the same for males and females (pp.59, 122). Women are mentioned again in terms of their contribution to the unemployment problem. No suggestion is made of how they are affected by the unemployment problem (p.66). Women are mentioned a fourth time when the authors point out that on certain issues there should be no regional variance in Canada; they give as an example that it would not be tolerable for women to have equal rights in Manitoba, but not in Ontario (p.108). The choice of wording in this sentence leaves it ambiguous as to whether the denial of equal rights to women would be intolerable, so long as there were no regional disparity involved.

However, I am not criticizing the Task Force for neglecting to deal with the issue of women's rights. In fact, I shall argue that given the two parameters of their study — namely, the principles of duality and regionalism — it is natural that women would not emerge as a separate group for special consideration. Furthermore, I suggest that these very principles illustrate the sense in which women, as a non-dominant group, differ dramatically from any other non-dominant group in our society. These differences will be found to roughly correspond with the differences between the egalitarian and the special status approach to rights, responsibilities, and goods. I shall argue that any constitution or any bill of rights which attempts to give specific consideration to non-dominant groups must, in the interests of justice, take account of such differences. With talk in the ranks of re-writing the Canadian constitution, this is an appropriate time to examine the subtleties of this issue very closely. If confederation is to provide a context within which individual and collective rights can be defined and promoted, then the nature of that context will differ significantly for women and for minority groups. In my argument, I will make extensive use of the two principles which the Task Force takes to define the lines of cleavage (p.25) in Canadian society, namely, duality and regionalism.

Neither of these terms is explicitly defined by the Task Force, but then their meanings are obvious enough. Duality is the fact of pairedness, or of twoness, or of alternation in the logical sense. The central duality in Canada is that defined by French and English. This duality has many different facets, among which history, language, and legal system predominate in importance. Since the "French fact", as the authors put it, resides *for the most part* in Quebec, they address themselves primarily to the dualism formed between Quebec and the rest of Canada. As the report indicates, however, the French/English dualism emerges in other contexts as well. For example, within Quebec itself an English/French dichotomy obtains. And there are many completely different dualisms, such as indigenous peoples and settlers, caucasians and non-caucasians, middle class and working class.

"Regionalism", as used by the Task Force includes both the notion of land and of multiplicity; thus they imply by the term the essential division of the *country* into *several* distinct regions. The composition of the regions varies with the criterion for differentiation. In terms of political units the provinces and territories each constitute a region; in terms of geography there could be five units consisting of British Columbia, the prairies, Ontario, Quebec, and the Maritimes. The Task Force views this first mode of division as the most vital to consideration of the future of confederation. It further notes in the report that dualism and regionalism are seldom separable quantities. Quebec itself, as one half of the central duality, is divisible into rural and urban regions, whereas Ontario, one of the central regions, manifests the feature of dualism through its minority population of French Canadians and mainstream population of English Canadians. In this complex mosaic of dualisms and regionalisms, it is important that there be an equitable sharing of benefits and power.

The Pepin-Robarts report recommends that "there be a new and distinctive Canadian constitution to meet the present and future needs of all the people of Canada" (p.124). This constitution should

> recognize the historic partnership between English and French-speaking Canadians, and the distinctiveness of Quebec; affirm the special place of the native peoples of Canada; recognize the richness and the contribution of Canada's other cultural groups; recognize the diversity among Canada's regions and the need to permit all regional communities to flourish; seek the promotion of the social, economic and cultural development and the equality of opportunity for all Canadians in all regions of Canada (p.125).

In this list of groups whose interests should receive constitutional consideration, women do not appear. Why? The answer is that they do not clearly match either of the two principles, duality and regionalism, which the authors select as crucial to sorting out the question of benefits and power. This seems an odd claim, as on the surface the female/male relationship is certainly one of duality. Subtle nuances of the male/female relationship sharply differentiate it from any other instance of dualism in Canadian society, however. There are in particular two distinguishing features. The first is that the very term "dualism" is suggestive of dichotomy, of confrontation, of opposition, of polarization, such that in referring to the dualism of English and French, for example, one is tempted to write English *versus* French. The female/male relationship, on the other hand, is more readily perceived as complementary, where the two units are not separate alternatives, but parts of a whole. The second distinguishing feature (closely related to the first) is that dualisms are generally understood to relate whole classes of people, rather than particular individuals. This is why the French/English dualism automatically suggests the dualism exemplified between the inhabitants of Quebec and the inhabitants of the rest of Canada. Yet the male/female relationship is not generally perceived as one of class, but rather as one of individuals, and often a private, highly personal relationship at that. On a personal, private, individual level, our society exerts relatively little pressure on members of different linguistic, racial, or ethnic groups to interrelate. In fact, in terms of the most private, personal and individual relationship possible, marriage, it is safe to say that society *discourages* such intermingling. Yet it is precisely in this area of highly private, personal, and individual relationships that society virtually coerces us into the male/female combination. Alternatives to the female/male combination incur such heavy social wrath that for most people they are not genuine alternatives. Furthermore, the personalization and privatization of male/female units mitigates against a wider political and social polarization of these groups. The present social and political polarization of the English and French in Canada would also lose its force if individual French and English Canadians were pushed into co-habitation. Thus the male/female unit does not represent a duality in anything like the sense that English/French forms a duality in Canada.

Even if one persisted in seeing the female/male relationship as a genuine duality, further peculiarities arise when we consider the principle of regionalism. Corresponding to the French/English dualism are parallel regions. In other words, French Canadians have Quebec. Smaller minority groups of Francophones also have their places. Francophones in Ontario occupy the region adjacent to the Quebec border; Francophones in New Brunswick occupy the northeast region. Where French Canadians have had no region, they have been assimilated by English Canadians; the use of the French language has tended to disappear in these instances (p.46). This is what has happened to women, who have no region of their own. Even relative to the middle class/working class dualism, women are without a region; for most Canadian cities are fairly distinctly regionalized in terms of class. Women, on the other hand, are forced by the nuclear family into the male/female unit. Even in the home, the woman has traditionally had no room of her own. Given the theory of a husband's right to sexual access, and given the difficulty, sometimes the impossibility, of obtaining an abortion, a woman's very body is not her own.

Since women cannot be said to occupy a distinct region, and since they do not form part of a genuine duality, it is not surprising that they virtually go unmentioned in the Task Force report, whose whole content is organized according to the principles of regionalism and dualism. Given these facts, it would be unwise for women to argue for a position of special rights as opposed to a principle of egalitarianism. Since women are given almost no choice about participating in the traditional male/female structure of the nuclear family, and since, unlike any other cultural, religious, linguistic, or racial group in the country, they are not easily able to meet together or to even perceive themselves as a class, I suggest that we could not count on women being able to work out their own definition of what constitutes their special status. What is more likely to happen is that the special nature of women would continue to be defined by and in the interests of men. Such "special status" has not in the past worked to the advantage of women, who were denied access to many relatively high paying job areas, for example, because men perceived the "purity of mind and of language" peculiar to women to be threatened by the harsh language of the industrial plant, or the court, or the operating room. Other non-dominant groups do operate and see themselves as a distinct class. There is less reason for the self-perception of native Canadians, for example, to be entirely a product of how the mainstream group perceives them; although a non-dominant group in this society, native Canadians have their own place in their own region, and this permits the possibility of solidarity and independence in their definition of self.

While native Canadians are undoubtedly exploited by the mainstream group, they are at least free to despise their exploiters. No additional penalty of love is exacted. This distinguishes their position from that of women, from whom love of their oppressors is demanded, by virtue of the fact that members of the exploiting group are husbands, sons, and brothers to the women.

Women, because they face special difficulties in independently defining their own special status, needs, and rights, would be better advised to argue for egalitarianism than for special rights, for they can count on the dominant group to look out for its own best interests, so simply to demand the same rights and privileges would seem to be a safe move. By opting for equal rights, women will be opting for the rights that men see as belonging to men. If women as well achieve these rights, they will have acquired the keys to a very powerful vehicle of self-determination. Ironically, by going the equal rights with men route, women will optimize their independence, making the development of their own perception of self a real and present possibility. On the other hand, women may attempt to *start* from a set of special rights, based on the notion of special female needs and female nature. This approach is problematic, since women are, at present both a non-dominant, generally disadvantaged group in the society and at the same time a group whose members are linked by bonds of love and family to the dominant oppressing class. Given what some writers have referred to in such strong terms as women's colonized position, we should expect this initial perception of self to be strongly determined by the male perception of what constitutes the special status of a woman. Such a self-perception is unlikely to be conducive to the independence and autonomy of women. In short, until women are in a position to *autonomously* define their own natures, needs, and rights, they will be advised to demand equal rights; from this plateau, they will be much better equipped to engage in self-analysis in a spirit of independent thinking, and to subsequently, if their analysis carries them in this direction, decide upon and fight for a set of special rights and needs.

The different paths to autonomy distinguishing women from other non-dominant groups are dictated by their different situations — specifically, because the concept of dualism is not applicable to women in the same way as to the other groups, and the concept of regionalism is not applicable to women at all. Consequently, different solutions will also be required. In particular, different patterns of socialization and training, especially for the young, will be needed. For example, while it may be quite appropriate and justifiable to limit the socialization and skills exposure of native Canadians to those demanded by their traditional life styles, it is imperative that the skills taught to females should *not* be limited to those traditionally associated with the female life style. It is also imperative that females be socialized into the value scheme traditionally associated with males — competitiveness, assertiveness, independence, and competence. Without such value acceptance and skill acquisition, women will continue to be disadvantaged economically and politically.

The responsibility of sorting out appropriate socialization patterns will fall to the school — more specifically, to the teacher. This would entail sweeping changes in the educational system, in the political structure of the school, and in the preparation of teachers but if, like the proposed constitution advocated by the Task Force, it could help "to meet the present and future needs of *all* the people of Canada" (p.124, my italics), such a task would carry its own categorical imperative.

NOTE

All page references are to Jean-Luc Pepin and John P. Robarts, Co-chairpersons, The Task Force on Canadian Unity, *A Future Together; Observations and Recommendations* (Hull, Quebec: Canadian Government Publishing Centre, January 1979).

NATURAL RESOURCE RIGHTS AND CONSTITUTIONAL CHANGE

Brenda M. BAKER

Recent constitutional debates have been marked by a lively sense on the part of the provinces of their legitimate rights, and an increasingly confident provincial posture in defence of those rights. It can scarcely be doubted that constitutional reform will reflect this assertiveness by according a larger place to provincial rights in any new division of powers. It is therefore very important that we think seriously about the grounds on which such provincial rights or powers should be justified, and about the proper extent and limits of such rights.

One provincial claim which has in recent years received unanimous support from the provinces, and which is of special concern to Western Canada, is the claim to ownership and control of natural resources. Indeed, the Alberta government position paper on constitutional change recommends "that the existing sections of the BNA Act protecting provincial ownership and control of natural resources be strengthened".[1] I hope then to present some reflections on the proper grounding and scope of provincial rights generally, by focussing on natural resource rights, and inquiring about their proper justification and scope.

How then can provincial claims to ownership and control of natural resources be justified? From the standpoint of justice,[2] provincial claims to natural resource ownership control appear morally arbitrary, and cannot be effectively defended by appeal to such traditional criteria of justice as desert, merit or need. The value of a province's natural resources is a function of many factors which lie outside provincial control or responsibility, and the extent of a province's natural resources depends in considerable part on historical and geographical accident and on other environmental contingencies, so that provinces can scarcely claim to deserve or to merit ownership or control of their natural resources. While it might be argued that certain earlier generations had some legitimate claim to ownership of natural resources based on the effort, courage and enterprise displayed by those generations in making resources accessible and usable for the benefit of individuals, this argument would at best establish a partial claim to limited natural resources, and would not warrant the transfer of that claim to later generations, including the present generation. And that the distribution of natural resources riches is not congruent with the distribution of economic needs throughout the country is obvious.

If provincial claims are not easily defended on grounds of justice, does Canada as a whole have a better claim to ownership and control of its natural resources, based on such grounds? We are often told, in a tone of moral fervour, that natural resources, after all, *"belong* to *all* Canadians" , as though they were something we could collectively lay claim to as a matter of right. But the same objections as were brought against provincial claims based on appeals to justice apply with considerable force to the claim of the country as a whole to be entitled as a matter of justice to possession and control of the totality of its natural resources. The resource wealth of the country is not something to which we have a special claim of desert based on effort and labour extended or on performances accomplished, nor which we can claim on grounds of special need.

There is one respect in which national claims to ownership and control of natural resources may be more defensible than provincial claims, from the standpoint of justice, namely, if we accept the principle that the benefits (burdens) with respect to which there are no significant claims of desert should be distributed as widely as possible, on the ground that every individual has an equal standing with respect to the enjoyment of such benefits (or the assumption of such burdens). However, this principle is itself controversial, even as a principle of justice, and it would in any event not ground an unassailable right on the part of Canadians to control their resources.

Possibly the discussion thus far has approached the question of the rightful ownership of natural resources from the wrong perspective. For the question before us at this time in our history is not, after all, what is the ideally just, or ideally right, allocation of powers[3] in a nation or in our nation; the question is, rather, what changes, if any, in the allocation of powers should be made in the constitutional framework that this country already has. We are not, then, engaged in a process of creating a constitution *ab initio*, from some idealized original position, but are concerned with the question of the legitimate reallocation and modification of an established existing division of powers. Those constitutional powers have over the past century served us reasonably well, and have given rise to established patterns of practice and expectation in thought and behaviour that in turn shape how we can and do approach the question of constitutional revision.

The provinces' claim to natural resource ownership and control is strengthened by being viewed in this context. Section 109 of the BNA Act provides for provincial ownership and control over all lands, mines, minerals and royalties, and this allocation of natural resource powers has been a cardinal feature of the division of powers distinctive of our federation. Proponents of provincial ownership and control over natural resources can therefore claim that what they are seeking is in large measure a clarification and reaffirmation both of the original intent of the articles of confederation and of an important pattern of established practice throughout our country's history. The effect of this approach is to shift the onus of proof to those who would argue against provincial claims — they will need to show that the present or future situation regarding natural resources is sufficiently different to displace this appeal to traditional practice and to constitutional objectives.

In addition to this 'constitutional' argument, I think it is arguable that placing resource ownership in provincial rather than federal hands will commonly result in a more effective and capable handling of those resources, with potential benefits for Canadians generally. Provincial bodies are better placed to avail themselves of specialized skills and expertise appropriate to the intelligent utilization of their resources, to monitor administrative use and abuse, and to make informed policy decisions about the relations between natural resource use and other economic and social provincial priorities, such as the development of secondary industry or the provision of recreational opportunities. Also, they can be made answerable to the democratic process. Provincial resource ownership may then be a very effective way of promoting certain social goods, such as economic benefits, increased opportunities for individual development, and more intangible benefits such as an increased self-esteem grounded in regional achievement.

What then are the difficulties facing the provinces' claims to natural resource rights of ownership and control? The most serious difficulties seem to be two. First of all, it is obvious that the virtues of provincial control of natural resource development are accompanied by certain limitations and risks, especially those attendant on the limited interests, perspectives and priorities of the particular provinces themselves. The interests of producing provinces are bound to be considerably at odds with the interests of consuming provinces, for example, and a policy which best answers to provincial needs may detrimentally affect the well-being of the country as a whole.

Secondly, provincial claims to resource rights are themselves disconcertingly vague. They fail to specify which complexus of rights and powers is being asked for. One expects that minimally claim is being made to certain rights to determine the use to which resources are put, and to rights of taxation and royalty-collection on the sale and management of natural resources. But 'ownership and control' might also embrace other rights of control over natural resources as commodities, including rights to determine marketing arrangements and to set prices within and outside the province concerned. In this area, the claim to provincial control becomes highly problematic because it is here that the interests of one province and another, or of one province and the country as a whole, can most clearly diverge and conflict.

Granting unfettered provincial rights to determine marketing agreements for the use of their natural resources would of course conflict with existing federal powers regarding interprovincial and international trade and commerce, with serious implications for national sovereignty. We should carefully consider here whether existing federal powers are sufficient to enable the federal government to fulfill its responsibilities to the Canadian people, or whether these should be enlarged or reshaped in a revised constitution.[4] It is not hard to think of situations where a province's exercise of natural resource rights might jeopardize important national interests, even without violating existing federal powers, e.g. a province's decision to leave its natural resource heritage in the ground, or to remove only enough for consumption within its boundaries, might result in national scarcity and serious hardship in other parts of the country.

If the discussion thus far is along the right lines, then there is need as well as opportunity to address ourselves to the question of how to frame a reasonable allocation of federal-provincial powers in the natural resources area. The tenor of my earlier remarks is that the best way to approach the question of such an allocation is to regard it as a means to the realization of various goals and values that are accepted by Canadians generally, having regard for the particular historical and political circumstances which are distinctive in our country. The goodness of any such allocation will be instrumental goodness, although nothing in my earlier discussion requires that these values and goals be strictly utilitarian in character.

Following this general approach, we should aim to identify a number of criteria and/or principles that can serve to underwrite and shape such an allocation of resource rights. The following questions, also important in themselves, should serve to give this enterprise a definite focus.

1. Should a revised constitution contain some provision empowering the federal authority to ensure that the use (etc.) of Canadian natural resources is not detrimental to the nation's serious interests? Such a provision might include the power to initiate, discontinue or redirect resource development or use where required by compelling national interest.

A full answer to this question would consider whether in general, and if so whether in the particular case of Canada at the present time, it is wise to ensure that desirable structures of resource rights are constitutionally embodied. It may be that more informal procedures are to be preferred.

2. On the supposition that some constitutional provision is desirable, how should such a power be specified and what should be its justifying grounds? Here I think there are strong reasons against giving our federal authority a broadly defined entitlement such as that of 'regulating natural resource use in the national interest'. The 'national interest' rubric is too vague and potentially too indiscriminate in its application; its availability would undercut the provinces' autonomy and planning ability unnecessarily, and it would invite abuse (by confusing national and party political interest, for example). If these considerations are persuasive, we need a more precisely defined and circumscribed set of warranting grounds (e.g., by a specification of harms to be avoided, such as prevention of serious hardship to significant portions of the nation's population, or of serious dislocation of the national economy). What should these be?

3. Should provincial ownership and control of natural resources extend to embrace *any* rights to determine marketing and pricing arrangements for the sale and use of its resources? One pertinent consideration here is that the case for such provincial rights is much stronger with respect to commerce *within the province* than it is in relation to interprovincial or international trade. For provinces are not constitutionally bound to take account of wider national concerns, nor are their executives answerable to many who could be directly affected, sometimes detrimentally, by extra-provincial marketing arrangements. In short, certain legal and political constraints that might serve to check the exercise of provincial resource-commodity-rights *within the province* would not similarly operate on extra-provincial arrangements.

Subordinate questions under this third heading include the following:

(a) Should individual provinces have the right to enter into marketing agreements with one another by mutual consent, or should the federal authorities instead play a decisive role in determining the acceptability and terms of such agreements?

(b) Should federal rights take priority over provincial rights in all matters relating to the sale or export of natural resources to parties representing interests outside Canada, or should there be concurrent federal-provincial jurisdiction over some aspects/areas of these activities?

It is hoped that these questions provide a framework for thinking constructively about the wider issue of a proper future allocation of resource rights and powers in Canada, so that this thinking can be conducted in a way which minimizes the aura of confrontation that often surrounds claims of rights.

NOTES

1. *Harmony in Diversity,* Alberta Government Position Paper on Constitutional Change, October, 1978 Sect III, (i), Recommendation 6.

2. The close tie between what are properly one's rights and what is owing to one as a matter of justice has frequently been noted philosophically. See, for example, J.S. Mill, *Utilitarianism*, chap. 5 and Joel Feinberg, "The Nature and Value of Rights" , *The Journal of Value Inquiry,* Vol. 4, 1970, reprinted in D. Lyons (eds.) *Rights*, 1979, p.78-91.

3. It may well be that framing our questions in terms of *powers* instead of *rights* will facilitate their profitable discussion and resolution. While powers can entail rights and vice-versa, powers lack the associations of 'absoluteness' that often attach to rights. Powers have to do with the actual, whereas rights can be actual or ideal. Rights can be stood on and demanded as unquestionably legitimate, in a way that brooks no argument, whereas powers are more readily seen as mechanisms for realizing certain purposes and fulfilling certain functions, and therefore as negotiable and adjustable. The absolute, non-negotiable nature of rights-claims has been more fully discussed by several other participants to this workshop.

4. In addition to these more immediate constitutional issues, there are underlying important moral questions about the nature and extent of provincial governments' obligations to Canada and its interests, supposing it to be the case that such collective obligations exist over and above the obligations had by members of provincial bodies as individual Canadian citizens. The examination of these questions is beyond the scope of this discussion paper.

DELIVREZ-MOI DE VOS DROITS!

Serge J. MORIN

D'après les derniers sondages d'opinions publiques le grand débat canadien, du moins tel que le jouent présentement nos politiciens, est aux Canadiens ce qu'est, pour nous des maritimes, la côte magnétique. Une explication possible pour ce manque d'enthousiasme chez nos citoyens se trouverait peut-être du côté du phénomène bien connu de l'influence de l'habitude: comme le soulignait Carlyle, "let but a Creation of the world happen *twice*, and it ceases to be marvelous, to be noteworthy or noticeable". Ou encore, et cette fois nous nous approchons un peu plus près de la vérité, il se peut qu'à toute fin pratique le phénomène ait tout simplement disparu de la scène. Plus précisément, je veux dire qu'à l'ombre du débat officiel ou traditionnel remue un autre débat de beaucoup plus important et intelligent; un débat qui, à mon avis, ne se joue pas essentiellement entre deux nations, deux peuples fondateurs, mais entre deux perspectives de notre réalité sociale — perspectives qui transcendent le discours "dueliste" traditionnel. Si on me pressait d'attacher un nom à chacune de ces perspectives, j'en nommerais une "les pionniers" et l'autre "les résidents".

Les résidents disent aux pionniers, "You have a blue guitar, you do not play things as they are". Et aux pionniers de leur répondre, "Things as they are are changed upon the blue guitar (Wallace Stevens)". Jouer de la guitare bleue représente ce que les pionniers sont en train de faire lorsque l'air qu'ils jouent vise la création de nouveaux modèles, non *de* ce qu'est la réalité canadienne mais *pour* ce que pourrait être cette réalité. Selon Thomas Kuhn, les pionniers sont des fabriquants de paradigmes ou de modèles (métaphores?) nouveaux pour le Canada. De leur côté, les résidents ne songent pas à remettre en question le paradigme ou le modèle dominant à l'intérieur duquel ils oeuvrent depuis Charlottetown, et avec suffisamment de succès, diront-ils. Il serait plus à propos de dire que ce modèle ou cette métaphore, justement en tant que modèle ou métaphore, n'apparaît plus comme tel aux yeux des résidents: il leur est invisible. Au début nos pères l'avaient proposé comme étant un modèle parmi d'autres *pour* cette réalité qui allait se concrétiser. Graduellement ce modèle — cette façon de voir leur espace, cette perspective originale — s'est concrétisé, voir même ossifié, et les citoyens ont senti qu'il leur devenait de plus en plus difficile de voir leur réalité autrement que comme un rapport de correspondance ou de stricte cohérence avec le modèle établi. En d'autres mots, ce qui, à l'origine était un modèle *pour* quelque chose à produire, est maintenant un modèle *de* quelque chose, d'une réalité donnée et définie. Ainsi ne peuvent-ils faire autrement que de continuer à dédoubler ou à étendre "from coast to coast" une seule et unique "réalité". Le sens ou l'aspect concret de cette réalité dite "Canada" dépend de la concrétisation de leur perspective. A mesure qu'une façon de voir devient habituelle nous oublions ou négligeons notre perspective. Elle devient invisible et nous croyons alors rejoindre les choses telles qu'elles sont — comme si les choses étaient connaissables indépendemment d'une perspective quelconque — éliminant ainsi toute rivalité ou compétition avec d'autres perspectives qui feraient ressortir des réalités radicalement différentes. C'est ainsi que les résidents pratiquent une sorte d'impérialisme paradigmatique, à travers lequel le Canada *en-soi* est atteint et connu. Le Canada n'est plus pour eux un projet mais simplement un nom ou une description d'un fait accompli. Comme une métaphore en devenant de plus en plus acceptée se transforme en "ce que les choses sont réellement", le Canada perd de sa vivacité en augmentant sa véracité.

Dans le camp opposé, les pionniers sont en train de forger des nouveaux modèles, des métaphores phénoménologiquement mieux fondées. Pour eux, la perspective dominante est comme un filet qui n'attrape que des poissons déjà morts. Ils lui substituent un nouveau code, un nouveau discours, invitant leurs lecteurs à dé-réaliser ou à dé-concrétiser leurs réalités conventionnelles afin de réaliser le nouvel espace qui est en train de se dessiner. Ils doivent re-connaître les faits anciens sous leur forme nouvelle. Ici la ressemblance à la réalité antécédente n'est plus un critère de succès, de vérité ou de beauté, car les pionniers, contrairement aux résidents, sont remarquablement peu intéressés à la représentation standardisée de la réalité et sont remarquablement intéressés à la voir sous sa nouvelle forme, isolée de la forme conventionnelle. Les pionniers en arrivent ainsi à briser ou à rendre visible la présence et l'influence de la perspective traditionnelle en même temps qu'ils nous offrent une infinité d'alternatives, chacune produisant son propre monde, son propre Canada, "The whole process of discovery and confirmation ultimately relies on our own accrediting of our own vision of reality" (Polanyi, *Personal Knowledge*, 1958).

Ils entraînent donc une transformation du monde; brisant et faisant littéralement éclater le réalisme traditionnel, les pionniers font naître l'angoisse et la détresse chez les résidents. Cette détresse est le reflet de quelqu'un qui a sur-investi dans *un* monde et qui doit maintenant se mettre à l'écoute des autres langages de l'Etre. "Thought can bring forth and make what did not exist into an object of experience, that is, into reality." (Jaspers, *Truth and Symbol*, 1959).

En somme, les pionniers sont en train d'écrire un nouveau scénario *pour* le Canada: ils ré-organisent notre perspective en des formes et associations nouvelles, incommensurables avec nos représentations habituelles. En inventant des nouvelles métaphores, les pionniers inventent des nouveaux programmes d'exploration car la métaphore définit son propre domaine d'application et l'invite ou, comme dirait Cassirer, la force à exister. Une salière étiquetée "DDT" n'est plus une salière, un pauvre reconnu comme une personne économiquement faible n'est plus un pauvre, un acadien vivant dans sa province n'est plus un minoritaire, une province souveraine n'est plus une province. Les nouveaux termes d'appellation changent 1) notre attitude vis-à-vis un être, et 2) changent l'être lui-même.

Je vois le Canada comme une métaphore, un "comme si" qui n'est plus vu comme une métaphore, i.e., une métaphore qui graduellement a été prise trop au sérieux, et nous savons que prise littéralement une métaphore doit être absolument absurde — l'homme n'est pas un rat. Un mythe n'est qu'une métaphore acceptée comme vraie; c'est accepter une absurdité comme vraie. Le Canada, celui qu'acceptent nos résidents, est un mythe. Ainsi nous entendons plusieurs gens qui croient que le Nouveau-Brunswick est un modèle *du* Canada ou un modèle pour le Canada: en tant que modèle *du* Canada, c'est un mythe, et en tant que modèle pour le Canada, ce serait une tragédie. Voyons d'autres mythes nationaux:

1) Canada, "*comme s*'il y avait deux peuples fondateurs": ici "deux peuples" et "fondateurs" constituent une absurdité empirique.

2) Canada, "*comme s*'il y avait deux mère-patries": l'amérindien est ainsi transformé en un batard, une personne sans mère, un orphelin, *comme* s'il n'était pas chez-lui.

3) L'acadien, un francophone vivant hors Québec — *comme si* le

terreneuvien était un anglophone vivant hors de l'Ontario, ou l'ontarien, un anglophone vivant hors de Terreneuve, ou un huron, un iroquois, un algonquin, vivant hors . . . de quoi?

4) L'Ungawa est devenu le Nouveau-Québec, *comme s*'il s'agissait d'une propriété privée.

5) Les Iles turcs et caicos veulent se faire voir *comme si* elles étaient un parc provincial du Nouveau-Brunswick.

6) En Acadie, 375 ans plus tard, on dit "On est venu, c'est pour rester" *comme s*'il n'était plus question d'une simple visite chez un étranger. C'est pourquoi notre hôte a quitté les lieux.

7) Université d'Ottawa — université franco-ontarienne — *comme si* les franco-ontariens pourraient un jour enseigner dans leur institution . . . (voir par exemple les départements de philosophie et d'histoire.)

Ainsi nos métaphores nationales devraient être démasquées, i.e., consciemment perçues "comme si". Cela ne veut pas dire qu'il faille les prendre comme si elles n'étaient que pure fiction car nous manquerions alors une occasion de les élaborer en modèles, puis en théories. De même il ne faut pas les accepter comme vraies, i.e. comme une *imitation de* quelque chose, car alors nous manquerions une occasion d'entrevoir leurs rivaux possibles. Le choix entre des métaphores rivales devient apparent seulement lorsque nous conservons consciemment le "comme si" de notre pensée métaphorique. A mon avis, les pionniers sont seuls à nous offrir un tel choix. Ceux-ci, par exemple, forcent la concrétisation d'une nouvelle perspective en demandant aux ontariens ou aux néo-écossais de se définir, de développer leur propre espace, leur propre identité — une identité autre que celle de n'être qu'anglophone. Ainsi le débat canadien de demain pourrait aussi bien se jouer entre le Yukon et l'Ile du Prince Edouard, ou entre Terre-Neuve et le Labrador. Il n'y aura plus deux opposants mais bien 2 X 2 X 2 X 2. En somme, en démasquant notre réalité comme étant dépendante de notre perspective, ils inventent une infinité d'alternatives.

Et le minoritaire dans tout ceci? Si le Canada est une métaphore, le minoritaire est l'ironiste par excellence. Plus que n'importe quel citoyen, il vit et perçoit l'absurdité dans laquelle le situe la métaphore dominante. Suivant Kuhn je dirais que le minoritaire est une anomalie vivante pour le modèle dominant. Pour le minoritaire, il lui semble que la société, que tel groupe de personnes, que la nature même se moquent de lui. L'esprit harmonieux, ou celui qui ne perçoit que l'harmonie, découvre difficilement cette malice. Par exemple, notre minoritaire perçoit son statut de minoritaire, non pas comme une description objective de sa réalité mais bien comme une *punition* malicieuse (voir ces belles métaphores de "reserve", "ghetto ethnique", "région économiquement faible", "dumb frog" ou "dumb indien", "le chiac", etc.). Le minoritaire sait trop bien que ce n'est pas le *fait* acadien, micmac, franco-ontarien... qui entraîne la répression, mais la répression qui entraîne le fait acadien, micmac, etc. Cette punition ou répression se poursuit sous une étiquette altruiste à travers toutes ces agences de services qui forcent l'acadien à devenir un objet servile, un esclave. Impossible pour lui de se défaire de ces étiquettes: s'il essaie, on y voit une autre manifestation de son statut de minoritaire. Donc, il doit constamment déjouer l'autre en agissant *comme si:* comme s'il était le vrai de vrai. R.D. Laing a très bien décrit le jeux ironique du patient face à son médecin — le patient simule l'absurdité. Ainsi donc, comme dirait Kierkegaard, dans *Le concept d'ironie*, quand le minoritaire "se montre autre qu'il n'est en réalité, l'on pourrait croire qu'il se propose de faire illusion aux autres; à vrai dire, ce qu'il veut proprement, c'est se sentir libre". Jouer à l'assimilé c'est pour lui de présenter un extérieur en contradiction avec l'intérieur, une sorte d'hypocrisie ou d'imposture — ça paraît bien. Mais cette hypocrisie renvoie immédiatement au modèle dominant, au système. L'assimilation comme libération? comme moyen qu'a le minoritaire d'empêcher qu'une situation obscène ne prenne réalité. Il veut sortir continuellement de sa situation de minoritaire; il bat constamment en retraite; il conteste la réalité quotidienne, en dévoile toute l'imperfection. Je ne veux pas entrer ici dans le détail de cette perspective qui voit le minoritaire comme ironiste. Je me contenterai d'y faire allusion comme une piste fructueuse.[1]

Mais déjà nous constatons que cette question des droits des minorités, posée à l'intérieur des métaphores en place, ne nous donnera comme réponse que des droits qui consistent à ne recevoir que des services; et la critique ne portera que sur la qualité ou l'absence de ces services. Les droits revendiqués seront du même ordre que les droits protectionistes que l'on porte vis-à-vis nos malades institutionalisés. Si le minoritaire est une personne que l'on punit, i.e. si notre société croit qu'elle a le *droit* de le punir ainsi, alors que reste-t-il comme droit au minoritaire? Seulement celui d'être puni moins sévèrement, d'être réhabilité, d'avoir un porte parole à la porte du pouvoir? Délivrez-moi de vos droits!

NOTE

1. Voir l'excellent ouvrage de Richard H. Brown, *A Poetic for Sociology*. London: Cambridge University Press, 1977.

APPENDIX

APPENDICE

LE QUÉBEC, LE CANADA: UN DIALOGUE

Stanley G. FRENCH et Storrs McCall

McCALL Voyons si je peux préciser ce que je vois comme étant les principaux points d'accord et de désaccord entre nous. Tous les deux, nous soutenons le maintien, la diffusion et l'épanouissement de la langue et de la culture québécoise. Stanley est de l'opinion que ce n'est possible que si le Québec assume le contrôle effectif des principales institutions reliées à la culture, telles que l'éducation, l'immigration, la politique sociale et économique. De plus, il croit que le Canada, dans sa structure actuelle, n'est pas un cadre politique viable pour la préservation et la promotion de la langue et de la culture québécoises, et que la souveraineté québécoise est nécessaire pour la réalisation de ce but.

Ici nos opinions divergent. A mon avis, le Canada fournit précisément un cadre viable pour la préservation et la promotion de la langue et de la culture, ce qui est démontré par l'évolution rapide de la société québécoise au cours des dix ou quinze dernières années. En outre, le million de francophones qui habitent hors du Québec a besoin, comme tout groupe minoritaire, d'être protégé de la domination de la majorité. Là aussi le cadre fédéral joue un rôle important, même indispensable. Si nous nous demandions ce que signifie la démocratie en général, nous serions autant porté à répondre "la protection contre la tyrannie" que "la loi de la majorité". Aussi longtemps que le Canada soutient et défend fermement les droits des groupes minoritaires - les droits des femmes, des francophones, des autochtones, des enfants, des vieillards, des minorités ethniques qui ont plus d'une centaine de langues et de traditions différentes - alors le Canada est la meilleure option pour nous tous. Si le Canada sanctionnait la discrimination contre les Québécois, ou nous niait nos droits démocratiques, alors je serais d'accord qu'il faudrait considérer sérieusement, comme alternative, l'indépendance du Québec.

FRENCH Du point de vue que je représente, tes remarques

préliminaires contiennent un nombre d'affirmations, et aussi d'attitudes, qui reflètent le côté anglophone bien exprimé de nos deux solitudes historiques. Par exemple, tu impliques que les francophones ne sont qu'une autre minorité ethnique canadienne dont les droits sont, bien sûr, à soutenir et à défendre "fermement". Compare ton point de vue avec celui affirmant qu'il y a deux (ou trois) peuples fondateurs au Canada, les anglophones et les francophones (et les autochtones).

La nation fondatrice francophone n'a pas joui des mêmes droits et des mêmes privilèges que l'anglophone dans cet état appelé le Canada. Les anglophones au Québec ont eu leur propre système scolaire financé par l'état. Les francophones au Canada ne l'ont pas eu. Les anglophones au Québec ont reçu les services médicaux et beaucoups d'autres dans leur propre langue. Les francophones ailleurs au Canada, non.

Tu fais référence à l'évolution rapide de la société québécoise au cours des dix dernières années et tu en conclus que le Canada fournit réellement un cadre viable pour la préservation et la promotion de la langue et de la culture québécoises. Il y a deux problèmes avec cette sorte d'argument. Le premier est que, étant un des peuples fondateurs, les Québécois ne devraient pas avoir été mis dans une position qui nécessite un rattrapage. Deuxièmement, quand on a été victime de discrimination, une solution gradualiste est insatisfaisante. On veut la justice immédiatement.

Le Canada ne soutient pas et ne défend pas fermement les droits des groupes minoritaires. Les droits des femmes (quoi qu'elles ne soient pas une minorité), les droits des francophones et des autochtones, n'ont été reconnus qu'à contre-coeur. Très peu d'actions positives ont été prises. La Déclaration des Droits du Canada n'a pas été incorporée dans la constitution, elle n'a pas préséance sur la législation antécédente, et on a montré qu'elle a peu ou pas de signification pratique. Nous créons des Commissions royales d'enquête et ensuite nous ne tenons pas compte de leurs constatations et de leurs recommandations. Les membres conscients des groupes victimes doivent peser les avantages d'une association continue contre les désavantages des situations parfois intolérables.

McCALL Je suis content qu'on dise que je m'exprime bien mais je ne suis pas aussi content de penser que je suis encore enfermé dans une des deux solitudes. Toutefois, permets-moi de faire de mon mieux. Je ne veux pas donner l'impression que je considère les francophones comme étant seulement un des nombreux groupes minoritaires du

Canada. Je crois réellement, comme toi, Stanley, à la notion de deux (ou trois) peuples fondateurs.

Je suis aussi d'accord que la nation fondatrice francophone n'a pas joui des mêmes droits et des mêmes privilèges que la nation anglophone. Deux exemples en sont la législation scolaire du Manitoba de 1890 et la Régulation 17 de l'Ontario. Mais mettre l'accent seulement sur les injustices du passé ne nous amène pas plus près d'une résolution dans le présent. Certes le progrès a été lent. Mais on a fait du progrès quand même, et ça continue. Par exemple, au cours des dernières semaines, la Colombie Britannique a adopté une loi qui accorde le droit, dans une communauté, à l'éducation publique en français à tout groupe composé d'au moins dix enfants francophones. D'un certain point de vue, c'est le gradualisme, mais d'un autre point de vue on ne peut pas s'empêcher d'admirer la façon d'agir directe et prompte du gouvernement de la Colombie Britannique.

Est-ce que la Colombie Britannique aurait agi de cette façon si elle ne faisait pas partie du Canada? J'en doute.

Je suis d'accord que le Canada a agi très lentement en ce qui concerne les droits des groupes minoritaires. Nous n'avons pas, comme tu le fais remarquer, jugé bon d'incorporer une déclaration des droits de l'homme dans notre constitution. Mais maintenant le climat semble changer. Au dernier congrès des premiers ministres provinciaux, la moitié de ceux-ci favorisaient son inclusion. N'est-il pas temps d'agir maintenant, et de lutter pour la reconnaissance explicite des droits individuels et ceux des groupes minoritaires, plutôt que d'abandonner et dire que le Canada peut aussi bien mourir?

FRENCH Je pense, Storrs, que nous abordons maintenant le vif de l'affaire. Il est évident que tu attaches une grande valeur à la prolongation de l'existence d'un Canada qui inclut le Québec. Je comprends, parce que cela a été — en effet, reste — une de mes propres valeurs. Une partie de moi regretterait profondément la création d'encore un autre état au monde. En tant que Canadien anglophone habitant, supposons, London-Ontario, le Québec est cette caractéristique du Canada que j'admire le plus. Enlever le Québec et vous enlevez le caractère unique du Canada, l'âme du Canada. A ce moment-là l'Ontario peut aussi bien s'annexer aux Etats-Unis.

Mais en tant que Québécois, je n'ai réellement aucun intérêt au maintien du Canada. Je ne sais où se situe London-Ontario et d'ailleurs, ça n'a aucune importance pour moi. Mon chez-moi est le Québec, pas le Canada. Visiter Toronto ou Edmonton est comme visiter un pays étranger. En fait, on m'accueille avec plus de courtoisie et de respect quand je visite New York, ou Miami.

Considérez Canada-Québec comme un mariage qui est en train de se désintégrer. Un partenaire dit que, dans l'ensemble, il a été content de son mariage. Il aime sa femme, quoi qu'il lui ait été infidèle parfois. Sans elle, il serait sérieusement appauvri. Ils sont déjà séparés, mais pas légalement. Quelques-uns des enfants vivent avec le père, quelques-uns avec la mère. Les enfants doivent être protégés par la continuation de l'institution. Un divorce aurait pour conséquence une épreuve économique pour les deux parties. Soyons pratiques, faisons une liste de nos différences, cherchons des compromis, voyons peut-être un conseiller matrimonial.

Je réponds que, d'une façon ou d'une autre, tu passes à côté de la question. D'abord, le mariage m'a été imposé. On s'est servi de moi. J'ai donné plus que je n'en ai reçu. A cause de ma langue (mon genre), tu m'as assigné des rôles qui faisaient ton affaire. Généralement parlant, j'ai fait le travail ingrat, le travail ennuyeux, les tâches ménagères. Tu as dit que ceci était l'ordre naturel des choses.

Tu m'as privée de ma dignité, du respect de moi-même. Le temps s'écoule pour moi. Maintenant, avant qu'il ne soit trop tard, je veux être autonome.

Je veux vivre seule, prendre mes propres décisions. Je suis prête à faire les sacrifices économiques nécessaires. Les anglophones à ma charge seront traités avec au moins autant de considération que le seront les francophones qui vivent avec toi. J'espère que nous resterons amis.

Ça ne sert à rien de voir un conseiller parce que je ne suis pas motivée pour essayer de sauver notre mariage. C'est typiquement toi de penser en fonction d'une liste déterminée de griefs négociables. Bien sûr, j'ai des griefs sérieux; mais en somme, mon désir pour l'autonomie est un sentiment non-quantifiable, non négociable. Laisse-moi vivre seule pendant un certain temps. Permets à mon respect personnel de s'enraciner solidement. Alors peut-être pourrons-nous former une association d'égaux fondée sur le respect mutuel.

McCALL Tu peins une image émotive, utilisant la puissante métaphore d'un couple malheureux qui va vers le divorce. Mais je ne sais pas jusqu'à quel point cette image émotive est appropriée. D'abord, je ne suis pas certain du nombre de Québécois qui partagent les sentiments que tu dépeins. Selon ma propre expérience, beaucoup ou la plupart d'entre eux ne les partagent pas. Deuxièmement, ce qui importe dans une discussion de cette sorte ne sont pas les émotions, mais les arguments. Qu'est-ce qui justifierait la séparation? Pas simplement un sentiment d'injustices passées, ou un désir pour l'indépendance. Ce qui est requis est un argument qui montrerait que ces injustices sont irrémédiables: que le Canada ne fournit pas, et selon toute probabilité, ne fournira jamais un cadre dans lequel le Québec peut vivre, grandir, et s'épanouir. Jusqu'à maintenant, je n'ai pas rencontré un tel argument.

En fait, en ce qui concerne les arguments, il me semble que la plus grande partie se trouve de l'autre côté. La langue et la culture québécoises n'ont jamais été aussi vivantes au Québec qu'elles le sont présentement, et par son exemple, les communautés francophones hors Québec sont animées par un nouveau souffle de vie. Ces changements ont eu lieu à l'intérieur de la confédération. Selon ce qui se produira au cours des prochaines années, nous aurons l'occasion de créer au Canada quelque chose de très rare au monde: une société dans laquelle plus d'une langue et plus d'une culture vivent côte à côte au profit commun de tous. L'alternative est de risquer de s'enfermer dans des états nationaux étroits, exclusifs, fermés sur eux-mêmes.

Avant qu'il ne soit trop tard, et avant que les attitudes des deux côtés ne s'endurcissent au point d'empêcher tout retour en arrière (les attitudes à l'extérieur du Québec, les "laissez-les se séparer", sont aussi destructrices que les attitudes séparatistes ici), agissons de façon à rapprocher les gens. Le Canada a besoin d'être recréé, non pas d'être détruit.

FRENCH Je veux maintenant décrire quelques-unes des options pour le Canada et le Québec. On peut discerner toute une série de modèles, allant du modèle (1), le maintien du statu quo, au modèle (5), la souveraineté du Québec en tant que état-nation.

Je ne dirai rien au sujet du premier, sauf que, par tes commentaires jusqu'à présent, tu sembles parfois favoriser le statu quo ("le Canada fournit précisément un cadre viable..."), et à d'autres moments tu sembles appuyer un autre modèle ("N'est-il pas temps d'agir maintenant et de lutter pour la reconnaissance explicite des droits individuels et ceux des groupes minoritaires...").

(2) **La Réforme constitutionnelle** Ce modèle implique (i) le transfert (le rapatriement) de l'Acte de l'Amérique du Nord Britannique, de la Grande-Bretagne au Canada; (ii) des modifications à l'Acte, y compris des changements substantiels quant à la division des pouvoirs fédéraux-provinciaux; (iii) une déclaration des droits de la personne, incorporée dans la constitution, incluant les droits

linguistiques et le droit à une éducation en français ou en anglais. Dans le modèle (2), le Canada demeure un seul état avec deux (ou trois) nations fondatrices. Il y a une constitution. La nouvelle constitution amendée peut déléguer certains pouvoirs au Québec, sujets aux contraires d'une charte des droits. Il y a quelques indications que tu appuyerais le modèle (2), mais il est possible logiquement que tu accepterais le modèle (3).

(3) **Le Statut spécial pour le Québec** Comme le modèle (2), ce modèle requiert le rapatriement de la constitution et une réforme constitutionnelle. La constitution amendée reconnaîtrait explicitement que le Québec n'est pas comme les autres provinces. Le Québec se verrait accorder des pouvoirs dont les autres provinces ne jouissent pas, des pouvoirs qui se rapportent à la préservation et à la promotion de la langue et de la culture québécoise. La déclaration des droits de la personne envisagée dans le modèle (2) peut être anathématique dans le modèle (3). Toutefois, nous avons un seul état avec une constitution asymétrique.

(4) **La Souveraineté-association** Maintenant nous sommes de l'autre côté de la barrière. Nous n'avons pas une constitution, mais deux. La constitution du Québec lui accorde une souveraineté illimitée sur A, B, et C (par exemple, l'immigration, les communications), tandis que X, Y, et Z sont partagés avec le Canada (par exemple, la défense, le système monétaire canadien). J'essayerai d'expliquer et de défendre le modèle (4) dans ma prochaine intervention.

(5) **La Souveraineté** Ici nous avons deux états, le Canada et le Québec, chacun ayant une souveraineté illimitée. Le Québec est le 146° membre des Nations Unies. Nous avons notre propre armée, notre propre système monétaire, notre propre compagnie aérienne financée par l'état et motivée par le prestige, et autre attirail étatique de cet acabit. Nous ne favorisons, ni un ni l'autre, le modèle (5) quoi que nos raisons puissent être différentes. J'opterais davantage pour le modèle (5) que pour le modèle (1), tandis que toi Storrs, presque certainement, tu ne le ferais pas.

Je t'invite à expliciter la position que tu défends.

McCALL Je suis content que l'on commence à discuter de façon plus concrète les modèles possibles pour le Canada et le Québec. Oui, tu as raison, je préférerais un des modèles du (1) au (3), et je n'appuie pas les modèles (4) ou (5). Je ne suis pas un expert en ce qui concerne la constitution et je ne sais pas vraiment quel serait le meilleur type de fédéralisme renouvelé, sauf que j'appuie fortement l'incorporation des droits de la personne et des droits linguistiques dans la constitution. Cependant, j'ai de sérieuses appréhensions que j'essayerai de préciser au sujet de ton modèle (4), souveraineté-association.

Tu dis que, dans le modèle (4), nous n'avons pas une mais deux constitutions, une pour le Québec et une pour le Canada. Je suppose que tu veux dire que le Québec serait souverain dans un sens, sous le modèle (4), mais non-souverain sous le modèle (3). Comment déterminer dans quel sens? Ceci est une question très importante mais à laquelle il est difficile de répondre. Le mot souverain étant un mot ambigu, ayant au moins deux significations distinctes.

Dans le premier sens, la souveraineté est une et indivisible: une population ou une nation est souveraine ou non. Si oui, ça constitue un état-nation. Si non, ça constitue beaucoup moins qu'un état-nation, comme par exemple une province, un territoire, une région ou secteur, ou alors dans le cas de la République Soviétique, une république autonome. Ces unités ne peuvent, de fait prétendre s'appeler souveraines car elles tombent sous la juridiction d'une autorité plus haute.

Dans le deuxième sens, la souveraineté peut, plus ou moins, être partagée. Au Canada, il est dit que la souveraineté est partagée entre le gouvernement fédéral et les provinces, le gouvernement fédéral étant "souverain" en matière de défense nationale, et les provinces en matière d'éducation. Dans le même esprit, les membres du Marché commun en Europe ont cédé un peu de leur souveraineté au Parlement Européen. Cependant, il est à noter que la Grande-Bretagne et la France, même si elles ont cédé une partie de leur souveraineté dans le deuxième sens, retiennent leur souveraineté dans le premier sens et peuvent se retirer du Traité de Rome. La Souveraineté dans le premier sens est indivisible et ne peut être partagée, malgré qu'elle puisse être entièrement cédée et se placer sous la juridiction d'un autre état.

Tu dis que, dans le modèle (4), nous n'avons pas une constitution mais deux, une pour le Québec et une pour le Canada. Est-ce-que cela veut dire que le Québec devient souverain dans le premier sens? Je présume que oui. Dans ce cas le Québec n'élirait probablement plus de représentants au Parlement d'Ottawa et la souveraineté dans le deuxième sens qu'elle partagerait avec le reste du Canada en matière de défense, du système monétaire, etc., serait exercée à travers les comités ministériels exécutifs communs. Est-ce possible? Est-ce qu'un état souverain peut confier des questions telles que la défense et la politique monétaire à un comité qui n'est pas contrôlé par sa propre assemblée élue? J'en doute.

Si le Québec devient souverain, il devra vraiment être souverain, et son assemblée élue devra avoir le contrôle de la monnaie et de l'armée. Un état souverain peut, bien sûr, entrer en association tarifaire et monétaire avec un ou plusieurs états, comme on peut le constater par l'exemple du Marché commun européen. Mais ceci nécessite, premièrement une période de souveraineté dans le premier sens, sans partager la souveraineté dans le deuxième sens. Il faut ensuite entreprendre des négociations et décider collectivement d'entrer dans une période où il y a souveraineté dans le premier sens et un partage de la souveraineté dans le deuxième sens. Il est à noter cependant qu'en Europe, il y a un Parlement européen et qu'à date il y a eu peu ou pas, de souveraineté partagée en matière de défense.

Ce qui est encore plus important est l'idée que la langue et la culture françaises peuvent être protégées adéquatement uniquement à l'intérieur d'un état souverain. Ceci me semble faux. De plus, comme j'ai dit auparavant, la transformation du Québec en un état souverain voudrait dire l'abandon des minorités de langue française à l'extérieur du Québec. Il est peu probable que leur langue et leur culture reçoivent l'appui dont elles jouissent présentement dans le système fédéral actuel.

FRENCH Dans ce dernier propos, tu as fait quelque chose qui me laisse perplexe. En fait, deux choses. Premièrement tu as refusé d'éclaircir les propositions que tu préconises, sous prétexte que tu n'es pas un expert en ce qui concerne la constitution. J'y reviendrai.

La deuxième chose est que tu n'as pas hésité à critiquer le modèle (4), celui de la souveraineté-association, quoi qu'il n'ait pas été pleinement développé. Tant mieux. Tes critiques devraient être utiles dans ce processus.

Une constitution est un système de principes fondamentaux selon lesquels sont gouvernés une nation ou un état ou un groupe. Dans le modèle (4), la nation québécoise a une constitution dans laquelle elle a la souveraineté absolue dans le premier sens sur des institutions tels que A, B, et C — en général, les institutions qui permettent la préservation et la promotion de la langue et de la culture. D'une certaine façon, le Québec demeure une partie du Canada. Les institutions qui ne se rapportent pas directement à la préservation et à la promotion de la langue et de la culture tombent dans la sphère de la souveraineté dans le premier sens du Canada-Québec et de sa constitution.

Dans le modèle (3), celui du statut spécial, le Québec n'a pas la souveraineté dans le premier sens. Dans le modèle (4), le Québec a la souveraineté dans le premier sens sur A, B, et C.

Dans le modèle (3), le Québec n'est pas un état-nation. Dans le modèle (5), il l'est. Dans le modèle (4), le Québec est un cas-limite: une nation avec une souveraineté absolue sur A, B, et C, à l'intérieur d'un état qui a la souveraineté absolue sur X, Y, et Z.

En réponse à une de tes questions, il y aurait un parlement Canada-Québec (possiblement analogue au Parlement européen) dans lequel des représentants élus par le Québec et les représentants élus par le Canada, exerceraient le pouvoir législatif sur X, Y, et Z. Le Canada et le Québec auraient chacun leur propre assemblée nationale pour s'occuper de A, B, et C.

Quelles raisons peuvent être données pour préférer la souveraine-téassociation au statut spécial? Premièrement, on présume que la préservation et la promotion de la langue et de la culture seraient mieux servies, le Québec étant souverain dans le premier sens sur A, B, et C. Avec le statut spécial cédé dans le modèle (3), la préservation et la promotion de la culture ne sont pas assurées par la constitution, elles sont toujours sujettes à la bonne foi de la majorité anglophone.

Une autre raison pour préférer le modèle (4) au (3) est que la souveraineté-association a de meilleures chances de nourrir la dignité ou le respect de soi recherchés. Avec le modèle (3), justement à cause du statut spécial, on est encore citoyen de seconde classe.

A part le fait qu'aucun précédent n'existe, le meilleur argument contre la souveraineté-association est que les droits des minorités au Québec, et au Canada, peuvent en souffrir. Je suppose ici, qu'en négociant la nouvelle constitution du Québec, du Canada, et du Canada-Québec, chacun essayera de protéger constitutionnellement les minorités vivant à l'extérieur par rapport à cette nation.

Revenant maintenant aux points que tu as relevés dans l'avant-dernier paragraphe concernant le modèle du Marché commun européen, il me semble qu'ils s'appliquent davantage au modèle (5) qu'au (4). Ce que tu dis peut aussi s'appliquer à la version de la souveraineté-association envisagée par certains membres du Parti Québécois. On ne peut pas en être certain, car le Parti Québécois a toujours refusé de préciser ce qu'il voulait dire.

Je cite *Le Bulletin de Liaison* du Parti Québécois (janvier 1979, p.4). "La souveraineté-association n'est pas encore définie, mais le terrain est déjà 'balisé', comme les ponts de glace sur les rivières durant l'hiver." Une telle réticence — on serait presque tenté de dire un tel stratagème politique — n'est cependant pas le domaine exclusif du Parti Québécois. Le député fédéral libéral de Westmount a dit dans *The Westmount Examiner* (11 janvier 79, p. 5): "What should the position of the federal government be if, say, 60 percent of Quebecers vote 'yes' to a referendum question asking whether Quebec should negotiate sovereignty-association with the rest of Canada?. . . My view is that no disclosure of federal strategy should be discussed in advance of knowing what the question will be and what the actual results are riding by riding and region by region."

En tant que philosophes, nous pouvons nous élancer là où les politiciens craignent de s'aventurer. Tu dis qu'il t'importe beaucoup que les droits de la personne et les droits linguistiques soient incorporés à la constitution. Peux-tu donner des exemples précis? Est-ce que le droit à l'éducation en anglais ou en français devrait être incorporé à la constitution? Si tu réponds à l'affirmative, comme tu le fais apparemment, alors réponds-tu à la proposition qu'une telle démarche, en fait, minerait la langue et la culture québécoises?

McCALL J'aime beaucoup tes paroles à l'effet que les philosophes s'élancent là où les politiciens craignent de s'aventurer. Nous sommes certainement plus libres que la plupart dans cette discussion et nous pouvons explorer le domaine des idées avec équanimité. Mais il y cependant quelques contraintes. Ton concept de la souveraineté-association me frappe comme étant intérieurement contradictoire. Ceci est quelque chose auquel on doit mettre de l'ordre.

Sous la souveraineté-association, est-ce que le Québec serait souverain dans le premier sens? Ta réponse est un genre de oui et de non. Il serait souverain, dans le premier sens, sur les institutions qui permettent la préservation et la promotion de la langue et de la culture. Sur les autres institutions, ce ne serait pas le Québec (ni le Canada) qui serait souverain dans le premier sens, mais une nouvelle entité appelée Canada-Québec. "Le Canada", c'est-à-dire, les neuf autres provinces, seraient vraisemblablement souveraines sur la langue et la culture dans leur territoire.

Ce modèle ne fonctionne pas, parce qu'il n'est pas cohérent. On est souverain dans le premier sens ou on ne l'est pas. On ne peut pas partager la souveraineté dans le premier sens. Ce qui peut être partagé, et ce qui est partagé dans le Canada fédéral et dans le Marché commune européen, est la souveraineté dans le deuxième sens. Alors cela n'a pas de sens de dire que le Québec peut être souverain dans le premier sens sur les institutions reliées à la culture et pas en d'autres matières.

On doit choisir entre deux alternatives. Ou le Québec sera souverain dans le premier sens, ce qui veut dire qu'il sera souverain ipso facto en toutes matières de langue et de culture, ou il ne sera pas souverain dans le premier sens. Si on choisit cette dernière alternative, le Québec fera partie d'un plus grand état, comme il le fait présentement, qui exerce sur lui la souveraineté dans le premier sens. Cependant il serait toujours possible pour le Québec, à l'intérieur de ce plus grand état, d'être souverain dans le deuxième sens. On ne peut jouer sur deux claviers. C'est pourquoi je persiste à demander si, sous la souveraineté-association, le Québec serait souverain dans le premier sens.

Tu peux croire que ces questions sur la souveraineté sont pédantes et plutôt d'ordre légal. En fait, elles touchent au vif de la question de la souveraineté-association. Supposons, par exemple, un Québec souverain dans le premier sens et qui entre dans une union tarifaire et monétaire avec le reste du Canada. Dix ans plus tard, il n'es plus satisfait de ces arrangements économiques, et il décide d'émettre sa propre monnaie. Etant souverain, il pourrait le faire. Il pourrait se retirer de l'union monétaire. La décision serait la sienne seulement. Cependant s'il n'était pas souverain dans le premier sens, la décision ne serait pas seulement la sienne. S'il voulait émettre sa propre monnaie ou lever une armée, il serait obligé d'en demander la permission à l'état souverain dont il fait partie, et il est peu probable qu'une telle permission soit accordée. La seule façon d'éviter la nécessité d'obtenir l'accord des autres est d'être souverain dans le premier sens.

Permets-moi maintenant d'aborder la question de l'incorporation des droits de la personne et des droits linguistiques à la constitution. Ceci est, comme tu le dis, un projet qui me tient à coeur. Je crois que les droits linguistiques suivants devraient être incorporés, entre autres:

(1) Le droit de tout Canadien de communiquer avec le gouvernement fédéral et le gouvernement provincial ainsi que d'obtenir des services en français ou en anglais.

(2) Le droit de tout Canadien dont la langue maternelle est le français ou l'anglais de faire éduquer ou instruire leurs enfants dans leur langue maternelle, là où le nombre le justifie.

(3) Le droit de tout Canadien de recevoir les services médicaux et de pouvoir comparaître devant la cour en français ou en anglais, là où le nombre le justifie.

Pourquoi ces droits sont-ils importants? Ils sont importants parce que, sans eux, nous n'avons aucune idée claire de ce qu'est la citoyenneté. Après tout, qu'est-ce qui me distingue d'un Américain, ou, quant à cela d'un citoyen de la France? Une chose très évidente c'est que j'appartiens à un pays qui est, dans un sens important, officiellement bilingue. Peu importe où je choisis de vivre à l'intérieur du Canada; peu importe si je suis francophone ou anglophone, je peux être assuré que je pourrais recevoir au moins certains services gouvernementaux dans l'une ou l'autre langue et que mes enfants pourront recevoir leur éducation dans leur langue maternelle. Ces éléments de base de la citoyenneté canadienne doivent être spécifiés dans la constitution et, le degré de générosité dont les provinces feront preuve en précisant la clause "là où le nombre le justifie", sera la mesure de la bonne volonté de tous les Canadiens.

D'après ce que je peux comprendre tu as deux appréhensions pour ce qui est de permettre au Canada, plutôt qu'au Québec, d'être le véhicule de la promotion et de la langue et de la culture. Premièrement, tu dis qu'une telle promotion dépendrait toujours de la bonne foi de la majorité anglophone. Bien sûr, tu as raison. Aucune constitution représentant un accord entre des parties contractantes n'est réalisable sans la bonne foi de tous. Mais si les garanties linguistiques et culturelles sont incorporés à la constitution, alors la préservation et la promotion de la langue et de la culture françaises reposeraient sur quelque chose de plus solide que la simple bonne foi. Deuxièmement, tu te demandes si un droit garanti à l'éducation en français ou en anglais ne pourrait pas, en réalité, miner la langue et la culture québécoises. Est-ce que tu pourrais commenter ce point en plus grand détail? Est-ce que la restriction à la langue maternelle, le français ou l'anglais, apaiserait tes craintes?

FRENCH Pour ceux de nos lecteurs qui ont eu la patience de se rendre jusqu'ici, je dois expliquer, Storrs, que nous nous sommes engagés dans ce dialogue pour plusieurs raisons: tous les deux nous nous préoccupons beaucoup de l'avenir du Québec, et du Canada et nous voulons aussi apporter quelques éléments au colloque du A.C.P. au sujet de l'avenir de la fédération canadienne; de plus pour le simple plaisir qu'on tire d'une telle activité philosophique.

J'espère que notre intérêt, et notre plaisir, nous amèneront à continuer ce dialogue au cours de semaines et des mois critiques à venir. Toutefois, ceci sera ma dernière contribution avant le colloque du A.C.P. Donc j'aimerais faire quelques commentaires d'ordre général avant de reprendre plus spécifiquement ce dont tu parlais plus haut.

Nous semblons partager les buts suivants. Nous soutenons activement le désir de préserver et de promouvoir la langue et la culture québécoises. Nous ne soutenons pas, ni un ni l'autre, la souveraineté du Québec dans le sens de la création d'encore un autre état mondial, le modèle (5), bien que je préfère une souveraineté totale au statu quo. Nous nous préoccupons des droits des groupes minoritaires. Nous favorisons le rapatriement et la réforme de la constitution. Nous éprouvons un certain sens de fierté et d'identité en tant que citoyens d'un état bilingue composé de deux- (ou trois-) nations. J'aime particulièrement le passage où tu parles de ce qui nous distingue d'un Américain, ou d'un citoyen de la France.

A cette phase du dialogue, nous n'avons pas réussi à nous mettre d'accord concernant les moyens à prendre pour arriver à ces fins. Utilisant les modèles trop simplifiés que j'ai exposés afin que notre discussion puisse devenir plus concrète, j'ai essayé de défendre un type de souveraineté-association pour le Québec. (Je reviendrai à tes critiques en temps et lieu.) Un autre modèle que je suis prêt à approfondir, en tant que deuxième choix, est le statut spécial pour le Québec. Tu t'opposes certainement à la souveraineté-association. Tu t'opposes probablement au statut spécial. Et bien que tu hésites à t'engager, il semble, d'après ton intervention précédente, que tu ne consentes pas à négocier plus loin que la réforme constitutionnelle.

Passons maintenant brièvement à ce que je considère comme étant le début de ton exposé et de ta défense d'un modèle de la réforme consitutionnnelle, j'aimerais faire les observations suivantes:

(a) Quelle est la raison fondamentale de ces droits? Est-ce que tu les considères comme étant évidents en soi?

(b) Pourquoi ces droits particuliers, au lieu d'autres, apparemment semblables? Prenons le deuxième, par exemple, nous avons les possibilités suivantes:

2.1 Le droit de tout Canadien ou de toute Canadienne à une éducation en français ou en anglais.

2.2 Le droit de tout Canadien ou de toute Canadienne, dont la langue maternelle est le français ou l'anglais, de faire instruire leurs enfants dans leur langue maternelle...

Pourquoi as-tu opté pour le 2.2 plutôt que le 2.1? Tu ne le dis pas.

(c) Chaque droit que tu proposes est destiné à protéger certains groupes minoritaires, les francophones au Canada, les anglophones au Québec. La protection de tels droits francophones au Canada peut coûter de l'argent, et peut occasionner certains inconvénients et certains ressentiments, mais la culture anglophone dominante en Amérique du Nord n'en serait pas menacée.

D'autre part, on peut argumenter que la protection de ces droits pour la minorité anglophone au Québec peut constituer une menace pour la survivance de la langue et de la culture québécoises. Par exemple, si ton (1), (2) et (3) étaient incorporés dans la constitution, le Québec redeviendrait, encore une fois, pour les Canadiens anglophones un lieu intéressant où vivre et où travailler dans leur langue maternelle. Ils émigreraient au Québec pour des raisons économiques, entre autres. La majorité québécoise, qui est une minorité nord-américaine, luttant pour sa survie, continuerait et accélérerait son glissement jusqu'à l'impuissance, jusqu'à l'existence purement symbolique. Je ne pense pas que je me livre tout simplement à un discours vide de sens. Dans un sens important, la protection des droits des minorités, quoi que sans doute désirable pour les francophones au Canada, aurait tendance à miner la tentative de faire du Québec un territoire national francophone sûr. N'admets-tu pas que ceci pose un problème spécial?

Passant finalement à ta critique de mon modèle de la souveraineté-association, il me semble que nous sommes devant une énigme philosophique typique. Dans ce domaine, nous avons défini 'la souveraineté', 'la souveraineté-dans-le-premier-sens', et 'la souveraineté-dans-le-deuxième-sens', Ceci a été fait *à priori*, pour ainsi dire. Maintenant tu dis que mon concept de la souveraineté-association est "intérieurement contradictoire", et que mon modèle "n'est pas cohérent...". Ton argument est basé sur nos définitions de 'la souveraineté'.

Permets-moi d'essayer de défendre ma position. Il y a quatre questions qui m'intéressent en ce qui concerne la souveraineté-association: (1) *En fait*, serait-il possible d'établir le type d'état composé de deux nations qui est esquissé au-dessus? Je pense que ce serait possible, et tu n'as pas argumenté à l'effet du contraire. (2) Même s'il s'avère possible d'établir ce type d'état, est-ce qu'un tel état composé de deux nations fonctionnerait? Encore une fois, je pense que oui, mais il faut développer davantage les modèles. (3) Est-ce que les avantages/désavantages de la souveraineté-association l'emportent sur les avantages/désavantages du statu quo, de la réforme constitutionnelle avec la protection des droits des minorités, du statut spécial, et de la souveraineté totale? Je crois que oui, mais j'aimerais approfondir davantage le modèle du statut spécial avant de reprendre une décision finale.

(4) Est-ce que la souveraineté-association est logiquement possible,

conceptuellement cohérente? Ta critique se limite à cette question. Or il me semble que si un modèle peut être mis en pratique et s'il pourait fonctionner, alors, s'il y a un problème logique ou conceptuel, nous devons reprendre notre définition de 'la souveraineté' pour résoudre la confusion. C'est ce que je me propose de faire.

Le mot 'souverain' signifie posséder le plus haut rang ou le plus grand pouvoir, être indépendant de l'autorité des autres gouvernements, être l'arbitre final, pour ainsi dire. Or on est souverain *sur* quelque chose, de la même façon qu'une propriété est une propriété de quelque chose. On peut être souverain sur *quelques* institutions dans une société (selon le sens employé par Rawls), ou on peut être souverain sur *toutes* les institutions. Ainsi, quand nous écrivons qu' "une population ou une nation est souveraine ou elle ne l'est pas", nous devrions écrire, pour être plus précis, qu'une population ou une nation est l'arbitre final sur toutes ces institutions, ou la population est alors l'arbitre final sur quelques-unes, ou aucune des institutions.

Il y a donc plusieurs distinctions à faire en ce qui concerne la souveraineté que nous avons omises dans la première partie. On peut être l'arbitre final sur toutes, quelques-unes, ou aucune de ces institutions. On peut avoir l'autorité cédé sur toutes, quelques-unes, ou aucune de ces institutions. Dans ce qui précède, je parle de l'autorité légale; mais il y a aussi la souveraineté *de facto* . Une population peut être l'arbitre constitutionnel final en ce qui concerne l'institution A, ou elle peut avoir une autorité *de facto* sur A, ou elle peut n'avoir aucune autorité sur A.

L'élément de base de la critique semble être une supposition, fondée sur la définition qu'on est l'arbitre constitutionnel final (l'état souverain traditionel), ou alors on ne possède que des pouvoirs cédés. C'est pour cette raison que tu écris que je dois "choisir entre deux alternatives". Or il y a plus de deux options, comme je crois l'avoir démontré.

La souveraineté-association ne peut pas être définie hors d'existence.

McCALL Tu as raison. La souveraineté-association ne peut être définie comme n'existant pas. Le problème ici est que tu n'a pas réussi à la définir comme existant. Ceci n'est pas surprenant, vu qu'il y a plus d'une douzaine de concepts de la souveraineté-association à travers le Québec. Néanmoins, nous ne ferons pas de progrès en discutant les mérites de la souveraineté-association avant d'avoir trouvé une formule générale pour la souveraineté-association.

Comme tu le dis, un peuple peut être légalement et constitutionnellement souverain sur quelques-unes de ces institutions, ou il peut être souverain sur toutes. Seulement dans le dernier cas est-il souverain dans le premier sens. Il est à noter que parmi les institutions qui tombent sous l'autorité de la souveraineté dans le premier sens est la constitution elle-même. Un peuple souverain dans ce sens peut modifier sa propre constitution, il peut changer les conditions de sa propre association avec d'autres peuples. Un peuple qui est souverain dans le deuxième sens, ne le peut pas. Etre constitutionnellement l'arbitre final de quelques-unes de ses propres institutions, mais pas toutes, veut dire qu'on est souverain dans le deuxième sens, dans le cadre d'un état plus grand qui est souverain dans le premier sens. Comme je l'ai déjà dit, la souveraineté dans le premier sens, c'est tout ou rien. Tu l'as ou tu ne l'as pas. Tu ne peux pas être souverain dans le premier sens sur quelques-unes des institutions mais pas souverain sur les autres.

Je conclus, par ce que tu viens de dire, qu'il est évident que sous la souveraineté-association, le Québec ne sera pas souverain dans le premier sens. Peut-être que je t'interprète mal sur ce point, mais je crois que ce que je dis est juste. Sous ton option (4) de la souveraineté-association ci-haut, "la constitution du Québec lui octroie une souveraineté illimitée sur A, B et C (tels que l'immigration, les communications), tandis que X, Y et Z sont partagés avec le Canada (tels que la défense, le système monétaire)". Ce que tu ne précises pas, c'est si sous le modèle (4) le Québec pourrait unilatéralement modifier les conditions de ses rapports avec le Canada. En toute probabilité, il ne le pourrait pas, puisque tu dis plus loin que le Québec "continuera, dans un sens, de faire partie du Canada". Ainsi soit-il. Si le Québec doit chercher l'approbation du parlement Canada-Québec pour des changements constitutionnels ou autres, qu'il désire y apporter, il n'est pas souverain dans le premier sens.

Pour donner suite à ça, il y en a deux points à discuter. Le premier est ton modèle de souveraineté-association, Stanley, qui diffère radicalement de celui du Parti Québécois. Selon leur modèle, le Parti Québécois n'élira pas de représentants au parlement Canada-Québec. Il ne sera pas sujet à une législation décrétée par celui-ci. Il peut, unilatéralement, modifier ses rapports avec le Canada, et il peut modifier sa propre constitution. La position du Parti Québécois par conséquent est *souverainiste* dans le plein sens du mot. Le tien ne l'est pas. Deuxièmement, si sous la souveraineté-association telle que tu la conçois, le Québec n'est pas souverain dans le premier sens, ton modèle (4) ne diffère pas, fondamentalement, de ce qu'on a maintenant. Sous le (4), tel que je le comprends, le Canada sera toujours ou encore une fédération. Ce sera peut-être une fédération rénovée; une fédération avec une nouvelle constitution; une fédération dans laquelle le Québec aura plus de pouvoirs qu'il n'en a maintenant; peut-être aussi une fédératin à deux-membres au lieu d'une fédération à dix-membres; mais, néanmoins ce sera une fédération. Ton option (4) par conséquent, tombe sous les options du fédéralisme, quoique à l'extrême bout de la rangée.

En résumé, tu as essayé de te tailler un mi-chemin, sous le nom de la souveraineté-association, entre une nation souveraine et les diverses options du fédéralisme. Mais il n'y a pas de mi-chemin. Si le Québec ne peut être un état souverain, la plus grande autonomie qu'il puisse espérer, c'est d'être un partenaire à l'intérieur d'une fédération. Croire le contraire, c'est une illusion.

En réponse à tes questions, laisse-moi dire quelques mots aussi sur l'inclusion des droits linguistiques dans la constitution. Tu me demandes pourquoi j'ai choisi les droits (1), (2), (3) que j'ai énumérés, et quelles ont été mes raisons. Bien, je n'ai pas essayé d'épuiser les possibilités; j'ai essayé plutôt de présenter certains droits, d'après moi essentiels, à la préservation d'un Canada bilingue. Par cela, je ne veux pas dire un pays dans lequel tout le monde parle les deux langues, mais un pays dans lequel tous les citoyens, au moins, reçoivent certains services gouvrnementaux soit en anglais soit en français et obtiennent une éducation dans leur langue maternelle pour leurs enfants. Si ces droits n'existent pas, que signifie le fait d'être citoyen d'un pays bilingue? Tu demandes si en accordant ces droits à la minorité anglophone au Québec, la langue et la culture québécoises ne seraient menacées. Tu évoques la possibilité que des anglophones venant d'autres provinces, encouragés par l'inclusion d'un droit linguistique pour leurs enfants, se rendent au Québec en nombre suffisant pour déborder la "majorité assiégée du Québec". Est-ce que tu plaisantes, ou es-tu sérieux? Pour nous ici au Québec, la question qui se pose n'est pas de savoir si la communauté anglophone va submerger les francophones, mais plutôt de savoir si dans dix ans, il y aura encore une communauté anglophone appréciable?

Enfin, pour conclure sur un ton plus positif, je suis enchanté de noter la liste de points sur lesquels nous sommes d'accord. La liste est substantielle: promouvoir la langue et la culture québécoises, éviter la création d'un nouvel état-nation, être conscient des droits minoritaires, hâter le rapatriement et la réforme de la constitution, encourager un sentiment de fierté et d'identité en tant que citoyen d'un état bilingue composé de deux- (ou trois-) nations. D'après moi, la liste aboutit à une conclusion: le besoin urgent d'une structure constitutionnelle rénovée dans l'ensemble du Canada qui pourrait englober et assurer chacun des points de cet accord. Comme je l'ai déjà dit auparavant, ce n'est pas le moment de détruire le Canada c'est le moment de le créer tel qu'il doit être. Il ne devrait pas être hors de notre portée de trouver une formule constitutionnelle pour le faire, une formule qui donnerait une réponse toute canadienne à la question qui se pose, notamment, est-ce que des gens parlant différentes langues et venant de différentes traditions peuvent vivre ensemble. Nous devons bâtir ensemble une société et un mode de vie fondée sur les deux cultures et y puisant sa force.

BIBLIOGRAPHY *BIBLIOGRAPHIE*

par/by
Myrna FRIEND
University of Toronto
1979

INTRODUCTION

The following bibliography was intended for the use of workshop participants at the *Conference on Philosophical Issues Related to the Future of Confederation.* It might best be regarded as a preliminary checklist; it makes no claim to be perfect or exhaustive.

The focus of the bibliography is material relevant to the Canadian situation.

We thought, however, that it would be useful to include section 1, Selected General Works, and Section 2, Studies of Other Countries. The former section draws attention to some recent works which provide general background, contain references to the Canadian situation, or discuss relevant theories, such as consociationalism which may not be widely known. The latter section may be useful because arguments about the Canadian situation often draw on parallels with other countries.

Section 3A, Government Documents, is provided for the use of those who wish to be certain of the legal facts or who wish to draw on data gathered by various government commissions.

Sections 3B and 3C are devoted to specifically Canadian material. The problem being dealt with by participants in the Conference has historical, legal, political, economic and sociological aspects as well as philosophical ones. These elements tend to blend together and to interact. Our collection reflects this fact. Moreoever, we have not attempted to designate certain works as specifically philosophical. First, because of the interaction mentioned above; and, second, because the drawing of boundaries, such as that between political philosophy and political theory, is itself a matter of dispute. We leave it to the users to draw such distinctions and boundaries as they see fit.

We also wish to acknowledge the helpful suggestions and advice of J. Plamondon, N. Kaufmann, F. Cunningham, D. Braybrooke, and S.G. French. Primary credit for producing the bibliography must go, however, to Myrna Friend of the Erindale College Library, University of Toronto.

J.T. STEVENSON

BIBLIOGRAPHY / *BIBLIOGRAPHIE*

Myrna FRIEND

1. Oeuvres Générales / General Works

Akzin, Benjamin. *State and Nation.* London: Hutchinson University Library, 1964.

Claude, Inis L. *National Minorities; an International Problem.* Cambridge, Mass.: Harvard University Press, 1955.

Cobban, Alfred. *The Nation State and National Self-Determination.* London: Collins, 1969. Rev. ed., 1970

Connor, Walker. "Nation-Building or Nation-Destroying?" *World Politics,* v. 24, no. 3 (April 1972) 319-355.

Dahl, Robert A., ed. *Political Oppositions in Western Demoncracies.* New Haven: Yale University Press, 1966.

Gross, Feliks. *World Politics and Tension Areas.* New York: New York University Press, 1966.

Jouvenal, Bertrand de. *Sovereignty; an Inquiry into the Political Good.* Tr. by J.F. Huntington. Chicago: University of Chicago Press, 1957.

Kedourie, Elie. *Nationalism.* Rev. ed. London: Hutchinson, 1966.

Laski, Harold Joseph. *Studies in the Problem of Sovereignty.* New York: Howard Fertig, 1968.

Lehmbruch, Gerhard. "Segmented Pluralism and Political Strategies in Continental Europe: Internal and External Conditions of 'Concordant Demoncracy'," International Political Science Association, *Round Table Meetings,* no. 6 (August 1969) 1-10.

Lijphart, Arend. "Consociational Democracy," *World Politics,* v. 21, no. 2 (January 1969) 207-225.

Lijphart, Arend. "Cultural Diversity and Theories of Political Integration," *Canadian Journal of Political Science,* v. 4 (1971) 1-14.

Macartney, Carlile Aylmer. *National States and National Minorities.* New York: Russell & Russell, 1934. 2d. ed. 1968.

Merriam, Charles Edward. *History of the Theory of Sovereignty Since Rousseau.* New York: Columbia University Press, 1900. Reprinted in 1972.

Minogue, Kenneth R. *Nationalism.* New York, Basic Books, 1967. (Ideas in action) Reprinted: Baltimore: Penguin Books, 1970.

Nordlinger, Eric A. *Conflict Regulation in Divided Societies.* Cambridge, Mass., Harvard University Center for International Affairs, Occasional Paper no. 29 (January 1972).

Pi-Sunyer, Oriol, ed. *The Limits of Integration: Ethnicity and Nationalism in Modern Europe.* Amherst: University of Massachusetts Department of Anthropology, 1971.

Shafer, Boyd Carlisle. *Nationalism: Myth and Reality.* New York: Harcourt, Brace & World, 1955. (Includes bibliography).

Smith, Anthony Douglas. *Theories of Nationalism.* London: Duckworth, 1971. (Includes bibliography).

Snyder, Louis Leo. *The Meaning of Nationalism. Foreword by Hans Kohn. New York: Greenwood Press, 1968. (Includes bibliography).*

Synder, Louis Leo. *The New Nationalism.* Ithaca, N.Y.: Cornell University Press, 1968.

Social Compass, v. 9, nos. 1-2 (1962) 1-164. Special issue on "Vertical pluralism."

Steiner, Jürg. "Conflict Resolution and Democratic Stability in Subculturally Segmented Political Systems," *Res Publica,* v. 11 (1969) 775-798.

2. Études Etrangères / Studies of Other Countries

Clough, Shepard. *A History of the Flemish Movement in Belgium: a Study in Nationalism.* New York: Richard R. Smith Inc., 1930.

Coupland, Reginald. *Welsh and Scottish Nationalism: A Study.* London: Collins, 1954.

Da Silva, Milton M. "Modernization and Ethnic Conflict: the Case of the Basques," *Comparative Politics,* v. 7, no. 2 (January 1975) 227-251.

Dunn, J.A. "Consociational Democracy and Language Conflict: A Comparison of the Belgian and Swiss Experience," *Comparative Political Studies,* v. 5 (1972) 3-39.

Hall, Raymond L., ed. *Ethnic Separatism: Comparative Dynamics — The Americas, Europe and the Developing World.* New York: Pergamon, 1978.

Lijphart, Arend. "Cleavages in Consociational Democracies: a Four-Country Comparison" (Paper presented at the Symposium on Comparative Analysis of Highly Industrialized Societies, Bellagio, 1971).

Lijphart, Arend. *The Politics of Accommodation: Pluralism and Democracy in the Netherlands.* Berkeley: University of California Press, 1968.

McRae, Kenneth Douglas. *Switzerland: Example of Cultural Coexistence.* Toronto: Canadian Institute of International Affairs, 1964. (Contemporary Affairs, no. 33).

Payne, Stanley G. *Basque Nationalism.* Reno: University of Nevada Press, 1975.

Rose, Richard. *The United Kingdom as a Multi-National State.* Glasgow: University of Strathclyde Survey Research Center, 1970.

Steiner, Jürg. *Amicable Agreement Versus Majority Rule: Conflict Resolution in Switzerland.* Rev. & enl. ed. Chapel Hill: University of North Carolina Press, 1974.

3. Canada

A. Documents Officiels / Government Documents

Actes de l'Amérique du Nord britannique et modifications y apportées. Ottawa: Imprimeur de la Reine.

Gt. Britain. Laws, statutes, etc. *British North America Acts.* (Consolidated with amendments, 1965).

Canada. Commission royale d'enquête sur le bilinguisme et le biculturalisme, *Rapport préliminaire.* Ottawa: Imprimeur de la Reine, 1966.

Canada. Royal Commission on Bilingualism and Biculturalism, *Preliminary report.* Ottawa: Queen's Printer, 1966.

Canada. Commission royale d'enquête sur le bilinguisme et le biculturalisme. *Rapport.* Ottawa: Imprimeur de la Reine, 1967-69. V. I-V. v.1: Introduction générale. Livre I: les langues officielles; v. 2. Livre 2: L'éducation; v. 3 A,B: Le monde du travail; v. 4: L'apport culturel des autres groupes ethniques; v. 5, Livre 5: La capitale fédérale.

Canada, Royal Commission on Bilingualism and Biculturalism, *Report.* Ottawa: Queen's Printer, 1967-69. V. 1-5 in 6. v. 1. General introduction; Bk. 1. The official languages; v. 2. Education; v. 3 a,b The work world; v. 4. The cultural contribution of the other ethnic groups; v. 5 Bk. 5 The federal capital; v. 6 Voluntary associations.

Canada. Parlement. Comité spécial mixte sur la constitution du Canada. *Rapport final.* Ottawa: Imprimeur de la Reine, 1972. Texte en français et en anglais.

Canada. Parliament. Special Joint Committee of the Senate and of the House of Commons on the Constitution of Canada: *final report.* Joint chairmen: Gildas L. Molgat and Mark MacGuigan. Ottawa: Information Canada, 1972. In French and English.

Canada. Dept. of Justice. *The Amendment of the Constitution of Canada.* Ottawa: Queen's Printer, 1965.

Canada. Ministère de la justice. *Modification de la Constitution du Canada.* Ottawa: Imprimeur de la Reine, 1965.

Canada. La Commission de l'unité canadienne. Jean-Luc Pepin et John P. Robarts. *Se retrouver: observations et recommandations.* Ottawa: Ministre des Approvisionnements et Services Canada, 1979.

Canada. La Commission de l'unité canadienne. Jean-Luc Pepin et John P. Robarts. *De finir pour choisir: vocabulaire du débat.* . Ottawa: Ministre des Approvisionnements et Services Canada, 1979.

Canada. La Commission de l'unité canadienne. Jean-Luc Pepin et John P. Robarts. *Un Temps pour parler: les commentaires du public.* Ottawa: Ministre des Approvisionnements et Services Canada, 1979.

Canada. Task Force on Canadian Unity. Jean-Luc Pepin and John P. Robarts, co-chairmen. *A Future Together: Observations and Recommendations.* Ottawa: Minister of Supply and Services Canada, 1979.

Canada. Task Force on Canadian Unity. Jean-Luc Pepin and John P. Robarts, co-chairmen. *Coming to Terms: The Words of the Debate.* Ottawa: Minister of Supply and Services Canada, 1979.

Canada. Task Force on Canadian Unity. Jean-Luc Pepin and John P. Robarts, co-chairmen. *A Time to Speak: The Views of the Public.* Ottawa: Minister of Supply and Services Canada, 1979.

Canada. Privy Council. Task Force on the Structure of Canadian Industry. *Foreign Ownership and the Structure of Canadian Industry* (the Watkins report) Ottawa: Queen's Printer, 1968.

Canada. Economic Council. *Living Together: A Study of Regional Disparities.* Ottawa: Supply and Services Canada, 1977.

Ontario. Legislative Assembly. Select Committee on Economic and Cultural Nationalism. *Final Report on Cultural Nationalism.* Ontario: Queen's Printer, 1975.

Québec (Province). Commission d'enquête sur la situation de la langue française et sur les droits linguistiques au Québec. *Rapport.* (Commissaires: Jean-Denis Gendron et al.) Québec: 1972. 2 v. T. I. la Langue de travail; t. II. les Droits linguistiques; t. III. les Groupes ethniques.

Quebec (Province). Commission of Inquiry on the Position of the

French Language and on Language Rights in Quebec. *Report.* (Commissioners: Jean-Denis Gendron et al.) Quebec: 1972. 2 v. Bk. 1. The language of work; bk. 2. Language rights; bk. 3. The ethnic groups.

Québec (Province). Commission royale d'enquête sur les problèmes constitutionnels. *Rapport.* Québec: 1956. 4 v. en 5. Thomas Tremblay, président. Sommaire: v. 1. Aperçu historique. Finances publiques. v. 2. La province de Québec et le cas canadien français. Le fédéralisme. v. 3. Analyse des besoins et recommandations. t. 1. La juridiction provinciale. T. 2. Les problèmes municipaux et scolaires. Les relations fiscales et financières. v. 4. Documentation. Bibliographic des ouvrages, articles et documents ayant servi au travail des commissaires (p. 381-409).

Quebec (province). Royal Commission of Inquiry on Constitutional Problems. *Report.* Quebec, 1957. 4v. in 5. Thomas Tremblay, Chairman. Contents: v.1. Historical outline. Public finances. v.2. The Province of Quebec and the French-Canadian case Federalism. v.3. Analysis of needs and recommendations. bk. 1. Provincial jurisdiction. bk. 2 Municipal and financial relations. v.4. Documentation. Bibliography of works, articles and documents consulted by the commissioners (p. 381-409).

B. Livres / Books

Abella, I.M. *Nationalism, Communism and Canadian Labour: The CIO, the Communist Party, and the Canadian Congress of Labour, 1935-1956.* Toronto: University of Toronto Press 1973.

Allemagne, André d'. *Le Colonialisme au Québec.* Montréal: Éditions Renaud-Bray, 1966.

Angers, François Albert. *L'option des États associés.* Montréal: Hurtubise HMH, 1967

Arès, R. *Dossier sur le pacte fédératif de 1867* (La Confédération: pacte ou loi?). Montréal: Bellarmin, 1967.

Arès, R. *Nos grandes options politiques et constitutionnelles.* Montréal: Bellarmin, 1972.

Axline, W., ed. *Continental Community?* Toronto: McClelland and Stewart, 1974.

Bailey, Alfred Goldsworthy. *Culture and Nationality: Essays by A.G. Bailey.* Toronto: McClelland and Stewart, 1972. (The Carleton Library, no. 58).

Barbeau, Raymond. *J'ai choisi l'indépendance.* Montréal: Éditions de l'homme, 1961.

Barbeau, Raymond *Le Québec, est-il une colonie?* Montréal: Éditions de l'homme, 1962.

Bélanger, André-J. *L'apolitisme des idéologies québécoises: le grand tournant, 1934-1936.* Québec: Les Presses de l'Université Laval, 1974.

Bercuson, David Jay, ed. *Canada and the Burden of Unity.* Toronto: Macmillan Company of Canada, 1977.

Berger, Carl Clinton, et al. *Approaches to Canadian History.* Toronto: University of Toronto Press, 1967.

Berger, Carl Clinton, comp. *Imperialism and Nationalism, 1884-1914; A Conflict in Canadian Thought.* Toronto: Copp Clark, 1969. (Includes bibliography).

Berger, Carl Clinton. *The Sense of Power: Studies in the Ideas of Canadian Imperialism, 1867-1914.* Toronto: University of Toronto Press, 1970.

Berger, Carl Clinton, and Ramsey Cook, eds. *The West and the Nation: Essays in Honour of W.L. Morton.* Toronto: McClelland and Stewart, 1976.

Bergeron, Gérard. *Le Canada français après deux siècles de patience.* Paris: Éditions du Seuil, 1967.

Bernard, André. *What Does Quebec Want?* Toronto: James Lorimer, 1978.

Bernard, Jean-Paul, ed. *Les idéologies québécoises au XIXe siècle.* Montréal: Boréal Express, 1973.

Bernard, Jean-Paul. *Les Rouges: libéralisme, nationalisme et anticlericalisme au milieu du XIXe siècle.* Montréal: les Presses de l'Université du Québec, 1971.

Black, Edwin, R. *Divided Loyalties: Canadian Concepts of Federalism.* Montreal: McGill-Queen's University Press, 1975.

Blanchard, Raoul. *Le Canada Français.* Paris: Presses universitaires de France, 1964. 2e éd., 1966.

Bourgault, Pierre. *Oui à l'indépendance du Québec.* Montréal: Quinze, 1977.

Bourque, Gilles. *L'état capitaliste et la question nationale.* Montréal: Les Presses de l'Université de Montréal, 1977.

Bourque, Gilles. *Question nationale et classes sociales au Québec (1760-1840).* Montréal: Parti Pris, 1970. (Collection aspects, 7). (Bibliographie: p.341-350).

Bourque, Gilles. *Question nationale et théorie.* Montréal: les Presses de l'Université de Montréal, 1976.

Boulet, G. *Nationalisme et séparatisme.* Trois Rivières, Qué.: 1962.

Bouthillier, Guy. *Le choc des langues au Québec 1760-1970.* Montréal:

les Presses de l'Université du Québec, 1972.

Brillant, Jacques. *L'impossible Québec. Essai d'une sociologie de la culture.* Montréal: Éditions du Jour, 1968.

Brossard, Jacques. *L'accession à la souveraineté et le cas du Québec: conditions et modalités Politicojuridiques.* Montréal: les Presses de l'Université de Montréal, 1976. (Bibliographie: p. [767] -783).

Brunet, Michel. *Canadians et Canadiens; études sur l'histoire et la pensée des deux Canadas.* Montréal: Fides, 1954 (Bibliothèque économique et sociale).

Burns, Ronald M., ed. *One Country or Two?* Montreal: McGill-Queen's University Press, 1971.

Calegoropoulos-Stratis, S. *Le droit des peuples à disposer d'eux-mêmes.* Bruxelles: Bruylant, 1973.

Cameron, David R. *Nationalism, Self-Determination and the Quebec Question.* Toronto: Macmillan of Canada, 1974. (Canadian Controversies Series).

Canadian Institute of International Affairs. *Human Rights, Federation and Minorities / Les droits de l'homme, le fedéralisme et les minorités.* Ed. by Allan Gotlieb. Toronto: Canadian Institute of International Affairs, 1970. (Contemporary Affairs, 43).

Canadian Institute of International Affairs. *Power and Independence: the Relevance of Nationalism and Sovereignty in the 1970's and Beyond; an Aid to Study Groups.* Toronto: Canadian Institute of International Affairs, 1970.

Careless, Anthony G.S. *Initiative and Response: The Adaptation of Canadian Federalism to Regional Economic Development.* Montreal: McGill-Queen's University Press, 1977. (Canadian public administration series).

Carr, D.W. *Recovering Canada's Nationhood.* Ottawa: Canada Publishing Co., 1971.

Chaput, Marcel. *Pourquoi je suis séparatiste.* Montréal: Éditions du Jour, 1961.

Chaput, Marcel. *Why I am a separatist.* Tr. by Robert A. Taylor. Toronto: Ryerson Press, 1962. Tr. of *Pourquoi je suis séparatiste.*

Chaput-Rolland, Solange. *Mon pays, Québec ou le Canada?* Préf. de Claude Ryan. Ottawa: Cercle du Livre de France, 1966.

Chaput-Rolland, Solange. *My country, Canada or Quebec.* Toronto: Macmillan of Canada, 1966. Tr. of *Mon pays, Québec ou le Canada?*

Chaput-Rolland, Solange. *Québec année zéro* Préf. de Judith Jasmin. Montréal: Cercle du livre de France, 1968.

Chaput-Rolland, Solange. *Reflections: Quebec Year One.* Tr. by Gretta Chambers. Foreword by Hugh MacLennan. Montreal: Chateau Books, 1968. Tr. of *Québec année zéro*

Chaput-Rolland, Solange. *The Second Conquest; Reflections II.* Montreal: Chateau Books, 1970.

Chaput-Rolland, Solange. *La seconde conquête.* Montréal: Cercle du Livre de France, 1970.

A Citizen's Guide to the Gray Report. Toronto: New Press, 1971.

Clement, Wallace. *The Canadian Corporate Elite: an Analysis of Economic Power.* With a foreword by John Porter. Toronto: McClelland and Stewart, 1975. (Carleton library, no. 89). (Bibliography: pp. 367-380).

Clement, Wallace. *Continental Corporate Power. Economic Elite Linkages Between Canada* and the United States. Toronto: McClelland and Stewart, 1977. (Bibliography: pp. 374-384).

Colas, Emile. *La troisième voie; une nouvelle constitution.* Montréal: les Éditions de l'homme, 1978.

Confederation of Tomorrow Conference, Toronto, 1967. *Proceedings.* Toronto: 1968.

Constitutionalism and Nationalism in Lower Canada: Esssays by Fernand Oeullet and Others. Intro. by Ramsay Cook. Toronto: University of Toronto Press, 1969.

Cook, Ramsay. *Canada and the French-Canadian Question.* Toronto: Macmillan of Canada, 1966.

Cook, Ramsay, ed. *French Canadian Nationalism; an Anthology.* Toronto: Macmillan, 1969.

Cook, Ramsay. *The Maple Leaf Forever; Essays on Nationalism and Politics in Canada.* Toronto: Macmillan of Canada, 1971.

Cook, Ramsay. *Provincial Autonomy, Minority Rights and the Compact Theory, 1867-1921.* (Studies of the Royal Commission on Bilingualism and Biculturalism, Vol. 4, Ottawa: Queen's Printer, 1969).

Creighton, Donald Grant. *Towards the Discovery of Canada; Selected Essays.* Toronto: Macmillan of Canada, 1972.

Crépeau, Paul André, and C.B. Macpherson, eds. *The Future of Canadian Federalism. L'avenir du fédéralisme canadien.* Toronto: University of Toronto Press, Montréal: les Presses de l'Université de Montréal, 1965.

Dion, Leon. *La prochaine révolution.* Montréal: Leméac, 1973.

Dion, Leon. *Quebec: the Unfinished Revolution.* Tr. by Thérèse Romer. Montréal: McGill-Queens University Press. Tr., with revisions, of *La prochaine révolution.*

Dofny, Jacques, and Nicole Arnaud. *Nationalism and the National Question.* Tr. by Penelope Williams, Montreal: Black Rose Books, 1977.

Dosman, Edgar J. *The National Interest: The Politics of Northern*

Development 1968-75. Toronto: McClelland and Stewart, 1975.

Dubé, Rodolphe. *Cent ans d'injustice? Un beau rêve: Le Canada,* par François Hertel. Montréal: Éditions du Jour, 1967.

Dumont, Fernand, et al. *Idéologies au Canada français, 1850-1900.* Québec: les Presses de l'Université Laval, 1971.

Dumont, Fernand, et al. *Idéologies au Canada Français, 1900-1929.* Québec: les Presses de l'Université Laval, 1974.

Esman, Milton J., ed. *Ethnic Conflict in the Western World.* Ithaca, N.Y.: Cornell University Press, 1977.

Faribault, Marcel. *Unfinished Business: Some Thoughts on the Mounting Crisis in Quebec.* Toronto: McClelland and Stewart, 1967.

Fournier, Pierre. *The Quebec Establishment; the Ruling Class and the State.* Montreal: Black Rose Books, 1976.

Gaboury, Jean-Pierre. *Le nationalisme de Lionel Groul, aspects idéologiques.* Ottawa: les Éditions de l'Université d'Ottawa, 1970.

Gagne, Wallace, ed. *Nationalism, Technology and the Future of Canada.* Toronto: Macmillan of Canada, 1976.

Glazer, Nathan, and Daniel P. Moynihan, eds. *Ethnicity, Theory and Experience.* Cambridge, Mass., Harvard University Press, 1975.

Grant, George Parkin. *Lament for a Nation; the Defeat of Canadian Nationalism.* Toronto: McClelland and Stewart, 1965.

Grant, George Parkin. *Technology and Empire; Perspectives on North America.* Toronto: House of Anansi, 1969.

Hardin, Herschel. *A Nation Unaware: The Canadian Economic Culture.* Vancouver: J.J. Douglas, 1974.

Harvey, Jean Charles. *Pourquoi je suis antiséparatiste.* Montréal: Éditions de l'homme, 1962.

Hayes, Carlton Joseph Huntley. *Essays on Nationalism.* New York: Macmillan, 1926.

Horowitz, Gad, et al. "Nationalism, Socialism and Canadian Independence." *Canadian Dimension Pamphlet,* 1969.

Hutcheson, John. *Dominance and Dependency: Liberalism and National Policies in the North Atlantic Triangle.* Toronto: McClelland and Stewart, 1978.

Johnson, Daniel. *Egalité ou indépendance.* Montréal: Éditions Renaissance, 1965.

Johnson, Harry Gordon. *The Canadian Quandary; Economic Problems and Policies.* Toronto: McClelland and Stewart, 1977.

Jones, Richard. *Community in Crisis; French-Canadian Nationalism in Perspective.* Toronto: McClelland and Stewart, 1967.

Joy, Richard J. *Languages in Conflict: The Canadian Experience.* Toronto: McClelland and Stewart, 1977. (The Carleton Library, no. 61).

Kontos, A., ed. *Domination.* Toronto: University of Toronto Press. 1975.

Kwavnick, David, ed. *The Tremblay Report: Report of the Royal Commission of Inquiry on Constitutional Problems,* ed. and with an Intro. by David Kwavnick. Toronto: McClelland and Stewart, 1973. (The Carleton Library No. 64). (Includes bibliography). This edition presents an abridgement of the original five volumes.

Lajoie, Andrée. *Expropriation et fédéralisme au Canada.* Montréal: les Presses de l'Université de Montréal, 1972. (Bibliographie: p. 319-325).

Lalande, Gilles. *Pourquoi le fédéralisme? Contribution d'un Québécois à l'intelligence du fédéralisme Canadien; essai.* Montréal: Hurtubise HMH, 1972. (Collection Constantes, v.29). (Bibliographie: p. 201-205).

Laxer, James, and Robert Laxer. *The Liberal Idea of Canada: Pierre Trudeau and the Question of Canada's Survival.* With a foreword by George Grant. Toronto: James Lorimer, 1977.

Laxer, Robert, ed. *The Political Economy of Dependency.* Toronto: McClelland and Stewart, 1973.

Leach, Richard H., ed. *Contemporary Canada.* Toronto: University of Toronto Press, 1968.

Leonard, Jean-François. *La Chance au coureur: Bilan de l'action du gouvernement du Parti Québécois.* Montréal: Éditions nouvelle optique, 1978.

Lévesque, René. *An Option for Quebec.* Toronto: McClelland and Stewart, 1968.

Lévesque, René. *Option Québec* . Montréal: Éditions de l'homme, 1968.

Lévesque, René, et Pierre O'Neill. *Un Pays qu'on peut bâtir.* Montréal: Mouvement Souveraineté-association, 1968.

Lévesque, René. *La solution; le programme du Parti québécois présenté par René* Lévesque. Montréal: Éditions du Jour (distributeur: Messageries du Jour, 1970).

Levitt, Kari. *Silent Surrender; the Multinational Corporation in Canada.* With a pref. by Mel Watkins. Toronto: Macmillan, 1970. (Includes bibliography).

Lijphart, Arend. *Democracy in Plural Societies; a Comparative Exploration.* New Haven, Yale University Press, 1977.

Litvak, I.A., C.J. Maule and R.D. Robinson. *Dual Loyalty: Canadian-U.S. Business Arrangements.* Toronto: McGraw-Hill, 1971.

Lumsden, Ian, ed. *Close the 49th Parallel, etc.: The Americanization of Canada.* Toronto: University of Toronto Press, 1969.

Mallea, John, ed. *Quebec's Language Policies: Background & Response.* Québec: les Presses de l'Université Laval, 1977. (International Center for Research on Bilingualism).

Manzer, Ronald Alexander. *Canada: a Socio-Political Report.* Toronto: McGraw-Hill Ryerson, 1974.

Marchak, M. Patricia. *Ideological Perspectives on Canada.* Toronto: McGraw-Hill Ryerson, 1975. (Series in Canadian Sociology).

McRae, Kenneth Douglas, comp. *Consociational Democracy: Political Accommodation in Segmented Societies.* Toronto: McClelland and Stewart, 1974.

McRoberts, Kenneth, and Dale Postgate. *Quebec: Social Change and Political Crisis.* Toronto: McClelland and Stewart, 1976. (Canada in Transition).

Meekison, J. Peter, ed. *Canadian Federalism: Myth Or Reality.* Toronto: Methuen, 1968. 3d. ed., 1977.

Milner, Henry, and Sheilagh Hodgins Milner. *The Decolonization of Quebec; an Analysis of Left-Wing Nationalism.* Toronto: McClelland and Stewart, 1973. (Carleton contemporaries). (Includes bibliography).

Milner, Henry. *Politics in the New Quebec.* Toronto: McClelland and Stewart, 1971.

Monet, Jacques. *The Last Cannon Shot; a Study of French-Canadian Nationalism, 1837-1850.* Toronto: University of Toronto Press, 1969. (Inlcudes bibliography).

Monière, Denis. *Le développement des idéologies au Québec; des origines à nos jours.* Montréal: Éditions Québec-Amérique, 1977. (Bibliographie: p. 379-381).

Morin, Claude. *Le Combat québecois.* Montréal: Éditions du Boréal Express, 1973.

Morin, Claude, *Quebec vs. Ottawa: The Struggle for Self-Government, 1960-72.* Toronto: University of Toronto Press, 1976.

Morin, Jacques-Yvan. *Le Fédéralisme: théorie et critique, cours télévisé* (polycopié), Montréal: Université de Montréal, 1963-1964.

Morin, Jacques-Yvan. *Le Statut particulier en tant que forme de gouvernement,* inédit, en dépôt à la bibliothèque de la Faculté de droit de l'Université de Montréal.

Morris, Raymond N., and C. Michael Lanphier. *Three Scales of Inequality: Perspectives on French-English Relations.* Toronto: Longmans, 1977, (Canadian Social Problems).

Murray, Vera. *Le Parti Québécois: de la fondation à la prise du pouvoir.* Montréal: Hurtubise HMH, 1976 (Cahiers du Québec, 28). (Bibliographie: p. 241-242).

Le nationalisme québécois à la croisée des chemins. Laval: Centre québécois des relations internationales. Institut Canadien des Affaires internationales.

Ossenberg, R., ed. Canadian Society: *Pluralism, Change, and Conflict.* Scarborough, Ont.: Prentice-Hall, 1971.

Panitch, Leo, ed. *The Canadian State: Political Economy and Political Power.* Toronto: University of Toronto Press, 1977.

Paquet, Gilles, ed. *The Multinational Firm and the Nation State.* Don Mills, Ont.: Collier-Macmillan, 1972.

Parti québécois. *Qui controle l'économie du Québec?* Montréal: Editions du Parti québécois, 1972. (Le Citoyen, 3).

Parti québécois. Conseil Executif. *Prochain étape. . . quand nous serons vraiment chez nous.* Montréal: Parti québécois 1972. ("Projet soumis aux membres du Parti québécois en vue du congrès d'octobre 1972").

Pelletier, Gerard. *The October Crisis.* Toronto: McClelland and Stewart, 1971.

Popovici, Adrian (dir.) *Problèmes de droit contemporain* (Mélanges Louis Beaudoin), Montréal: les Presses de l'Université de Montréal, 1974.

Porter, John. *The Vertical Mosaic; an Analysis of Social Class and Power in Canada.* Toronto: University of Toronto Press, 1965. (Studies in the structure of Power: decision-making in Canada, no. 2).

Pour l'autodétermination du Québec, par G. Desautels, G.W. Kashtan, B. Magnuson, H. Fuyet, et S. Walsh. Plaidoyer Marxiste. Montréal: Editions Nouvelles Frontières, 1978.

Presthus, Robert Vance. *Elite Accommodation in Canadian Politics.* Toronto: Macmillan of Canada, 1973,

Prévost, Jean Pierre, comp. *La crise du fédéralisme canadien.* Paris, Presses universitaires de France. 1972. (Dossiers Thémis, 52. Série Institutions politiques).

Le Québec dans le Canada de demain. Montréal: Éditions du Jour, 1967. 2 v. (Éditions du jour. [Publications] 62-63). "L'idée de statut particulier, hier et aujourd'hui, par Jacques-Yvan Morin: Complément." (Supplément, *Le Devoir* , Montréal, le 30 juin, 1967). Sommaire: t. 1. Avenir constitutionnel et statut particulier. t. 2. Vers un meilleur partage de pouvoirs.

Quinn, Herbert Furlong. *The Union Nationale; a Study in Quebec Nationalism.* Toronto: University of Toronto Press, 1963.

Rapprochements. Extracts reprinted from *University News.* Halifax: Dalhousie University, 1978.

Rioux, Marcel. *Quebec in Question.* Tr. by James Boake. Toronto: James Lewis & Samuel, 1971. Tr. of *La Question du Québec.* (Includes bibliography). 2nd ed.Toronto: James Lorimier, 1978.

Rioux, Marcel. *Les Québécois.* Paris: Seuil, 1974. (Collection Microcosme. Le Temps qui court, 42). (Bibliographie: p. 186-188).

Rioux, Marcel. *La Question du Québec.* Paris: Seghers, 1969. Ed. revue et augm. d'un chapitre: Montréal: Parti pris, 1976 (Collection Aspects, no. 30).

Rocher, Guy. *Le Québec en mutation.* Montréal; Hurtubise HMH, 1973.

Rotstein, Abraham, comp. *Power Corrupted: the October Crisis and the Repression of Quebec.* Ed. by Abraham Rotstein for *The Canadian Forum.* Toronto: New Press, 1971. (Articles published in the Janurary 1971 issue of *The Canadian Forum).*

Rotstein, Abraham, and Gary Lax, eds. *Independence: The Canadian Challenge.* Toronto: Committee for an Independent Canada, 1972.

Russell, Peter, ed. *Nationalism in Canada.* Toronto: McGraw-Hill, 1966.

Ryan, Claude, comp. *Le Québec qui se fait.* Montréal: Hurtubise HMH, 1971.

Ryerson, Stanley Bréhaut. *Unequal Union; Confederation and the Roots of Conflict in the Canadas, 1815-1873.* Toronto: Progress Books, 1968.

Sabourin, Louis. *Le système politique du Canada, institutions fédérales et québécoises.* Ottawa: Editions de l'Université d'Ottawa, 1968. (Cahiers des sciences sociales, no. 4). (Bibliographie: p. 475-502).

Saul, John, and Craig Heron, eds. *Imperialism, Nationalism and Canada.* Toronto, New Hogtown Press, 1977.

Savard, Jean-Guy, and Richard Vigneault. *Multilingual Political Systems: Problems and Solutions.* Québec: Presses de l'Université Laval, 1975.

Schwarz, Mildred A. *Public Opinion and Canadian Identity.* Berkeley: University of California Press, 1967.

Scott, Francis Reginald, and Micnael Oliver, eds. *Quebec States Her Case: Speeches and Articles from Quebec in the Years of Unrest.* Toronto: Macmillan, 1964.

Seguin, Maurice. *L'idée d'indépendance au Québec: genèse et historique.* Trois-Rivières. Qué., Boréal Express, 1968.

Serbyn, R. éd. *Fédéralisme et nations.* Montréal: Presses de l'Université du Québec, 1971. (Cahiers de l'Université du Québec, 27).

Sheffe, Norman, comp. *Canadian / Canadien.* Toronto: Ryerson

Educational Division, McGraw-Hill, 1971. (Issues for the Seventies).

Simeon, R., ed. *Must Canada Fall?* Montreal: McGill-Queens University Press, 1977.

Sloan, Thomas. *Quebec; the Not-So-Quiet Revolution.* Toronto: Ryerson Press, 1965.

Smiley, Donald V. *Canada in Question: Federalism in the Seventies.* 2nd. ed. Toronto: McGraw-Hill Ryerson, 1976.

Smiley, Donald V. *The Canadian Political Nationality.* Rev. ed. Toronto: Methuen, 1970.

Smith, Denis. *Bleeding Hearts. . . Bleeding Country; Canada and the Quebec Crisis.* Edmonton: M. Hurtig, 1971.

Teeple, Gary, ed. *Capitalism and the National Question in Canada.* Toronto: University of Toronto Press, 1972.

Thomson, D.C., ed. *Quebec Society and Politics: Views from the Inside.* Toronto: McClelland and Stewart, 1973.

Thorson, Joseph T. *Wanted: a single Canada.* Toronto: McClelland and Stewart, 1973.

Touret, Bernard. *L'aménagement constitutionnel des États de peuplement composite.* Québec: Presses de L'Université Laval, 1973 (c1972). (Centre international de recherches sur le bilinguisme, Publications, 6).

Tremblay, Rodrigue. *Indépendance et marché commun Québec-États-Unis; manifeste économique.* Montréal: Éditions du Jour, 1970. (Collection Les Idées du jour, D-56).

Trudeau, Pierre Elliott, comp. *The Asbestos Strike.* Tr. by James Boake. Toronto: J. Lewis & Samuel, 1974. Tr. of *La Grève de l'Amiante.*

Trudeau, Pierre Elliott. *Federalism and the French Canadians.* Toronto: Macmillan, 1968.

Trudeau, Pierre Elliott. *Le Fédéralisme et la société canadienne-française.* Montréal: Éditions HMH, 1967. (Collection Constantes, v. 10).

Trudeau, Pierre Elliott, éd. *La Grève de l'Amiante.* En collaboration, avec Gilles Beausoleil et al. Montréal: Éditions du Jour, 1970.

Vadeboncoeur, Pierre. *La dernière heure et la première; essai.* Montréal: L'Hexagon, 1970.

Vallière, Pierre. *Choose!* Tr. by Penelope Williams. Toronto: New Press, 1972. Tr. of *L'urgence de choisir.*

Vallières, Pierre. *Nègres blancs d'Amérique.* Montréal: Éditions Parti Pris, 1968.

Vallières, Pierre. *Un Québec impossible.* Montréal: Éditions Québec-Amérique, 1977.

Vallières, Pierre. *L'urgence de choisir; essai.* Montréal: Éditions Parti Pris, 1971 (Collection Aspects, no. 13).

Vallières, Pierre. *White Niggers of America.* Tr. by Joan Pinkham. Toronto: McClelland and Stewart 1971. Tr. of *Nègres blancs d'Amérique.*

Wade, Mason, ed. *Canadian Dualism: Studies of French-English Relations.* Toronto: University of Toronto Press, 1960.

Wade, Mason, ed. *Regionalism in the Canadian Community, 1867-1967.* Toronto: University of Toronto Press, 1969.

Watkins, Mel, ed. *Dene Nation: The Colony Within.* Toronto: University of Toronto Press, 1977.

C. Articles

Bobet, Jacques. "Laïcité, nationalisme, sentiment national," *Liberté,* v.5 (1963) 189-192.

Bonenfant, J. C., and J.C. Falardeau. "Cultural and Political Implications of French Canadian Nationalism," *Canadian Historical Association Report* (1946) 56-73.

Bourque, Gilles, et Nicole Laurin-Frenette. "Classes sociales et idéologies nationalistes au Québec 1760-1970" *Socialisme québécois,* nos. 20-22. For an English language translation and commentary, see D. Roussopoulos, "Nationalism & Social Classes in Quebec," *Our Generation,* v.8 no. 2 (April 1972) 37-57.

Braybrooke, David. "À la recherche d'une justice de structure au Nouveau-Brunswick," *Philosophiques,* v.3, no. 1 (avril 1976) 123-129. (commentaire sur l'essai de Morin).

Breton, Albert. "The Economics of Nationalism," *Journal of Political Economy,* v. 72 (February-December 1964) 376-386.

Brossard, J. "Le droit du peuple québécois à l'autodétermination et à l'indépendance," *Études internationales,* v.8, no. 2 (1977) 151-172.

Brunet, Michel. "L'évolution du nationalisme au Canada français de la conquête à 1961," *Le Magazine Maclean,* (mars 1961) 19, 54-62.

Brunet, Michel. "Trois dominants de la pensée canadienne-française," *Ecrits du Canada Français,* v.3 (1957) 31-118.

Careless, J.M.S. "'Limited Identities' in Canada," *Canadian Historical Review,* v.50 no. 1 (March 1969) 1-10.

Couturier, Fernand. "Le pays de la culture," *Philosophiques,* v.5, no. 1 (avril 1978) 195-199.

Forsey, Eugene Alfred. "Canada: Two Nations Or One?" *Canadian Journal of Economics and Political Science,* v.28, no. 4 (November 1962) 485-501.

Fortin, Gérald. "Le nationalisme canadian-français et les classes sociales," *Revue d'histoire de l'Amérique française,* v.22, no. 4 (mars 1969) 525-535.

French, Stanley G. "Considérations sur l'histoire et l'esprit de la philosophie au Canada français," p.146-163 in: Yvan Lamonde, *Historiographie de la philosophie au Québec 1853-1971.* Montréal: Hurtubise HMH, 1972.

French, Stanley G. "Droit à la sécession," p.85-99 in: *Philosophie et Droit.* Montréal: Bellarmin, Paris: Desclée, 1979.

French, Stanley G. "Le thomisme au Canada français," *Cité Libre,* (juin-juillet 1964) 20-26.

French, Stanley G. "La Volonté du peuple," p.115-117 in: *Tradition et Avenir,* v. 1. Abidjan: Société Ivoirienne de Philosophie, 1977.

French, Stanley G., and A. Gutman, "The Principle of National Self-determination," p.138-153 in: *Philosophy, Morality and International Affairs,* ed. by Virginia Held, Sidney Morganbesser, and Thomas Nagel. New York, London: Oxford University Press, 1974.

Gagnon, Charles. "Je venais de loin quand j'arrivai à Montréal en Septembre 1960," *Le Magazine Maclean,* v.10, no. 7 (juillet 1970) 31-35.

Gagnon Charles. Rebuttal of Pierre Vallière's declaration. *Le Devoir* (5 et 6 janvier 1972).

Gagnon, Lysiane. "Les Conclusions du Rapport B.B.: De Durham à Laurendeau-Dunton: Variation sur le thème de la dualité Canadienne" dans: *Écomonie Québécoise.* Montréal: les Presses de l'université du Québec, 1969.

Garigue, Philippe. "Organisation sociale et valeurs culturelles canadiennes-françaises," *Canadian Journal of Economics and Political Science,* v.28, no. 2 (May 1962) 189-203.

Goldstick, Dan. "The Right of Nations to Self-Determination," p. 96-112 in: *Contemporary Issues in Political Philosophy,* ed. by William R. Shea and John King-Farlow. New York, Science History Publications, 1976.

Hartz, Louis. "Violence and Legality in the Fragment Cultures," *Canadian Historical Review,* v. 50, no. 2 (June 1969) 123-140.

Hughes, Everett C., and Margaret L. McDonald. "French and English in the Economic Structure of Montreal," *Canadian Journal of Economics and Political Science,* v.7, no. 4 (November 1941) 493-505.

Lambert, R. "Hegel, Eric Weil, et la situation politique du Canada," *Pourquoi la Philosophie?* C.S.M. -II, 83-90.

Lamontagne, M. "Fédéralisme ou association d'États indépendants," *Études internationales,* v.8, no. 2 (1977) 208-231.

Léger, J.M. "Aspects of French-Canadian Nationalism," *University of Toronto Quarterly,* v.27, no. 3 (April 1958) 310-329.

Léger, J.M. "La souveraineté, condition de salut," *le Devoir,* (23-25 octobre 1967).

Lemieux, V. "Quel État du Québec," *Études internationales,* v.8, no. 2 (1977) 254-266.

Lijphart, Arend. "Linguistic Fragmentation and Other Dimensions of Cleavage: a Comparison of Belgium, Canada, and Switzerland" (Paper presented at the Ninth World Congress of the International Political Science Association, Montreal, 1973). Bruxelles, International Political Science Association.

Maheux, Arthur. "Le nationalisme canadien-français à l'aurore du XXe siècle," *Canadian Historical Association Report* (1945) 58-74.

Maintenant. "Un Québec libre à inventer." Montréal, 1967. Cahier spécial issued as nos. 68-69 of the periodical.

Marcil-Lacoste, Louise. "The Proclamation of Human Rights," p.78-95 in: *Contemporary Issues in Political Philosophy,* , ed. by William R. Shea and John King-Farlow. New York, Science History Publications, 1976.

Marx, H. "The 'Apprehended Insurrection' of October 1970 and the Justicial Function," *University of British Columbia Law Review,* v.7, no. 1 (1972) 55 f. (re Gagnon and Vallières v. the Queen, 1971 C.A. 454).

Marx, H. "The Emergency Powers and Civil Liberties in Canada," *McGill Law Journal* (1970) 39 f.

Marx, H. "Language Rights in the Canadian Constitution," *Revue juridique* Thémis (1967) 239 f.

Mayer, R.A. "Legal aspects of scession," *Manitoba Law Journal,* (1968).

Meunier, J.G. "Nationalisme, langage, langue et philosophie," *Pourquoi la philosophie?* (éd. Ste-Marie), CSM -II (1968) 73-81.

Milner, Henry. "The Implications of Vallières' Declaration," *Our Generation,* v.8, no. 2 (April 1972) 27-35.

Minville, Esdras. "Les conditions de l'autonomie économique des Canadiens français," *Action Nationale,* 37 (1951) 260-285.

Morin, Claude "La politique extérieure du Québec," *Études internationales,* v.9, no. 2 (1978) 280-289.

Morin, Jacques-Yvan. "Le fédéralisme canadien après cent ans," *Revue juridique Thémis,* (mars 1967).

Morin, Jacques-Yvan. "Liberté nationale et fédéralisme," *Thémis,* (mai 1964) 91 s.

Morin, Jacques-Yvan. "The Need for a New Canadian Federation, "

Canadian Forum v.44, no. 521 (June 1964) 64-66.

Morin, S.J. "Sur l'injustice de structure," *Philosophiques,* v. 1, no. 1 (avril 1974) 171-192.

Nadeau, Robert, Georges-A. Legault, Louise Marcil-Lacoste, et Claude Panaccio. "Autour de la loi 50," *Philosophiques,* v.2, no. 2 (octobre 1975) 341-375.

Oeullet, Fernand. "Les Fondements historiques de l'option séparatiste dans le Québec," *Canadian Historical Review,* v.43, no. 3 (September 1962) 185-203.

Oeullet, Fernand. "Le Nationalisme canadien-français: De ses origines à l'insurrection de 1837," *Canadian Historical Review,* v.45, no. 4 (December 1964) 277-292.

Ouellet, Fernand. "Nationalisme canadien-français et laïcisme au XIXe siècle," *Recherches Sociographiques,* 4 (1963) 47-70.

Paradis, W.H. "Le nationalisme canadien dans le domaine religieux," *Revue de l'histoire d'Amérique française,* 7 (1953-1954) 465-482; 8 (1954-1955) 3-24.

Rioux, Marcel. "Sur l'évolution des idéologies au Québec," *Revue de l'Institut Sociologie,* no. 1 (1968) 95-124.

Roussopoulos, Dimitrios. "Social Classes and Nationalism in Quebec," *Our Generation,* v.8, no. 2 (April 1972) 37-57.

Simoneau, P. "Les principes du fédéralisme," *Revue juridique Thémis,*(1972) 13 s.

Soucier, Pierre. "B & B ou l'inégalité à perpetuité," *Maintenant* no. 73 (5 janvier-15 février 1968) 16-18.

Taylor, Charles. "Nationalism and the Political Intelligensia; a Case Study," *Queens Quarterly,* v.72, no. 1 (Spring 1965) 150-168.

Tremblay, M. "Réflexions sur le nationalisme", *Ecrits du Canada Français,*5 (1959) 9-44.

Trent, J. "Terrain d'entente et territoires contestés: les positions fédérales et provinciales à l'égard de l'avenir constitutionnel du Canada", *Études internationales,* v.8, no. 2 (1977) 172-197.

Trudeau, Pierre Elliott. "L'alienation nationaliste," Cité Libre, 12 (mars 1961) 3-5.

D. Bibliographies

Boily, Robert. *Québec 1940-1969. Bibliographie: le système politique québecois et son environnement.* Préf. de Jean-Charles Bonenfant. Montréal: les Presses de l'Université de Montréal, 1971.

Clement, Wallace, and Daniel Drache. *A Practical Guide to Canadian Political Economy.* Toronto: James Lorimer, 1978

Cotnam, Jacques. *Contemporary Quebec; an Analytical Bibliography.* Toronto: McClelland and Stewart, 1973. English or French.

Monière, Denis, et André Vachet. *Les idéologies au Québec: bibliographie.* Montréal: Bibliothèque nationale du Québec, 1976.